INTIMACY AND TERROR

SOVIET DIARIES OF THE 1930S

INTIMACY

and

TERROR

EDITED BY

VÉRONIQUE GARROS,

NATALIA KORENEVSKAYA,

and THOMAS LAHUSEN

ENGLISH EDITION DIRECTED BY THOMAS LAHUSEN

TRANSLATED BY CAROL A. FLATH

THE NEW PRESS · NEW YORK

English translation by Carol Flath

copyright © 1995 by The New Press

Library of Congress Cataloging-in-Publication Data

Intimacy and Terror / edited by Véronique Garros, Natalia Korenevskaya, and Thomas Lahusen; translated by Carol A. Flath.
p. cm.
ISBN 1-56584-200-6
1. Soviet Union—Biography. 2. Soviet Union—Social life and customs—1917-1970. I. Garros, Véronique. II. Korenevskaya, Natalia. III. Lahusen, Thomas.
DK268.A1867 1995
920.047—DC20 95-1967
CIP

The New Press prepared this volume
in conjunction with Progress-Complex Publishers, Moscow.
Progress-Complex Publishers will publish a Russian edition.
Published in the United States by The New Press, New York
Distributed by W. W. Norton & Company, Inc., New York

Established in 1990 as a major alternative to the large, commercial publishing houses, The New Press is the first full-scale nonprofit American book publisher outside of the university presses. The Press is operated editorially in the public interest, rather than for private gain; it is committed to publishing in innovative ways works of educational, cultural, and community value that, despite their intellectual merits, might not normally be commercially viable. The New Press's editorial offices are located at the City University of New York.

Book design by Charles Nix

Production management by Kim Waymer
Printed in the United States of America

95 96 97 98   9 8 7 6 5 4 3 2 1

To the memory of
Mikhail Yakovlevich Gefter

Contents

ACKNOWLEDGMENTS

This project would not have been possible without the help of a true "International" of colleagues, friends and institutions. We would like to thank in particular the historians Marc Ferro (Paris), Mikhail Gefter (†), and Moshe Lewin (Philadelphia), as well as a number of colleagues and fellow travelers, who have given advice or donated part of their time to read, reread and copy: Ivan Bannov, Olga Blinova, Alain Blum, François Castaing, Yves Cohen, Myriam Désert, Evgeny Dobrenko, Irina Dolgova, Ogniana Eneva, Valentin Gefter, Marie Hornisberger, Elena and Andrei Illesh, Claudio S. Ingerflom, Andrei Khmara (†), Anatoly Kirillov and his students, Mikhail Korenevsky, Yaroslav Leontev, Roland Lew, Marie-Hélène Mandrillon, Marina Miroshchnikova, Anatoly Naiman, Denis Paillard, Elena Predtechenskaya, Vladimir Pyatnitsky, Tatiana and Oleg Renzin, Marina Rozhanskaya, Mikhail Rozhansky, Nikolai Sorokin, Igor Chubykhin, Yao Yuan, Viktor Zhigulin.

We are thankful to Kirill Markovsky, our photographer, who gave much of his time to the project; to Konstantin Lagunov for having given us a photograph of Arzhilovsky's diary; to Jochen Hellbeck for his assistance in obtaining the photograph of Podlubny's diary as well as biographical details of the author; and to Robin LaPasha, research assistant at Duke University.

Our gratitude goes also to Andrei Bogachev, Frederick S. Choate and Mikhail Korneev of the SovLit Database Project (Berkeley–Moscow) for their professionalism and the rapidity of their services. Without their help — the copying in electronic format of a number of diaries, many more than those published here — this project would have been difficult to achieve.

Portions of this research have been funded by: the French Research and Space Ministry (Project "URSS/Russie: les enjeux de la mémoire," directed by Marc Ferro. Appel d'offres 1992/1993), the French National Center of Scientific Research (CNRS), Duke University, and Perkins Library at Duke. A grant from the International Research & Exchanges Board (IREX) made Natalia Korenevskaya's research trip to New York in the fall of 1994 possible. We would also like to thank Charlotte Douglas

(New York University), who indirectly enabled the meeting of the editorial team during the final stage of production.

Finally, our special thanks go to the editorial staff of The New Press, in particular to Grace Farrell, Matthew Weiland, Anja Grothe, and especially to its director André Schiffrin, who has expressed interest in this project from the beginning to end.

Editors' Introduction

This collection of diaries from the Soviet 1930s is the result of a collabo-
ration involving many participants from three countries — Russia/the
Soviet Union, France, and the United States. We were determined to discover the daily lives of the citizens of the Soviet Union during the tragic
1930s. Though much has been published about the Stalin purges, the
Moscow trials, and the Gulag Archipelago, very little is known about the
ordinary doings of the majority of Soviet citizens. Even less is known
about their thoughts — and dreams.

But how to go about this difficult task? A few years ago things were, in a
sense, easy: one "belonged" to this or the other side; even for "dissidence"
there was a status; the "evil" was identifiable. A parallel can be drawn
between the lessons of August 1991 and the present crisis of Soviet studies: the disintegration of the Soviet Union and the fall of communism did
not bring "democracy," and the opening of the Soviet archives did not
yield the simple truth about the Soviet past. What we three editors have
in common, despite our different geographic and intellectual locations
and origins, is an acute sense of the increasing impossibility of writing
this past in the way the preceding generation did, and the urge to write it
nonetheless.

We decided to seek out the private, mostly unpublished diaries of a
broad cross section of the population. During several years of research we
consulted about two hundred diaries of the period 1934–39 from official
and private archives, located in many places within the former Soviet
Union, including Moscow, Leningrad, Kalinin, Sverdlovsk, Irkutsk, or
Khabarovsk. Some people gave us their precious writings — or those of
their relatives — thinking that "historians would make good use of them;"
some were happy to get rid of the dusty rubbish; others requested money
(and it is hard to blame them in today's troubled times). Many texts had to
be deciphered with the help of a magnifying glass, letter by letter; some
were entirely copied out by hand. On the basis of this work, initiated by
Véronique Garros in the late 1980s, about fifty diaries were gathered; of
these fifty, a final selection of ten diaries was made.

The voices of the diarists, collected from the era of (and preceding) the "Great Terror," between 1934 and 1939, speak out in the following pages. After nearly sixty years, their experiences have become "history." Fyodor Shirnov, Lev Gornung, Galina Shtange, Vladimir Stavsky, and Oleg Frelikh were neighbors without knowing it. Their most intimate thoughts and feelings languished until now in the Russian State Archives for Art and Literature.[1] Ignat Frolov bided his time on the shelves of the Lenin State Library in Moscow.[2] Lyubov Shaporina's diary is kept in the Saltykov-Shchedrin Public Library in Leningrad/Saint Petersburg.[3] Andrei Arzhilovsky was brought back to life thanks to Aleksandr Petrushkin, who undertook the Russian publication of his diary in the journal *Ural*.[4] Only two diarists are alive today: Leonid Potyomkin, whose writings are conserved in the author's private archives, and Stepan Podlubny, who deposited his diary in 1989 at the Central Popular Archives in Moscow.[5]

One could say that the Soviet 1930s began on 1 October 1928, with the official launching of the First Five-Year Plan, which marked a turning point in the history of the Soviet Union.[6] Priority was given to industrialization, requiring the development of a numerous, low-skilled labor force and the modernization of technology. The necessary energies were mobilized by a certain "spirit of the plan," but also by material incentives and a system of increasing coercion of the Soviet worker. The greatest change however, concerned the Soviet countryside: on 27 December 1929, Stalin announced the end of NEP, the implementation of mass collectivization, and the "liquidation of the kulak as a class." At the beginning of 1933, the First Five-Year Plan was declared accomplished — nine months ahead of time. About eighty percent of arable land was collectivized, with 210,000 collective farms and 4,300 state farms. Overall, the outcome of the "big drive" was a catastrophic drop in agricultural production, which led to a major famine in 1932–33 and the disproportionate destruction of human and material resources (despite the proclaimed 273 percent increase in heavy industrial production). There were profound and long-lasting social consequences. As Moshe Lewin describes the situation in *The Making of the Soviet System*, Russia was propelled into a general state of flux and gigantic social turnover, with a "constant interplay of influences between a backward agricultural sector, which acted as a brake on industrialization, and a too rapidly growing industrial sector, which weakened agriculture."[7] The "superstructure," that is, the state bureaucracy, itself contaminated by the flux and social mobility that it encountered and had provoked, "rushed ahead," attempting to master the chaos by strengthening the administrative, controlling, and coercive mechanisms of the state.[8]

The purges of the 1930s can be understood in this context, at least in part, as the reaction of the official ideology against those who stood in the way of the creation of a new statehood. This strikingly recalls the principles of "Autocracy, Nationality, Orthodoxy" and other ideological devices of the imperial past and church history.[9] The number of victims of the purges has long been debated, but the opening of the Soviet archives has supplied an abundance of new data, like this recent count of those who were sent to the labor camps (the numbers in parentheses refer to the "political" prisoners, that is, those sentenced for "counterrevolutionary crimes"):[10]

1935	965,742	(118,256)
1936	1,296,494	(105,849)
1937	1,196,369	(104,826)
1938	1,881,570	(185,324)
1939	1,672,438	(454,432)

These figures do not include the prisoners in jails (for example, 350,538 in January 1939), those who were deported and sent to remote places for a term or for life, and those who were executed. And still, these numbers are far below those of "Dostoevsky's prophecy," according to which "socialism will cost Russia over a hundred million lives."[11] Some, in the spirit of a kind of reverse — and perverse — revisionism, wanted the prophecy to be true: the use of fantastic and unfounded figures by diverse Sovietologists of the cold war era manifests the same contempt for the "unit" of history. Millions were not enough, tens of millions were needed to juggle with.

The whole is of course not explainable by the addition — or subtraction — of its parts, but the contrary is also true: every (hundred) thousand starts — or ends up — with a unit, each digit represents by itself a whole, a *cipher* that history has to decipher. Where to situate a cipher like the journalist Aleksandr Starchakov, shot in 1938, who, drunk on wine, and also on tragedy, used to beat up his wife with volumes taken from his Shakespeare collection? Where to situate Baranov, a prisoner of this mysterious "there" that was not yet named Gulag, whose son was exulting at every movement forward of the republican front on the map of the Spanish civil war? Or Kirillov, who committed suicide on the shores of the Siberian exile that had been imposed on him, a Party member above reproach? Or the writer

Olga Berggolts, who composed odes to Stalin's glory and declaimed them to her grateful fellow prisoners? These people wrote diaries that space considerations have excluded from our collection, but they are *also* representative of those hundred and fifty million or so, who, in 1937, were counted but did not count in the official statistics of the time. The Soviet citizens submitted themselves to the census of 1937 freely, yet the findings of this census were never published. One of the reasons was the high percentage of citizens who declared their religious faith.

In the very heart of the defiance of "reason," enacted in the great Moscow trials of 1936–38, in the very courtroom that witnessed the triumph of insanity, the journalists who are usually so prompt to rationalize the "event," had no recourse other than to borrow from the language of tragedy or of the madhouse, and to confess their incapacity to "understand": "The great sessions of the Salpêtrière[12] that the psychiatrists of the nineteenth century devoted to the phenomena of hysteria and autosuggestion are nothing compared to the Moscow trials"; "Personal rivalry and hatred, the most exacerbated revolutionary passion, all this cannot explain everything and the Russian tragedy will remain for a long time an enigma"; "One ceases to understand. One constructs hypotheses to seek for an explanation of the phenomenon, to tally it with reason. And one finds nothing. One is left with a mystery."[13]

To add up the numbers of millions of victims does not solve the mystery of "how all this could happen." Nor, however, do those who today choose their own camp, track down the culprits, and rewrite history in the context of the new political agenda produce the meaning that we – the survivors of these years included – are still searching for. Our choice has therefore been to distance ourselves from the temptation of any interpretative reading of the period. Instead we have sought out the quivers of the soul, the most intimate gesture: the inscription of the chronicle of one's self. In a diary, *everything* has meaning: the weather, the prosaic details of life, the political event, memory, the sequence of time itself. We believe that the essence of a diary is the space of tension between different – often heterogeneous – times, between the personal, the intimate, sometimes the bodily, and the social.

But is it not shameful or indecent to violate the intimacy of those men and women of the Soviet 1930? Is there not also the danger of coming dangerously close to the "professional populism" of those who attempt to rewrite history, purging the canon of its "great texts," an operation that, as Dominick LaCapra has warned, "engenders the vicious paradox by which a certain class of scholars establish their own disciplinary hegemony through a vicarious appeal to the oppressed of the past."[14] But as the reader will see, it is precisely the notion of oppression that is being challenged by our texts.

In our attempt to recreate the historical landscape of the "Great Terror" through its "intimate" chronicles, we certainly share a certain helplessness in regard to the "mystery" of those times that cannot be thoroughly explained, but we also have the responsibility of listening to those voices that have come to us and should remain, as much as possible, the subjects of their stories. In the "age of mechanical reproduction," enough remains of the wondrous freedom of the diarist, whose present resists the sieve of historical memory—the smoothing out of the past, the rationalization for the sake of intelligibility. The diary leads us to those unpredictable shores, where choices can still be made, where interpretation remains still possible. It delivers a material that is blurred, disparate, discontinuous, irreconcilable, and recalls perhaps what the Russian historian Mikhail Gefter understood as the "world's asymmetry." What freedom the diarist has who can experience within one sentence a growing stoutness with the conquest of the North Pole, the first snow with a capital execution, a kiss with an earthquake, a trip to the bathhouse with the arrest of an acquaintance.

The reader will find a narrative, made of nine diaries. Some of them are reproduced in their entirety (Shirnov, Gornung, Arzhilovsky); others have been shortened, even significantly in the case of Podlubny, to "match" the years that we have decided to focus upon, or for reasons of space. The motives for writing and the themes that surface in these texts recall other diaries of other times and places. Often the sole reason to write appears to have been the need to stem the "flow of time." But the flow of time is always uneven, even in the Soviet 1930s. The details of everyday life found here may surprise more than one reader. Stalin's slogan "Life has become better, comrades, life has become happier," for example, not only appears as the cynical leitmotif of Andrei Arzhilovsky's writings (a man who was shot, partially for having written a diary), but is also part of life "itself." Does *Izvestiya* "lie" on 6 August 1937, when it describes the carnival at the Moscow Park of Culture and Recreation, the fireworks, the dances, the colorful crowd, the jazz bands, the "sense of brotherhood," the feeling that "we are all friends, in the time-honored tradition of the masquerade"? "Let my life ascend as a beautiful firework, be it only a momentary flash, at mankind's celebration of its triumph," writes Leonid Potyomkin, a student of the Sverdlovsk Mining Institute in 1936 (and future vice minister of geology of the USSR). Where is the deeper truth, what is more "objective" in Lyubov Shaporina's diary (she was a member of the artistic and literary intelligentsia of Leningrad): the memory of Alyona, her little daughter dead for three years, the terrible lucidity of her analysis of the ongoing repression, or her anti-Semitism?

We have decided to risk an exercise of *montage*, entitled "Chronicle of the Year 1937 as recorded by the newspaper *Izvestiya* and collective farmer Ignat Frolov," which introduces the diaries per se, to underline our distrust of "historical objectivity," to make explicit the subjectivity of our own choices. The contrast that we hope to produce by juxtaposing these two radically different texts goes well beyond some narcissistic and "literary" play. A universe seems to separate the epic stream of the notes of collective farmer Frolov about the weather or about "planting Potatoe" and the "state's voice" of *Izvestiya*, but both voices are far from being monolithic. One day *Izvestiya* celebrates the Moscow trials, another day, the fresh cucumbers that have appeared in the stores of Komsomolsk-on-Amur. In what time does Frolov live? Difficult to say, because this diarist lives *simultaneously* in a sacred and a profane time:[15] during all his life he notes the weather in using the "old (prerevolutionary) style," thirteen days behind the new, as in the following entry:

> 29-th of June. a holiday. the feast day of the apostles Peter and Paul. fine Sunny and hot weather all day long with a mild southwest breeze all day the collective farmers dried grass and green fallow. there's an awful lot of mowed fallow and grass.

In fact, if we look at the "real" calendar of the year 1937, this 29 June 1936 was Monday 12 July, "new style," the day when — as *Izvestiya* reports — "*The Tales of A Thousand and One Nights* are being published in the Chechen language by the State Publishing House of the Chechen-Ingush Autonomous Republic." All this shows the presence of a real polyphony (in Bakhtin's sense), the very possibility of "conflicting" idioms, thoughts, stories, experiences, in "1937."

Finally, this "Chronicle" may also serve as an invitation to proceed with one's own "vertical" reading. We refer the reader, for example, to those entries of Andrei Arzhilovsky's relatively peaceful summer (two months before his execution) in July 1937, and to Oleg Frelikh's "unconscious," that is, his dream about fortunetelling during the same month of July 1937 in which the following dialogue between "him" and "her" appears: He asks, "You mean I'm in for bad luck?" She answers, "Misfortune, misfortune." One might also compare the "rapturous" days of "practical training" that the student Leonid Potyomkin lives through one year earlier, in July 1936, during which he "pushes fulfillment up to 152%," to the "corresponding" entries in July 1936 when our most *public* "character" — the poet Anna Akhmatova — was living very private and idyllic moments in a dacha near Kolomna.

The reader might also explore what the diaries *do not tell*. Stepan Podlubny summarizes the entire year of 1937 in one sentence: "No one will ever know how I made it through the year 1937." Galina Shtange "won't write" about the trial of the right Trotskyite bloc on 2 March 1938, since she is "saving the papers and it all can be read there." Vladimir Stavsky, General Secretary of the Union of Soviet Writers, does not mention his denunciation of the poet Osip Mandelshtam in his diary, which led to Mandelshtam's arrest and eventual death in a labor camp. Some omissions are less explicit: we learn from two entries of *Izvestiya* (18 and 21 July 1937) that both Yezhov and Vyshinsky were awarded the Order of Lenin, the first "for his outstanding work directing the NKVD" (the State Security), the second "for his successes in strengthening law and order and the offices of the Public Prosecutor." For what successes *Izvestiya* does not specify, because "everybody knows."

We have attempted to provide part of the knowledge shared by the readers of *Izvestiya* by adding a number of notes to the "Chronicle" and to our diaries, as well as a short biography before each author's text. The facts provided represent our attempt to establish a frame of reference. As well as making known these chronicles of the years 1934–39, where memory is brought as close as possible to the ungraspable of "life" — from banality to poignancy, from truth to lie, from cowardliness to courage, from the abject to the sublime — the volume is intended to deconstruct a "given," the precariousness of which has caused much disarray to both professional and casual readers of the Soviet past, especially after the "opening" of its archives. We hope that the reader of this book will benefit from the process as much as its editors have.

NOTES

[1] RGALI (Moscow), F. Shirnov: f. 1337, op. 1, ed. khr. 296; L. Gornung: f. 2813, op. 1, ed. khr. 1; G. Shtange: f. 1837, zh. 5, ed. khr. 48–52; V. Stavsky: f. 1712, zh. 4, ed. khr. 8; O. Frelikh: f. 2760, op. 1, ed. khr. 6.

[2] Russian (formerly Lenin) State Library (Moscow), F. 218, n. 1283, ed. khr. 13.

[3] Saltykov-Shchedrin Public Library (St. Petersburg), F. 1086, ed. khr. 5, 6.

[4] *Ural* (Ekaterinburg), No. 3 (1992): 138–60.

[5] Tsentr Dokumentatsii "Narodnyi Arkhiv" (Moscow), F. 3o, op. 1, ed. khr. 16.

[6] The following lines, as well as the chronology that follows the translator's note, are quoted in part from *Les grandes dates de la Russie et de l'URSS* [The Great Dates of Russia and the USSR], ed. Francis Conte (Paris: Larousse, 1990), 211–33.

[7] Moshe Lewin., *The Making of the Soviet System: Essays in the Social History of Interwar Russia* (New York: The New Press, 1994), 115. See also chapter five, "Who Was the Soviet Kulak?" 121–41.

[8] Ibid., 264–65.

[9] Ibid., 304–10.

[10] See Moshe Lewin, "Figures From the Dark," Appendix to his *Russia/USSR/Russia: The Drive and Drift of a Superstate* (New York: The New Press, 1995), 343. Lewin quotes from V. Zemskov, *Istoriya SSSR* 5 (1991), 152. Source: GARF, NKVD Fund. See also J. Arch Getty, Gábor T. Rittersporn, and Viktor N. Zemskov, "Victims of the Soviet Penal System in the Pre-war Years: A First Approach on the Basis of Archival Evidence," *The American Historical Review* 98, 4 (October 1993): 1017–49.

[11] Alexander Solzhenitsyn, quoted in *Le Monde* (September 25, 1993).

[12] Reference to Jean-Martin Charcot who founded the hospital of the Salpêtrière in Paris in 1882. One of his students was Sigmund Freud.

[13] Quoted by Nicolas Werth, *Les procès de Moscou* [The Moscow Trials] (Bruxelles: Editions Complexe, 1987), 57–59.

[14] Dominick LaCapra, *History & Criticism* (Ithaca and London: Cornell University Press, 1985), 132–33.

[15] About religion and peasantry in the 1930s, see Lewin's "Popular Religion in Twentieth-Century Russia," in his *The Making of the Soviet System*, 57–71.

Translator's Note

The texts you are about to read were not written for publication. Whatever their reasons, our diarists wrote down their daily thoughts. We do not know who, if anyone, they imagined might read their diaries, but surely they could not have imagined the fate of their notebooks—that some sixty years after their appearance on paper, these private thoughts would be collected, joined with those of strangers, printed in a different language, and published between glossy covers, to be read by inhabitants of a radically different world and time. The process of translation from Russian to English is thus only one of a great number of changes that these texts have undergone—transcription from notebook to typed manuscript, editorial cutting and sequencing with other diaries, the process of publication itself—in their metamorphosis from the most private of documents into public property.

It has been my primary goal as a contributor to this process to respect and preserve the integrity of the authors' styles and intentions. Our diarists represent a broad spectrum of educational levels, and even those who wrote elsewhere for publication naturally tend to be careless in their private writings. Each diarist has a unique style. Andrei Arzhilovsky's language sparkles with aphorisms and wry, culturally embedded social commentary. Galina Shtange writes her most private thoughts in the cliches of Soviet public discourse. In emotionally charged moments, Leonid Potyomkin has a tendency to lose his thoughts in a heady and utterly impenetrable gush of formulas from Soviet Marxist-Leninist ideology. The diaries of Ignat Frolov and Fyodor Shirnov lack the most rudimentary attention to spelling, grammar, and punctuation, though Shirnov's style changes noticeably after he returns from his Arctic expedition. For each writer, I have tried to find ways of conveying in English the texture as well as the sense of the language of the diary. Ultimately, this is an impossible task. But after all, this can be said of any translation.

Editorial cuts are indicated by ellipses in brackets. All other ellipses are the author's own. All misspellings are intentional: they reflect the diarists' writing. In order to reflect the diaries' inconsistencies, we also kept abbreviations as used in the original texts and avoided the dates and numbers to be styled uniformly.

In the interest of the non-Russian speaker, we have chosen a simplified, nonscholarly transcription system.

CHRONOLOGY

The following chronology lists a series of important dates and events. Some of them are reflected in the "Chronicle of the Year 1937 as Recorded by the Newspaper *Izvestiya* and Collective Farmer Ignat Danilovich Frolov," in the notes and, of course, in the diaries themselves.

1934

26 January–10 February. Seventeenth Congress of the Communist Party. The outcome of the congress is usually considered as a compromise between J. Stalin and moderate members of the Politburo. The former opposition submitted itself to autocriticism. Bukharin was elected a candidate member of the Central Committee. The new secretariat was comprised of Stalin, L. Kaganovich, A. Zhdanov and S. Kirov. On the Politburo were: Stalin, V. Molotov, L. Kaganovich, K. Voroshilov, G. Ordzhonikidze, V. Kuibyshev, S. Kirov, A. Andreyev, S. Kosior; candidate members: A. Mikoyan, V. Chubar, G. Petrovsky, P. Postyshev, I. Rudzutak.

16 April. Creation of the title of Hero of the Soviet Union.

7 May. Creation of the Jewish Autonomous Region of Birobidzhan on the Manchurian Border.

8 June. Law on "high treason" (death penalty, collective responsibility of family members).

10 July. The OGPU functions of police and security were transferred to a People's Commissariat of Internal Affairs (NKVD), reorganized by G. Yagoda. The NKVD was also in charge of the prison camps, which were rapidly expanding.

17 August–1 September. First Congress of the Union of Soviet Writers.

18 September. The USSR accepted as a member of the League of Nations.

1 December. Assassination in Leningrad of S. Kirov by L. Nikolayev. Assumed to have been instigated by Stalin, this assassination signalled the onset of a period of unprecedented repression and terror. In the evening, a decree was issued, speeding up the judicial procedure and immediately instituting the death penalty in cases of terrorism. During the following days, expeditious executions of alleged "White guards" and political prisoners were carried out in Leningrad, Moscow, and Kiev.

16 December. Arrest of L. Kamenev and G. Zinoviev. A. Zhdanov replaced S. Kirov at the Party secretariat of Leningrad.

20 December. Creation of the Mordvinian Autonomous Socialist Soviet Republic.

28 December. Creation of the Udmurt Autonomous Socialist Soviet Republic.

29 December. The official news reported the executions of L. Nikolayev and his "accomplices."

1935

1 January. Rationing cards for bread and flour were withdrawn, but their prices sharply increased.

15–16 January. Trial in camera of the "Moscow Center," accused of having encouraged the assassination of S. Kirov. G. Zinoviev was sentenced to ten years of prison, L. Kamenev to five years. Wave of arrests and deportation of the last "bourgeois" elements of the Leningrad region.

26 January. Announcement of the death of V. Kuibyshev, responsible for the Gosplan (State Plan). The official reason was heart attack.

28 January–6 February. Seventh Congress of the Soviets, which decided on the redaction of a new constitution.

February 1. Plenum of the Central Committee. A. Mikoyan and V. Chubar are elected full members of the Politburo. A. Zhdanov and R. Eikhe are named candidate members.

17 February. Adoption of new statutes for collective farms by the Second Congress of Shock Collective Farm Workers. It specified the limits of the privately farmed plots.[1]

23 February. N. Yezhov (secretary of the Central Committee who replaced S. Kirov) took the direction of the Central Party Control Committee.
23 February. Pravda announced N. Khrushchev's nomination as first secretary of the Moscow Party Organization.

7 March. A circular ordered the withdrawal from all reading rooms and all libraries of the works by L. Trotsky, G. Zinoviev, L. Kamenev. Several months later, the names of E. Preobrazhensky, A. Shliapnikov, A. Lunacharsky, and many others were added to the list.

23 March. Signing of an agreement between Japan and the USSR, which sold Soviet rights on the Chinese Eastern Railway (KVZhD) to the state of Manchukuo.

8 April. Children over twelve years became legally responsible and subject to the death penalty.

15 May. The first line of the Moscow subway began operation.

June. A. Vyshinsky became general prosecutor of the USSR.

10 July. Approval by the Central Committee and the Sovnarkom (Soviet of People's Commissars) of a plan for the reconstruction of Moscow.

13 July. Signing of a trade agreement with the United States. Soviet imports from the United States increased from 7.7 percent in 1934 to 28.5 percent in 1938.

25 July–25 August. Seventh and last congress of the Comintern (Communist International): ratified the tactics of "popular fronts," which gathered all the forces of the left against fascism.

Night of 3o–31 August. Aleksei Stakhanov, a minor of the Irmino mine of the Donets region mined 102 tons of coal (fourteen times the norm), in a single shift.

3 September. New school law enforced discipline and the authority of the teacher.

22 September. Reestablishment of ranks in the Red Army. The first five marshals were K. Voroshilov, N. Tukhachevsky, A. Yegorov, V. Bliukher, and S. Budenny.

29 September. The consumers cooperatives of the cities were replaced by state enterprises.

1 October. Withdrawal of rationing cards for meat, oil, fish, sugar, potatoes. Increase of controlled prices, which approached those of the free market.

25 October. Creation of the Kalmuck Autonomous Socialist Soviet Republic.

14–17 November. First conferences of the Stakhanovite workers of the USSR. Stalin's speech: "Life has become better, comrades, life has become happier."

3o December. End of the restrictions on access to higher education on the basis of social origin.

1936

Creation of the Autonomous Socialist Soviet Republics of Mari, Chechen-Ingush, North Ossetia, and Kabardin-Balkar.

January. Beginning of a new purge in the Party, with the renewal of Party cards. The exchange of official documents had the goal of maintaining "social purity."

1 April. Devaluation of the ruble.

15 May. Opening of the Central Lenin Museum in Moscow.

12 June. Publication of the draft of the new constitution, submitted for public discussion.

18 June. Death of Maxim Gorky, the circumstances of which remain mysterious. André Gide, traveling at that time in the USSR, delivered the funeral oration on Red Square.

27 June. "Mothers' Assistance Law." It made abortion (which had been legalized by a decree of 1920) illegal, made divorce more difficult, and raised family subsidies.

August. The USSR officially espoused the policy of nonintervention in the Spanish civil war.

18–24 August. First public trial in Moscow ("Trial of the Sixteen"): the defendants included G. Zinoviev, L. Kamenev, G. Evdokimov, and I. Smirnov. Accused of having formed a "terrorist Trotskyite-Zinovievist center," the sixteen defendants acknowledged their contacts with Trotsky, their participation in Kirov's assassination and in a plot against Stalin and other leaders. Sentenced to death, they were executed on 25 August.

23 August. Suicide of M. Tomsky, the former head of the trade unions.

10 September. An investigation against N. Bukharin and A. Rykov was officially closed for lack of a "legal basis" for arraignment.

22 September. Arrest of K. Radek.

25 September. Stalin and A. Zhdanov ordered the replacement of G. Yagoda by N. Yezhov as the head of the NKVD.

23 October. I. Maisky, the Soviet ambassador in London, protested against the help provided to Franco by Germany and Italy and announced that the USSR was no longer bound by the nonintervention agreements. The Soviet Union sent military materiel and experts, but no Soviet volunteers participated in the International Brigades. The help to the Spanish Republicans was accompanied by a fierce struggle against Trotskyites and anarchists.

25 November–5 December. Eighth (Extraordinary) Congress of the Soviets, adopted on 5 December the new constitution, which eliminated restrictions on the universal suffrage, guaranteed individual freedom, declared the Party's leading role, and made references to planning and collectivization. The equality of the federate Republics was institutionalized (they increased from seven to eleven, after the promotion of the Autonomous Republics of Kazakhstan and Kirghiz and the splitting up of Transcaucasia into the three Republics of Armenia, Azerbaijan, and Georgia). Election by the citizens, every four years, of a Supreme Soviet, composed of two houses (the Soviet of the Union and the Soviet of Nationalities). The president of the Supreme Soviet functioned as the head of state. The widely publicized constitution, "the most democratic in the world," according to Stalin, was drafted under the direction of N. Bukharin.

1937

6 January. Census of the population of the USSR. The results were not published.

23–30 January. Second Moscow Trial ("Trial of the Seventeen"): the defendants included G. Pyatakov, K. Radek, L. Serebryakov, G. Sokolnikov. New accusations against this "Trotskyite anti-Soviet Center": economic wrecking, treason, and spying for Germany and Japan. Charges were also brought up against N. Bukharin and A. Rykov. Thirteen death penalties (including G. Pyatakov and L. Serebryakov), four prison terms (ten years for K. Radek and G. Sokolnikov).

18 February. Death of G. Ordzhonikidze, allegedly caused by a heart failure. In reality Ordzhonikidze committed suicide.

25 February–5 March. Plenum of the Central Committee, which decided to exclude from the Party ranks N. Bukharin and A. Rykov, who were arrested on 27 February.

1 April. Achievement of the Second Five-Year Plan, after four years and three months. According to the declaration, production had increased by 137 percent (100 percent in consumer goods).

May. Restoration of the power of political commissars in the army.

31 May. Suicide of General Ya. Gamarnik, who headed the Political Direction of the army.

11 June. The press announced the arrest and trial in camera of eight military commanders, accused of espionage, treason on instructions from the German General Staff and Trotsky, and participation in a counterrevolutionary fascist conspiracy to overthrow the Russian government. The death sentences were carried out on 12 June. It was followed by an extensive purge in the army.

15 June. The political commissars in the army were given the same rank as military officers. All orders were to be signed jointly. Opening of the Moscow-Volga Canal.

18–20 June. Nonstop flight from Moscow to Portland (over the North Pole) by the pilot V. Chkalov.

21 August. Signing of a nonaggression pact with China, to which the USSR delivered military materiel.

12 December. First elections to the Supreme Soviet: 98.6 percent of the votes went to the bloc of "Communists and non-Party."

1938

1 January. Official start of the Third Five-Year Plan.

January. Khrushchev became first secretary of the Communist Party of the Ukraine and succeeded to the post of P. Postyshev as candidate member of the Politburo.

12–19 January. Session of the Supreme Soviet. M. Kalinin confirmed as head of state.

1 March. Trade agreement between Germany and the Soviet Union, extended the agreement of 24 December 1936.

2–13 March. Third Moscow Trial ("Trial of the Twenty-One"): the defendants included N. Bukharin, A. Rykov, Ch. Rakovsky, and the former chief of the NKVD G. Yagoda. The accusations against the "bloc of rightists and anti-Soviet Trotskyites" include plotting against Lenin and Stalin, the assassinations of Kirov, V. Kuibyshev, and M. Gorky, sabotage, and treason.

Death sentences for all the defendants, except Ch. Rakovsky, who was executed in October 1941.

13 March. Decree that imposed the teaching of Russian in all schools of the non-Russian republics.

15 March. Protest of the Soviet Union against the Anschluss (the attachment of Austria to Germany on 11–13 March).

20 July. Beria appointed assistant to N. Yezhov at the NKVD.

End of July. Jan Rudzutak, member of the Politburo, was executed without a public trial.

29 July–11 August. Armed conflict between the USSR and Japan in the region of the lake of Khasan, on the Manchurian-Korean border.

September. Crisis of the Sudetenland.

29–30 September. Munich Conference to which neither Czechoslovakia nor the USSR were invited. Agreement between Germany, Italy, France, and Great Britain concerning the annexation of the Sudetenland by Germany. Protest of the USSR on 2 October.

1 October. Publication of the *History of the All-Union Communist Party: Short Course*.

23 November. Announcement of a purge of officials of the Komsomol (Young Communist League).

8 December. L. Beria succeeded N. Yezhov at the head of the NKVD.

20 December. Extension to all workers of the obligation of the labor book, which further restricted their freedom.

27 December. Creation of the Title of Hero of Socialist Labor.

28 December. Decree on the enforcement of labor discipline. Social mobility was discouraged by the reduction or the cancellation of benefits in case of the change of work place.

1939

January. Census of the population. The results (170.6 million people, 33 percent of whom resided in urban centers) seem to be exaggerated. They nevertheless are indicative of a demographic catastrophe.

10–21 March. Eighteenth Congress of the Communist Party in which only fifty-nine delegates of the preceding Congress participated (1,108 out of the 1,956 were arrested). Announcement of new statutes, the end of the massive purges, and of a new campaign of recruitment. Enforcement of centralized Party control over economic life. Adoption of the third Five-Year Plan.

Zhdanov and Khrushchev entered the Politburo as full members, Chvernik and Beria, as candidate members.

3 May. M. Litvinov, People's Commissar of Foreign Affairs, was replaced by V. Molotov. End of the attempt to institute a collective security system.

1 August. Inauguration of the All-Union Agricultural Exhibition.

24 August. Signing of the German-Soviet Non-Aggression Pact, accompanied by a secret protocol (the existence of which was denied by the USSR for the following fifty years). It divided Eastern Europe into zones of influence: Western Poland and Lithuania to Germany; Finland, Estonia, Latvia, and Eastern Poland to the USSR, which also expressed an interest in Bessarabia.

NOTES

[1] For this point, see Lewin, *The Making of the Soviet System*, 178–88.

PAGE FROM FROLOV'S DIARY (1937)

CHRONICLE OF THE YEAR 1937
as Recorded by
THE NEWSPAPER IZVESTIYA
and
COLLECTIVE FARMER
IGNAT DANILOVICH FROLOV*

Friday, January 1. The momentous dates of last year will stand out as a monumental column in the chronicles of socialism. They will enshrine the epic simplicity, the sense of elation and excitement that filled our days, and the grandeur and beauty of our celebrations; they will encompass the inspiring songs of the Ukrainians and Cossacks, the daring of Chkalov, Levanevsky, Kokkinaki, and Yumashev,[1] the bravery of the border guards Captain Ageev and Karatsupy, and the courage of Nikolai Ostrovsky.[2] From each and every date threads will stretch forth into the future, like those extending from the storming of the Bastille to the "Ode to Joy" and from the "Ode to Joy" to the majestic chords of the Ninth Symphony sounding forth on the day of the adoption of the Stalin Constitution.[3] The sun of our epoch will cast its beneficent rays ever wider, and a new Gorky, a new Pavlov,[4] a new Karpinsky[5] will mature and grow on our earth, tens of thousands of Galina Osipenkos and Praskovya Kovardaks will ascend onto the Kremlin tribune, hundreds of thousands of Makarovs and Mazyaevs[6] will arise to take their places in the factories, and millions of Soviet women will reflect with gratitude upon the Mothers' Assistance Law.[7] The winds of history will disperse the contemptible ashes of the

---

* The diary of Ignat Danilovich Frolov was acquired by an archeographical expedition of the Lenin State Library in the fall of 1965. The manuscript was given to Nikolai Borisovich Tikhomirov, a resident of the expedition, by Ignat Frolov's son Timofei Ignatovich Frolov, inhabitant of the village Verkhnee Khoroshevo, district of Kolomna, region of Moscow. The dates of the entire diary are March 20, 1936 (April 2, 1936, new style)–October 31, 1939 (November 13, 1939, new style).

  All dates in Frolov's diary, which is printed in italics, are old (Julian) style, thirteen days behind *Izvestiya*; thus although the Frolov entries that follow each *Izvestiya* entry bear different dates, both concern events of the same day; temperatures are given in Celsius; spelling, odd punctuation, and so forth reflect the original.

Trotskyite-Fascist terrorist gang, leaving no trace, the rains will cleanse the earth of their rotten blood, and millions of people will stride forward, trampling under their feet the detested, disgraced names. This great year in history overflows with momentous events. It is too great, too broad, to be contained within its 366 [sic] days. An epoch unto itself!

*　*　*

On New Year's Eve nearly A QUARTER OF A MILLION HOLIDAY TREES were lit up in the capital alone. The spruce tree has come to symbolize our country's happy youth, sparkling with joy on the holiday.[8] The tree was the centerpiece of New Year's balls, masquerades, and parties. One celebration was held in the spacious club of the Kauchuk Factory. The guests danced to jazz, to the sounds of brass bands, pianos, bayans (a kind of accordion), the radio. Mysterious masks hastened to the gymnasium, where a luxuriously decorated tree rose right up to the ceiling. The clinking of filled glasses filled with champagne. At the stroke of midnight, hundreds of thousands of hands raised them in a toast to the health of their happy motherland, giving tribute in the first toast of the year to the man whose name will go down through the ages as the creator of the great charter of socialism.

19-th of December. overcast weather with a Southwest wind it was warm even thawed a little the roofs are dripping.

Monday, January 4. Soon the Soviet people will mark a sorrowful date in the history of human culture — the centennial of the tragic death of our nation's great poet Alexander Sergeevich Pushkin, murdered by agents of a reactionary clique of noblemen led by the Russian tsar.

22-nd of December. Overcast weather with a Southwest wind it was warm and we had a little damp snow fall in the afternoon. today we went to the mill ground the last of the rye and wheat 310 kilogram. from which they took 30 kilogr. leaving 280 kil. or 17 pood.

Sunday, January 24. The best representatives of Soviet society fill the courtroom. Medals gleam on the breasts of Stakhanovites, pilots, and academics. Among those present are the writers A. N. Tolstoi,[9] Lion Feuchtwanger[10], Fadeev[11] and others. Unflinching hatred, insurmountable scorn, inexpressible disgust fill their gazes as they stare at the defendants. The seats reserved for the Soviet press are filled to overflowing. Some thirty correspondents of the major foreign press agencies and newspapers took their places long before the opening of the trial. Numerous representatives of the diplomatic corps are present in the hall, including the American Ambassador Mr. Davis, the French Ambassador Mr. Coulondre, and others. Will they confess—Pyatakov, Sokolnikov, Radek, Serebryakov, Livshits, Muralov, Drobnis, Boguslavsky, and the 9 others—to all these atrocious crimes?[12] The interrogation of defendant Pyatakov, which began in the morning, continues through the entire evening session. The questions addressed to him by Com. Vyshinsky, Chief Prosecutor of the USSR work like a surgeon's scalpel to dissect this walking corpse.[13]

11-th of January. weather still fine and sunny with a mild north wind it was down to 28 Below in the morning. today was the first day of manure hauling from the stable out to the cabbage patch up by the bridge

Tuesday, January 26. "It's hard for me, an ordinary collective farmer, to find the words to express what is going through my mind as I sit here in the courtroom. One thing I can say: it never even crossed my mind, even in my dreams, that the earth could spawn such villains. What they did, and what they planned to do, cuts me to the quick and I feel like shouting out at the top of my voice: 'Death to you, you damned butchers!' I can barely restrain myself. As a collective farmer, naturally I took special note of the fact that Trotsky and his gang had been planning to disband the collective farms. I tell myself, I bet they were going to force you, Ivan Ivanovich, back out into the fields to work as a farm laborer again. But this will never be!" Ivan Ivanovich Vidyushonkov, worker in the artel[14] of the Bolshevik Collective Farm, Leningrad Region.

13-th of December [sic] Fine weather with a north west wind, 20 below today we took all the horses to the vets. to be Checked. Manya went to Kolomna again for cabbage she bought (2 pood) 30 kilogr. at 50 k. for 15 rub.

Thursday, January 28. The Central Executive Committee of the Union of the SSR resolves: to confer on Com. YEZHOV Nikolai Ivanovich, People's Commissar of Internal Affairs of the USSR, the title of General Commissar of State Security.

15-th of January. Fine weather real cold with a north wind, 20 below the Collective Farm is still. hauling manure to the vegetable bed at the market hay was up to 20 r. a pood today.

Saturday, January 30. Lion Feuchtwanger: "The trial that has just ended is of enormous psychological, political, and historical interest. The people of Western Europe, however, do not fully understand the reasons and motivations underlying the deeds of the defendants and their behavior in court. The crimes of the majority of these people warrant the death penalty. But abusive epithets and outbursts of indignation, understandable though they may be, cannot completely expose the souls of these people. The crime of the defendants and their punishment can only be adequately explained to the people of Western Europe by the pen of a great Soviet writer. The trial has shown that the path to the right is the path to war. This constitutes the true historical significance of the trial; it has erected a new barrier against war."[15]

17-th of January. fine sunny weather real cold with a north wind. 35 below today they checked our war readiness

Monday, February 1. Over 200 thousand Moscow workers gathered in a public rally to show support for the sentence of the Supreme Court and express their devotion to the party of Lenin and Stalin.

19-th of January. Overcast weather with a light Northwest wind not terribly cold the frost let up, today it was up to 6–8 below. they took 6 carts out past Shurovo to get hay for the collective farms they paid 13 rub. a pood.

Thursday, February 4. Within the next few days a radio-telephone line will be put into operation, linking Moscow with Khabarovsk. The length of the line, the longest in the USSR, is around 7000 kilometers. It has been installed in such a way as to make it impossible to listen in to a conversation using an ordinary receiver. The cost of a three-minute conversation is 15 rubles.

22-nd of January. The weather in the morning was not too cold 10–8 below with a light Southeast wind. overcast. today at 5 3/4 in the morning the Cow calved she stuck it out the whole 287 days she had her fling on April 10 today manya went to Kolomna to get hay for the Collective Farm, and today the 22-nd of January Ivan Zakharovich Stepanov passed away at 5 o'clock in the morning at the age of 72 from a chronic digestive problem for a long time his stomach wouldn't take any food, just liquid.

Friday, February 5. Moscow will take on a festive appearance as it prepares for the Pushkin Centennial.[16] Special care will be devoted to the decoration of Sverdlov and Pushkin Squares, as well as the Bolshoi Theater, as specified in the government resolution. A gigantic portrait of Pushkin reading his poems will be installed at the top of the belfry of the former Strastnoi Monastery. The facade of the former Strastnoi Monastery will be covered with a magnificent panel depicting a Soviet youth demonstration, with the marchers shown carrying books by Pushkin and portraits of the leaders.

23-d of January. Overcast weather with a Southeast wind it wasn't cold just a slight frost. 5–6 below there was some snow flurries off and on.

Friday, February 10. Writers and workers, collective farmers, academics, Red Army soldiers, school children, teachers — millions of people in our country have been preparing for the momentous occasion, the centennial of the death of Pushkin; they have been rereading and studying his works and, inspired by his genius, have themselves joined in the joyful process of artistic creation. The whole country has joined together to celebrate the Pushkin centennial as a genuinely national holiday.

Rostov-Don: A radiogram received in Tuaps from the tanker Batumi, presently located off the California coast, reports that the whole crew is working on preparations for a celebration to honor the Pushkin centennial. The tanker Emba, presently located in the Black Sea, has issued a special Pushkin brochure and album containing a collection of materials about Pushkin. Tuaps itself is planning a big Pushkin celebration to be held in its new Palace of Culture. Excerpts from *Eugene Onegin, Boris Godunov*, and *Poltava* will be performed by the sailors and their wives.

28-th of January. Fine weather again with a strong wind and frost at 2 o clock we left lovtsev with the hay. There was 7 carters including me I went too. the first night the 27-th we spent in a hut by the haystacks

Thursday, February 11. The population of Detskoe Selo[17] has enthusiastically welcomed the resolution of the Central Executive Committee of the USSR to change the name of their town to Pushkin. The "Second Five-Year Plan" Knitwear Factory, machine plants and railroad installations, sanatoriums and vacation homes have held public celebrations. On February 11 the District Committee of the Communist Party, the District

Council and District Committee of the Komsomol,[18] together with Stakhanovite workers, will conduct an expanded Plenary Session dedicated to the life and works of A. S. Pushkin.

29-th of January. Fine weather the wind has let up a little and its not as cold as yesterday. still bringing the hay we got home around half past 5 but we spent last night in Pirogi.

Wednesday, February 17. Two a.m. A drunken old man sits on the floor in the middle of the store, wrapt in affectionate conversation with a dog who wandered in from the street. Another drunk, completely covered with dirt, has snuggled up in the corner next to the heating unit and gone to sleep. A disorderly crowd of people pushes and shoves to get up to the cashier's booth. Dozens of hands hold out their checks, and the clerks run frantically to and fro, trying their best to figure out who wants what. The line is in disarray, the customers are raucous, and the majority of them have had too much to drink. Occasionally a fight breaks out. Someone knocks a bottle out of someone's hand, the glass shatters on the floor, and fists fly. The store is stuffy, the air is thick with fumes from the stove and tobacco smoke, and it reeks of spilled vodka. And where, might you ask, is all this going on? In Moscow, on Gorky Street...right down the street from the Moscow City Council. And it's the same scene in the other all-night stores of Moscow.

4-th of February. Fine weather with a light Southeast wind and a slight frost 5 below but when the sun is out theres some dripping from the roofs.

Saturday, February 20. The crowds gather in front of every building, factory, school and office, and proceed solemnly and slowly toward the Columned Hall.[19] When they learn of the death of the great revolutionary, Sergo Ordzhonikidze,[20] passengers switch to a different tram or metro train and hasten to the Columned Hall. Pedestrians notice the flags that have been raised, ask what they're for, and then they too head for the Columned Hall. The people make their way slowly along the streets by the House of Unions. No one says a word. The misfortune struck suddenly, without warning. Workers, Red Army soldiers, school children, engineers, academics — they are all there in the crowds. They walk for hours and hours; the line, several versts long, fills the streets to overflowing. They enter the hall, where black ribbons cut across the white columns, halfway down, expressing all the grief in our broken hearts.

7-th of February. overcast weather with a strong Southwest wind but no new snow, its freezing cold 10 below. the wind makes it real cold.

Sunday, February 28. Speaking after Fadeev, B. Pasternak[21] declared that in spite of the numerous mistakes, errors and lapses, both in his poetic works and in his oral statements, he never considered himself entitled to stand opposed to the masses in the sense expressed by Com. Fadeev. "In all my thoughts and intentions," stated Pasternak, "I am with you, with the country, with the Party." Commenting on the vile anti-Soviet libel expressed abroad by André Gide,[22] Com. Pasternak told angrily and indignantly of Gide's persistent attempts to meet with the poet, even showing up once on his very doorstep in an unsuccessful attempt to obtain material for the filthy and defamatory concoction he was cooking up. "We are not at all hostile to Pasternak," said V. Kirshon, the next speaker, "We believe him when he says that he is completely with the Party and the people. He is a talented poet, but he lives in a kind of extremely limited creative environment, closed off from the atmosphere of ordinary Soviet life. It is absolutely essential for him to understand this and to renounce his identity as — a special poet in this sense, without losing his creative originality along the way, of course."

15-th of February. Fine cold weather with a mild northwest wind 15 Below. Degrees. today I come home from Moscow. at 2 in the afternoon.

Monday, March 15. 135 boxcar loads of oranges and 95 loads of lemons, bought in Spain, will arrive in stores in Moscow and the Moscow region during March and April.[23]

2-nd of March. The weather was overcast with a Southeast wind it was warm and not freezing outside it was wet and the roofs are dripping from the melting snow.

Tuesday, March 16. In accordance with the will of the workers of the capital, the Presidium of the Moscow City Council has resolved to change the name of Bukharin Street to Volochaev Street. The Bukharin Tram Park and Tram Workers' Club will henceforth be known as the Kirov Tram Park and Club. The Rykov Workers' School has been renamed the Kirov Workers' School.[24]

3-d of March, 1937. Overcast weather in the morning a little snow fall. with a Southeast wind but after noon it got clear and sunny and it was warm and humid the melting snow pored down the roofs all day long.

Sunday, March 21. Party elections must be conducted in strict accordance with the decision of the Plenum of the Central Committee of the Communist Party, made on February 27, 1937. It reads: "Voting a straight ticket in Party elections is prohibited. Each position must be voted on individually, thereby guaranteeing to all members of the Party the unlimited right to reject or criticize candidates. Secret balloting is to be instituted in Party elections."

"In its discussion of the case of Bukharin and Rykov, the Plenum of the Central Committee established that the renegades on the right constitute a gang of bandits who have set themselves the goal of restoring Capitalism in our country. A huge gulf separates them from us, for they have slipped irretrievably down, together with the Trotskyites, into a stinking swamp of treachery." From Com. Zhdanov's speech reporting on the Plenum of the C.C. of the Communist Party.[25]

8-th of March. fine calm weather with a slight morning frost it was warm in the afternoon a lot of the snow melted again and the roads got bad, today I went to Kolomna again for firewood and brought back 1/2 Cubic meter.

Tuesday, March 23. Today, March 23, 1937, the Bolsheviks will command the Volga to stop, and the mighty river will crash helplessly against a wall of concrete and come to a halt.[26]

10-th of March. Fine sunny weather with a Southeast wind its warm and the snow is melting in the fields the water is poring through the ravines like crazy. today we went to Kolomna again to get Hay for the collective farmers. and Oats for the Collective Farm Today I went to Kolomna to buy me some things and got some sanding cloth for 44 k. at 3/8 d. for 2 r. 10 k. Tomatoe seeds for 75 k. 1 loaf of bl. bread 1 r. 78 k. 3 rolls 1 r. 08 k. 2 apples 80 k. 3 packets of mustard 1 r. and 2 glasses of Coffee 70 k. red powder 32 k.

Wednesday, March 24. The chronicles of the Moscow-Volga Canal will contain this entry: "On March 23, 1937, at 10:37 a.m., the Volga, for the first time in its entire long existence, was halted by the power of man." Imagine the excitement that ran through the crowd standing atop the Volga

Dam when the Director of Construction issued the order: "Close the sluice gates tight. Don't leave even a 25–centimeter crack! Bring the Volga to a complete halt! For several minutes!" And then the Volga, stopped by the dam, panting heavily through a single narrow crack, began gasping for breath. The 150-ton sluice gates gripped her by the throat. It all lasted for just three minutes.

11-th of March. Fine weather in the morning but with a strong Southeast wind at 5 in the afternoon it rained it was warm and the roads got real bad and we had a whole lot of snow melting and coming in from the fields The water in the rivers is going real strong the slay route is about done for today we brought the last 1/2 cubic meter. of firewood and the collective farmers brought themselves from Kolomna 4 cartloads of pressed straw and we took 5 carts to the mill but we only got 5 bags of rye ground and brought the rest back unground on account of all the water they had to stop the mill and take down the dam.

Friday, March 26. Fresh cucumbers have appeared in the stores in Komsomolsk-on-Amur. They are the first products from the greenhouse of the town's recently established farm production center.

13-th of March. Overcast weather foggy with a strong Southeast wind warm no frost the snow in the fields has just about all melted no more slay riding. Today a lot of people in the village and us sandbagged the Cellars. but in the Collective Farm the Potatoe in the storage cellar was flooded. the water went up to 1 1/2 arshins (42 inches) from the top from their carelessness they couldn't get the snow dug out and let the water run through in time. Today Mother left for Kolomna to get herself on the right track, she's fasting. because with the flooding the priest couldn't get here to Lukeryino and also because of his weak health Today they took everyone's passports for exchange[27] and also took the meat supply contracts for checking.

Thursday, April 1. On March 27, a train pulled out of the Vspolye-on-Mogilyov Station. Shortly thereafter, terrible shrieks could be heard coming from one of the cars. The train was stopped and everyone rushed to the car. It turned out that the elephant Shango had suddenly gone on a rampage and destroyed the inside of the car. A monkey and parrot in the car were killed.

19th of March. Fine weather but with a north wind and heavy morning frost, but

*during the day it all melted again today I went to the bathhouse and spent 1 r. 60
k. on my bath including the train ticket plus tea and a snack for 2 r. 75 k.*

Friday, April 2. At dawn on April 1, N. Ilyin, a carter from the Meat Processing Plant, was on his way from the Krestyanskaya Gate to the Ilyich Gate
in Moscow. Three robbers came after him at the Rogozhsky Riverbank.
One of them jumped up onto the cart and started trying to pull off the
driver's leather coat. Ilyin set the horse into a gallop, and a struggle began
between him and the robber, with the other two chasing after them. Suddenly a Moscow Police Administration van carrying a load of prisoners
appeared around a corner. The police escort in the van saw what was
going on on the cart, and some of them rushed off in pursuit of the robbers: They made a futile attempt to get away, but all three were appre-
hended, and they were added to the ranks of the prisoners in the van.

*20-th of March. Fine weather with a north wind in the morning and frost it melts
during the day where the sun shines. but not in the shade. today we went to
Kolomna for beet husks to feed the cows and calfs on the Collective Farm we
brought 1 ton we got for 150 r.*

Saturday, April 3. TROTSKY[28] Ivan Ivanovich, from the village of Peski,
Kharkov region, announces the change of his surname to GRANOVSKY.
  ZINOVIEVA[29] Yevgeniya Mikhailovna, originally from Kiev, now living
in Kharkov, announces the change of her surname to KLIMOVITSKAYA.
  TROTSKY Vladimir Aleksandrovich, originally from the village of
Kolotovitsa, Leningrad Region, announces the change of his surname to
KARPINSKY.

*21-st of March. The weather is just like yesterday Today Manya Went on the work
train to Shurovo to get Sauerkraut she brought 15 kilogr. she got for 8 r. 40 k. at
56 kop. a kilo.*

Sunday, April 4. In view of recently discovered official malfeasance of a
criminal nature committed by People's Commissar of Communication
G. G. Yagoda,[30] the Presidium of the Central Executive Committee of the
USSR resolves: 1—to suspend G. G. Yagoda from his duties as People's
Commissar of Communication; 2—to turn over the case of G. G. Yagoda to
the investigatory agencies.

22-nd of March. Fine weather with frost in the morning and a light North wind everything melted again during the day it got warm in the sun today Manya went to sell 12 liters of milk she sold 14 r. 30 kop. worth at 1 r. 20 kop. and had to spend all the money on food.

Monday, April 5. On April 2, a group of hooligans showed up at the last showing of the day in the Taganka Movie Theater (Moscow). There were 8 of them. The film had barely begun when the hooligans began whistling loudly and shouting and arguing among themselves at the top of their voices. The police had to be called in. The hooligans resisted arrest and even tried to disarm one of the policemen. The case is under investigation.

23-d of March. The weather in the morning there was a light frost with a northeast wind between 9 and 10 it looked like snow but not for long after lunch it cleared again and got sunny and warm but then toward evening it started to freeze up again

Today Manya went to the railway station in Kolomna to get pressed Straw for the collective farm And today we took the Cow to the bull for the second time.

Friday, April 9. LOST: Ivan Petrovich, age 7, and Olga Petrovna, age 5, Filenko. Last seen in 1933 in the city of Kharkov. Anyone having any information as to their whereabouts please respond to: P. O. Budyonovskoye, Prolet. District, AChK, Lozova Farm, P. P. Filenko.

27-th of March. Fine mild sunny weather with a slight frost in the morning but warm in the afternoon after noon thick clouds moved in

Wednesday, April 14. Kalinin. The regional and district authorities are utterly negligent in their selection of radio broadcasting staff. And look what it leads to. In the town of Velikie Luki the announcer on the local radio station reads, "cheater" instead of "leader" and "enemy commander" instead of "army commander," etc. And it's just as bad in the Kalinin Radio Committee itself. The Kalinin local "Radio News" is taken up either with blatant lies (like the report about a regional record of 18 centners of flax-fiber from a single hectare) or with utterly boring information, which no one listens too. 200 districts out of 60 simply don't receive the regional station at all; the others prefer to tune in to Moscow.

1-st of April. Fine weather mild and warm in the morning there was a slight frost today Manya didn't leave for Rostov until 1 in the afternoon. but Olya went to visit Manya and see her Mama, whose back from her operation, Sanya

Friday, April 16. It was a lively night outside the Moscow Art Theater.[31] Theater lovers hoping to get tickets to the premiere of *Anna Karenina* began waiting in line at 8 p.m. They were not intimidated by the prospect of standing there all night long, waiting for the ticket booth to open. The tickets to the shows on April 21 and 24 sold out within three hours.

3-d of April. Cloudy mild and calm weather with no frost the wind was very mild from the Southeast our Lida got sick on April 2-nd it looks like the mumps and with her Face all swelled up people are calling her Piggy

Saturday, April 17. Not so long ago there used to be settlements along the border in many neighboring countries, where the inhabitants made their living almost exclusively by smuggling contraband into the Soviet Union. This situation has changed now, thanks to the growth in prosperity in our country. The sharp reduction in contraband can also be explained by the fact that our borders have been closed and are now kept firmly under lock and key.

4-th of April. Cloudy weather with a strong Southeast wind its chilly but there's no frost they're already sowing a mixture of peas and oats for fodder on the land plowed in the fall. today they took Lidushka to the hospital on the 3 o clock train. so far the weather is dry no rain.

Thursday, April 29. Achievements in the area of industrial production and the early fulfillment of the second Five-Year Plan have enabled the state to accumulate new material resources, thereby allowing for further reductions in the prices of manufactured consumer goods. Accordingly, the Council of People's Commissars of the USSR has resolved to lower the retail prices for manufactured consumer goods, effective June 1.

16-th of April. Overcast weather with a North wind its chilly but there's no rain they're still replowing the land for potatoe and planting Potatoe.

Saturday, May 8. A question for Com. Lyubimov, People's Commissar for Light Industry of the USSR: "Dear Comrade Lyubimov: Allow me to ask you a question that concerns all the women of our country. What are you doing to guarantee the supply of decent quality women's stockings to the population, and why have there been such shortages in this area?" — E. Chudinova (Archeda Station, Stalingrad Railways)

25-th of April. Overcast weather with a mild east wind and scattered showers all day long. but late in the afternoon and at night it started raining good and heavy but not warm at night with a strong east wind, they're still planting Potatoe.

Sunday, May 9. One occasionally encounters children in Sverdlovsk with Spanish names. Recently we were on the square, and we heard a nanny calling a little boy José. She told us that the child's parents had named him in honor of the Spanish Bolshevik José Dias.[32] A. N. Ponomareva, a maid in one of the student dormitories, named her baby girl Dolores.[33]

26-th of April. Overcast weather with a cool east wind it rained pretty hard all day and soaked the ground real good. Today is Sunday! The week after Easter. Fedot Danilovich come from Moscow on his vacation, the collective farm had the day off no one worked

Monday, May 10. What kind of mothers would abandon their children? The majority of them are maids, cleaning women, and transients. A casual affair, no place to stay; with a child on their hands they can't get an apartment or a job, and it's hard to take one out into the country, too. They leave their children at the train station or in the entryways of a building somewhere, then hide and watch to see where they're taken.

27-th of April. Cloudy and cold weather in the morning with a north wind but it cleared up in the afternoon got sunny and warm but after all that rain they didn't plant no potatoe today

Tuesday, May 11. Beginning today, the prices for meals in Moscow restaurants have been lowered by 10 percent.

* * *

On May 12 thousands of Moscow runners will participate in the first cross country meet of the spring season. Some 20 thousand runners have registered for the race.

28-th of April. Fine cool weather with a north wind in the morning there was a light frost but it got warm later in the afternoon in the evening there was a few bugs, the first ones. may bugs

Friday, May 14. A comment on Com. Lyubimov's answer to Com. Chudinova's question: "Dear Comrade Lyubimov: I don't know whether your answer will satisfy Com. Chudinova and the many thousands of consumers who have been searching the stores for women's stockings, but as someone who knows the stocking and knitwear industry well, I find it inadequate. You are mistaken, Com. Lyubimov, when you claim that the Soviet stocking industry is just starting out. Like it or not, this branch of manufacturing has existed for 20 years now; isn't it about time to stop justifying its backwardness on the pretext that it is still new? Over the course of those 20 years, our country has mastered the technology of blooming mills, slabbing mills, and wonderful airplane engines, and no one goes around bragging about it. Meanwhile the knitwear manufacturers can't seem to 'get the hang' of stockings." S. Arlatov, Director of the Tushino Stocking Factory.

1-st of May. Fine sunny and very warm weather with a mild Southwest wind late in the evening some storm clouds and thunder come through from the west but it just sprinkled a little and then stopped without hardly wetting down the dust. In the orchards the plum and cherry trees are coming into bloom, with real bright color today we planted early cabbage and Today we started painting our roof.

Saturday, May 15. Due to the peculiarities of its historical past, more centers of religious obscurantism have remained active in the Gorky region than anywhere else. There are a great many active churches, a variety of sectarian groups, and a large number of priests and church councils, surviving monastery "cadres," etc. The clergy and their activists here are using all means in their power, often not without success, to strengthen their influence among the masses. This was particularly in evidence over the Easter holiday. In Kochergino, Balakhnino District, representatives of the church campaigned so effectively in the village council that they prevailed upon the chairman of the Collective Farm to declare May 1 a working day, and May 2—Easter—a general holiday. Naturally the church representatives took full advantage of this to disrupt 3–4 days of sowing in the Collective Farm. In the village of Ananyevo, the local priest offered his services to the village council as manager of the Collective Farm Club, since, as he put it, he is now a citizen in his own right, and the village lacks a program of cultural activities.

2-nd of May. Fine warm even hot weather in the afternoon a couple of good strong thunderstorms come through from the Southwest direction

Sunday, May 16. At the train station and the dock in Kiev one used to encounter deaf mutes selling postcards with various scenes. Occasionally a deaf mute would acquire the gift of speech and attempt to sell pornographic postcards to the trusting buyer. The gang of "deaf mutes" was headed by a certain P. Gornesevich. This character, calling himself a "free artist," produced the pornographic postcards at home and used the "deaf mutes" to sell them. Gornesevich has been arrested.

3-d of May. fine weather in the morning with a good strong Northwest wind it started out cold but got very warm in the afternoon today Kav. Isaev. Bragina. gave a ball to celebrate Pavlova's Wedding

Friday, May 21. Pavel Nikolaevich Abramov's first surprise awaited him at his front entrance. The doorman pretended not to hear the usual greeting and made a point of turning to look the other way as he passed. Pavel Nikolaevich could make no sense of it. Things got worse and worse. When Com. Abramov showed up at the office his subordinates and coworkers seemed surprised to see him. Everything became clear when Pavel Nikolaevich picked up the latest edition of the regional newspaper *Uralsky Rabochy* (The Ural Worker) from April 18. In a report on the X-th Plenum of the Regional Executive Committee he read that Abramov had been dismissed from the plenum as an enemy of the people. And of course everyone knows that Pavel Nikolaevich Abramov is a member of the Regional Executive Committee. People avoided Pavel Nikolaevich for 10 days: who wants to be seen hob-nobbing with an enemy of the people? On the 11-th day – April 29 –, an "Editorial Clarification" appeared on the last page, in fine print: "The editors consider it necessary to inform their readers that it was Ya. K. Abramov, the former director of Kizilugol, who was dismissed by the plenum." Truth prevailed, and Pavel Nikolaevich Abramov was rehabilitated. But it should be noted that the editors of *Uralsky Rabochy* have been resorting rather frequently to clarifications of late.

8-th of May. Fine weather very warm in the afternoon even hot but it cooled down by evening the wind is coming from the east. there was some storm clouds but no rain. today was Ivan Zakharov's funeral, he drunk himself to death on vodka Today they tore down our shed from the estate and took it over to the collective farm for building over Gavrilov's old cellar.

Saturday, May 22. The incredible news raced across the entire planet: The red banner of triumphant socialism billows in the air at the northern extreme of the earth's axis. The North Pole has been conquered by the Bolsheviks. Soviet people have settled at the North Pole. Yesterday Otto Yulyevich Shmidt[34] reported to the party and the government: "At 11:10 the airplane USSR N-170 flew over the North Pole. Vodopyanov[35] made a brilliant landing at 11:35. Today we can announce, with great and joyful emotion, with enormous pride, that we have taken the North Pole. Four brave men — Papanin, Krenkel, Fyodorov, and Shirshov — will remain at the Pole. These men set forth voluntarily and consciously to accomplish this feat in the name of science, in the name of service to their motherland."

9-th of May. Fine warm weather with a mild Southeast wind.

Friday, May 28. In April and May in Moscow and the Moscow Region, as well as in a number of other areas in the northern and central USSR, there has been observed a sharp increase in the number of cases of malaria.

15-th of May. fine weather in the morning but with a very strong Southwest wind and then at about 4 in the afternoon a rainstorm come through with thunder and a strong wind it rained again at 9:00 in the evening and give the ground a good soaking.

Saturday, May 29. It took the Omsk Regional Court seven days to unravel a dense tangle of despicable crimes committed by the former leaders of the Velizhansk District. In the fall District Committee Chairman Nikolaev issued a subversive, criminal directive: "Shred the private farmers like cabbage." Inspector Bydashin of the District Executive Committee, together with the chairmen of several village councils, set about collecting "arrears." The criminals broke locks and confiscated all the peasants' property, shot and killed their pigs and divided the meat among themselves on the spot. They went to the farm of Kovalyova, an old woman of 65 who lives alone and has no debts; they seized her last possessions and several kilograms of grain. Skishev took everything, right down to the last wisp of hay, from Kostko, a blind old man of 73. Laptev committed an actual armed robbery in the village of Slavlenka; he rounded up all the livestock and drove them away, taking all the grain with him as well. Nikolaev, the brains behind these operations, was given a suspended two-year sentence. Clearly the Omsk Regional Court underestimated the political significance of this case. Nikolaev and Ivanov discredited collectivization in the district. The court chose not to take Nikolaev's political identity into account, in spite of indications that he had praised the bandit Zinoviev after his execution.

16-th of May. Overcast weather all day there was rain clouds and it rained a few times with a Northwest wind the Air was cool.

Tuesday, June 1. On May 31, Ya. B. Gamarnik,[36] former member of the Central Committee of the Communist Party, having become entangled in contacts with anti-Soviet elements and evidently fearing discovery, committed suicide.

* * *

Yesterday afternoon the well-known Russian writer A. I. Kuprin[37] and his wife arrived in Moscow from Paris by trans-European express after many years spent living abroad. "I am infinitely grateful to the Soviet government for allowing me to return to my native country after so many years away, years of isolation which caused me great suffering."

19-th of May/1-st of June. Fine warm weather with a moderate Southwest wind today I went to the bathhouse in bobrovo and stopped in to see my daughter's father-in-law in his new apartment and stayed overnight at Gegorushka's.

Sunday, June 6. Baku. An old man -- Makhmud Nur Mamed-Ogly, a Collective farmer, was guarding Collective Farm property near the border at night. During a flash of lightning the old man noticed a stranger making his way along the border. Makhmud Nur Mamed-Ogly realized that he was faced with an enemy. He summoned the workers from the Collective Farm, and together they captured the border violator. He turned out to be the ringleader of a major counterrevolutionary band. Makhmud Nur Mamed-Ogly is enjoying a well-deserved fame. He has already captured some dozen spies, saboteurs, smugglers and bandits as they tried to cross over the border into the land of the Soviets.

24-th of May. Sunday! Fine weather with a cold North wind it was warm in the afternoon but toward evening it got real cold today they're carting manure from our farmyard using 3 carts they hauled away 53 loads.

Wednesday, June 9. The editors asked several members of trade unions why they've gone so long without paying their membership dues. Here is the answer of I. E. Starshy, caretaker of No 26 M. Bronnaya Street: "Here's my Union Card. It's true I haven't paid my dues for several months now. But whose fault is that? I haven't been paid for 1 1/2 months now. And what has my union done to get the House Tenants' Cooperative Association[38] to pay me on time? Not a thing!"

26-th and 27-th of May. fine sunny weather with a lot of dew in the morning it was hot in the afternoon with a north wind. Today the 27-th I come back from bezpyatovo at around 8 in the evening.

Thursday, June 10. The Moscow Regional Conference of the Communist Party. Restructuring (Perestroika) must proceed on the basis of increased vigilance, self-criticism and a strict observance of intra-Party democracy. We must remember that there are enemies all around us. Com. Khrushchev[39] is calling for strictest maintenance of Party secrecy, for a resolute struggle against idle gossipers and frivolous and careless people. Unfortunately we still have plenty of people prone to idle chatter who don't know how to keep State and Party secrets. Someone has to know something and you tell him, "from me to you," and next thing you know you're hearing it "from corner to corner," says Com. Khrushchev, to the general approval of the audience.

28-th of May. Ascension Day! fine weather it got cloudy and very warm and calm after lunch there was rain clouds but no rain. the Collective Farm didn't work today they gave us the day off.

Friday, June 11. Investigation of the case against Tukhachevsky M. N., Yakir I. Z., Uborevich I. P., Kork A. I., Eideman R. P., Feldman B. M., Primakov V. M. and Putna V. K., arrested individually by the NKVD, has been completed and turned over to the court.[40] The above-mentioned defendants are accused of violation of their military duty (their oath of allegiance), treason against their motherland, treason against the peoples of the USSR, and treason against of the Army of the Workers and Peasants. All the accused pled guilty to the crimes they are charged with. The case will be tried today, May 11, at a special Judicial session of the Supreme Court of the USSR, to be held behind closed doors.

* * *

By decision of the Regional Committee of the Communist Party of the Ukraine, a day of Party unity was conducted in Kiev for discussion of the question of maintaining State and Party secrets. Disturbing cases of carelessness were brought to light by the Communists of the Party Organization of the Kiev Regional Land Office. Any citizen can drop in at the Regional Land Office and learn anything he might want to know about the status of machines and equipment at the Machine-Tractor Station,[41] along with other information of vital importance; the data is there for the asking.

* * *

On June 9 a drunken man entered the menagerie located on the territory of the Yaroslavsky market (Moscow). Taking from his pocket a half-liter bottle of vodka, he started giving it to one of the bears. The bear quickly drank up all the vodka and, having become intoxicated, he bit into the bottle and broke it, severely lacerating his jaws and tongue. Menagerie workers managed to apprehend the hooligan. His name is I. Bazykin.

Saturday, June 12. The spies Tukhachevsky, Yakir, Uborevich, Kork, Eidemen, Feldman, Primakov and Putna, who sold out to the sworn enemies of socialism, had the audacity to raise a blood-stained, criminal hand against the lives and happiness of the people, one hundred seventy million strong, who created the Stalin Constitution. The sentence of the court is a humanitarian act, aimed at defending our motherland and our progressive people from the vicious, bloodthirsty agents of bourgeois espionage. The whole country, which had unanimously demanded that the band of eight spies be wiped off the face of the earth, welcomes the decision of the court. Execution by shooting! Such is the sentence of the court. Execution! Such is the will of the people.

29-th and 30-th of May. Fine calm and hot weather with a very light breeze from the North the collective farm finished hauling manure on the 30th. they're weeding onion and they've started mowing the grass along the roads and between the fields.

Tuesday, June 15. Gorlovka.[42] When Com. F. Dreev, a coal-hewer in the Stalin Mine, learned of the sentence of the band of spies, he marked the occasion by setting a new productivity record. Extracting 120 tons of coal in a single shift, he exceeded the quota by 800 percent.

* * *

Only bungling on the part of the leaders in the field of light industry can explain the huge number of complaints from citizens about the completely unjustifiable absence of thread and stockings on the store counters and the shortages and miserable quality of other consumer goods. Sabotage by Trotskyites, Bukharinites and others has done enormous damage to our light industry. The saboteurs have aimed their blows against the most vulnerable places and have been active in many factories and central administrative offices, taking advantage of the idiocy and scatterbrained negligence of workers in light industry. A meeting of activists of the People's Commissariat of Light Industry has also shown that light industry has not yet developed the necessary level of Bolshevik self-criticism. People's Commissar Lyubimov has been remarkably close-lipped on the subject of the weaknesses in the work and leadership of the People's Commissariat itself. It would seem that the People's Commissariat and its own leaders have very little to do with these major weaknesses.

* * *

Com. Stavsky[43] made a statement summarizing the meeting of the Party group of the Soviet Writers' Union: "Our overall goal," he stated, "is to expose the methods used by the enemy to conduct its sabotage activities in the area of literature. The enemy will continue to infiltrate literature. It is the task of the party organization to expose saboteurs before they can do any damage. Our investigation exposed outright sabotage and a complete breakdown in the work of the editorial staff of the journal *Novy mir* (New World).[44] Suffice it to say that in the July issue there was not a single article about Gorky, although in July we mark the first anniversary of his death."

2-nd of June. Cold overcast weather with a strong north wind you couldn't go outside in your summer clothes only wearing a padded jacket there was scattered showers here and there. the collective farm is mowing the grass and clover now they're still weeding the onions.

Wednesday, June 16. In response to subversive activity by fascist spies, the workers have asked the government to issue bonds for strengthening the defense capabilities of our motherland.

3-d of June. Fine sunny weather but with a strong north wind it was cool today I went into the woods for a cubic meter of aspen. and today we finished bringing all the firewood from These woods.

Thursday, June 17. People living in the Far East usually receive newspapers from the capital with a ten- or eleven-day delay. Today mailcarriers delivered to subscribers the central newspapers from the eleventh, that is, five days earlier than usual. The newspapers were delivered to Khabarovsk by the pilot Vsevolod Ivanov. Today postal airplanes will begin regular delivery of the central newspapers to Khabarovsk; papers will arrive, at the latest, on the fifth day after their publication.

4-th of June. Fine warm sunny weather with a light north breeze in the afternoon it was hot but the evening it got fairly cool the collective farm is mowing the clover at Kashirka's. with a mowing machine and weeding beets in the vegetable beds.

Sunday, June 20. In response to numerous requests from the workers of the city and the collective farmers of the countryside, the Council of People's Commissars of the USSR has instructed the People's Commissariat of Finances of the USSR to submit for government approval, with all due speed, a draft law in the series "Bonds for Strengthening the Defense of the USSR."

7-th of June. Trinity day Sunday fine sunny Weather hot during the day after noon storm clouds come in from the north with thunder but all we had was just a tiny little drizzle a strong wind come up and blew it all away today the Collective Farm had the day off

Tuesday, June 22. The task set by Comrade Stalin and the Government of the USSR has been accomplished: a nonstop flight, unparalleled in history, has been made from Moscow to North America over the North Pole. The dream of mankind has come true.

9-th of June. Fine sunny weather with a light Northeast breeze its hot the Collective Farm has been mowing clover near Kamenka with mowing machines for two days and the women are weeding Potatoe today we started mowing on the old estate the grass is very good we hardly ever see it so good.

Wednesday, June 23. "The Land of the Soviets is rejoicing. Turning a new page in the history of world and Soviet aviation, our Bolshevik pilots have again shown the whole world the wonders of heroism and skill of which the sons of the great Socialist motherland are capable," declare the workers of the People's Commissariat of Light Industry of the USSR. "Your example will inspire us onward to even better work," write the workers of the mechanical shop of the Kalinin Lead Works in Chimkentsy in their telegram to Com.s Chkalov, Baidukov and Belyakov. "Our beloved heroes' crossing along the second Stalin route is the best answer to the machinations of the enemies of the people," states Com. Chelidze, a worker at the Tbilisi Shoe Factory.

10-th of June. Fine calm and hot weather with a very light northeast breeze.

Thursday, June 24. By decision of the Moscow City Committee of the Communist Party, from June 19 to July 1 businesses, offices and educational institutions in Moscow will conduct a Day of Political Education for the purposes of informing the workers about the goals, methods and practices of sabotage, espionage and diversionary activities being conducted by foreign intelligence agencies and their right-Trotskyite secret service.

11-th and 12-th of June. fine sunny calm and very hot we're having a drought I wish God would send us down a little rain otherwise all the vegetables will dry up. today the 12-th we went into the woods past kamenka to mow grass and stack clover. Timochka and Manya left us This year the Grass harvest is very good, one in a million!

Saturday, June 26. Thousands of Muscovites gathered yesterday to welcome the heroic conquerers of the North Pole upon their arrival in Moscow. Millions of Soviet people all over the country tuned in at this exciting hour to the live radio broadcast from the rally at the Central Airfield. From the airfield the participants of the heroic expedition to the North Pole set off in a triumphant procession to the Kremlin. The workers of Moscow lined the streets, applauding the heroes and throwing flowers, and a veritable snowstorm of welcoming leaflets poured down on them from above. Soviet composers and poets sing the praises of the heroic conquerors of the North Pole in music and verse. The State Music Publishing House is issuing a series of songs for the masses, dedicated to the intrepid conquerers of the North Pole. One of them, "The Pole is Ours," music by M. Sirer, words by N. Tikhonov, has already been published.

13-th of June. Fine calm and very hot weather the drought is terrible we could really use some rain! today the mowers come back from Kamenka they finished up with the Clover the mowing is all done

Monday, July 12. A physical fitness parade is scheduled to take place today on Moscow's Red Square. Forty-five thousand of the country's best athletes will take part—members of amateur sports clubs, gymnasts of the Red Army of Workers and Peasants, pilots, parachutists, and combined columns of young pioneers and bicyclists. The procession of amateur athletes will be led by the "Locomotive" club. "Locomotive" will be followed by gymnasts from "Torpedo," "Pravda," "The Builder," "Arrow," "Motor," "Tempo," and "Red Confectioner."

* * *

The *Tales of A Thousand and One Nights* are being published in the Chechen language by the State Publishing House of the Chechen-Ingush Autonomous Republic.

29-th of June. a holiday. the feast day of the apostles Peter and Paul. fine Sunny and hot weather all day long with a mild southwest breeze all day the collective farmers dried grass and green fallow. there's an awful lot of mowed fallow and grass

Saturday, July 17. For allowing loaded combines to stand idle, for poor organization of the work of the combines, for not assisting the combine drivers, for intentional underreporting of the harvest, for allowing grain to be lost during harvesting, and for poor organization of grain transportation, Com. N. N. Demchenko, People's Commissar of State Farms of the USSR, has removed Pavlov, director of the Dorenburg State Farm, from his post and turned his case over to the court.

People have forgotten that art consists of service to the people; it is a difficult path that demands knowledge, hard work, and patience. Neither an artificially tacked-on label; "Collective Farmer," "Stakhanovite," "Shock Worker of the Socialist Fields," nor coloration and other tricks can redeem a false, incomprehensible, crude, or technically inferior work of art. We have a colossal need for sculpture. In a remote corner of the woods outside Perm, on one of the tributaries of the Kama, I saw a woman, a Collective farmer, on a barge. In her arms, like a precious treasure, she was cradling a bust of Ilyich.[45] Many sculptors have lost touch with real life. They sit in their studios and laboratories solving problems

33

of "monumentalism," which they understand to mean the depiction of impossibly fat legs, exaggerated to the point of caricature.

4-th of July. Overcast weather it rained all day from early morning until late at night stopping at times it was very heavy with thunder and lightning the road got all mudded up and impassible and they had to stop the harvesting. This evening my sister Sanya come from Moscow on the work train with her land-lady, Alexandra Ivanovna and her son Fedya They will stay with us for a few days but Sanya has to go back to work in Moscow tomorrow.

Sunday, July 18. The Central Executive Committee of the USSR has resolved: for his outstanding work directing the NKVD,[46] to award Comrade N. I. YEZHOV[47] with the ORDER OF LENIN.

5-th of July. Sunday! The weather in the morning was rain but then it cleared and it was fine with no rain we went out after lunch to stack the green fallow it was badly spoilt. today I got 5o r. for my Bookcase and Sanya went back to Moscow.

July 21. The Central Executive Committee of the USSR has resolved: for his successes in strengthening law and order and the offices of the Public Prosecutor, to award Comrade A. Ya. Vyshinsky with the Order of Lenin.

* * *

In all cities and rural localities of the Soviet Union inspectors and special agents of the State Insurance Agency are accepting orders for insurance of household property. The following items may be insured: furniture, clothing, musical instruments, food and fuel supplies, etc. The cost for each 1000 rubles valuation, depending on the fire-resistant qualities of the building, is: in cities and workers' settlements, 1 to 4 rubles, in agricultural localities and dacha communities, from 3 to 9 rubles.

8-th of July. the Feast Day of the Kazan Virgin, fine sunny and very warm and calm weather with a Lot of dew today we bought 6 kil of fresh cabbage in the collective farm for 3 r.

Thursday, July 22. Early in the morning lines start to form in various cities outside the doors of pawnbrokers' shops. The shop is usually small and cramped, there are not enough appraisers, they can barely accommodate one or two hundred people a day; and people have to get in line early in order to make it to the appraisal counter.

9-th of July. In the morning the weather was fine sunny and hot but in the afternoon storm clouds started moving in from the Southwest direction with thunder but a strong wind come up and blew it away there was just a little bit of rain it just drizzled all day but nothing big we had a good days work out in the meadows.

Friday, July 23. One often encounters poorly educated people working in Soviet offices. What a mass of errors, what incoherence do we find in the documents that emerge from under the pens of police office clerks, building managers, court workers, wardens, and stewards! Here's how Khripunova, chief clerk of the People's Court of the Luxemburg District of Orenburg Region, expresses herself: "Guiding arts. 319–320 of the cr. cod. the court sentenced: Sosov Semyon Peramonovich based on art. 73 of the cr.c. to be subjected to corrective labor for a term of six months serving on general grounds to rescind the Sentence of resettlement with confiscation of his residence permit. Crediting Sosov with preliminary incarceration from November 20 to 23 as 3 days. The sentence is final but it may be appalled to the Regional Court within a 5 day period."

10-th of July. Fine sunny calm and hot weather with lots of dew in the morning storm clouds come in in the evening but it didn't rain at all. today they started mowing the rye.

Monday, July 26. Leningrad. Yesterday the Moscow and Leningrad Dynamo Soccer teams played at Lenin Stadium. The game ended in a 3–3 tie. It should be noted that the Moscow team played a very rough game. During the second half the Leningrad soccer players A. Fyodorov, P. Dementyev, and Kuzminsky were injured by them and had to be carried off the field.

13-th of July. Fine calm and warm weather today the factory had the day off and we mowed and bound rye we got a lot done there was two binding machines working too Today Alexander come to see us. Grigoryevich with Sanya Manin's sister Nyusha and her husband and Gegorushka with Manya

Monday, August 2. In the Ivdel and Garin regions of the Northern Urals lives a tribe of seminomadic people called the Mansi. In recent years some of the Mansi have settled down into a sedentary existence. But many Mansi continue to lead a nomadic way of life. They live in small, scattered nomadic settlements, 500–600 kilometers apart, setting up camp around sites where they have killed a bear or an elk.

20-th of July. the Holy Prophet Elijah. Fine weather all day long no rain the collective farm worked harvesting mowing and binding wheat today Vitya come over

Wednesday, August 4. In No. 20 B. Serpukhovskaya Street there is a store with a sign saying "Groceries and Provisions." An intolerable stench overwhelms the customer at the entrance. Inside, a broken jar full of dirty raisins stands on a filthy counter, with bits of broken glass mixed in with the raisins. A raisin-cheese ball is set out in a prominent place. You look a little closer and notice that some of the raisins are stirring—they're flies! We have already learned how to conduct trade in a civilized, Soviet manner. So why do such "stores" still exist?

22-nd. Wednesday fine sunny and warm weather with a good strong east wind they're still mowing and binding wheat and tonight they thrashed rye too.

Thursday, August 5. The People's Commissariat of Social Security of the Russian Republic is responsible for the welfare of up to two million citizens: disabled workers and war veterans, children who have lost their parents, retired people and temporarily disabled workers. What is the quality of service offered by the agencies of social welfare? Are the disabled, the aged and chronically ill given the sensitive care that they need? The People's Commissariat of Social Security does not use a pass system, but it's not that easy to get access to the upper stories, where all the main administrative offices and departments of the People's Commissariat are located. The guard on duty stems the flow of visitors, detaining people at the complaints bureau on the first floor. There is no particular solicitude for visitors in evidence here either. The little reception room is crammed with people, the room is stuffy and dirty, and people are addressed rudely, grudgingly, and only through the window.

23-d of July. Thursday. Fine sunny and warm weather with a mild Northeast wind the wheat harvest is still going on they're mowing and binding the rye and hauling it to the thrashing floor they stack it there and then do the thrashing at night.

Friday, August 6. The openings in the cardboard mask have paper eye-lashes pasted over them. This somewhat narrows your field of vision. But you don't want to take the mask off. You want to maintain your cheerful, festive appearance. There is something magical in these red paper curls, in the hilarious papier-mâché nose. A carnival mask is essentially a cap of invisibility. Comrades, acquaintances, relatives and coworkers walk past without seeing you. And how marvellous to be jostled about in the bois-terous, colorful carnival crowd, where you don't recognize any of the "faces"; precisely for that reason there are no strangers here. That splen-did carnival sense of brotherhood — we are all friends, in the time-hon-ored tradition of the masquerade. At the stroke of nine sharp fireworks blaze up, leaving light trails of smoke across the sky, and the entire color-ful crowd at the Moscow Park of Culture and Recreation presses onto the parapet of the Moscow River embankment. Now tradition takes over, masks are the rule, and the carnival begins. Glittering green, red, blue, and yellow pathways and avenues, a diamond labyrinth of electric light. Light and music, everywhere you look. Musical groups roam the avenues and pathways. Jazz bands play in the pavillions. People dance in the open areas, on the pathways and the embankment. A colorful blizzard of con-fetti. Everything blends together — Spaniards, harlequins, jokers, enter-tainers and guests, a huge giraffe, a bear with a pipe, exotic sailors, friends and strangers, familiar and unfamiliar faces, Ukrainian and Uzbek girls, a domino...The lightly rustling paper streamers that twist around the peo-ple dancing, strolling, and running, are like fetters binding them all together in a single, tightly wound ball of carnival spirit. It's already mid-night, but new crowds keep flowing in from Kaluzhskaya Square, from the Krymsky Bridge. People put on their masks before they come, and the streets leading to the Park of Culture and Recreation are completely filled with crowds of people in masks, comical paper hats of all kinds, and brightly colored jabots, carrying carnival lamps. Even the ice-cream and chocolate-ice sellers are wearing masks. Overcrowded trams pull up and disgorge impatient passengers in colorful costumes. Carnival night!

24-th of July. Fine sunny and very warm weather with a light breeze from the East the collective farm is real busy with the wheat harvest, they did all the mow-ing they finished that and now they're binding. And they're bringing in the rye they stack it on the thrashing floor and do the thrashing at night. They've bound the rye from 50 hectares. 447 stacks.

Tuesday, August 10. Nenets reindeer herders have gathered here on the shore of the Karskoye Sea in Anderm. They have come to mark their national holiday — Reindeer Day. The celebration was enthusiastic and festive. Athletic competitions were followed by meetings at which the Nenets people listened to reports on the international situation and the new election law.[48]

28-th of July. Fine calm and warm weather with a very mild east wind.

Wednesday, August 11. The young people on the Collective Farm in the village of Guta can barely remember the wealthy kulak Alexander Arkhipenkov. Arkhipenkov and his kulak brood are long gone from Guta; the waves of Collectivization swept him up and bore him away from the village, never to return — he wouldn't dare! And indeed, Arkhipenkov did not come back to Guta, not the first year, or the one after that, or five years later. Nor did he show up after Guta had become a Collective Farm; instead, he burrowed into the depths of the Suzemsky woods and made them his new lair. Posing as a forestry worker, Arkhipenkov settled down on the rich earth of the forest. Before long he had built up a farm with six cows, three calves, and a dozen or so pigs. Every year this self-styled "worker" sows several hectares of cereal crops alone, twelve times more than the collective farmers plant on their individual plots. Arkhipenkov's clan followed him out into the woods, they all settled down there. These are not isolated cases. The settlements of Earth, State Farm, and Town have also disappeared into the woods.

29-th of July. Fine sunny and hot weather they're working full steam on the grain harvest. they bring the wheat straight in from the field and thrash it they use harvesting machines on the oat fields.
    Today we got 129 kil. 600 gr. of wheat and 116 kil. 200 gr. of rye in Advance its all been milled, also 9 stacks of wheat straw.

Friday, August 20. P.B.L. these three mysterious letters usually adorn the shabbiest and most unsightly business establishments in our cities. They stand for Public Bath and Laundry, which, for some strange reason, also includes hairdressers and barbers. We are in the process of building new apartment houses with baths and cooperative laundries. But for the time being the majority of the city population still has to go to the public bath, and people still have to go to all kinds of trouble getting their clothes laundered every month. What gives our City Council officials the right to ignore this state of affairs? It's really quite simple: just make sure the faucets don't spray boiling hot water all over the place, that the water—hot and cold—runs whenever it's needed, that everything is clean, comfortable, and adequately ventilated, and that people are treated with courtesy, care, and attention. That's all there is to it.

* * *

A year ago a campaign was initiated against noise in the city. Drivers of trams and other vehicles were forbidden to use their horns except when absolutely necessary. The well-intentioned initiatives of the Moscow City Council soon fell by the wayside. Take some time to observe the traffic, and you will notice how often drivers use their horns when they don't have to. Moscow does have some quiet streets where the tram doesn't go and there are very few cars. But even there, things are no better. Several loud radios broadcasting three different stations simultaneously—it's enough to drive even the most patient of men out of his mind.

7-th of August. Overcast weather beginning at 10 o'clock or so there was a very strong heavy rain it interrupted all the harvesting the sowing of winter rye and wheat has been going on since the beginning of August.

Saturday, August 21. A resolution passed by the Zhizdra City Council could no doubt serve as a guide for good form, though it does give a somewhat strange impression of the manners and customs of the population of Zhizdra. Its authors—two colleagues named Belov, the chairman and the secretary of the City Council—exercising the authority entrusted to them, have embarked on a resolute campaign to improve the manners of the town. If the authors of the old manuals delicately "admonished," Comrades Belov "institute" and "prohibit." For example, traffic on the city streets shall be "*instituted*" until 1 in the morning," whereas "aimlessly walking the streets after the above-indicated time shall be *prohibited*." These two items are only the first steps in the Belovs' program to "civilize" their town. But the population has shown itself to be utterly ungrateful even for them. The first item has aroused obvious displeasure among collective farmers, who occasionally arrive late at the station and have to walk home through the town after 1 a.m. As for the second item, reliable sources inform us that the town's lovers showed such a unanimous solidarity in defending their time-honored right to go walking in the moonlight that the Zhizdra District Executive Council was forced to repeal it.

8-th of August. Warm overcast weather again with a Northeast wind its been raining hard all day long it got so muddy outside they had to stop harvesting the sowing stopped too a lot of mowed oats is lying unbound in the fields

Monday, August 30. Krasnodar. A girl leaps out past the checkpoint at the entrance of the Chapaev Factory and takes off running down the street, lickety-split. The guard rushes off after her, yelling at the top of his voice, "I'll show you how to run away from a lecture!" But the "criminal" Klochkova escaped. The guard Zheltobryushenko gave up the chase and returned to "take up his post" again, closing and locking the front door behind him. Zheltobryushenko has been given unambiguous instructions by Ivankin, the cultural director: "Keep people in!" It's not the first time the factory has used this method to achieve "one-hundred-percent attendance" at lectures and meetings, and so the incident with the worker Klochkova did not surprise or disturb anyone. Rudolf, the chairman of the shop committee, did not ascribe any significance to it, and Party Committee Secretary Dedyaeva just laughed and issued the guard a gentle rebuke.

[There is no entry date in Frolov for August 17 (his August 30)]

Thursday, September 2. Having become entangled in anti-Soviet contacts and evidently fearing accountability before the Ukrainian people for his betrayal of their interests, on August 30 Lyubchenko, the former chairman of the Council of People's Commissars of the Ukraine, committed suicide.

20-th of August. Overcast weather in the morning with a north wind but then it cleared up it was sunny and warm from about 10 o'clock this afternoon Olya went mushroom picking and filled a whole basket to the top with different kinds of mushrooms.

Friday, September 3. Tbilisi. Pilots in the Transcaucasus transport unusual cargoes every day. Recently, the airport inspector on duty was receiving an airplane on a scheduled flight from Akhalkalaki. When he opened the door of the cabin, several four-legged passengers leapt out at him, bleating loudly, and he had to struggle to stay on his feet. The plane had brought some 150 poisonous snakes from Yerevan to Sukhumi. They all came through their flight very well. Every day after they finish with their regular passenger flights, pilots Lykev and Lakhno deliver to the civil workers in Baku fresh, fragrant peaches, apples, and pears from the town of Zakataly. Aviators Raingarten and Kolesnikov make up to twelve flights a day. They work the Kutaisi-Mestia route, delivering flour, manufactured goods and fruits to the mountain regions.

21-st of August. The weather in the morning was fine sunny and warm with a light Northwest wind after lunch it started to cloud over but it didn't rain Today Olya went out to the woods again for mushrooms and got a lot of different kinds but mainly white ones. a whole big basket of just white ones. at night they brought us 1 cartload of threshed oat straw from the Collective Farm for 20 eggs in Potrebilovka mother got 3 meters of cloth and 4 spools of thread she paid in cash 6 rubles 90 kop. 2 kilograms of sugar 7 r. 60 k.

Saturday, September 4. Where not so long ago the walls and towers of the Strastnoy Monastery stood, now you see big piles of bricks and debris. By September 20, the demolition work should be complete, and workers will begin paving the site for an expansion of Pushkin Square, which will nearly double in size. The demolition is proceeding at an extremely unsatisfactory rate, however. At the Central Park of Culture and Recreation, construction work is being completed on one of the most beautiful embankments of the Moscow River—the Pushkin Embankment.

22-nd of August. Fine sunny weather with a strong Northwest wind it was warm a lot of apples were blowed down. Olya went out for mushrooms again she got a lot again a whole basketful of white ones. the Collective Farm is bringing oats in from the field they stack it all and bind it they've bound 400 shooks

Thursday, September 9. A review by the Soviet Control Commission has established instances of criminal storage and damage of grain at a number of processing plants, the State Assorting Fund, warehouses, and State Farms. To address the problem, the Council of People's Commissars of the USSR has instructed Com. Vyshinsky, Prosecutor of the USSR, immediately to summon the persons responsible for these criminal acts to account for themselves before the law.

27-th of August. fine sunny and warm weather in the morning with a mild Southwest wind but it got cloudy and overcast in the afternoon though it didn't rain by evening it all cleared up again and we had a clear sunset and the night was starry and cool today on August 27 Olya went out mushroom picking again and filled a basket with white mushrooms and 1/2 a basket with different kinds of black mushrooms the Collective Farm is bringing in the Onion.

Tuesday, September 14. Kiev. The Presidium of the Kiev City Council has decided to establish a children's home for 150 school-age children. The home will be specially designated for Spanish children living in the USSR.[49] The children's home will have its own school, electric generating station, club, and gymnasium. Special rooms are being furnished for teaching personnel and residential advisors.

1-st of September. Fine sunny weather and it was very warm but with a good strong Northwest wind and storm clouds started moving in toward evening and at night it rained with thunder and lightning Today we took 6 bags of wheat and 2 bags of rye to the North mill.

Saturday, September 18. Izhevsk. The city of Mozhga in the Udmurtsk Autonomous Soviet Socialist Republic planned to conduct a "Soviet Day." Meetings and discussions had been scheduled to explain the "Regulations Governing the Elections for the Supreme Soviet of the USSR." The City Soviet and the citizens prepared for the occasion. But it did not take place. A few hours before the meetings were to begin, a woman started making the rounds of the different institutions. Claiming to be a City Council courier, she informed everyone, on behalf of the City Council, that the meetings had been cancelled. The next day it became clear that no such order had been given, no courier had been sent, and in fact that there hadn't been a courier at all. The false courier has not been identified. This is not the first time the class enemy has made an appearance.

5-th, 6-th, 7-th and 8-th of September. Fine weather it was calm and very warm even hot I was in Moscow from the 6-th to the 8-th I went to stock up for the holiday in the Collective Farm they're spending all their time bringing in the potatoe but they don't get along with each other and hardly anyone shows up for work.

Wednesday, September 22. A meeting for the elderly was held in the Zeltsky National District of Odesshchina for discussion of the new election law. Four hundred people attended the meeting.

9-th of September. the weather is still fine sunny warm and calm today I got my hands on a case of straight spirit for the holiday they brought us another load of potatoe today small ones with some big ones too

Tuesday, September 28. Following the example of the village of Chapaevka, Kiev Region, Dnepropetrovshchina designated ten villages to receive major improvements. The Novospassky Village Council of the Berdyansk Region has achieved extraordinary results. They've built a theater in the collective farm and developed a beautiful park; construction is proceeding on a stadium, a radio broadcasting relay station, and a bathhouse, and the finishing touches are being put on a defense shelter.

15-th of September. Fine sunny weather its calm and warm but cold at night

Thursday, September 30. Yesterday the First Model Printing Office of the Association of State Publishing Houses completed the publication of 1,600,000 copies of the textbook *A Short Course of History of the USSR*, under the editorial direction of Prof. A. V. Shestakov. The work was completed by Stakhonovite printers two days before the deadline. One hundred thousand textbooks were issued in a deluxe edition (in a leather binding). The printing office completed, also before the deadline, a quarterly publication schedule for standard textbooks for primary and secondary schools. Schoolchildren will receive eighteen million bound books.

17-th of September. The weather in the morning we had a light frost again but the day stayed fine they're bringing in the potatoe

Saturday, October 2. Ishim (Omsk Region). "More and More Slander" — such is the motto proclaimed by hostile elements. A priest in the village of Karasulo subscribes to the central newspapers (although the town reading room, one might point out, does not) and conducts loud public readings. He distorts the text when he reads, accompanying it with slanderous "commentaries." He'll give a brief rejoinder or an extensive explanation that twists what he has read and makes it mean the opposite of what was intended. Meanwhile the village council is delighted with its priest: look how well he keeps up with things! One could list dozens of ways in which enemy elements try to "get involved" in the election process. The enemy uses all means in his power to spread his influence among the collective farmers.

43

19-th of September. The weather at night rained a little and in the morning it was overcast but then in the afternoon it cleared up and got fine and calm today they brought us some more potatoe big ones, 4 cartloads 1455 kil. in all a total of 87 pood it's the second time we've got this much

Monday, October 4. The Moscow Zoological Park, overrun with alien elements, has suffered direct acts of sabotage. Several valuable animals were poisoned by someone's malevolent hand. As a result of an improper, unscientific feeding regime, a large number of animals have died of stomach and intestinal disorders. The man responsible for the feeding regimes at the zoo is Kalmanson, the Deputy Manager of the Zoo Department, who until recently had been closely associated with a known spy who has now been arrested. The Culture Section of the Moscow City Council has decided to suspend Zoo director Ostrovsky and to dismiss Kalmanson and turn his case over to the Prosecutor's office. The decision also provides for an immediate review of the staff of the Zoo, with subsequent removal of alien and hostile elements.

21-st of September. Overcast weather in the morning but it cleared up in the middle of the day and there was a calm South wind and no rain all day long Today they brought 50 bush. of large potatoe, 1600 kilogram or 100 pood on 5 carts one cartload of pears 25 pood was sold in Lukeryino.

Wednesday, October 6. Lipovo Valley. In many villages of the Lipovo Valley District of the Poltava Region, collective farmers have begun writing the history of their villages over the past twenty years. Young people, Red Partisans, and veterans of the Civil War have joined special circles to compile these histories. The books they write will be published to mark the twentieth anniversary of the October Revolution.

* * *

Wednesday, October 6. Before the Revolution, people living in Bashkir villages had never even heard of the telephone. Now the Lower Bashkir Telephone Network has 13,750 kilometers of wires. Eight hundred Collective Farms, 987 village councils, 96 MTS, and 40 State Farms now have telephone service.

23-d and 24-th of September. Fine weather warm during the day with a mild northeast wind this morning we had a very light frost they kept on bringing in

44

potatoe and today they finished it they got it all in and started delivering it to peoples houses one Kilogram per day worked[50]

Friday, October 8. The Red Triangle Factory (Leningrad) is expanding its production of moulded galoshes. In the fourth quarter of the year the factory is scheduled to produce 2,600 pairs. Tests have proven them to be much more durable than glued galoshes.

25-th of September. Fine warm weather but it started clouding over toward evening and after 8 o'clock it started raining. today they brought us 2 more cart-loads 638 kilogram. or 39 pood. of large potatoe on 2 carts.

Saturday, October 9. "Our main task is to overcome tendencies toward sabotage among the population and to destroy saboteurs. A few words about what we plan to do. Until now it has been generally believed that the only thing that can be used on steep slopes is a miner's pick, that mechanical tools are ineffective. This is completely false. We must overcome such antimechanization sentiments and get down to business introducing coal-cutters into steep-sloped mines. Com. Kaganovich[51] recommended installing four coal-cutters. We plan to install ten." From the speech of Com. Kartashev—manager of the "Artemugol" Trust at the All-Donetsk Rally of Stakhanovites and Mining Shock-Workers (in Gorlovka).

* * *

Kursk. If an office or private person chooses not to redeem an I.O.U. it is burned. The editorial board of a local newspaper learned about a number of unredeemed I.O.U.'s that had accumulated in the Communications Department and were to be burned. They invited leaders of organizations who had chosen not to respond to correspondence addressed to them to come to the Communications Department. First they went through the letters and picked out ones addressed to Com. Sorokin, the District Prosecutor. What did the letters say? Collective farmer T. writes that the Dairy of the Northern Collective Farm is in trouble, the cattle are dying off. Collective farmer E. S-n appeals to the prosecutor for help; there's a plot against him. In a letter to the District Land Department, team leaders of the Land of the Soviets Collective Farm write that the chairman of the Collective Farm is not crediting them for the days they worked. There are dozens of such letters, and they were about to be burned. And how many have already been destroyed...

26-th of September. Fine warm weather, they're thrashing on the thrashing-floor. They brought all the Potatoe and oats in from the field they pulled up all the beets too and they're hauling them to the shed for storage

Sunday, October 10. Yesterday a citywide meeting of writers was held in the Moscow House of Scholars. Com. Vyshinsky, Prosecutor of the USSR, reported on the election law. The writer's community of the capital gave Com. Vyshinsky's detailed report a warm reception. A number of writers spoke. Vs. Vishnevsky shared his recollections of the October Revolution. The poet S. Kirsanov, who has promised to write his best poetic work about the creator of the Constitution of the USSR, gave an emotional speech. The writers A. Barto, L. Nikulin, and others gave interesting speeches, full of examples illustrating the shared goal of the writers' community — to give the Stalin Era its proper reflection in their works. The writers at the meeting unanimously approved a greeting to send to the Leader of the Peoples, Comrade Stalin.

27-th of September. Fine calm warm weather though its cloudy still there's no rain today I went to the bathhouse in Kolomna I went to the nursery and bought myself two roots for planting one seedless pear and one black apple tree 3d type I paid 1 r. 50 k. for the apple tree and 3 r. for the pear tree 4 r. 50 k. in all

Friday, October 15. A number of new brands of confectionaries, tobacco, and perfumes will be put on the market in anticipation of the holiday.[52] The Moscow Bolshevik Factory is preparing special varieties of high-quality cookies to be called "Happy Childhood" and "Union." The cookies will be packaged in beautifully designed boxes. The Red October Factory will produce various candies, including a caramel called "Pioneer," and chocolates called "Soviet North Pole." Leningrad's Samoilova Confectionary Factory will produce beautifully packaged chocolate candies (with pictures of the Soviet Pavilion at the Paris Exhibition, etc.). 197 million cigarettes are being manufactured by the Glavtabak Factory in anticipation of the holiday. Mass quantities of surprise boxes of cologne, perfume, soap, and powder are also being produced.

2-nd of October. Overcast cold weather in the morning we had a heavy frost and it snowed in the afternoon off and on with a Northwest wind they're pulling onions, cutting and carting cabbage and cleaning it up for the Contractation

Sunday, October 17. Yesterday the newly renovated Museum of the Revolution of the USSR reopened in Moscow. Its exhibits were redone in accordance with the instructions given by Com. Stalin in his letter to the authors of the textbook on the history of the Communist Party.

4-th of October Fine weather again with a mild frost and a Southwest wind

October 20. Soon a small-production theater will open in Leningrad. The theater will stage vaudevilles, short operettas, parodies on current events, lyrical scenes, heroic monologues, etc. The Artistic Director of the theater is Distinguished Artist I. Dunaevsky.[53]

7-th of October. Fine weather with a light morning frost and a northwest wind They're still thrashing Oats and bringing cabbage in from the vegetable bed.

Thursday, October 21. "I work as a propagandist in the village of Lubyanka in the Borodyansk District. This is uncharted territory for a propagandist. In the past the village was overrun by Petlyurovites.[54] Now, of course, things are different. Work still remains to be done, however, not only to prepare people for the elections, but also in the areas of linen processing, potato digging, etc. The main problem is the weakness of the leaders. The chairman of the Village Council is new, and he hasn't gotten oriented yet. The Party Organizer has no authority at all—inside or outside the Party. Andrei Kravets, chairman of the Collective Farm, has has been taken in by class enemies and is destroying the Collective Farm before everyone's eyes. I have already helped the Party, the Komsomol and the Collective Farm conduct meetings on election issues. One large obstacle encountered by the propagandist is the shortage of supplies of literature and educational materials. You have to fall back on what you have memorized." (From a letter to *Izvestiya* from E. Ponomarenko, worker at the Kiev Railway Junction.)

* * *

Leningrad. Work has been completed on the dismantling of the monument to Alexander III, which had stood on Insurrection Square in front of the Moscow Train Station. The bronze figure, weighing over 20 tons, and the huge granite blocks of the pedestal were removed without damage. Now the roadway where the monument stood is being cleared.

* * *

Ten thousand Collective Farms in the USSR have electrical power. The total capacity of rural electric generating stations this year has reached 230 thousand kilowatts.

8-th of October. Overcast but warm with a Southwest wind there was no frost at all today I paid 2 installments of agricultural tax. 9 r. they're still threshing oats and carting in cabbage from the vegetable bed.

Saturday, October 23. At their campaign meeting, representatives of the workers of the Stalin Election Precinct of the city of Moscow have unanimously nominated as their candidate for Union Council Joseph Vissarionovich Stalin.

* * *

Tbilisi. The scaffolding has been taken down from the front of the remarkable building of the Tbilisi Branch of the Institute of Marx, Engels and Lenin. The building facade is adorned with sixteen monumental columns of dark gray marble. The ground level of the building is finished in dark gray granite. The pediment features sculptures illustrating scenes taken from letters written by Georgian workers to Comrade Stalin and bas-reliefs of Marx, Engels, Lenin and Stalin. The furnishings for the building were specially commissioned by the Institute.

10-th of October. Fine sunny weather with a light frost in the morning but the afternoon was warm with a very mild Southwest wind they're thrashing wheat Today they hauled government Contract cabbage on 4 carts. I had an Accident today, I cut my right hand bad with a chisel.

Sunday, November 7. "Greetings to the Soviet Union on the occasion of its twentieth anniversary. Greetings also to all the readers of *Izvestiya*. Congratulations to the Soviet film industry for its achievements. Sincerely yours, Charlie Chaplin."

25-th of October. Ovecast weather but with a light Northwest breeze its dry and not too cold. today I was at the demonstration in Kolomna and we celebrated. at Sanyas and Gegorushkas. I stayed there at Sanya's overnight.

Wednesday, November 10. At about 3:00 p.m. on November 7, in spite of bad weather and a 400–meter cloud cover, the first airplanes appeared over Red Square. Over 300 airplanes—modern high-speed aircraft of all types—participated in the military show. In a departure from previous years only the latest models were shown—modern high-speed bombers, fighters and reconnaissance aircraft. In spite of severe turbulence, the airplanes maintained their precise formation, as though bound together by invisible ribbons; they formed an inscription that droned triumphantly across the sky: XX USSR.[55] Power and daring, speed and exceptional skill—such is the impression left by the air show commemorating the twentieth anniversary of the Great October Socialist Revolution.

* * *

Gori. On November 8 a ceremony was held to celebrate the formal opening of the house where Joseph Vissarionovich Stalin spent his childhood years, newly restored on the initiative of Com. Beria.[56] The little house with its two tiny little rooms has been restored to the condition it was in a half-century ago. The house is enclosed in a decorative stone and granite pavilion with a glassed-in roof and columns finished in black marble lining the sides. The central part of the pavilion offers a fine view of the facade of the house, with the front door and two windows opening on to the street. Over 2,000 people attended the public ceremony celebrating the ceremonial opening of the museum and monument.

28-th of October. Overcast weather cloudy in the morning but warm with some thunder and scattered showers. in the evening it started really coming down though not for long and there was no rain overnight.

Thursday, November 11. Organizations that mass-produce sculptures are often guilty of distorting the image and likeness of Lenin, Stalin, Pushkin, and Gorky. To address this problem, the All-Union Committee on the Arts has ordered all organizations that mass-produce sculptures to have their models approved in advance: portraits of Lenin and Stalin, by the Central Museum of Lenin and portraits of Pushkin and Gorky, by the Gorky Institute of Literature.

29-th of October. Overcast weather but it was calm and warm with no rain today they finished up the pea thrashing.

Saturday, November 20. In spite of temperatures that dropped to 20 below, strong wind and deep snow, Red Army soldiers and commanders of the N. Infantry Division of the Northern Caucasus Military District accomplished a mass climb to the peak of the Kazbek, where they conducted a shooting exercise using machine guns and rifles.

7-th of November. Fine weather with a Southeast wind there was a frost and some snow fall but not much at all still not enough for slays

Tuesday, November 23. The New Ukraine Electoral District has selected as its candidate for Deputy in the Union Council the distinguished Director of the Odessa Institute of Breeding and Genetics, Trofim Denisovich Lysenko.[57] Flesh of the flesh of his people, Academician Lysenko is a compelling example of a non-Party Bolshevik and an ardent patriot. In a speech at the Second National Congress of Collective Farm Shock Workers, he said: "In our Soviet Union people are not born, what is born is organisms; in our country, people are made: tractor drivers, engine technicians, mechanics, academics, and scholars. I myself am one of those people who were made, rather than born; I was not born a man, but made one. And to feel oneself a part of such an environment—it is something much greater than mere happiness." "Bravo, Comrade Lysenko, bravo!"—these words of Comrade Stalin rang out as high praise for the remarkable work of the revolutionary and scholar. Together with Stalin, the whole Soviet people enthusiastically applauds its scholar: "Bravo, Comrade Lysenko, bravo!"

10-th of November. Tim had a Son, his parents decided to call him Anatoly. recording it old style. Overcast weather with a mild Southeast wind not cold its warm

Wednesday, November 24. Stalino. A foreign delegation has come to Gorlovka to visit the distinguished coal hewer E. P. Yermakov. Yesterday the delegates went down into the mine with Com. Yermakov, to see the Stakhanovite miners at work with their own eyes. In the presence of the foreign guests Com. Yermakov set a remarkable new record, hewing 180 tons of coal in a single shift, exceeding the plan by 1,288 percent.

* * *

People living in the southern part of the Kara-Kumy desert never had their own vegetables before. This year the collective farmers here harvested a beautiful crop of honeydew melons, watermelons, onions, and corn. Next year mass quantities of melons and vegetables will be planted in southern Kara-Kumy.

11-th of November Overcast weather very warm with a real light frost but no snow today I went to the bathhouse in bobrovo and they went out to Kamenka today for the 2-nd time with 9 carts to get clover

Friday, November 26. On November 24 millions of workers listened to a radio broadcast dedicated to the Secretary of the Central Committee of the Communist Party, People's Commissar of Internal Affairs of the USSR, candidate for Deputy on the Union Council from the Gorky-Lenin Electoral District (city of Gorky), Comrade Nikolai Ivanovich Yezhov. The actor V. N. Yakhontov read a story about the life and revolutionary activity of N. I. Yezhov. The literary-musical part of the program included: *Poem about People's Commissar Yezhov*, by native Kazakhstani poet Dzhambul, *Thoughts about the Motherland*, by native Dagestani bard Suleiman Stalsky,[58] poems by Perets Markish,[59] and the "Voroshilov March," "We are on guard," and "Song of Valor," by the composers Ilyin, Listov and Fere.

13-th of November. Overcast but calm and warm weather with no snow fall, but now the surface is good enough for slays our collective farm is still carting clover from Kamenka.

Saturday, November 27. A telegram arrived in Moscow: "to Valentina Grizodubova, Gorky Squadron, Vybornaya, Moscow. Dear Comrade Grizodubova, the collective farmers of the Chuisk Electoral District of the Kirgh SSR are nominating you as their candidate for Deputy in the Council of Nationalities. Please agree to run in our district. Please come by airplane. A landing field has been prepared for you."

"I am deeply touched," says Grizodubova, "by your trust in me. I understand this trust as follows: I must be devoted to our great people, to the Communist Party, to our dear, beloved father, the greatest man of our age, Comrade Stalin. I must devote every last bit of my strength to the struggle against the Trotskyites and Bukharinites, the Fascist spies, bourgeois nationalists and other counterrevolutionary scum, in defense of our motherland. Could I ever have become a pilot in the old days? My mother was a seamstress, my father — a worker. We just barely managed to make ends meet. Soviet power has enabled me not only to become a pilot, but also to break four world records. And there are thousands of people like me in our country."

* * *

Collective Farmers of a village in the Odessa Region detained a wandering monk named Starozhuk. He was going around spreading priestly nonsense. The monk was conducting anti-Soviet propaganda telling people that the end of the world was at hand, and encouraging them to nominate priests for the Soviets.

14-th of November. Overcast but not too cold weather with a mild Southeast wind and a light frost.

Wednesday, December 1. The editors of the "Latest News by Radio" are planning a radio broadcast dedicated to the memory of Sergei Mironovich Kirov, to be aired at 18:30, Moscow Time, on the Comintern Radio Station.

18-th of November. Overcast weather again with a mild Southwest breeze not too cold snow flurries the whole time. they're still carting clover.

Friday, December 3. From the stenographer's report of the December 2 meeting of elderly voters of the Stalin District of the city of Moscow. The speech of Com. M. V. Makarova (age 73): "I had a bad life before. I lived in the country. My father died, leaving my mother with five of us children on her hands. No one bothered to educate us. We wandered around barefoot and hungry. When I was eleven my mother hired me out as a nanny. I worked from six in the morning until twelve midnight for fifty kopecks. I married at sixteen and soon found myself alone—my husband was drafted and sent off to war. I came to Moscow and got a job at a factory. Then I worked in a laundry, washing 150 pounds of linen a day for five rubles a month, plus a room. But now I live well. I've been given a little room of my own, I have an easy life, and for that I thank Comrade Stalin from the bottom of my heart." [applause]. The chairman: "In a few days, as we elect Comrade Stalin, we will be sure to reflect on our lives, the way they used to be and the way they are now. The whole country says, Thank you, Comrade Stalin. The children add, for our happy childhood. And you can say: thank you Comrade Stalin for my happy old age."

52

20-th of November. Overcast cold weather with a Northeast wind it just keeps on snowing. I worked in Lukeryino today fixing up cabs

Saturday, December 4. On the anniversary of the adoption of the Stalin Constitution, December 5, and on the 6-th as well, huge, open-air celebrations will be held for the people in all the central squares and parks of the capital. A large network of portable stalls and booths is being organized to serve the workers. Food service enterprises are planning buffets on the squares where hot lunches will be sold.

* * *

"Who, if not the Soviet people, has the right to smile, to laugh and be joyful! And who in the whole world has more right than we to bask in a justified pride that arises from the awareness of victories achieved! The audience has the right to expect from us art that is jubilant, joyful, and sunny. That is why National Artist of the USSR V. I. Nemirovich-Danchenko[60] was right yesterday in bestowing on Leningrad the premiere of *The Fair Helen* in the Musical Theater that bears his name. One might think that the plot of this famous Offenbach operetta is hopelessly out of date. This parodic re-creation of the ancient world was intended to have an explosive effect on its bourgeois audiences, made up of people who had endured the torment of memorizing Latin vocabulary and Greek irregular verbs in school. And that's exactly what happened when Parisian audiences of the 60s were suddenly faced with majestic Greek heroes dressed in the risqué costumes of operetta characters. But for us, antiquity is a fascinating period of genius and national artistic creativity, not an instrument to inflict suffering on school children, not something to hold up to ridicule. Nemirovich-Danchenko most certainly had this in mind when he shifted the center of gravity in the show away from the mocking, parodic aspect of Offenbach's work and emphasized its joyfulness, passion and genuine lyricism. The cloudless Hellenic world, a cheerful song of love – such is the look of Nemirovich-Danchenko's operetta. Its great and profound human wisdom is confirmed by the fact that it is the most venerable and eminent producer in the family of Soviet directors who has created the show that is the most passionate and free of affectation and petty bourgeois primness." From a review by S. Radlov.

21-st of November. overcast weather with a Northeast wind and cold its snowing. but not too heavy

Sunday, December 5. The People's Commissariat of Internal Trade of the USSR has prohibited the sale of preprocessed sausage meat. The customer must be allowed to personally select the meat he will buy, and it must be prepared in his presence.

*   *   *

Border Guard Com. Dolgikh detained a major foreign spy at the Northwestern border. The spy had been cleverly made up to look like an old man. A Browning automatic pistol and a bag containing encoded espionage information were discovered on his person.

22-nd of November. Overcast but calm weather and we had a real thaw it got wet and the roofs dripped pretty heavy. Today Alexander's sister come from Moscow for a 2 day visit and in the evening Alexander Grigoryevich came over with Sanya

Tuesday, December 7. "Comrades! I will speak in the verse of old Dzhambul, native poet of Kazakhstan, of the contributions made by Nikolai Ivanovich Yezhov to the Party and the country:

> Bands of Trotskyite spies were creeping up on us
> Bukharinites, sly snakes from the swamps,
> An embittered mob of nationalists.
> They exulted as they drew near us with their fetters at ready,
> But into Yezhov's traps fell the beasts.
> Devoted friend of the Great Stalin,
> Yezhov destroyed their treacherous circle...

I urge you to give your vote to N. I. Yezhov on December 12." From a speech given at a rally in Gorky by Com. Ivanov, an engineer from the New Sormov plant.

24-th of November. Overcast weather from early morning and at one p.m. it started to snow hard but it warmed up by evening we had a thick fog and scattered showers. the roofs are dripping heavy again.

Thursday, December 9. The other day V. Panina was arrested at the Leningrad Train Station in Moscow. In her pocketbook were three paper fans, with nineteen bags of opium cleverly concealed in their folds. Subsequently her accomplice, Yu. Ven-yan, was also arrested. They had been supplying opium to addicts.

26-th of November. Overcast weather with a Northwest wind cold with a good heavy 8 degree frost today mother went to sell Onion, 1 1/4 measure, she sold 17 rubles worth

Saturday, December 11. Yesterday campaign rallies were held for young voters in twelve districts in Moscow. The young Stakhanovites, students, and Red Army soldiers who spoke at the rallies enthusiastically pledged to go to the polling places on December 12 and unanimously submit their ballots for the candidates proposed by the coalition of Communists and non-Party voters. Yesterday's youth rallies in Moscow were attended by 260 thousand voters.

* * *

The Moscow Council has requested that the Trust for the Dismantlement and Transfer of Buildings develop a plan for the removal of buildings located on Gorky Street between the Moscow Hotel and the Manezh Building. This work is part of the major project to create the Palace of Soviets Avenue. A monument to Pavlik Morozov[61] has been proposed for the site of the demolished buildings.

* * *

Arkhangelsk. Four corpses of mammoths have been discovered on the island of Vrangel.

28th of November. The weather was stormy last night just before dawn, with a strong Southeast wind a snowstorm and everything iced over in the afternoon the wind died down and it got warm in side even damp, today I went to the Struev factory bathhouse.

Monday, December 13. Preliminary data show that no less than 95 percent of the electorate turned out to vote in the cities and regions of the USSR.

30-th of November. Fine weather with a Southeast wind it was real cold today they brought the last of the clover from Kamenka on 6 carts.

Tuesday, December 14. Afterwards, many people confessed to each other that during those eighteen hours of election day that turned the whole city into one single family, they felt this thought pulsing in their heart over and over again: "This is how it will be every day, every hour of human life in that near future when Communism will become an actual reality won by us on earth." The thought arose in the atmosphere of cordiality, sincerity and warmth with which thousands and hundreds of thousands of people treated each other on December 12. The invisible boundaries between "I" and "you," between individual families, apartments, houses, streets and districts seemed to disappear and merge into a single, shared desire to elect the supreme organ of the state and to do it unanimously, all together, in an atmosphere of universal understanding...

* * *

Today New Year's trees go on sale in Moscow. Trees will be sold on all the main squares, streets and markets of the capital. Arrangements are being made to accept advance orders, to arrange for the delivery of trees to people's homes, and to provide help in setting up trees in homes, kindergartens, schools, and offices.

1-st of December. Overcast weather with a strong east wind and a snowstorm today they started thrashing the clover. but the motor broke. the chairman of the Collective Farm left today for Moscow for talks on illuminating the village with Electricity.

Friday, December 17. In order to eliminate abuse and fraudulent use of passports, all passports will be issued with photographs of the bearers. In large businesses, photographs will be affixed by police workers specifically assigned to the task.

* * *

The national exhibition of children's art that recently opened in the Home of the Teacher (Moscow) is a great success. The children's works on exhibit offer a broad range of subject matter: portraits of Lenin and Stalin, drawings, stories and poems about those October days of 1917, the Civil War, the events in Spain, the conquest of the Arctic, and Collective Farm life, etc.

* * *

The premises of beer stands and "American" bars in Moscow that have been closed down are being turned over to food service establishments. district food organizations, and trade cooperatives. Snack bars, sandwich shops and cafés, etc, will be opened in them.

4-th of December. Overcast weather with a weak Southeast wind and warm it got damp with the roofs dripping there's no frost at all. today we started hauling firewood home which was sawed in the spring two cubic meters each

Monday, December 20. The Party organization of the Meyerhold Theater held a meeting to discuss Com. Kerzhentsev's[62] article and other press materials. The meeting demonstrated yet again all the stagnancy and decrepitude of the atmosphere in the Theater. This time, as in the past, no real self-criticism of any significance took place. At a time when the whole Soviet public clearly understands that all attempts to turn Meyerhold onto the correct path have been fruitless, the Communists of the theater could find nothing better to do than entreat him to carry on his work. And the meeting resolved to do just that: to request that the Committee on the Arts release V. Meyerhold[63] from his duties as director, but keep him on as artistic director of the Theater. What a corrupt, politically spineless decision! The Party organization of the theater did not draw the necessary conclusions from the statements that have been appearing in the press. It has limited itself to criticism that is purely formal, while in essence defending the shamefully bankrupt leader of the Theater.

7-th of December. Overcast weather warm and damp with a fairly strong Southeast wind it started to rain several times there's a thaw the snow is really melting and poring down from the roofs.

Wednesday, December 22. The People's Commissariat of Internal Trade of the USSR has determined that leaders and local workers in the Soyuzlesprodtorg and the Soyuzlesprodtyazh[64] have been committing flagrant violations of the principles of Soviet trade. These organizations are conducting trade based on lists, for all practical purposes turning stores into closed distribution centers. The proposal has been made to turn over the cases of those responsible for violations of the principles of Soviet trade to the prosecutor's office so that criminal proceedings can be instituted against them.

9-th of December. Overcast weather with a mild breeze from the Southeast and a light frost but its not cold they're still carting their rotten firewood and the Collective Farm is hauling manure out to the fields from the Stable

Wednesday, December 29. The Lunacharsky Musical Instrument Factory in Leningrad has begun production of instruments for Neapolitan orchestras. The factory has manufactured protopypes of a semi-oval mandolin that produces an especially delicate sound timbre.

16-th of December. Fine weather with a light Southeast wind freezing cold 23 below and 20 below at the end of the day

Friday, December 31. The Felix Dzerzhinsky[65] Commune for Homeless Children in Kharkov is now ten years old. Over the time it has been in existence the Commune has given a new start in life to almost a thousand formerly homeless children. Now there are more than 2,500 children living in the Commune.

* * *

1937, now on the wane, was the historic year of the great Stalin Constitution of triumphant Socialism. A year when the entire Soviet people demonstrated to the world its moral and political unity at the elections for the Supreme Soviet of the USSR. This year our country displayed its enormous power, the power of a country in which man is truly free. And no enemies, no Trotskyite-Bukharinite band of spies and saboteurs, no fascist agents will be able to shake this ever-increasing power. The year to come, 1938, will be a year of yet more remarkable triumphs of Socialism. The great Soviet people will step over the threshold of this new year cheerfully and boldly, as they move forward and continue their work building the majestic edifice of Communism, the bright future of all mankind, under the leadership of the Party of Lenin and Stalin.

* * *

A children's carnival is being planned at the skating rinks and stadiums of Minsk.

18-th of December. Overcast weather with a slight frost 10 degrees or so below with hoar frost on the trees. the collective farm is still carting manure from the stable into the potatoe field

NOTES

[1] Famous Soviet pilots, who were the subject of a cult at that time.

[2] Nikolai Ostrovsky, 1904–1936, Soviet novelist, author of the socialist realist "classic" *How the Steel Was Tempered*. He died, bedridden and blind, while writing his second novel *Born of the Storm*, devoted to the civil war.

[3] The new constitution was adopted on 25 November 1936 by the Eighth Congress of the Soviets. Replacing the constitution of 1924, it was characterized (by Stalin) as "the most democratic constitution in the world." It guaranteed to the Soviet citizens, among other rights, the freedom of religion, the freedom of press and of speech, the right to assemble and to demonstrate.

[4] Ivan Petrovich Pavlov, 1849–1936, physiologist, mainly known for his development of the concept of the conditioned reflex and the study of higher nervous activity in animals and humans. Pavlov received the Nobel Prize in 1904.

[5] Aleksandr Petrovich Karpinsky, 1846–1936, geologist and geographer, author of works on the geography of the European part of the USSR, in particular of the Ural region. President of the Academy of Sciences of the USSR from 1917 to 1936.

[6] Famous Stakhanovites, who broke their "records" during the year of 1936, itself proclaimed the "Stakhanovite year." The movement's name comes from Aleksei Stakhanov, a Soviet miner, who mined 102 tons of coal (fourteen times the quota), in a single shift on 30 August 30 1935. The shock worker movement was one of the forms of socialist competition. The title of shock worker was awarded to workers who made outstanding contributions to enhance productivity. The movement was at its height during the First Five-Year Plan (1929–1932). Around 1935 the movement was replaced by the Stakhanovite movement. Subjects of a cult, the Stakhanovites received considerable material privileges.

[7] The title of this decree of 27 June 1936 was a terrible euphemism: it made abortion illegal, made divorce more difficult and raised family subsidies. It was preceded by an extensive debate in the press during which citizens were invited to speak out.

[8] The Christmas tree had been outlawed for a long time. It was authorized again as "New Year's tree" in 1935–36, which was a real event for the population if we believe the diaries of the time. "Happiness" refers here directly to Stalin's famous slogan "Life has become better, comrades, life has become happier."

[9] Aleksei Nikolaevich Tolstoi, 1883–1945, nobleman by birth, one of the major Soviet writers and apologists of the Soviet regime. Before the revolution, he began his career as a poet, playwright, and novelist. After his emigration in 1918, he wrote for émigré journals in Paris and Berlin; he returned to the Soviet Union in 1923. The first volume of his trilogy *Road to Calvary* was published in Paris, and the whole cycle was completed in Moscow. He was a

remarkable stylist and prose writer and highly cynical in his political choices. He was an ardent defender of Stalinism. His works include science fiction novels, such as *Aelita*, the controversial historical novel *Peter the First*, and war reports (*The Russian Character*).

[10] Lion Feuchtwanger, 1884–1958, German Jewish novelist and playwright. Author of *Jud Süss* [American title: *Power*] (1921), the *Josephus-Trilogie*, and other works.

[11] Aleksandr Fadeev, 1901–1956, Soviet novelist and major literary bureaucrat during the Stalinist era. Fadeev came to fame with his civil-war novel *The Rout* (1927). Member of the Central Committee of the Communist Party from 1939 until his suicide in May 1956, he held also high posts in the Writers' Union since 1934. (He was general secretary from 1946 to 1954.)

[12] This is a report on the second Moscow trial (23–30 January 1937) during which the "old Bolsheviks" (Pyatakov, Sokolnikov, Serebryakov, Radek) and high officials from the economy were tried. As during the first trial (August 1936), the defendants confessed their "counterrevolutionary crimes." Thirteen of the defendants were executed and four were sentenced to long prison terms.

[13] Andrei Yanuarevich Vyshinsky, 1883–1954, Soviet statesman, diplomat, and lawyer. Chief prosecutor during the Great Purge Trials in Moscow in the 1930s.

[14] Agricultural association with some elements of private ownership.

[15] In his, at that time, famous book, entitled *Moskau 1937. Ein Reisebericht für meine Freunde* [Moscow 1937: A Report on a Journey for My Friends], Feuchtwanger reiterated his conviction of the guilt of the convicted at the trial. He was far from being alone. The International Human Rights League also concluded, after investigation, that the defendants of the Moscow trials were guilty. On Feuchtwanger and the Moscow trials, see Michael Rohrwasser, *Der Stalinismus und die Renegaten: Die Literatur der Exkommunisten* [Stalinism and the Renegates: The Literature of the Former Communists] (Stuttgart: Metzler, 1991), 151–157.

[16] Elaborate preparations were made for the hundredth anniversary of Pushkin's death. The centennial marked an important moment in the state's reappropriation of the "great Russian culture."

[17] Detskoe Selo is a suburb of Saint Petersburg. Until the October Revolution it was called Tsarskoe Selo; in 1937 it became the city of Pushkin.

[18] Acronym for Leninist Young Communist League of the USSR.

[19] The Great Columned Hall of the House of the Trade Unions, where the Moscow trials were held.

[20] Sergo Ordzhonikidze (Grigori Konstantinovich), 1882–1937, old Bolshevik. Member of the Central Committee since 1921 and of the Politburo from 1930 to 1937. From 1932 to his death he was the People's Commissar of Heavy Industry. The whole country mourned Sergo's death, allegedly caused by a heart failure. In reality he committed suicide after a violent dispute with Stalin, caused, according to recent sources, by the arrest of some of his close colleagues and his own brother.

[21] Boris Leonidovich Pasternak, 1890–1960, one of the great masters of modern Russian literature, author of some of the best Russian poetry written in the twentieth century and of the novel *Doctor Zhivago*, completed in 1955. His words here illustrate his difficult and ambiguous position during the 1930s.

[22] André Gide's famous report *Retour de l'URSS* [Return from the USSR], was written after the writer's visit to the USSR in 1936. After its publication, Gide became the object of a violent campaign launched by the Communists in the USSR and in France.

[23] The Soviet aid provided to the Spanish Republicans and other "Spanish" themes were recurrent in the Soviet press of these years. In fact, the Soviet aid was limited to the delivery of (insufficient) military equipment and of two thousand specialists, made up of political cadres, police, and military forces. It seems, however, that there existed a real movement of solidarity among the Soviet population.

[24] What the "workers of the capital" did not know at that time was that N. Bukharin and A. Rykov had just been arrested during the recent Plenum of the Central Committee (February 1937). They were to become the principal defendants of the third Moscow Trial (March 1938) and were sentenced to death; Sergei Mironovich Kirov, 1886–1934, was first secretary of the Central Committee of the Party of Azerbaijan from 1921 to 1926. From 1926 to 1934, he was first secretary of the Regional Committee of Leningrad, member of the Politburo from 1930 to 1934. His assassination on 1 December 1934 was presented as the result of a vast "antirevolutionary conspiracy" and is interpeted by many as the signal initiating the great purges. It is generally assumed that his assassination was orchestrated by Stalin.

[25] Andrei Aleksandrovich Zhdanov, 1896–1948. From 1934 to 1948, Zhdanov was first secretary of the Regional Party Committee, first secretary of the Party Committee of the city of Leningrad, as well as secretary of the Central Committee. Zhdanov was the chief spokesman of Stalinist cultural politics. He directed the vast campaign of ideological mobilization (mainly against the intelligentsia and the nationalities), launched after the "Great Patriotic War" (World War II).

[26] Report on the completion of the Volga-Don canal. The navigation on the canal was inaugurated on 15 July 1937.

[27] The system of internal passports was introduced in 1932. It was explicitly intended to restrict the "Kulak infiltration" to the urban centers, to limit the rural exodus, and to maintain the "social purity" of the great construction sites and new cities. Later, the various programs for the exchange of official documents, such as passports, Party cards, trade union cards, and so forth, had the same goal of "purification."

[28] Homonym of Trotsky, Lev Davydovich, 1879–1940. Trotsky organized the seizure of power in 1917; he was later commissar of foreign affairs and of war, founder of the Red Army, theoretician of the "permanent revolution," and founder of the Fourth International. Expelled from the Soviet Union in 1929, he remained the leader of anti-Stalinist opposition abroad until he was murdered by one of Stalin's agents in 1940.

29 Homonym of Zinoviev, Grigory Evseyevich (pseudonym of Ovsel Gershon Aronov Radomyslsky), 1883–1936. One of the leaders of the revolution of 1917, central figure in the Communist Party leadership in the 1920s. Member of the triumvirate with Kamenev and Stalin that eliminated Trotsky as a serious contender in the power struggle after Lenin's death. Stalin eventually turned against his former allies, including Zinoviev. Several times expelled from the Communist Party and readmitted, Zinoviev was arrested in 1935 and secretly tried for "moral complicity" in the assassination of the Party leader Sergei Mironovich Kirov and sentenced to ten years imprisonment. He was retried at the first great purge trial in 1936, found guilty on the fabricated charge of forming a terrorist organization to assassinate Kirov and other Soviet leaders, and executed.

30 Genrikh Grigorevich Yagoda, 1891–1938. Since 1924, vice president of the OGPU; General Commissar of the State Security in 1935; from 1934 to 1936, People's Commissar of Internal Affairs; from 1936 to 1937, People's Commissar of Transports. Yagoda was sentenced to death and executed in 1938 after the third Moscow trial for his participation in "the bloc of Trotskyites and Rightists."

31 The Moscow Art Theater (MKhAT), founded in 1898 by Konstantin Stanislavsky and Vasily Nemirovich-Danchenko, was named after Maxim Gorky. It was one of the leading theaters of the USSR and was famous for its production of the plays of Chekhov and Gorky.

32 José Dias was the leader of the Spanish communist party.

33 La Passionaria Dolores Ibarruri.

34 Otto Yulyevich Shmidt, 1891–1956, Soviet mathematician and geophysicist. Shmidt headed several Soviet polar expeditions: in 1929–30, 1932 and 1933–34 (see Shirnov's diary page 67, and note 13). In 1937 he directed an expedition by air to the North Pole.

35 See note 1.

36 Yan Gamarnik, chief of the Red Army's Political Administration in 1937, accused of participating in the alleged "Tukhachevsky conspiracy." (See note 40).

37 Aleksei Ivanovich Kuprin, 1870–1938, Russian writer who emigrated in 1917. He was awarded the Nobel Prize in 1933.

38 A cooperative organization, renting dwellings from the local Soviet for its members. It existed until 1937.

39 Nikita Sergeevich Khrushchev, 1894–1971, Soviet political leader, first secretary of the Central Committee from 1953 to 1964. Khrushchev had held several important posts in the Ukraine after the end of the civil war before climbing the Party ladder in Moscow. From 1935 to 1938 he was the first secretary of the Moscow Party Committee. In 1938 he became the first secretary of the Central Committee of the Party of the Ukraine.

40 Marshal Tukhachevsky and the leading generals of the Red Army were accused of espionage, treason on instructions from the German General Staff and Trotsky, and participation in a counterrevolutionary fascist con-

spiracy to overthrow the Russian government. The death sentences were carried out on 12 June and were followed by an extensive purge. The Red Army lost nine-tenths of its high-ranking army commanders and 35,000 officers (out of 80,000).

[41] MTS, a state agricultural enterprise hiring out agricultural machines and skilled operators to collective farms. The Stations served as an instrument for exerting pressure on farms to ensure that they complied with Party directives.

[42] The place where Aleksei Stakhanov established his famous "record."

[43] See Stavsky's diary.

[44] *Novy mir* was one of the major Soviet "thick" literary journals. It started its publication in 1925. Stavsky was its chief editor between 1937 and 1941.

[45] The use of only Lenin's patronymic has an "intimate" connotation.

[46] Acronym for People's Commissariat for Internal Affairs. In 1934 one of its departments, the Chief Administration of State, took over the functions of the OGPU, the Organ of the Security Police. From 1936 to 1938 its head was the notorious Yezhov, who carried out Stalin's purges.

[47] Nikolai Ivanovich Yezhov, 1895–1940, People's Commissar for Internal Affairs from 1936 to 1938; General Commissar of State Security from 1937 to 1939; from 1938 to 1939, People's Commissar of River Transportation. He was arrested on 10 June 1939 "for having committed unjustified exactions toward the Soviet people" and was executed on 4 February 1940. The period of the great purges, which he supervised as the head of the NKVD, entered history under the name of "the Yezhov business" (*Yezhovshchina*).

[48] Following the implementation of the new constitution of 1936, this law reestablished the civil rights of those who had lost them after the October Revolution on the basis of their social origin.

[49] Children of the Spanish Republicans who emigrated to the Soviet Union.

[50] Instead of a fixed wage, collective farmers were paid according to the number of "work day units" (*trudoden*) they accumulated during the year. The unit was calculated to represent a day's work of average difficulty and intensivity. Unskilled work (e.g., that of a cleaner or a night watchman) rated only 0.5 of a unit, whereas the most highly skilled work (e.g., that of a tractor driver) earned around 2.5 units. At the end of the year the worker was paid in accordance with his or her tally of units, partly in cash and partly in produce. This system was introduced in 1931.

[51] Lazar Moiseevich Kaganovich, 1893–1992. People's Commissar of Routes of Communication and then People's Commissar of Heavy Industry (until 1939). Member of the Politburo from 1938 to 1947, vice president of the Council of People's Commissars. Kaganovich was director of the Ural Potassium Industrial Complex from 1957 until he retired in 1961.

[52] The celebrations of the twentieth anniversary of the October Revolution (25 October 1917; 7 November new style).

[53] Isaak Osipovich Dunaevsky, 1900–1955, famous Soviet composer of popular

songs and operettas. His name was associated with the mass success of many musical film comedies of the Stalin period, such as *Happy Fellows*, *Circus*, *Volga-Volga*, or the *Kuban Cossacks*.

[54] Followers of S. Petlyura, 1877–1926, one of the founders of the Ukrainian social-democratic party, minister of the independent Ukrainian government (July 1917). Eventually, Petlyura became an ally of the Polish occupants of Kiev in 1920. After the reconquest of the Ukraine by the Red Army, Petlyura emigrated to France, where he was assassinated.

[55] In honor of the anniversary of the October Revolution, celebrated with great pomp. The USSR was founded on 30 December 1922.

[56] Lavrenty Pavlovich Beria, 1899–1953. Beria was at this time the first secretary of the Central Committee of the Georgian Communist Party. In 1938, he replaced Yezhov as People's Commissar for Internal Affairs. He was executed as an enemy of the people in 1953.

[57] Trofim Denisovich Lysenko, 1898–1976, Soviet agrobiologist, theoretician of a "science" that attempted to accommodate Marxist determinism with the possibility of influencing nature and the human being in order to negate the laws of heredity altogether. His nomination to the post of president of the Lenin All-Union Academy of Agricultural Sciences marked the beginning of a witch hunt against scientists who were opposed to his theories, among them the noted botanist and geneticist Nikolai Ivanovich Vavilov, who died in prison in 1943.

[58] Suleiman Stalsky (Gasanbekov), 1869–1937, poet from Dagestan. His works include "Our Power" (1930), "Our Strength" (1934), the epic cycle of poems *Dagestan* (1935–36), and *Thoughts about the Motherland* (1937).

[59] Perets Davidovich Markish, 1895–1952, renowned Soviet Jewish writer. He was arrested in 1948 with many other Jewish artists and intellectuals and executed in 1952.

[60] Vladimir Ivanovich Nemirovich-Danchenko, 1858–1943, Soviet theater director. Founder with Stanislavsky of the Moscow Art Theater.

[61] Pavlik Morozov is a martyr of the Collectivization and subsequently was declared the "Hero of Soviet Children": at the age of twelve he reported his father for hiding grain. He was murdered in 1932, together with his younger brother, by "antirevolutionary *kulaks*."

[62] Platon Mikhailovich Kerzhentsev, 1881–1940, writer and literary activist, one of the important members of the Proletkult (postrevolutionary organization attempting to foster a culture proper to the new class of the industrial proletariat) and one of the propagators of the "Scientific Organization of Work," the Soviet version of Taylorism. From 1933 to 1936, Kerzhentsev headed the All-Union Radio Committee and between 1936 and 1938 he was the chairman of the committee for artistic affairs of the Council of People's Commissars.

[63] Vsevolod Emilievich Meyerhold, 1874–1940, theater, opera, and film director, one of the main theoreticians of the Russian avant-garde, eventually con-

demned as "formalist." His theater was closed in 1938, and he died soon after his arrest in 1939.

[64] Sections of the All-Union Lumber Association of Timber Industry enterprises.

[65] Felix Eduardovich Dzerzhinsky, 1877–1926, founder and president of the Extraordinary Commission (Cheka) after December 1917. People's Commissar for Internal Affairs from 1919 to 1923, as well as People's Commissar of Transportation. He held other important posts in the Soviet government, including the direction of the State Security (OGPU).

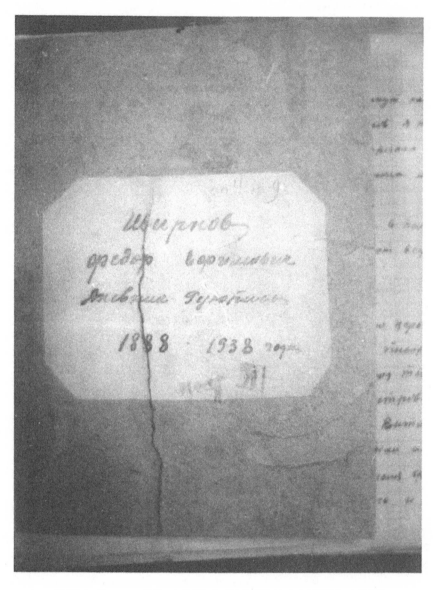

COVER OF SHIRNOV'S DIARY, WHICH HE KEPT FROM 1888 UNTIL 1938

FYODOR EFIMOVICH SHIRNOV

How the diary of Fyodor Efimovich Shirnov ended up in the Central State Archives of Literature and Art remains an enigma: the diary has no relation whatsoever to belles lettres. *About Shirnov we know no more than what is written in his diary. The reader will learn from the entries made in 1938 how he came to narrate his own birth in 1888, "in the middle of nowhere" and about the very circumstances that made him write his "manuscript diary."*

Two entries that we did not include in our text are short ones from 1931: we will quote them here. The first one gives some of the author's reasons for writing. The second is revealing about Shirnov's social standing before the 1932 "Kalyma Expedition."

1931. (After my son's death). I felt a kind of emptiness in my life, like I was already one foot in the grave and heading for the next world, I was writing a diary to leave a memory of me behind for my generation, but I couldn't keep it up, so I decided to just write up to age 50 and then stop after that.

4 June [1931]. I took a job at the Union Paper Trust, where I lasted only 4 months before I got transferred to the People's Commissariat of Waterways, as Housing manager, and from there they sent me out to the reorganizing River Transportation Administration of the Kalyma-Indigir State Shipping Office with its location in the town of Sredne-Kolymsk.

Diary of Fyodor Efimovich Shirnov
Traveller's Notes. From "Manuscript Diary," March 1, 1888–October 1, 1938.

May this here thing live on forever.

1888

3/1 — At five-twenty in the morning after the second roaster-crow I saw the light of day (I was born) on the stove Grandma Yevgenya cut my umbilical cord wrapped me in a blanket and put me aside my sick mama.

3/2 — Grandma washed me off and swaddled me rubbed my head with goose grease and stuck a knotted rag into my mouth for me to suck on.

3/3 — In the morning I took the tit (breast).

3/5 — They took me to the parish church in Vekshni to get christened. My godfather was the village clerk Nikolai Kotovich. My godmother was my aunt and my mothers sister Marfa Petrovna my parents wanted to name me Vitalisi. But my godfather and godmother forgot along the way there and father Vasily the priest christened me Fyodor at home Mother didn't like that name and they just called me Vitaly anyway.

3/6 — Grandma took me to the bathhouse for my first bath.

1932

My Trip on the Kalyma Expedition[1]

When on the third day the locomotive wistle blowed and the train left the station, I got settled on my seat by the window and tried to read the paper my favorite, *Gudok*, but I was so worn out I couldn't make no sense out of it, I just stared at the lines without seeing them. And there was something in that monotonus clattering of the wheels that touched my heart, a kind of joy inside. I look out the window. The trees flashing by, they seemed unusually kind and beautiful like they was saying goodbye and wouldn't see me again for a long time. The train was delayed because of land slides on the Baikal Ring Line, and I didn't get to see my friend in the town of Verkhne-Udinsk, where I worked back in 1924–26 in the Selenga State Shipping Office.

I got to Vladivostok at three in the morning the twelfth or fourteenth of May, the city was asleep, the silence of the tender enchanting night over the calm sea was interrupted only by bursts of raucus singing coming from sailors up late on ships anchored out on the bay.

In our expedition Headquarters work went on non stop, since we was getting the first ship ready for departure with a load of people and materials, since it was, a geology research vessel Captain Sidnev, an old and experienced sailor was appointed captain.

6/25 — Before setting out, all the workers on the expedition had to get a Medical examination and a Sanitation Check done and they had to be checked carefully against the lists which the captains staff used for a strict accounting of all the sailors as they boarded. So workers wouldn't get through without a Medical Check, who wouldn't be accepted on the steamer and would be returned back to headquarters.

Our River Transportation workers was unsteady on their feet on account of their tipsy condition. And a lot of them said more than they should have, but they was forgiven all that because they was going so far away and for three years too.

On the night we left, it rained mercilessly and inspite, of my new raincoat it seeped in under the collar and made me shivver off and on from the cold stream of water trickling down my spine. There was a cold nasty wind blowing. The ship rushed full speed ahead, in the un penetrable darkness of that roaring Japanese sea. On either side, now on the left, now on the right, red and green lights flashing from ships passing by. I strained my eyes to look into the dark abyss ahead and not seeing nothing except the pale white crests of the heaving waves.

I was bored in the cabin. Everyone was asleep. except for my storeman, Shura Yakanin from the Komsomol,[2] who run around with a flashlight from one hold to the next fussing with things. He was on his feet from morning to night and from night to morning never stopping a moment to rest he was always on alert, on land on the sea or out at anchor. When he found some thing wrong in the cargo he would narrow his thin reddish eyebrows into a frown. He would get all agitated at the slightest thing, like if one of the workers in our group spitted into one of the holds after getting their rations, he got all red, frowned and throwed himself on the culprit and humiliated him for his rude behavior involving the provisions hold, and that if everyone done that what would it lead to and what would become of our provisions.

But when Shurka[3] come up out of the hold on deck and saw them comrades he'd a just been lecturing, he would go right up and take them by their arm again and remark cheerfully in his usual good natured tone of voice that he used when he wasn't on duty. Hey Volodya! Don't be all upset that he chewed you out. Its just one of them things thats got to be done. Listen, work is work, friendship is something else my friend.

Shurka spent all his time that way, never bored, not minding the monotony of his work all absorbed in his service, he seemed completely satisfied and happy right where he was, he didn't even seem to miss his family his mother or his wife and children he had left in Moscow. His only thought and concern was for the contentment and happiness of all the comrades on the expedition. But suddenly and most un fortunately we heard a loud, terrible crash and the ship shuddered all over, some how listed and apparently grinded to a halt all of a sudden. There was a moment of stunned silence. The passengers was scared stiff and just stared at each other with their eyes wide open, and no one could get a word out. I took off a running out of my cabin and up the stares to the deck and went straight for the captain's bridge, which I was immediately asked to leave. At first I had no idea what happened and was gripped by terror which I tried to overcome with all my might, my heart sunk and I felt hot all over, then everything went dark and a chill run through my body but I tried to get a hold of myself.

Our ship was out in the open sea, still wrapped in un penetrable darkness. You couldn't tell what was going on on the main deck and the 'tweendecks. The sea was roaring real loud the wind whistling plaintively in the riggin and in the un penetrable night. The small waves lifted the ship then dropped her hard again and then again onto some under water stone. Each time she hitted, such a terrifying crash shook the entire ship, that it seemed like she couldn't possibly stand the torture and would snap in two any minute. Lord have Mercy. its all over! the passengers was huddled in little clusters on the deck and yelling plaintively we're going to wreck on this stone. Now what. We're really in a fix now, we're done for. So much for Kolyma. So much for them big salaries. And them fox fur collars, bare fur coats, so much for all that easy money. She knew it! She had a bad feeling about it when we was leaving. Back when she was getting on board. Should I go or not. That's just about enough out of you Aunty Anisya, commented Shurka from the Komsomol who was standing aside of the ship with his flashlight. What good does it do to whip up panic you just climb on up there into the hold and go to sleep, whats the point of all that blabbering. Our bald carpenter, he was already pushing sixty, stood there hanging onto the stareway with one hand, and squeezing his new galoshes tight against his side under his left arm. Snivelling some thing under his breath. Hey Baldy why all the moaning and groaning you'll be bawling on us any minute, asked Shurka from the Komsomol. I'm not crying, but the tears is running down his cheeks, he's got all them little grandbabies, we've all just started, living in this new, happy country. Its all well and good to realize that grandpa But shame on you crying like that bringing everyone down, yourself and others, you're not a little boy no more. We're not in no danger, and just because the sailers has got on their life preservers and let down the life rafts like the captain told them to, don't mean nothing, its just in case, who knows what might happen, after all we're not on land here, but out at sea. A voice blares out from the loud-speaker on the captains deck, all the regular passengers got to clear the deck. The officer on watch bussled around sending everyone to their places and not to panic.

I got a little spooked myself, you could feel the danger, but I didn't let on to nobody. and all I could think was if anything happened to save peo-ple. The wind picked up, the waves was splashing and hammering up against the sides of the ship. If only she would just hurry up and come off the rock! It had been over two hours since we ran up on the rock. But on that mem orable night them minutes seemed like an eternity. The captain come down off of the bridge and nodded to me as he ran past. meaning we're out of danger. Shurka from the Komsomol runs up to me without his jacket on, carrying a life preserver. What was that the captain said? Everything is all right so far we'll be all right I answered.

The captain hollers down from the deck through an open porthole to the engine room: How are the pumps? Is everything working? And back up again onto his bridge.

Two honks, one after the other. The engine. The captain giving orders into the machine room through a pipe. Is she moving? No, and to prove it she wasn't moving the ship beated helplessly again against the stone again, real heavy. This time was worse than before, the poor ship wouldn't give none, it was like she was bolted down to the spot. Another honk. The engine had started up. Is she moving no answer for several seconds. What have you all gone to sleep asks the voice from the captains bridge. She moved someone on the deck shouted. The unknown voice shouted more cheerfully it's cranked up and in another second we could hear voices she's moving. She slips down off the rock. The captain hastily gives the order full speed a head. The ship strains and scrapes real loud across the stone and delighting in her freedom her whole body sighs and she dives her nose down into the water then parting the dark waves of the rough stormy sea. This great un expressible joy comes over me a loud sigh of relief sweeping over the deck and a bittersweet, defiant smile plays across my face.

The ship flew on full speed ahead through the gloom of night nine knots just like a wounded Swan floating on the waves, licking her wounds.

After all these frightening experiences and a few hours of sound sleep. Me and Shurka from the Komsomol sat together in the cabin putting together the menus, for the next five days. The sea started acting up again the ship listed and the barometer showed stormy weather. The portholes of the cabin was closed tight, which plunged into the water then come out again, through the clouded panes of daylight.

There wasn't no one to be seen on deck except the sailors and the ships crew the passengers was sitting in their cabins and the 'tweendecks. It was real hard to walk on the deck, it jerked out from under your feet and it took special skill to choose just the right moment to walk across.

The waves was surging up high like the Kazbek mountains. Me and Shurka from the Komsomol barely made it across the deck when we went out to see how our comrades was doing. It was im possible to make sup per at a time like that and we had to just hand out cans of food to each comrade. When you went downstares into the 'tweendecks, it was stuffy and damp and a nasty sour smell from it being all closed up. Because of the violent rocking none of the passengers had eaten and they didn't want to, they just laid in their beds groaning like they was asfixiating.

In the Left corner near the door our metal workers wife Anisya laid on her bunk, groaning and cussing through her teeth at her husband. What the devil was she doing out here in Kalyma. And on the damn ocean too. May it rot in hell. She's got no more strength, she's done for, she cant eat and puking so bad that if she don't look out she'll puke all her guts right out. O lordy, save her little soul so's she can live on just a little more, life is so wonderful back home on land, just sit back and enjoy it. Just her luck to wind up on this here ship, over there a bench just come loose, like we run into something. I heard what my old man Ivanushka said, the idiot, you won't make it your going to croak. You old devil, you hairy old drunk. Whats the matter with you just lying there you lazy bum, you still drunk from Vladivostok or what, Anisya yelled at her husband, why don't you go see the captain he's a good man everyone says so, get him to turn back to dry land. All this time her husband had just kept quiet and laid quietly on his bunk, he really did have a headache but he couldn't restrain himself no more and come back at Anisya. You blitherin idiot, what do you mean dry land we done left it behind three days ago. Why don't you just take a drink and you'll feel better. What I do is just bottoms up all at once, it puts you right to sleep. and he don't even remember about us being stuck on that stone if you hadn't told him he wouldn't have knowed, that's what a drink'll do for you. And where was you before, why didn't you tell me. Here's the key to the trunk go open it and lift up the blue silk blanket inside you'll see a bottle there in the corner. and make it snappy. Ivan jumps for joy down off his bunk and gets the bottle of spirit like his wife told him to opens it and pours Anisya half a glassful, he don't forget to pour one for himself first so's to pull himself together, looking around the whole time to protect his dignity. Anisya drunk it up and immediately konks out face down into the pillow.

Meanwhile Ivan manages to drain the bottle with the aid of his friend in the next bunk and to assertain how much more she had in the basket. Anisya hadn't been down ten minutes before she got curious about what Ivan was up to. But the moment she leans her head down the spirit pours out of her onto the floor (she throwed up) and it was all Ivans fault, who Anisya started cussin out saying he meaned to drive her to an early grave. As for me I could use a little more says Ivan. But you can't hold your spirit. So you've no call going on at me Anisya. he wanted to make things better for you but it didn't work out so there ain't nothing you can do about it. how could you forget the time Mikolai Mikitich come to see us and telled about all them years he worked on the steamboats on the river Angar, in Irkutsk and his wife never throwed up, not even once, and she brung him lunch everyday on the boat and even had a glass of spirit with him too. Shut up you Old Devil and don't make excuses all you care about is getting yourself drunk you don't even notice your wife here suffering before your very eyes. Give that key here or else you're going to drink up all the spirit we have he and his neighbor had already drunk up that bottle he'd got out of the trunk, but they didn't touch the others, what others? the ones left in the basket and the trunk. — Oh you derelick you've already sniffed them all out. Well you can just wait on that vodka in the trunk, you won't see it before Kolyma, you get that strait you pitiful drunk. Go see the doctor you said just now there was doctors on the ship, maybe he's got some medicine he could give me. Ivan feels around behind his head and gets the bottle out from under his pillow goes up onto the deck starts making his way to the doctors cabin, its heaving so much he loses his balance and falls and brakes the bottle comes back and tells Anisya a whole sob story about how when he went up on deck the water was just pouring over the ship, he almost got swept out to sea, but grabbed onto a windlass at the last minute, he broke the bottle and never did make it to the doctors. You're just going to have to be patient Anisya, you ain't the only one sick, some might even be worse off. That does it, Anisya just blowed up and jumped down from her bunk grabs a pan and just whacks her Ivan on the head with it. Take that, that'll show you how much worse off others is than her, just look at her you alkoholic, she's all wet from being sick and she lit into poor Ivan, cussing him out and they'd still be at it if she hadn't started throwing up again.

As we got closer to the Japanese shore the waves started to calm down. The passengers went up on the deck to get some fresh sea air and talked about yesterdays storm. They'd opened the hatches and portholes and the 'tweendecks had already lost that sour smell.

After issuing rations to the galley for supper. Shurka from the Komsomol put together a musical group made up of the regular passengers who had brought musical instruments along. There was games, music, singing and dancing and everyone Cheered up and it got to the point that even the old men crawled out of the 'tweendecks and started doing the *prisyadka*[4] two by two with everyone singing little ditties:

> On the sea its marvellous
> With "Stalin" watching over us
> We don't fear no storm and squall,
> Protected by the Komsomol
> Into Arctic cold we're reaching
> Bringing Bolshevistic teaching
> which we will gladly share
> with the people living there
> Port of Archangelsk Kolyma
> Murmansk and Kamchatka.
> Vrangel-Lena-Anadyr
> Dixon and Pechera.
> !!!!!!!!!!!
> With our dear Stalin at the helm.

Our Shurka from the Komsomol was so pleased that he even danced with the guys himself a few times. Time just flew for everyone and before we knew it our ship was crossing the Gulf of Laperuza leaving behind the shores of the island of Sakhalin on the left and the Kuriles on the right. The sea was calmer, but the fog, clung low over the water. From the deck you could see seals poking up their little black heads and playful fish was leaping up out of the water. Through binoculars you could just barely see a whale spouting tall vertical fountains of water in the distance, and over on the right a Japanese torpedo boat diving in the fog observing our ship or simply following us. The crossing into the open ocean from the Okhotsk Sea was real rough and a couple of pigs and a cow was washed overboard. But the passengers was used to it by now and they didn't even bat an eye.

When we entered the bay at Petropavlovsk we was met by brass bands that had come out with red banners from local organizations. The working class of the city office workers and officials along with the leaders of the bolshevik Comunist Party gave us a hearty welcome, as young pioneers on our way to work and open up the Kalyma region.

To give us a chance to recover after the nine-day crossing, which was so difficult for the passengers who wasn't not used to it especially with the unusually bad storms of the sea journey. The Captain of the ship gave an order for everyone to go a shore, where I made a deal with the bathhouse to give everyone who wanted to the chance to have a bath and the state shipping office and the Kolyma branch office would foot the bill.

In the evening Shurka from the Komsomol organized a special Komsomol evening for our organization to get together with the Kamchatka one, where everyone was delighted and pleased, the hall was packed, of course our visiting organization was given priority. A few of our comrades was even surprised that out here so far away from the capital people here knew just about everything that was going on there, that just goes to show how concerned the soviet government is about all its far distant corners.

On June 11 at 14:00 we casted off from the Bay and tossed on the waves of the Kamchatka Sea, where we saw a whole lot of sea creatures swimming in big herds, walruses, dolphins, seals, others, too, we went on into providence Bay without stopping in at the bay of Amotor, but because of the dark and foggy night the captain put the ship to anchor, letted down a small boat and hollered to one of the sailors, Akhonka-Maly you're the bravest of all, get in and take this boat over to shore and make sure we're not going to run a ground anywhere. Yessir captain. Off he goes brave Akhonka and pretty soon a shout come back through the fog. Comrade, captain, I can see everything, what do you see? Near the shore there's an encampment with deer hides hanging all around a lot of game carcass and even some polar bear heads strung up, nothing to worry about and can the ship pass near shore shouts the captain through his megaphone, I don't know, but the boat got through answers Akhonka. You get right back here. you blockhead. You looked every which way but didn't pay no attention to the rocks underneath. He spits. You may be a hell of a sailor but you don't have no sense, he just don't get it. akhonka yells back, to comrade, Captain I can see a Chukotsk yurt[5] on the other side of the encampment and a tungus[6] sitting on the shore smoking a pipe and fixing a boat looks like he's getting ready to go out a fishing. Well just let him shout himself hoarse he still won't understand. he'll yell awhile then come back, he won't get nothing done anyway and you there, boatswain, check all the signal lights and make sure everything works, we're expecting the Lazovsky tonight and starting tomorrow morning we'll be unloading coal from her. put fomka Bezstrashny on watch you can count on him and have grishka Pyatkin on standby until our brave idiot gets back to help get the boat up and meanwhile he's going to his cabin to get three or four hours of sleep good night says the captain and goes on down to the first mates cabin.

Shurka from the Komsomol heard ducks quacking in the bay and took it into his head to do some hunting he kept at me asking permission to go a shore. This favor for Shurka was granted by me. But on condition that he would organize a hunting group since there was rifles on board and a whole lot of passengers who liked hunting too.

Before sunrise. The whole bay was surrounded by hunters, and a desparate offensive against the ducks was underway. The ducks tried every possible escape route but they ran into cross fire at every turn. So by 10 in the morning forty seven of them had been killed and the cook roasted some and made a delicious duck soup for supper.

When the Lazovsky arrived all hands was called up to unload the coal from her onto our ship, the work went good, the only problem was it poured down rain and everyone got completely soaked and they had to all be given a glass of port to warm them up and to stir their taste buds.

After we left providence bay several days passed and we started seeing ice flows here and there. The air changed it got cold on board, that meant we was entering the cold arctic, even with the suns rays warming us our ship, running day and night, couldn't cover no more than one or two miles in twenty-four hours, since the pack ice slowed us down. The ship approached the cape of Serdtse-Kamen where we got stuck in the ice and spent fifteen days trying to get free. Shurka from the Komsomol managed to lift everyone's spirits here, too, and got them to sing:

> Serdtse-Kamen don't be so proud!
> Your shards of ice so sharp and thick,
> Your wind may blow all fierce and loud,
> but you can't scare a Bolshevik.
>
> Here we sit our second week
> We'll hold out another one
> But after that we won't be meek
> we'll crush you flat, won't that be fun.

This engineers wife was travelling with us in a first class cabin, an Interesting lady, she spent all her time walking up and down the deck with a lornet like some high society Lady and she always had something to complain about, wasn't nothing suited her taste, one minute the ice is making too much noise and she can't sleep, the next thing you know she don't like the scenery, or dinner or supper is no good or she's bored from sitting here waiting for the ship to break out of the ice, or she didn't get the telegram her daughter sent from Moscow, and if Shurka from the Komsomol suggests some thing she can do to help with the social activities on board, she announces she can't work under these circumstances.

I got a telegram from the central office telling me to collect the work records of several comrades for them to return back to arkhangelsk, to do what, I didn't know. But the telegram said to send only people who avoided work, who caused trouble and was a bad influence on the others. And naturally our high society lady got what was coming to her.

When the entire expedition was united with our command ship the icebreaker Litke, a meeting was called for all the captains and the head of our state shipping, where the decision was made to return some of our workers to Kolyma to spend the winter there with the ships Shmidt and Kalyma and we was to meet up with them in Kamochinsk inlet.

8/15 — After finally breaking through the densest stretch of permanent ice our caravan of ships come out into open water where there wasn't so much ice and it floated in patches. We was no longer in any danger of having to spend the whole winter here, and still though we went through all sorts of difficulties we made it to the Bay of ambarchik on September 4. We started unloading the ships, but ran into some trouble because of severe storms that started up and the bins overturned spilled their loads into the sea. We had to stop unloading the ships and they left to winter in Chaunsk Inlet and I went with the Lenin down the Kalyma River to winter in the town of Sredne-Kalymsk, but we wasn't even within a hundred kilometers when the river iced up and the ship had to stop for the winter in a place called "Monzhelsk," all the workers had to leave the ship on foot, I had some kind of fever and felt terrible. but I didn't want to stay there and so I decided to leave too on foot somehow I managed to cover 20 km in 13 hours and reached a settlement called "Banskoe" where a woman named N. I. Yaglovskaya lived who met me and seeing the miserable state of my health she made me a bed on the floor and brewed me up some tea. And I slept like I didn't have no back legs just the ones in front. In the morning I couldn't stand on my own I had to use crutches. Natalya Ivanovna and her older daughter took me out behind the shed where they left me alone to tend to my needs. So I'm sitting there on a log and here comes this willow grouse out of the bushes running up the narrow path toward me, and she don't stop till she's right up under my nose just three paces away. It really bugged me that I couldn't even scare a little bird and I grabbed a handful of snow and throwed it at her, the grouse turned and headed back down the same path, I gathered my strength to go back to the hut, but I couldn't move and had to wait for Yaglovskaya and her daughter to come and get me. When I told them about what had happened to me and the grouse the older son Nikolai bust out laughing, it's a good thing she didn't poke your eyes out, your lucky there. But that's nothing, they've seen worse. Like last spring when their father was still alive they'd gone fishing and left a bag of food on the bank while they went out onto the river to set their nets. Coming back there was a bear sitting next to the bag. the father starts yelling at him and waving the oar, but Mishka[7] didn't pay no mind, he just kept on taking things out of the bag and eating them, bread fish he even set the fish bones aside specially and throwed them at them, and when he'd ate everything he crumpled the bag into a ball and throwed that at them too, then just walked off into the bushes. And other times when it was cold and windy and they was out catching fish they'd bury it under the snow to shelter it from the wind and keep it fresh, and that very same Mishka with his accomplices the white polar foxes and red foxes, and also sometimes with ermines, would steal that fish they had hid and would carry it off lickety split into the bushes where they buried it in snow or moss. But then later on these little critters would run circles around Mishka watching him while he gobbled up all the stolen goods by himself. So why don't You kill them I asked Kolya. They don't kill bears because they don't do nothing. In fact they even like running into bears in the woods, except theres one thing the bears don't like, thats if some one pulls in to shore and leaves his gun in the boat there, well then Mishka is sure to break the gun and he'll overturn the boat with everything in it, and throw it into the water, then he'll just walk off into the woods.

A week later I felt a little better and Nikolai took me by dog sled to the settlement of Kuldino and from there I was taken to the camp at Lobuya.

10/15 — Heavy frosts set in. The workers was living in tents and worked as hard as they could building yurts; by the start of winter they was already built and all the workers moved in. so that Lobuya, which before we got there had been just an ordinary old river bank out in the wilds now already had 28 yurts on it, a hospital a Radiostation a canteen, Bath,

Machine shops, an electric generating station and other buildings and what used to be nothing now had a population of some five hundred souls. Where on the shore of the river Kolyma and the mouth of the river Lobuya no human foot had ever trod, suddenly Ilyich's lamp[8] blazed up, hammers rung out and the red red banner unfurled. The sound of ships whistles filled the air and the River Kalyma abandoned long ago shook itself awake after its long hibernation. Now a whole fleet of ships sails its waters.

1933

Because the ships arrived late in the bay of ambarchik and the stormy weather had made it impossible to unload them the settlement of Lobuya was left without provisions. Though some did get delivered, still it was not enough and so people started coming down with scorvy, which I got too and took to my bed they put me in the hospital, and I stayed there almost until May. and I was officially instructed to leave the Kalyma region right away.

The management kept me on the job almost into August in the Liquidation Committee since state shipping was transferred to Dalstroi. There wasn't any ships at that time in Sredne Kalymsk, they'd all been sent to ambarchik to unload the sea vessels there, and so we was stuck, all we had was rowboats. We couldn't expect no help from the administration and so 4 of us crippled with scorvy got to gether and set out in a rowboat.

8/6 — We left Sredne Kolymsk at 4 in the afternoon going downstream on the river Kolyma, trusting ourselves to the good will of the river which seemed to have took it on herself to deliver us to the bay of ambarchik. The 1st stop was in the settlement of Zabartsevo. Where fishermen lived temporarily in these little huts winter and summer while they fished. It was already 8 a.m. local time, day was breaking, and after a rest we got started again on our journey.

We made it to Kuldino: a short rest. Without stopping in any of the huts we just boiled some water for tea right there on the shore ate some smoked yukola[9] and started off again. It was quiet and the river was calm without even a window, as we called it. Semashkevich laughed, and said that if the whole trip was going to be like this, then fine, it might take us longer, but at least we'd stay on course. Maybe so, I said, but don't forget that the ships ain't going to wait for us, they'll unload and leave and what, are we just going to sit on the bank there till we croak? Yes, that wouldn't be too good neither, so it would be better if we got some help from a tail wind, that'd be easier and we'd get a move on.

We passed the Settlement of Banskoe, that's where I had stayed almost a week on the way to Kalyma when I had been so sick and couldn't walk. I also remembered that grouse who hadn't been afraid of me. Ketka and Yuliya didn't know about that yet I had told Semashkevich about the grouse back in Lobuya and how I'd shooed her back into the bushes. Late in afternoon my comrades rowed as best they could, though some had only one good arm meanwhile I sat helpless at the rudder steering like I didn't have no arms at all. We tried to make it to the settlement of Moizhenko to spend the night since it was a dark night and the sky was covered with dark clouds it looked like rain, the wind picked up and waves started rising and breaking on the river. It was getting some dangerous to be out in the middle of the river like that and we moved in under the steep cliffs on the left bank. Suddenly our boat catched onto something and wouldn't budge when we stuck our oars down into the water they didn't hit bottom. whats going on here. we had no idea and we couldn't see nothing in the darkness of night. Our Yuliya, who was a real scardey cat, starts bawling, it's a Wood Goblin done trapped us, we're stuck now. There we was on our last legs but we just bust out laughing. That really set Yuliya off she got all mad at us for being in good spirits. Semashkevich started poking his oar in the water and it caught on some fine threads under the surface but he didn't say nothing and just started singing, O sick ones, let us pray, we're stuck in a net and can't get away, The devils aim is sure and true and now whatever can we do. We'll have to spend the night here. The river was roaring and the waves beated up against the steep rocky banks and we was about to be smashed to bits.

Semashkevich and Keshka tried to push the nets down deep into the river with their oars so we could get through but it didn't work. Till we figured out what was wrong, it was a small but thick screw on the bottom of our boat that had got caught in the nets.

We reached a place where the river divided into several channels branching out to the sides. In the darkness we couldn't see the nautical markers we strayed into one of the channels and got lost. We only realized it when we ran a ground and the channel disappeared.

Semashkevich got out of the boat to have a look around and he realized there was no where to go, we just had to wait till morning. We drug the boat onto the swampy mud at the waters edge to get onshore we had to wade through mud up to our knees. and we had to wait through the night in this treacherous channel surrounded by the low thick woods of the taiga. But there wasn't no cause to feel ashamed about being stuck like this in the taiga. Even the local people have stories they tell about getting lost in the taiga and not finding their way out for several days, and it was no wonder people like us strangers travelling here for the first time would wind up in such a fix. It was just bad luck it wasn't our fault, what made it hurt was we was so sick. Well anyway there we was up on the bank. Keshka felt around in the darkness and gathered some kindling and we got a fire going. we just sit there laughing. Here we are in this awful predicament and we're acting like chumaks[10] of the far north, not a care in the world. The only thing on our minds is how to get out of here, we've already forgotten about the ship and that we might miss it. We've got two rifles an axe a saw and two ropes we still have bread, salt too and two packs of matches some makhorka[11] and a few old newspapers for rolling cigarettes, salted fish and yupala,[12] what else do we need. our health, but we done lost that already, there's no getting it back, so meanwhile all we can do is ignore everything but how to get to the ships.

Dawn broke. Yuliya got to work cleaning the fish. Keshka gathered wood, Semashkevich made two new oars to replace the broken ones and I was just about helpless by then and just sat on the ground adding wood to the fire. Keep it burning yelled Yuliya, quiet like, but I didn't pay no attention, then she run up to me and said that she heard something rustling near the boat. like there was someone stirring down there. Keshka went down the steep bank and clum back up in a tearing hurry. His face was white with terror and he couldn't get a word out. Yuliya rushed over to him, what's the matter. Keshka starts in about some Shaggy no leg monster down by our boat. Semashkevich grabs the axe I get the rifle and we go down and right there by the boat is a real bear big as life standing in mud up to his belly rocking the boat back and forth trying to tip it over when Semashkevich shouts at him Mishka sees this ain't a good time to overturn the boat so the bastard starts taking things out of the boat and throwing them into the mud. There wasn't no point in shooting at him with the shotgun it would just stir him up and who knows where that would lead to. But Mishka apparently got bored with messing around in the mud and climbs up out of it and heading straight for us, we take off running back up the bank grabbing whatever we could use to defend ourselves. But Mishka just turns and heads off down the shore in the opposite direction.

While Yuliya got the food ready, we straightened things up in the boat, dried out the soaked things packed them back in the boat and got everything ready to leave we're just waiting for food we start back up the shore and suddenly here comes Yuliya tumbling head over heels down the bank yelling and getting all scratched up on the underbrush, what's the matter Yuliya. A bear come up to our camp tried to grab her with its paw but she broke away and took off running down here to the river. Whats going on here! They's all over the place you can't escape. We're at their mercy. to hell with them. Keshka snuck up peeked through the bushes and seen Mishka having his breakfast by our campfire, when he ate up everything we had there he started throwing the dishes down into the river what could we do, just leave, or else who knows what travails might befall us. the only thing is the frying pan we need it for the trip, and the tea kettle, but the rest we can get in the settlements said I to my friends.

Lets get in the boat right away, he might come after us, something is crackling over there is it the bear coming down the bank. We're just getting clear of the mud and theres Mishka again on the shore right down by the water. We turn the boat sharp and head for the other shore to get away as quick as we can, but Mishka the clumsy devil sees we're already pretty far off, so he roars and grabs this piece of wood floating on the water and throws it at us real hard and sprays us on the boat. The farther away we get, the madder he gets and he starts heaving big old logs at us, but he couldn't get to us, exspecially when the bank got real steep and evidently our Mishka had to go back inland to get around it. Yuliya sits in the boat cussing out the channel and keeps looking down at her scratched up arms and legs and she's got big blue bruises under her eyes. The whole rest of the way she got all upset if one of us brought up the idea of stopping somewhere on the shore, she didn't want to run into no more bears in the woods. And she'd ruther just stay on the river hungry with nothing but dry bread to eat.

We catched up with our boats in Karlukovye, each one was hauling three large barges of cargo to Sredne-Kalymsk and along the way we learned that the ships hadn't been unloaded yet, but that we wasn't hardly half way there. The river widened out we went as fast as we could the weather was favorable almost totally dry after which, it got stormy and I have to admit it was downright dangerous we been on the river twenty-five days already and right at the mouth of the river, where it ran into the ocean the waves was real rough, we was all right so long as we stayed close to shore, but when we turned to cross over to the other side, we think its all over now, anyway, we made it across and was just starting to move in to shore, when a huge wave heaved us way up onto the rocky bank, the water fell back and there we was stuck on the rocks. Our boat was damaged and we couldn't use it no more. So we set off along the bank on foot spent two nights along the way we made it to the bay of Ambarchik and saw our ship the "Khabarovsk" standing at anchor five miles off shore. 8/31. We cast off from ambarchik. There was over forty of us, all sick. We made a good start thanks to comrade Shiffrin he let us have some provisions for the trip and we was already home free except for being so sick. Which we figured we'd get over when we reached Vladivostok and we was all excited about that. But fate was so un ceremonious and mean to us that it let us reach our goal and then forced us sick as we was to wait all through the winter at the cape of Bilinsk. Our ship got stuck in the ice and the captain announced we all was going to have to stay through the winter, since the three ships was lined up side to side while the Chelyuskin[13] hoping to break through to the island of Vrangel had already started off but she was in danger too at that time, because of all the ice coming in from the sea.

All the passengers was moved to the holds for the winter, where life was real hard for us. The stoves burned dirty the hold was full of smoke and we was sick enough already. just coughing and hacking. There wasn't enough medicine to go around. The only thing that saved us was the doctors Lyapunov and Skorokadomsky who done everything they could. To keep us alive and get us back safe and sound.

The polar night come on, blizzards and snowstorms howling constantly and there wasn't a minutes peace. the winds whistling oppressed everyone with its howling and all us sick people was in a state of deepest depression and feeling totally nasty and even disgusting.

The captain come down to see us calmed us down, promised to evacuate us by aeroplane back to shore. but these was just empty promises. Life was hard. The ship wouldn't give us no fresh water and our sick comrades was forced to take sledges from heaps of ice exposed to the wind to get water for cooking or washing. and also, about food, if it hadn't been for doctor Skorokadomsky who ordered them to issue us fresh provisions, like vennison, or fresh slaughtered pork from pigs he raised on board, but still a lot of people died anyhow, some of them was throwed overboard, and some was buried onshore between the cape of Biling and Yakan.

1934

New years was fun. The guys on the ship put on a show. our comrade Yer-molai played his accordion, in spite of him being sick, in general we kept our spirits up, we lived for the day. and just wait and see what the morrow holds in store. and we'd sit around drinking tea and shout, hey Yermoshka play The Irkutsk Maiden and I'll shake a leg, our Tamonov he was always laughing. Now give it all you've got, make that accordion sing so loud maybe someone back at home will hear it and think how much fun we're having out here in the arctic so they won't feel sorry for us, let's see him dance some fancy jigg, what do you mean jigg we ask each other. The one he danced just now, and if that ain't enough let him do another one, and he starts up like a circus acrobat going around like a wheel, our old Botswain Binderei. Whats the matter with you Mishka, chin up, all that thinking won't get you nowhere. Thinkings for the high and mighty, not for the likes of us, we got someone looking after us now while we're all crippled and sick, and when we get better we'll return the favor. So come on now, give us a good dance before supper. After supper we'll have a political lecture. today the captain of the North is going to talk, it'll be worth listening to, he speaks so slow and clear, its real easy to understand even if you don't have no education, and if he has to, he'll repeat it over and over and make sure you get it. Take Foma bezstrashny look how much he learned in just three months. Just you try having a conversation with him now. The other day he asks a question and the second mechanic just stands there with his mouth hanging open and cant say one word, just mumbling. It just goes to show what learning will do for you.

Over supper the first mate read us a telegram from the northern cape saying to clear a landing place tomorrow for a plane to come and get the people who was sick. I don't know where these sick men found the strength inside them but everyone who could still move at all announced their willingness to help out. It was like we got a surge of energy from people knowing about us stuck out here on the ice for the winter and suf-fering all kinds of ailments.

2/12 They started moving us off the boat everything went fine forty people in all was evacuated I'm supposed to go today. Telegram, the plane's not coming, then another one the Chelyuskin has had an accident.

84

2/13 A third telegram the ship the Chelyuskin was crushed by ice.

2/14 It sunk down to the bottom. The passengers and crew was all saved except for one. Everyone was evacuated onto an ice flow. with enough provisions for two months. We all feel our legs buckle under us, we just sit there in shock and wonder so now what. there's people stuck out there on the ice. Someone has to save them. We can't, we're sick, and its hard to say what our crew can do either.

With this calamity all of us forgot about our own predicament, and all we could think of was them people out on the ice and was they going to get rescued. We all gather round day after day and listen to the reports from Camp Schmidt.

The days start getting longer the sun come out, it was like the winds got gentler or maybe we was use to them and they didn't feel so scary and dangerous no more.

In the afternoon my friend Semashkevich went out with the sailors and caught a nerpa seal in a net. They drug her over to the ship and let her loose in the water in a hollow in the ice. The nerpa takes off with the sailors on her back for a ride they slipped into the water and got all soaked and exhausted and when they clum up the steps to their rooms they was exhausted and wet as frogs.

I'll never forget those minutes when the explosions team blowed up the ice with amonal and broke through the last stretch of ice and everyone yells and cheers we're free and our ship started forward after its long frozen winter, straining its utmost to get out of that ice that everyone was so sick and tired of.

When our ship cleared the ice and got out into open water at last, it felt like her whole body was breathing easy, it rocked gently from side to side and you could see the captain pacing back and forth up on his bridge with his hands behind his back, grinning his head off and looking down at the deck where we was all basking in the fresh air talking to each other well comrades, the captain asks from the bridge, you feeling better or worse now he asked? All us sick men yells back we're just about over it. thank you comrade captain. lets go on to the Arctic! Why not. We ain't scared of the Arctic, what scares us is this damn scorvy. So many people on the boat, and what use are they? Eat like bulls at dinner, but at work a puff of air lays them out like so many mosquitoes.

Our ship dropped anchor in the Bay of Lavrenty to take on some coal brought by the Kirov. The next day we was all systems go and on our way to Kamchatka. And then we stopped in Dakastri on Sakhalin to load up the weather was favorable and three days later when we entered the bay at Vladivostok there was a brass band blaring out music to welcome us on the beautiful long awaited pier. I waited with utmost patience for everyone to get off then they carried me out last of all onto the deck and then lowered me down the steps and they took me under the arms to certain citizen Lukin's apartment. to rest from the trip, and then they sent me to Moscow under the care of a doctor, Sarygin, Aleksandr Andrevich, who was returning home from Kamchatka, who took care of me during the trip and in Moscow at the train station he signed me into the hospital at Yauza. That's how my long journey I was on from 1932 to August 1934 come to an end and to commemorate this I entered some words to express my sentiments upon parting with the Arctic. Farewell you cold arctic

> Farewell ice and icebergs.
> Farewell seas and oceans,
> Farewell Chukchi and Lamut.
> Farewell Yakut and grouse,
> Farewell Nerpa seal and whales
> Farewell Dolphins and killer whales
> Farewell Fishes and polar foxes
> Farewell Tungus and Yukagir [14]
> Farewell blizzard and snowstorms
> Farewell channels and lakes
> Farewell eternal snows.
> F.Sh.

I append herewith an itinerary from the ship Khabarovsk and a list of the settlements where we — I stopped during our trip by boat down the river Kolyma:

town of Sredne-Kalymsk	679 k/m.
inlet of Lobuya	664 -"-
Zabartsevo fishing spot	652 -"-
Zabartsevo	649 -"-
Kuldino	636 -"-
Banskaya	622 -"-
Lower Banskaya	616 -"-
Former settlement	609 -"-
Petrovo -"-	599 -"-
Locality of Voronkovo	588 -"-
Upper-Zhirkovo	577 -"-

Zhirkovo	575 -"-
Mysovaya	551 -"-
Urna Settlement	547 -"-
mouth of the Bystraya	542 -"-
Tonya. yama settlement	527 -"-
Chakchanu -"-	509 -"-
Pomazkina -"-	495 -"-
Gornitsa -"-	492 -"-
Tulukanova Tanya settlement	489 -"-
Cape Cherny	483 -"-
Ytyrtakh	474 -"-
Kytyn	465 -"-
Yugus-toman	460 -"-
Kondakovo	444 -"-
Ulovo-Skovorodnik	436 -"-
Kresty	431 -"-
Begunovo	420 -"-
Komarok	415 -"-
Surukhtakh	408 -"-
Yevseika	394 -"-
Gornitsa	386 -"-
Kuzakovka	384 -"-
Nyasovka	380 -"-
Sukhanovo	376 -"-
Upper Konzaboi	375 -"-
Lower -"-	372 -"-
Karlukovo	369 -"-
Mouth of the Krivaya	362 -"-
Locality of Aleshkina	350 -"-
Upper Kholmy	339 -"-
Lower -"-	329 -"-
Kamskaya	323 -"-
mouth of the Amalok river	321 -"-
Winter Cape	303 -"-
Summer Cape	301 -"-
Voronskaya	295 -"-
Dubanskaya	285 -"-
Lapeevka	271 -"-
Dolgoe pole	258 -"-
V. Timkinskaya	237 -"-
Volochek	229 -"-

Yermolovo	229 -"-
Yamki	215 -"-
Lower Kalymsk	200 -"-
Kresty	160 -"-
Kamen I	125 -"-
Woods Edge	100 -"-
Shore of Damnation	
(our own name for the place	
our boat was wrecked)	75 -"-
Sharaurovo	45 -"-
bay of Ambarchik	00 -"-
	679 -"-

9/15 They sent me to the Mainaki mud-baths in Yevratori with my wife, who come along to accompany me to the hospital in place of the orderly assigned to me.

They brung me here to get the cure
Mud and Massage will work their sure
Arms and legs they twist and turn
pull my fingers till they burn
This'll work the doctors said
But I still can't get up out of bed

So I just laid around at the resort, six weeks rushed by like a single day. When my wife and I got home it took three people to get me into the apartment it turns out that the scorvy is stronger than any doctor.

1935

I spent the winter at home on bed rest, my wife Nataliya Georgievna took care of me, who got basins of hot water for me morning and night, first my legs, then my arms. She massaged me with methylated spirits and Ointment and dosed me constantly with Valerianin drops and bromide — because of the bad shock to my nervous system. and by April I felt better. I started walking on my own using a cane, I got rid of the crutches and on the advice of Ivan Nikitich Darichev, who took me on as a manager at the second building materials factory, where he is the Director where I started work, I got involved in community activities, started writing up topical notes for the wall newspaper and the workers who lived in the dormitory who had been living in bad conditions, read them and begun taking themselves in hand. it was dirty in the dormitory and there was drinking and brawling and knife fights when I come everything gradually started to improve. In the evening I read them newspapers, explained things and told about my trip up north, they was very interested and that took care of all the disorderly conduct at the factory, and plus we got us a new Director, also the dormitory and yard started getting some attention. so things started going like they should and the workers was satisfied. Though in practically every wall newspaper I put up Notices about problems, like for example:

> O Bed, miserable bed
> Always the same.
> Rumpled and unmade
> My constant shame
>
> Mattress crumpled like before,
> Pillow lying on the floor
> From the table by the bed
> A stream of muddy tears is shed.
>
> MECHANIC WHERE ARE YOU?
> Day follows night,
> it's almost been a year,
> Beg as we might
> The Mechanic won't appear
> The sink is leaking on the floor
> Around the bathroom theres a moat,
> Boards are rotting near the door,
> I guess we'll have to build a boat.
>
> BEDBUGS
> We all know without a doubt
> that bedbugs are out and about.
> In dormitory number 2
> there are more than just a few
> Take a look on your sheet
> you'll see a whole fleet.
> You may think that they're a curse,
> But disinfectant is much worse.

SOCIALIST COMPETITION IN THE BARRACKS
I bring from work my dirty shoes
and put them on the floor, I'm neat
My room is clean, how can I lose?
But at bedtime I find them on the sheet.

IMMACULATE CLEANING WOMEN
Intrepid Irina,
celebrated Polina
They're supposed to work
but all they do is shirk:
One sweeps underneath the bed
the other underneath the table,
They sweep the dust into a pile
but carry it out? They are unable.

NOVOSELTSEV TAKE A LOOK AROUND!
Where, my darling, are you from
From what crevice did you come?
All night long you plague my sleep
O you worthless little creep.

First you bite me in the side
Then you crawl into my ear
The only place I let you hide
is by my collar, right up here
    I cherish every little louse
    I stay away from the bath house
    I'll grow another hundred head
    in the mattress on my bed.

What with various slogans and funny little poems like this our friends the
Workers living there started taking themselves in hand, and it spreaded to
others too. Or take this other case: Before the weekend I instructed everyone to take a bath, led by the barracks monitor who was responsible for
making sure everyone got bathed, but Novoseltsev refused to go to the bathhouse and so he stayed dirty. Well, before their baths everyone was always
given fresh sheets. And this Novoseltsev laid down right on the clean sheets
in his dirty clothes, without even taking off his boots. His comrades lit into
him, but Novoseltsev wouldn't budge then all the workers got together and
hauled his bed outside with him in it and it was pouring down rain at the
time. Novoseltsev flew off the handle and starts yelling and cussing. Thats

when I came along and asked what was going on. and why was Novoseltsev laying out there in his bed in the rain. After which the bed was carried back into the barracks and I had to have a heart to heart talk with Novoseltsev. Why hadn't he gone to the bath answer. he didn't have no clean underwear. well did he have some that was dirty? I asked. he did. well so why didn't you, get it washed? There was no one to do it. Polina, I call the cleaning woman over and ask her to wash the mans underwear. with pleasure answered Polina. All right, who here has clean underwear, I do, I do and so on. Everyone does? yes. Someone give the man a change till tomorrow morning, while his is being washed let him go on and get a bath. Novoseltsev left.

Coming back from the bath, he didn't want to lie down on the dirty bed sheets no more and he asked me for some clean ones.

After that I asked Novoseltsev his opinion about his work and was he paid enough? Novoseltsev answered of course. You're right. So please make an effort to pay Polina the cleaning woman for washing your dirty underwear, why of course, he gets some money out of his trunk and pays her for the washing. So tell me how do you feel after your bath? Fine I feel refreshed, thank you answered Novoseltsev. From that time on I never had to remind him to go bathe and our Novoseltsev started taking care of himself and his bed even more than the others and during the October celebration he got a prize for cleanliness. It just goes to show what the right treatment can do for a man.

1936

Working at that same factory I participated actively in community activities along with my regular job, and I managed to redo the whole interior of the living quarters, plaster and white wash them inside and out, put up pretty tulle curtains in the windows, gave each barracks a clock and a mirror to hang on the wall, pathways flowers, decanters for the tables, tablecloths pretty lamphades benches outside the barracks, flower beds accordions, balalaikas, guitars, draughts and chess sets, a piano and portable gramophones, portraits, paintings and even thermometers on the walls. The medical clinic also got some attention and we trained the workers in the cafeteria to serve food fit for people, not barnyard animals. We brung in teachers to teach the workers and sent dozens out to take special courses. when our mechanics come back from the courses, they was already completely trained. They changed their way of working methods like it was nothing, Stakhanovites installed themselves firmly at the helm and our factory started buzzing, it went from a yearly volume of two million to thirteen million and in 1936 it rose even higher, keep pushing it higher and higher so all of us can live happier.

And now it would not be a bad idea to describe about Katya Sorokina about an average lubrication worker. How she wound up in Moscow.

Katya Sorokina was an ignorant uneducated woman, she walked all the way from Saratov Province to Moscow during the years of famine.[15] She found work with a market gardener who at that time still ran his own private business just outside Moscow. At first Katya worked for him practically for nothing just her daily bread. Then the gardener started paying her, but Katya still couldn't afford to buy her clothes, Katya asked for a raise but her boss not only turned her down but he fired her too. Katya found herself a place as a guard in the city parks where the work wasn't appropriate for her neither she was too young she kept wanting to get work at some factory or plant, and she found herself a job as a cleaning woman in the dormitory at a factory in Moscow. Katya didn't forsake the church, she had an icon of Nikolai the Miracle worker she kept under lock and key in her chest. But seeing that this chest wasn't helping her in the least and after pondering on it for a long time, Katya decided to part with that icon. Early one morning when everyone was still asleep Katya got out her icon took it down to the bank of the Yauza river and throwed it into the water, and stopped, going to church and praying to god. But she didn't see nothing better in her life, and she decides to get that icon back out of the river. She takes her rake and pokes it down into the water all over the place but she couldn't find it. Katya figures that Nikola the Miracle worker had saved himself got up out of the river and walked away. She stands there on the bank thinking she done a grave sin in the eyes of god. Right then Baranov, a shop master at the factory walks by on his way to work, Katya didn't know him yet, but Baranov knowed Katya. Seeing Katya standing deep in thought by the shore of the Yauza with a rake in her hand muttering to herself under her breath. Baranov goes up to her asks her Katya tells him everything and doesn't hold nothing back, Baranov claps her on the shoulder and says to her good for you Katya for doing what you done with that icon, your way in the world will be easier from now on and he orders her to come on along to the factory with him.

The shop master Baranov fixed Katya up with a job in the shop, where she earned up to two hundred rubles a month. Katya was very capable and quick minded, she learned everything real quick and became a shock worker,[16] completed the literacy program learned to read and write, and the shop master Baranov took Katya on as an assistant, Katya throwed herself into her work, Seeing how sensible and smart this diligent woman was, the Party Cell of the Factory invited Katya to join the party, where Katya completed the political education program, and then they sent this Katya to the Party School and after she graduated our Katya got appointed director of a big Factory in the Urals. It just goes to show what can come of it when our government and politically conscious Party members who know how to approach these ignorant people show their concern for them and rid them of their addiction to that priestly hocus pocus they've got circulating in their blood. After which we get big people with big talents and knowledge of our Great socialist society.

1937

I was still working in the same old place and in the same factory making sports equipment but when the Yauza River was reconstructed[17] our factory was torn down and afterwards the workers was let go.

7/2 I was offered a transfer to the sales department of the Bauman Industrial Trust as a sorter and inspector at the Sports and Games factory that was in the courtyard of No. 10, Sportokovskaya Square.

I didn't know much about inspecting manufactured goods and I didn't have no experience, and so, the shops tried to trick me and turn out inferior products. But this cheating was discovered by me and one fine day I rejected the entire whole days production and didn't put my official stamp on it and didn't accept it for our stocks. They ganged up on me but I didn't pay no mind. And I didn't waste no time and informed the trust by official notification that such phenomenons in the factory was unacceptable, for cheating the sales department and the customer. Several times an authorized commission was designated, that recognized I was right to reject all that stuff. After them commissions the management saw they wasn't going to get away with it and they started being more conciliatory with me and agreeing with my opinion and even started improving things making less rejects. But that's not all, I used that wall newspaper in which I didn't beat around the eyebrow I went straight for the eye. Like for example:

> What's the matter with our plant,
> It could before but now it can't,

It used to make the boss so glad,
And now its got so nasty and bad
Causing nothing now but woe
Producing stuff we cannot show.
The star we make is shaped all right,
The paint on it acceptably bright,
The paper too will do just fine,
But it's all covered with spots of grime.
Just whose handiwork is this
And whose business is it to fix.
If the foreman gave it the all clear,
While in the bar sipping his beer,
And the careless boss let it slip too.
But still there's something we can do
And what's sorters for after all,
If somethings wrong they make the call,
And also what is there to stop
Quality Control out of the shop?

After those difficulties there the loss at the end of the year was only 6000 rubles while in 1936 the factory had losses of over one hundred thousand. It just goes to show what a wall newspaper and attention to your work can do.

1938

This is the most difficult and painful year for me not because there is anything wrong with the year itself, but because my health took a sharp turn for the worse this year and I am no longer able to continue my labors on this manuscript diary, and so with an aching heart I bring my fifty year work to a close and with it I consider my life at an end too. I still want to live, but its no use. Though Mind and memory have not betrayed me yet, my hands refuse to work and my legs to walk. And something is wrong with my heart it goes once, twice, but then skips the third beat. My mouth starts to open but my body is all ready for the crematory, it's just hanging on waiting for that last breath.

I ask my readers forgiveness for the bad style in my wretched little manuscript diary. All the education I had was a village school way out in the middle of nowhere where I was born and spent my childhood up to the age of 14.

I hope that some of my readers might wonder what my goal was and

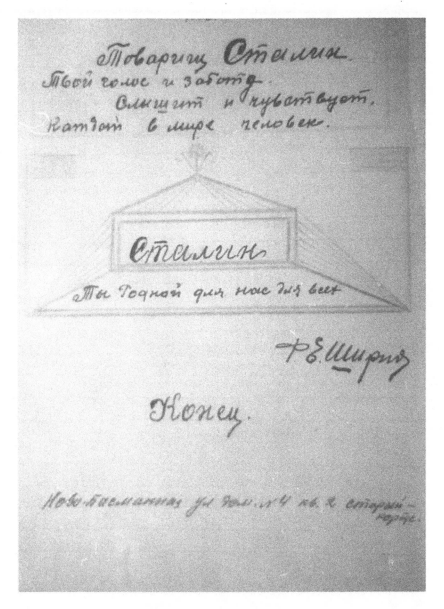

LAST PAGE OF SHIRNOV'S DIARY, DEDICATED TO STALIN

what made me write this diary the answer is simple. It was my fathers notebook got me started. My father didn't have no formal schooling, but he jotted down notes about my whole life from the day I was born. One day when I was in the second grade at the village school I was working on a history and geography assignment and my father told me at the time that a literate person always had a better life in his village and easier work. Thats when I asked my father for his notes about my life that was just beginning and he gave them to me on condition that I would continue to write down notes about my life no matter what difficulties I might encounter along the way. So from then on I took over the writing, first I'd write on scraps of paper, then after that put things down in a real diary.

I lost interest in this scribbling many times during my travels around Russia and I gave it up for a year or two at a time, in spite of the fact that I wrote in notebooks at home and when I accumulated several notebooks I would go around and collect them all to burn them, but then for some reason I would recall my fathers words and that would make me start scribbling in the manuscript diary again. Before the October revolution of 1917 I didn't write much just brief notes, but at least I kept it up, and afterwards when I felt freer and stronger, I got so I wanted to describe everything I saw and heard on my different jobs, where I went, what I done and so on. But now my health is ruined from my trips to the north, and I have brung my diary manuscript to a close.

> I hope this work I've done
> will be of use to everyone.
> Barely literate I may be
> but I've composed this diary,
> Fifty years of notes here in
> I send on to the Kremlin
> to the Great Stalin.
> —F. Sh.

> Comrade Stalin
> Your voice and your concern
>   is heard and felt
> by every man the world over

> Stalin
> You is dear to us all
> THE END   F. E. Shirnov

NOTES

[1] The author's spelling varies between "Kalyma," reflecting his pronunciation, and the correct "Kolyma," a river and region of the Far East where many labor camps that were part of the system of Dalstroi were to be located from the 1930s to the beginning 1950s .

[2] Acronym for Leninist Young Communist League of the USSR.

[3] The diminutive of Shura.

[4] Russian and Ukrainian folk dance, in which the performer, in a sitting position, throws his legs back and forth.

[5] Reference to Chukotka, or the Chukchi Peninsula, in the extreme northeast of Russia, opposite Alaska. The yurt is a a circular, domed tent used by the Mongols of Siberia and other nomad ethnicities.

[6] Also called Evenk, the Tungus are people of the Siberian Far North. See note 14.

[7] Affectionate name for a bear.

[8] Common reference to "electricity" in Soviet political mythology. The peasants of the village of Shumenskoe, where Vladimir Ilyich Lenin was exiled in prerevolutionary times, had allegedly created a small power station, and the first electric lamps that "blazed up" were named after the leader of the Russian revolution.

[9] A type of dry-cured fish, eaten by the peoples of Siberia and the Far East.

[10] The Chumaks were cossacks or peasants, trading salt and fish in the Ukraine between the sixteenth and nineteenth centuries.

[11] A kind of cheap tobacco, often rolled in newspaper.

[12] The same as yukola, or a misspelling.

[13] The "Chelyuskin" was a ship built in 1933 in Denmark by order of the Soviet government. In 1933, the ship sailed out for an expedition headed by Otto Yulevich Shmidt (1891–1956), with the goal of navigating directly from Murmansk to Khabarovsk. In the Bering straight, the Chelyushkin was caught in the ice. It drifted to the Chukhotka Sea and was crushed by the ice in 1934. The survivors of the expedition were rescued by air.

[14] Chukchi, Lamut, Yakut, Tungus, Yukagir: peoples and tribes of the Russian north and Far East. For an excellent recent history of these peoples, see Yuri Slezkine, *Arctic Mirrors: Russia and the Peoples of the North* (Ithaca and London: Cornell University Press, 1994).

[15] The famine of 1932–33 in the Ukraine and Volga regions.

[16] See note 6 of the "Chronicle of the Year 1937."

[17] In the context of the reconstruction plan of Moscow, adopted by the Central Committee and the Sovnarkom in July 1935.

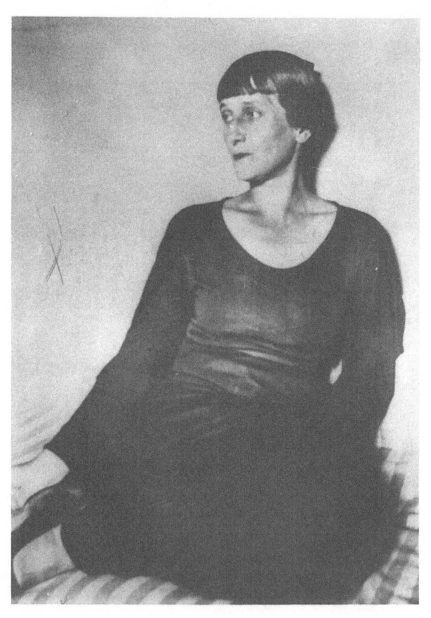

Anna Akhmatova, posing for Lev Gornung at Peski (July 1936)

LEV VLADIMIROVICH GORNUNG

Lev Vladimirovich Gornung, born in 1902, was a Moscow poet and transla-
tor. From 1920 to 1922 he served in the Second Moscow Reserve Artillery
Brigade of the Red Army. After his demobilization, during the 1920s, he
illustrated the manuscript journal Hermes. *In 1925 he was invited to work*
for the State Academy of Artistic Sciences (GAKhN) at the People's Com-
missariat of Education. His activity was mainly devoted to the organiza-
tion of artistic exhibitions. He had started to write poems during his youth.
In the 1930s he completed a number of translations, including works by
Racine and Corneille, as well as by Armenian and Serbian poets. From
1941 to 1945 he took part in the Tula front battles and those around Moscow.
After the war he worked as book designer in the Moscow Arts Fund.

These data were obtained from the Central State Archives of Literature
and Art (TsGALI). They were given to the archives by Gornung himself,
who delivered various documents in 1975, 1985, and 1989. Gornung died in
October 1993.

DIARY OF LEV VLADIMIROVICH GORNUNG

7/14/36

I finally left for Peski on the six-o'clock train. An. And.[1] has been there
for over two weeks now. It was already after nine when I arrived and no
one was out on the terrace; they had all gone into the dining room for
evening tea. So no one saw me. S.V.[2] met me by the kitchen and suggested
I take a pitcher out to the well in the garden to wash up, it's so much more
refreshing that way. I tossed my shirt onto a jasmine bush and S.V. rinsed
me with water from the pitcher. After the train ride in this hot weather, a
wash and change of clothes made me feel like a new man.

The professor,[3] who's forty, the family doctor,[4] Val. Iv.,[5] El. Vl.'s aunt[6] and
An[na] And[reevna] were sitting around the table in the dining room, in the
light of a shaded kerosene lamp. An[na] And[reevna] welcomed me warmly,
like an old friend. As during my last visit, El. Vl. was in bed, since she had

99

stayed out in the water too long again. It was dark in the bedroom and I hesitated about going in to see her, but she sent S.V. out to get me and I went in just for a minute. At the table no one had much to say. Val. Iv. poured the tea, and when she left the room, An[na] And[reevna] got up to serve me.

After tea the three of us sat out on the dark stone terrace, she, S.V. and I, and talked about Osip,[7] about our trip to Kolomna, and looked up at the stars and clouds in the night sky. A[nna] A[ndreevna] got up to go down to the river with Val. Iv., who was taking her female sheepdog for a walk. The dog has to spend practically the whole day inside, since there are other dogs and cats around.

7/15/36

After tea A[nna] A[ndreevna] invited me to walk down to the river with her.

We sat under the willows. I asked her about Mand[elshtam] and we talked about this and that.

At the dacha A[nna] A[ndreevna] never takes off her pale pink satin shawl. She is very modest and refined in the way she carries herself. When people reproach her at tea or dinner for not eating enough, she gets flustered and makes excuses, just like a child. She tries to play with the Shervinsky girls (Katka is the one who seeks her out more often), but she's awkward; it doesn't come naturally to her. And still you feel as though you're in the presence of something extraordinary, something that comes along only once in a hundred years, it's somehow strange to see A[nna] A[ndreevna] doing such ordinary things.

She's changed a great deal since I saw her last; it's not just that she's gotten older, she's turned into a tight bundle of nerves, she has an unsteady way of walking and her voice is shaky and uncertain, it breaks when she talks.

She's been consulting doctors and says that for several days now she hasn't felt her heartbeat. Vas. Dm.[8] found an abnormality in her thyroid.

After dinner I photographed Bayan[9] by the river. A[nna] A[ndreevna] and Val. Iv-na were there too. After sunset S.V. read three scenes from Faust. He's editing Bryusov's translation for the State Publishing House for Belles-Lettres [Gikhl].

We had supper by lamplight out on the stone terrace.

7/16/36

At tea S.V. said he thought today would be overcast and we decided to go to Kolomna. It was already too late to make the first train. Before tea I photographed the front of the house and took a picture of myself standing in front of it with the two girls.

Somehow S. V. found out about a work train leaving Peski for Kolomna at 1:00. On our way to the station, we realized how hot it was, but after some hesitation A[nna] A[ndreevna] decided to come along anyway.

She seemed interested in the town. There are a lot of old churches and small Empire-style buildings in Kolomna. While S. V. and I went up to the corner to take a close look at one of the houses from the other side, she sat on a bench in the shade by the gate. On our way back we saw her sitting there and decided to capture the moment, and I took a picture. Then we went to the Dmitry Donskoy gate, which is now called Pyatnitskie. I took two pictures here, one of A[nna] A[ndreevna] under a tree in front of an Empire-style building that used to be an almshouse, and one of her standing with S. V. in front of the Pyatnitskaya Tower. We stood in the church square and admired the church and the yellow buildings of the monastery. A[nna] A[ndreevna] said that this place reminded her of Pisa and S. V. agreed, saying he'd noticed the similarity long ago. We walked around the Marina Mniszek Tower.[10] Both entrances were closed. A[nna] A[ndreevna] was tired, worn out by the heat. I went to find someone from the museum who could let us in, which turned out to be more trouble than I'd thought. While I was away, the two of them sat on some logs at the entrance of the tower. We didn't spend too much time in the tower itself. On our way up the dark brick stairway, the sole of A[nna] A[ndreevna]'s shoe started to come off, and it embarrassed her a great deal to have to tell us about it. She asked to borrow my knife, but S. V. just tore the sole right off, since it was his wife's shoe anyway, A[nna] A[ndreevna] had just borrowed it for the trip (which I hadn't known).

On our way back to the station we passed a bar and A[nna] A[ndreevna] herself suggested we stop for a drink. We had some beer and hard-boiled eggs. Then S. V. and I went into a store next to the central square to pick up some things. We noticed an interesting flower, which S. V. called "*glokasinia*," in a window of one of the houses. He took us through the flower garden on the square, one of the local attractions, and showed A[nna] A[ndreevna] his favorite flowers, the purslanes. He suggested that she "expand her botanical knowledge" by learning to identify the cariolipsis, and she practiced repeating the names, but got mixed up with gloxinia and some of the others. Some photographers had set up their backdrops next to the collective farm market; one of the scenes showed a horse with a hole cut out where people could put their faces. We decided that if A[nna] A[ndreevna] would have her picture taken on the horse, it would be the best of all her photographs. That idea made A[nna] A[ndreevna] a little nervous, and S. V. assured her that he would get his own picture taken on the horse too.

When we got to the station we bought some peppermint cookies; we arrived home completely exhausted and thirsty from the heat.

A[nna] A[ndreevna] even got sunburned from being outside that afternoon. I asked her if she usually tried to stay out of the sun. "No it doesn't bother me, these days I don't worry at all about how I look."

7/17/36

I got up early in the morning as usual and at 7:00 I was already out photographing the big old pink church. Val. Iv. went down to the river with Bayan. I took a picture of everyone together at morning tea. When I developed the film afterwards, this picture didn't turn out. Light had gotten into the cartridge. Someone had brought Vas. Dm. some traditional buckwheat kasha, which he had been sharing with A[nna] A[ndreevna]. He gave her some this morning and said, "You will remember me back in Leningrad whenever you have this kind of kasha." To which A[nna] A[ndreevna] answered, smiling: "I'll remember you for more than just kasha."

We sent Anyuta to check the time, and when she came back and told us, A[nna] A[ndreevna] confessed that she "couldn't tell time until I was 14."

At tea today I reminded her, as I must have done ten times already, that she had forgotten to take her (endocrine) medicine, and she thanked me and said that she was going to have to take me with her to Leningrad, since she always forgets, and the local doctors have instructed her to continue taking it when she goes back. I expressed the hope that sooner or later she would get used to it, there had been times when she had remembered to take her medicine at tea herself.

Akhmanov's little boy had come down with meningitis and I went with Anyuta and the others to Cherkizovo to check up on him.

El. Vlad. is still on bed rest, but she's feeling better.

Before supper S. V. read Faust again, 5 scenes (the scene with Margarita and others). A[nna] A[ndreevna] came out in a simple black dress and El. Vlad.'s checkered shawl since it was chilly. Afterwards we went in for supper. When she saw the fried eggs with their runny yolks A[nna] A[ndreevna] recalled one time when she was visiting a friend and had a new dress on, and the friend wouldn't give her any fried eggs, she said, "Anichka, you mustn't eat anything that might stain."

After tea S. V. sat down with his accordion and sang a few songs. A[nna] A[ndreevna] was unmoved by the old Russian romances of Gurilyov's[11] music to poems by Lermontov.[12] I now recall the wondrous moment[13] — she said she doesn't like that poem, that it's false and contrived, and S. V. agreed with her! She liked one Italian romance (in Italian) and the Schubert serenades, which I love so much myself. Ogarev's translation.

7/18/36

Yesterday when S. V. was with us I told A[nna] A[ndreevna] that I would like to read her some poems of mine that she hadn't heard yet.

This morning after tea A[nna] A[ndreevna] asked me to read her the poems. I went home to get my notebook and we sat on a large bench that had been built in the form of an octagon around the trunks of three linden trees — the "three sisters"[14] —, which had grown from a single root. The bench stands at the end of a broad avenue.

I recited some 20–25 poems. She commented on a few of them during the reading itself. Then when I was done, she said that she liked them a great deal and that they were mature works. If I could get them published they would make quite a good book.

After that we started walking up and down the avenue, and for some reason she started telling me about herself. Then we sat on the bench again. Val. Iv. came up and got A[nna] A[ndreevna] to go down to the river with her for a swim, remarking pointedly, "Ah, so he's been reciting poetry to you!" I must say that she doesn't know A[nna] A[ndreevna]'s poems either and teases her about them too. The only things she takes seriously are her medicine and her dog.

Last night during Faust El. Vl.'s friend arrived from Moscow–Tat. Alekseevna. After dinner I photographed the two of them together in the park. S. V. and I had to leave for Moscow after tea. Before dinner I asked A[nna] A[ndreevna]'s permission to photograph her alone using the large camera. We were alone on the terrace except for Vas. Dm.

She was standing next to a column, leaning against it. She answered with a note of despair in her voice, "I can't pose for pictures any more, I'm too old." I did my best to change her mind. All the other times when I took group pictures she had been very reluctant, but joined in so as not to spoil the mood. That was probably just after Akhmanov, whose pictures of her were so awful. They make her look older than she is. After dinner she asked what dress she should wear for the photographs, and started in again: maybe it's not worth doing, but S. V. backed me up. I said to wear the black dress she had on yesterday.

She went to her room to change and when I went in with the camera, I got the impression that she was a little angry with us for insisting. In the light of day yesterday's black dress turned out to be dark blue; it was made of a very cheap, home-dyed material that you could see through. Besides that one, A[nna] A[ndreevna] had brought three simple cotton dresses and one pair of worn-down canvas-topped shoes. She sat down in the corner of the sofa with her knees forward. I asked her to change her position, she didn't understand right away, or didn't want to understand, and she mumbled something about how she shouldn't have her picture taken in such old shoes. I explained to her how I wanted her to sit, but she said, "go ahead and take it, just get it over with," and she sounded so desperate that for a moment I wondered if I should even try at all, and regretted that I had gotten into this. But it was too late to turn back, and I managed to focus and take the picture; then I let her go. I couldn't help asking if she was angry with me and told her that they don't make them like her any more, that she was wonderful and that for a long time I had dreamed of taking a good picture of her. She looked embarrassed and mumbled boyishly (I mean, girlishly), "No, no, no, that's not true. But I'm not angry with you." I kissed her hand.

Afterwards, at tea (after everyone else had finished and left), she said that she had intended to read some of her poems for me, but then Val. Iv. had shown up. We decided that she would read them to me the next time we saw each other.

7/20/36

I spent the day yesterday developing and printing. Today I took a letter to the Regional Administration asking for a postponement of my work there. What can I do? If they don't agree, I won't get to go to Novgorod with S. V., but a promise is a promise!

In the afternoon I found out that Sonya had been bitten by a dog out at their dacha and she and Mar. Iv. [Frenberg][15] had came to Moscow to get some shots.

I took the evening train to Peski. When I arrived at Starki[16] there wasn't a soul out on the terrace, and it was An. Andr., walking behind the house again with Val. Iv-a, who saw me first. She said, "Well, look who's here, look who's here!" and came over to meet me. After a few words of greeting, the ladies sent me to wash up after my trip, since S.V. was going to start his reading of Faust in half an hour.

But before the reading A[nna] A[ndreevna] asked me to show her my photographs, and she and El.Vl. looked at them by candlelight. S.V. came in to hurry them up, since everyone else was already out waiting on the terrace. A[nna] A[ndreevna] told him that she liked her pictures. But it was so dark, she couldn't have gotten a very good look.

S.V. repeated several times that he was very glad to see me, though he had been sure I would come, since I had missed him in Moscow yesterday.

After Chapters VII-XI, the guests left and we sat down to supper, and the photographs I had brought were subjected to a general inspection in the lamplight, and were a rousing success. A[nna] A[ndreevna] said that she liked the large one very much, and also the one of everyone together, where she is wearing her dress. The best proof of this came when she said she wanted to send the large one home to her husband immediately, without waiting until she went back herself, and she offered to sign two photographs, one for me and one for our generous hosts.

Val. Iv. was dissatisfied with how she had turned out on all three of the photographs, and she cut herself out of them all, over the protests of the professor.

When I went to S.V.'s study to make up my bed, S.V. was sitting there on the sofa and we talked for a long time about A[nna] A[ndreevna], sharing our impressions, and it turned out a lot of them were the same. He recited me the poem he had written for Anna And. here in Starki and talked about how well her photo had turned out etc.

7/21/36

Today was the holiday of the Kazan Holy Virgin, and Nastya left at dawn to go to the market that had opened in Kolomna for the occasion; we expected her back by tea-time with fresh bread. So everyone except the professor was just wandering around not doing anything, waiting for her, and El. Vl. had even left for church with the children. So A[nna] A[ndreevna] had time before tea to read several of her poems to me, and after tea she finished the rest, a total of some 15 new poems. After that we took a stroll in the avenue, and it was just like the last time (she read her poems to me, just as I had to her, sitting on the circular bench in the park), and again she told me about herself until Val. Iv. called her to go swimming.

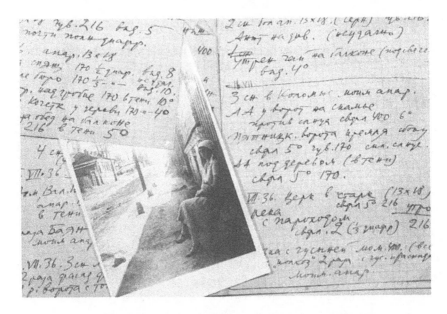

FRAGMENTS FROM GORNUNG'S DIARY ALONG WITH A PHOTOGRAPH
OF ANNA AKHMATOVA DURING THEIR EXCURSION TO KOLOMNA (JULY 1936)

Late in the afternoon a dozen or so of us got together to play volleyball.
It was a pleasant group of people, and everyone got caught up in the
game.

While we were playing, A[nna] A[ndreevna] took a walk with Val. Iv. on
the other side of the river and, as she told us later, they put out a fire that
had started on the edge of the woods. They scooped up handfuls of dirt
from the road and threw them onto the fire.

They got back toward 9. The volleyball game had just ended and it was
almost time for the day's reading of Faust. S. V. finished the last chapters
on the stone terrace.

* * *

7/22/36

In the morning after tea I gave A[nna] A[ndreevna] some of S. Ya.'s
unpublished poems to read.[17] She hadn't seen them before. I read a few
aloud. After the reading she said: "We're so rich, with poems like these, we
have nothing to complain about." And when she heard the last poem he
wrote before his death, she said, "How awful, just like Esenin's."[18]

Before lunch S. V. and I went for a swim, while Kochetkov[19] sat on the bank. Afterwards we went to play a game of croquet, and El. Vl. joined in.

After the game, when everyone was getting ready to leave for lunch, we started talking about food and got so carried away that Kochetkov suggested we all get together later and make supper. We were finishing lunch when Mar. Serg. arrived from the station with Stazya.

In the evening the guests all came out and sat on the stone terrace in the lamplight. A[nna] A[ndreevna] joined them. El. Vl. and Kochetkov prepared some raspberry punch, with the others helping out. When everyone at last was settled, S. V., acting as master of ceremonies, offered some toasts. A[nna] A[ndreevna] wouldn't touch the wine because of her doctors' orders. I sat between Stazya and Ksen. Konst. I got along well with Stazya. Maybe it had something to do with the wine, but I felt relaxed with her; she really does seem to be an unusually nice person.

7/23

Kochetkov and I had planned to go to Moscow on the early train, but the steamer was delayed and we just missed the train by a nose. A. S. was quite upset at first, but since he had overindulged himself at last night's dinner, he realized he really would rather spend some time at home in bed. We went back.

I arrived just in time for morning tea. Everyone made fun of me, "welcoming me from my trip," but in general, for some reason they seemed glad to see me. But I decided to leave that afternoon anyway.

Over tea we talked about last night, when we'd had our fortunes told. A[nna] A[ndreevna]'s fate was to suffer a major stroke in her old age, followed by insanity, and she said that when she was 17, she had been told she would die in prison.

Yesterday she signed her large photograph and gave it to Vera Adr. [Merkureva][20] Vera was in seventh heaven.

NOTES

[1] Anna Andreevna Akhmatova, 1889–1966, is considered one of the greatest Russian poets of the twentieth century. Her famous *Requiem* is devoted to the victims of terror.

[2] Sergei Vasilevich Shervinsky, 1892–1991, poet, translator, playwright, and literary scholar. A collection of his poems, written in 1916 and 1924, was published only in 1984. He is also the author of a historical adventure novel *East-India* (1933), of a volume on poetics, and of articles on Pushkin and Bryusov. He translated Sophocles, Virgil, Ovid, Catullus, Propertius, and other Western and Eastern classics, as well as poetry from the Baltic countries, the Caucasus, and Central Asia. A member of the Writers' Union of the USSR since 1934, he was part of the Permanent Committee on the *Igor Tale*, which he translated into Russian. About Anna Akhmatova's acquaintance with the Shervinskys, see Emma Gershtein, "The Thirties," in *Anna Akhmatova and Her Circle*, ed. Konstantin Polivanov, trans. Patricia Berioskina (Fayetteville: University of Arkansas Press, 1994), 140.

[3] Vasily Dmitrievich Shervinsky, professor of medicine, father of Sergei Vasilevich Shervinsky.

[4] Probably V. I. Zhmurovaya, a long-time friend and family doctor of Anna Akhmatova, mentioned by S. V. Shervinsky in his essay "Anna Akhmatova v rakurse byta" (Anna Akhmatova: A Foreshortening of Every-Day Life), in S. V. Shervinsky, *Ot znakomstva k rodstvu* (Yerevan: Sovetakan grokh, 1986), 246.

[5] "Val. Iv." is probably V. I. Abakevich.

[6] "El. Vl." refers probably to Elena Vladimirovna Shervinskaya, Shervinsky's wife.

[7] Osip Mandelshtam, 1891–1938, major Russian poet of the twentieth century, member of the Poets' Guild (1911–14). Friend of Akhmatova. He died in a Soviet labor camp in 1938. At the time of this conversation, he was already subject to persecution.

[8] Vasily Dmitrievich Shervinsky. See note 3.

[9] Evidently the name of Val. Iv.'s female sheepdog.

[10] Marina Mniszek (1588–1614), daughter of the Polish magnate Jerzy Mniszek. She was directly involved in the attempts to seize the Russian throne when she became the wife of the False Dmitry I and of the False Dmitry II. She died in captivity in Kolomna. Heroine of Alexander Pushkin's *Boris Godunov*. S.V. Shervinsky depicts the same excursion to Kolomna as Lev Gornung, but attributes it to the year 1938. "Anna Akhmatova v rakurse byta" (Anna Akhmatova: A Foreshortening of Every-Day Life), 253–54.

[11] Aleksandr Lvovich Gurilyov, 1803–1858, composer, author of romances and songs that were very popular in Russia.

[12] Mikhail Lermontov, 1814–41, major poet and novelist of the nineteenth century. Author of *The Hero of Our Time* and others works.

[13] Reference to Alexander Pushkin's famous love poem "To…" (1825).

[14] Reference to Anton Chekhov's play *Three Sisters*.

[15] Not mentioned in Shervinsky's essay.

[16] A village not far from the city of Kolomna in which Anna Akhmatova spent the summers of 1936, 1952, and 1956 in the house of the Shervinskys.

[17] Sofiya Yakovlevna Parnok, 1885–1933, Acmeist poet, translator, mainly from French (Baudelaire, Proust, Barbusse, and others), and critic (pseudonym: Andrei Polyanov). She was also the author of opera libretti.

[18] Sergei Esenin, 1895–1925, famous poet of the 1920s, member of the "Imaginist" literary group. He committed suicide in 1925.

[19] S. V. Shervinsky mentions a poet and translator A. S. Kochetkov. "Anna Akhmatova v rakurse byta" (Anna Akhmatova: A Foreshortening of Every-Day Life), 251.

[20] Added in pencil in the manuscript. Vera Aleksandrovna Merkureva, 1876–1943, was a poet and a translator. She published a cycle of poems in 1918, some translations, mainly from Shelley, and several articles. Mentioned by S. V. Shervinsky, "Anna Akhmatova v rakurse byta" (Anna Akhmatova: A Foreshortening of Every-Day Life), 251.

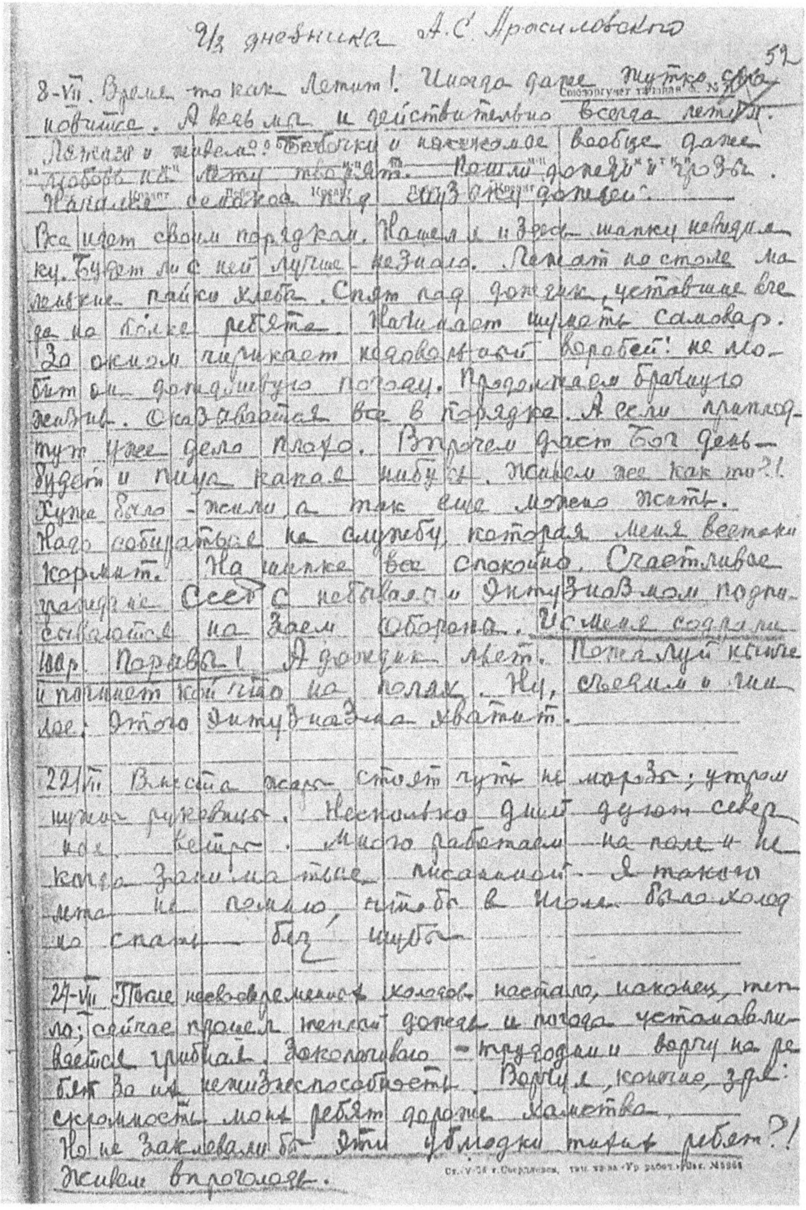
Из дневника А.С. Аржиловского 52

Page from Arzhilovsky's diary

ANDREI STEPANOVICH ARZHILOVSKY

The following biographical information is excerpted from the preface of the Russian publication of Arzhilovsky's diary by Konstantin Lagunov in the journal Ural *(Ekaterinburg), 3 (1992). The diary was given to Lagunov by Aleksandr Antonovich Petrushin, employee of the KGB of the Tyumen region.*

Andrei Stepanovich Arzhilovsky, born in 1885, was a peasant of the Chervishev district, Tyumen region. He had five children and lived on a farm. The fact that he had attended the rural school and was therefore able to read and write correctly enabled him to become a member of the Tyumen land administration just before the October Revolution. Under the government of Kolchak,[1] he became a member of the civil committee of inquiry. In October 1919 the Cheka of the Tyumen Province arrested Andrei Stepanovich, which was not unusual in those times. In his deposition before the revolutionary tribunal, Arzhilovsky denied ever having been a political activist. He had been enrolled against his will in the committee that kept Soviet activists out of the government in power, but never participated in any repression of Party activists or other Soviet citizens. He had left the committee of inquiry and the land administration for reasons of bad health and returned to his normal farming business. After the Whites had left under the pressure of the Red Army, he felt that it would be dishonorable to escape. He did not fight against the Soviet constitution, although he did voice his protest against some particular Soviet officials and their illegal actions, discrediting the Soviet authorities. The revolutionary tribunal sentenced him to eight years of imprisonment. Instead of keeping a low profile and quietly waiting for his liberation, after which he could vanish, far from the eyes of the Tyumen Security organs, he addressed a letter to the authorities, requesting a leave from prison for the time of fifty days, so that he could rebuild his farm and save his family from hardship and poverty.

In 1923 Arzhilovsky was liberated by an amnesty, given upon the formation of the USSR. He returned to his farm and in a short time was able to bring it into shape. He organized a peasant cooperative, joined the administration of a consumer society and the inspection commission of the rural

Soviet, became a juryman of the people's court and the editor of the local wall newspaper. But the Soviet power did not condone that kind of muzhik socialism. In 1929 Arzhilovsky's farm was classified as belonging to a peasant of average means. Andrei Stepanovich was the owner of a house with its outbuildings, of two horses, two cows, petty livestock, and three desyatinas (8.1 acres) of cultivated land. He was accused of counter-revolutionary agitation against the collective farms and was sentenced to ten years of imprisonment. In 1936, after seven years of labor camp, Arzhilovsky was released for reasons of bad health, and allowed to come home to die. Again, he chose not to run away, and took a job as an accountant at the Tyumen woodworking factory, The Red October, so that he could feed his numerous family. In July 1937 the local NKVD "uncovered" a "counterrevolutionary kulak sabotage organization," composed of twelve "special migrants," among them Andrei Arzhilovsky. During his interrogation, he declared that his opinions, unfortunately, were not purely Soviet, that he was a landowner and did not believe in the building of world socialism, but that these opinions had never left the pages of his diaries.

Authors of diaries rarely sign their work, but Arzhilovsky signed his in 1937. At the end of the manuscript, we find this note: "This diary was confiscated during a search in my home. It contains forty pages." Arzhilovsky's signature and the date, 29 August 1937, follow. Seven days later, Andrei Stepanovich was executed by a firing squad.

The passages in italic within Arzhilovsky's diary represent what an anonymous employee of the NKVD, searching for "evidence," had underlined in red.

DIARY OF
ANDREI STEPANOVICH ARZHILOVSKY

10/28/36. From force of habit, I can't resist the temptation to write down my thoughts and feelings. I feel the need to salvage something in my memory from the scattered ruins left after the storm and get as much as I can down on paper. I'm sitting in a new little house out behind the Red October timber mill. My family was given temporary use of this house in exchange for the one taken away from us in Zyryanka. By the grace of Moscow I was released back in May and am now beginning to forget my ordeals in the camps. I work as an accountant in the mill office, earning 150 rubles a month. Converted into bread that comes out to 166.5 kg. or 594 pounds. Just 8 rubles worth by the old reckoning. And my wife, Liza, still young as ever, pulls in another 200 rubles. We don't have any to spare but we're not starving either. Five kids in all, three at school, two here with me at the table. Muza is reading; she's got a head on her shoulders. Arseny, one of our twins, is drawing. I think he's a little slow, he's having trouble learning to read and write, which bothers me. But I'm probably overdemanding and too hard on him. A bad habit of mine. We had a light snowfall, but it has melted already, and now it's warm again. There's a full moon in the sky, and the lights of the town are sparkling. Liza is out at the dairy—that's where she works. While waiting for everyone to come home for the evening, I write down my recollections of the camps. My work at the office wears me out.

10/29. This morning was quite cold and I slipped on the frozen ground when I went outside. We—that is, Liza and I,—usually get up at five. The stove and samovar are my responsibility, and I have to bring in the firewood. There's no end to it: the firewood is not too far away, of course, but I have to carry each log by hand, and that takes its toll. We're getting used to doing without horses. I walked to town to get some dough. People used to shop just once a week, but now you have to chase around looking for bread every day. We're so used to the lines, we can't imagine any other way of life. Today I was lucky—there was no line at the bread stand. This little bitty girl runs up, all out of breath, and from habit asks, "Who's last?" And there were only three of us...I had a dream today. I'm in some European city. There's a crowd out on the square: they've come to see a giant. Sure enough, he shows up and crosses the square, and in fact there are two of them: the other one is a little smaller. He's wearing a loose gray suit and no hat. It's amazing what comes up in dreams. Liza was just given a contract and she signed up for 25 years. It's all the same, no matter where you live. We eat soup made from pig heads and count our blessings for it. I was at my brother Mikhail's recently. He's still keeping up appearances, with his valuable dog and his mistress. A modern Mazepa[2]...Just now Galina piped up, "If I can get a neckerchief I'll join the Pioneers."[3] So all it takes is a neckerchief. She's not too bright. Every once in a while she'll spout such nonsense, you wouldn't even believe it. They study geometry and algebra, but they're utterly empty, spiritually. And they're going to feed us in our old age?

10/30. I've turned 51. The very picture of youth. Mother and Galina are at the dairy, Gennady and Tamara are gnawing away at the granite of learning, and the little ones are listening to Grandma Darya tell a fairy tale. She came to wish her son a happy birthday. The story she's telling is marvellous, though utterly preposterous, but the kids hang onto every word. *We need to cherish and preserve this old woman, with her tales of old Russia: there are so few people left who can remember life as it used to be.* The fire burns brightly in the stove. Today to celebrate we had baked bread dumplings spread with just a touch of margarine. So we're still getting by. Gennady is an avid reader, though he's not methodical about it yet; Tamara is reading Chernyshevsky's *What is to Be Done?*[4] It is on the wreckage of the past that people come to grips with the present. At the factory where I work, people transgress, and *rather seriously: pilfering socialist property.* But I think that it's better not to interfere, since *the one who blows the whistle always winds up paying for it in the end*: find something, hold your tongue, lose something, hold your tongue. I have absolutely nothing to do with the community activities in our settlement, and the party activists have started to sit up and take notice. It's too bad I didn't buy a newspaper. I feel compelled to write for old time's sake: I want to write and I have things to say. *But how? Open your soul to these revolutionary philistines*, that is, tell them what you were, and they'll immediately come up with an axe to grind. No, we'll just keep quiet. Not everybody has to join in, it is also possible just to stand on the sidelines.

10/31. Grandma Darya is gone: she paid her maternal duty to her aging son, then dragged the smouldering embers of her life to lay at the feet of her orphan Masha. Today she'll be telling her fairy tales again to bright-eyed granddaughters in Masha's tiny little hut. *Live on, you marvellous old tales: reality for us, dislodged as we are from our old way of life, is so cruel that we find ourselves drawn inexorably back into the fairy-tale world of the past.* The younger children are asleep, the older ones are finishing up their lessons in what used to be the private school and they have to walk 5 kilometers to get home. I was just thinking about how frantic our pace of life is, especially these days. The pendulum of our grandfather clock has thrown its traces and is racing along as though it's trying to make it to the bazaar before all the cheap potatoes sell out. *Before, even the pendulum of the clock was aloof and stately...* Everything is different now. I look at the young people and it amazes me how they can bear all the burdens that are placed on their shoulders. And when I'm in the city, *surrounded by masses of people scurrying about their business, I always find myself thinking the same thing: all it would take would be one good war to cut the anthill down to size. Otherwise we will devour ourselves.* Anyway, I have to try and *salvage something from the recent past.* I think I had stopped at the prison infirmary. Things went so well for me that I started putting on weight and women started flirting with me (though I didn't actually sin—I was too scared to). I drank two liters of milk a day, and that does amount to something. During that time I got involved in community activities, I ran wall newspapers, wrote catchy little rhymes on topics of current interest, set them to music and performed them myself. One melody I used was the Kamarinskaya tune.[5] I also put quite a lot of work into the camp newspaper itself. I was a card-carrying leader and correspondent. In a word, I had reached the top. It's a lot worse to write small-scale opinion pieces locally than to be an editorial writer on the national level: everyone knows you personally and everyone recognizes himself in your criticism. What happens is people get resentful and malicious, they gossip behind your back and gang up against you. I showed a lot of nerve, pointing out and ridiculing all the mistakes in the way things were done, and it attracted a lot of hostility. People started digging around in my past and they all but devoured me. Ultimately that same camp newspaper that had printed my comments and had paid me an honorarium (though, to tell the truth, it didn't amount to anything), turned against me: some new hack writer turned up and wrote a couple of satires, aimed against me personally, calling me the "man in the case."[6] *It's not just people like me, even Trotsky, now that he's down off his pedestal, is an easy target.* I caught it both ways, both in my community activities and at work: I already had a position as a bookkeeper at a transit point, and they dismissed me and sent me to work as a low-level clerk at an out-of-the-way post, with a boss who was a little Napoleon. They were suspicious about me at first, and kept a close watch on me for awhile, though in fact after a couple of weeks my rotten mood began to improve. But my material welfare took a sharp turn for the worse, I had lost all my connections; other people had moved in, and I had to fall back on what I had managed to squirrel away before. The newspaper campaign against me dealt a serious blow to my morale; the only conclusion I could come to was: we are cursed to the end of our days and no matter how you try to change, no one will believe you, and at the first opportunity they'll gang up on you, chew you up and spit you out. *These knights of the revolution are so good at ruining a man's good name, they'll stop at nothing and they stand up for each other,* so they are capable of devouring greater men than a sinner like me. During this same difficult time I had to swallow yet another bitter pill. Exercising my right to request early release after serving half my time, I sent in two applications, one to Moscow, the other to the main court in Mordova, which had been granted the exalted right to release people from the camps. I receive a summons. A glimmer of hope. *I arrive in court and see that I still haven't learned* my lesson about the Communists, they were releasing the thieves and *murderers, they released one guy in particular, a parricide, who showed clear signs of a genetic predisposition to criminal behavior; embezzlers were treated with tender solicitude; but the moment they got to Article 58,[7] a stern expression came over the faces of the judges and the prosecutor, and the presiding judge snapped out a set phrase,* "Refused, as a class alien." My turn comes up. They scrutinize me. "Was that you they were just writing about in the newspaper?" "Yes." "Well, what do you want?" "I'm appealing for early release." They dig up from somewhere an awful evaluation from Vishera, stating in no uncertain terms that I am an incorrigible prisoner...I immediately sense I'm not going anywhere, not now, and not after I've served my time either. This new way of lying, this collusion of actions against a man when he is to be destroyed, hit me so hard that I just crumbled psychologically and aged several years, right on the spot. *But it is so natural: they sense the truth and can't forgive us our protests against their violence.* I went around for a long time afterwards like a man struck by lightning. Fortunately, the 12-th Post was slated for closure and we had to finish the job without the administration or guards. The Camp was emptied out, the towers vacated and the gates thrown open; at first we even felt a little ill at ease. A few of us were left behind. We did our own cooking and laundry and washed in the abandoned canteen. It's a good thing when they close a camp. Somehow we got a barter arrangement going: we got eggs and milk from a nearby village and gave them bread and fish in return. It was during spring. Mitrofan Semyonovich (an old clerk who was waiting for his release) and I delighted in the silence, we watched hungry rats and fed them, we cooked dinner together, chased an impudent sparrow out of a swallow's nest, told each other about our pasts, discussed our dreams. We took walks together, talking about whether it would be possible to live out here in the woods if we were given our freedom, and concluded it would be; he had a passion for beekeeping and there were a lot of bees in the woods. Mitrofan Semyonovich expected to get his release any day, but it didn't come and it didn't come. The poor man even started to lose weight. He was a wreck. How many times have I been in that position myself?! The wild strawberries ripened, and every day I brought home fresh, sweet berries to have with our tea. Those woods have a wealth of berries! And suddenly something totally unexpected happened, Moscow sent me my release! Mitrofan Semyonovich and I were summoned to get our releases and, loaded down with heavy bags of miscellaneous junk, we made our way to the camp center to pick up our documents: the old man's prophetic dream about being released together with someone else came true. It took a long time to sink in. And even when they handed me the document certifying my conditional early release, I still couldn't believe it. With great difficulty we made it through our last ordeals in the camps and finally, after enduring our final search, we found ourselves on the platform at the station. Clenching our tickets between our teeth we climbed up into the brightly painted green cars of the train. And it wasn't a dream, it was the beginning of a new life in freedom. As we waited for the train at the little station, we bought eggs and milk from dirty Mordvinian tradeswomen there, whose chests were covered with masses of coins and crosses. We resumed our lives as independent, free men: it was sweet, but also terrifying at the same time. The clatter and bustle of life deafened us. Granted, I hadn't been in chains, but still I had spent 6 years and 9 months in the clutches of the camp. Quite a solid chunk of my life. In freedom, Mitrofan Semyonovich and I had nothing in common, and we went immediately our separate ways, he set off for his cretaceous mountains, and a loudmouthed locomotive hauled me home to the old grey Urals.

11/3. The hot stove is too much for me, I don't feel like getting up; it's the inertia and decline of old age creeping up on me. The kids are asleep; there's no one else here. I'm battling with Arseny: he's doing badly in school, and I pretend that there's something really awful about that; I try to make myself take him to task. I'd like to awaken his self-esteem. Something is squeaking somewhere near the ceiling, but it doesn't sound like a mouse, exactly. People at work keep up their guard around me, they don't want to get too close: a former convict, shabbily dressed, unshaven and in general a sorry-looking old devil; *this bunch of people are on the whole pretty impressed with themselves, they've harnessed technology, they're the salt of the earth. Salt, all right, but not much flavor. Their interests are very narrow: all they think about is their careers and getting fitted for new clothes. The 19-th anniversary* [of the October Revolution] *is coming up, they're making huge banners and posters. The triumph of "Socialism" is at hand, but they could go bankrupt on the decorations.* Things have been dragging on in Spain, the

Whites have mounted a revolt and are marching on Madrid. Who's going to come out on top is hard to tell at this point. I just might give up talking about the camp: *people have the same happy life there; some are stuffed to the gills, while others are "on their last legs." Exploited and fleeced for all they're worth.* Take our so-called orderlies, for example. We didn't have servants, of course, only "orderlies." This lackey had all the same duties as a servant, but he never got his own hands dirty: he delegated all the hard work to people who were starving, and they were paid in food — there was enough grub to go around. As a result the orderlies who work for the high-ranked bureaucrats lived high on the hog, putting on airs and lording it over the others: they were clean, neatly shaven and well fed, well dressed etc. One of the bosses wanted to put a stop to it, and he wrote about "lackeys with lackeys," but nothing came of it: the people at the top weren't about to give up what they had gained. And they didn't. The same thing with the system of "connections." The camp learned all its ABC's from this primer and completely mastered the technique. I sat in the clean train car, savoring every minute of the ride. It was a long trip, and the transfers made it even longer. My happiness made me careless with money, and I spent a lot along the way. The excitement started to build as I approached Tyumen; after their long sleep, all the springs of my soul began gradually to well up again. We arrived in Tyumen in the evening. I barely made it to Marfusha's; I had to stop twice along the way to rest. My old mother and Marfushka and her family met me with tears. I started bawling myself, my nerves couldn't hold out. Kolya took me home to my own family.

11/7. Yesterday's mud dried out overnight. I made two trips to the river to get water, then I started up the stove; we're planning a huge feast to celebrate the anniversary. For the first time in seven years, I celebrate among free citizens. I received an invitation to the formal ceremony at the factory. Set to begin at 5:00. The comfortable factory cafeteria with its tiny Red Corner for the presidium. The musicians arrived right on time. Some twenty guys showed up; some workers came, a group of women and five men. The organizers showed up and started decorating the cafeteria. By the way, *the portraits of party leaders are now displayed the same way icons used to be: a round portrait framed and attached to a pole.* Very convenient, hoist it onto your shoulder and you're on your way. And all these preparations are just like what people used to do before church holidays...They had their own activists then, we have ours now. Different paths, the same old folderol. I sat through exactly two hours of it, no one else showed up. With this standard of punctuality in mind, I decided it would be best to go home before it was too late. And that was the end of the celebration for me. What happened after that, I don't know; I'm sure they're way behind schedule and everything is dragging on and on. *A panorama has been installed at the factory entrance: our Socialist Motherland with a border post and a sentry, and the Fascists are attacking from the other side. Toy soldiers trying to attack our happy land; naturally the Red Army soldier is smiting them and they're falling right and left in panic. All this is a lot of fun for the little kids, of course. But the fact is, it's a real waste of money. On the whole, extremely contrived and false.* On October 10 there was a meeting for the office workers. With much fanfare, they resolved to publish a special anniversary edition of the newspaper in three days; almost a whole month went by, and the newspaper still hadn't appeared: they got a special border ready and put clean paper into the galleys, but didn't actually get around to writing anything. Like taking a cow to the bathhouse, all blaw and no go. That's the way things were left, and apparently that's the way things will stay....We also came up with the idea of issuing our own periodical, a journal, no less. Gennady got inspired, but the girls couldn't care less; it looks as though there's no hope of making good citizens out of them. Though it's too early to say for sure. Materially, we're still getting by; there are people worse off than we are. Yesterday I went to town, I wanted to get a shave, but just try to find someplace to do it! There are 10 people waiting at each chair. That's how we live. Nothing but trouble. Everyone eats on the run. *They've poured money into posters and banners; but then, why dwell on it, it's all just so much tinsel.* Kolya and I arrived at the new workers' settlement outside of town. It's a purely socialist village, consisting of 100 households. Rows of identical little houses line the streets, single file. The place is still brand new; the streets haven't been tramped down yet, people just walk right over the bushes. Kolya forgot what house our family lives in, and we spent several minutes wandering around until we finally arrived at our doorstep. Liza leapt out into the yard like a mother hen with her chicks: they'd recognized me. We didn't make a big fuss over our reunion, we're quiet people. Liza has hardly aged at all; Tamara is grown now, she's a little stoop-shouldered; she looks tenderly up at me from under her brows. Galina has grown by leaps and bounds; lively little Muza and skinny Arseny, who has just started playing his home made balalaika, Chinese melodies, of course; Genya grew like a weed while I was gone, he's a quiet, rumpled-looking teenager. My family did not have an easy time of it, the hardships of their life left their traces on all of them. The one good thing was that they had their own separate house and didn't have to live in a barracks: at least they didn't get in anyone else's way. Grandma Mavra was no longer here among her grandchildren: she died not long before my return. It was right during the flood; they were living in the bathhouse of the Collective Farm, that's where Grandma died. I couldn't sleep the first night: I was too worked up; it was all like a dream. I was terrified to let myself go to sleep, what if it turned out I was still in the camp after all? *After all, though I was destitute, practically in exile, still I was a free man, and though these people were crushed and beaten down by life, they were my dear ones, and we were together. I had 100 rubles from the camp. That's just a drop in the ocean, but at least it gave something to build on. Soon I began the ordeal of trying to find a job.* I spent three days just trying to get a residence permit: lines everywhere, something always went wrong, and I myself had forgotten what it was like in this crazy, senseless life of ours.

11/8. I went into town yesterday. It was a bright, cheerful day. The parades were a great success. It seemed as though the entire city had come out onto the streets: not so much to march in the parades as just to gawk. Lots of people and noise, everyone all decked out in their best. Enormous achievements. Life has become easy. People sing songs that say this is the only place in the world where a man can breathe free. It's a fact. A foreigner would get a most unlikely impression: you sure live well, God grant everyone such a life. It would be interesting to calculate the amount of vodka and beer drunk to celebrate the anniversary. That seems to be the general tendency: in the morning there's the show; after the parade, the juices start to flow. Take your choice. History will figure it out; what we do goes by the wayside. I'll go out myself today and do my part.

11/9. The celebration is over, but the festive mood remains: with the state the workers are in, work is out of the question. You can still hear singing; some people are still out staggering around in the streets. Washing down the holiday with holy water. It's all literally come down to that: all anyone talks about is their holiday escapades. All the political hoopla was drowned in a blatant flood of drunkenness. I was in town myself, I downed some English bitters at Marfusha's place; I went twice to D. I. Yevdokimov's house and knocked at the gate, but I couldn't get a response either time. My own mood, on the other hand, is terrible: my complaints about the way things are being done at home have led to a big battle with my wife. Of course, I do have a nasty habit of poking my nose into dark corners, where there's always a lot of all kinds of "property" piled up: the firewood alone has taken up a huge amount of space by the stove. With only the best of motives, I wrote a humorous little poem for Arseny, making fun of the way he's always losing things. And now Mama is on her high horse: how could I?! But the real problem is that she interpreted the satire as aimed against her.... The latest scene of family solidarity. A whole campaign of boos and catcalls directed against me. Naturally, this has thrown me for a loop and I've decided to go on temporary strike: I'll chop the wood, but she can light the stove herself. You really have to keep an eye on the stove, and nobody around here is capable of doing it right. No one appreciates my services, and in fact, no one even seems to want them either. Get the fat lady off the cart, and the mare will have an easier time of it. Let her fuss and fume. Of course it is all my fault: I started it with my journal, started making fun of people. So now are they going to banish me from the house for my satires? But you need something like that if you want to get along. I can't come up with a better way! You can't teach the children, their mother takes everything personally, but you have to try, you can't just leave them to grow up on their own in this awful darkness and gloom.

11/11. We were just about to be frozen in, but last night it rained, and now it feels more like September than November. Frustrating weather. Yesterday I killed some time at the flea market and bought a few ready-made shirts: the workers drank up all their money during the anniversary celebrations and now they're selling off their possessions. We're working out our conflict; maybe it really is my fault: to demand that a child of eight be able to read?! Maybe there's still a chance he'll get motivated to study.... Also, I've started going out and trying to sell my labor. When I run into people I know they nod sympathetically and say that I have to find something, etc. I tracked down advertised positions and also tried places just off the street, but the answer was always the same: nothing. The first question was "Where did you work before?" An honest answer put them on their guard. A pensive expression would come over their faces, then they'd turn me down: "We don't need anyone just now." A few even questioned me in detail about what I was convicted for, who was involved, etc. Picky! But the main thing was the pathetic suit I wore and my overall appearance, which was even worse. After some twenty days of this I realized that I could forget about finding a job in my specialty. *It turns out there are a lot of unemployed people. And they're all young, with good references etc. So what is there left for the likes of me?*. I got a job doing excavating work, but I wasn't strong enough for it. I thought I'd try chopping firewood, but no one needed any. I seized upon an ad that said, "Workers needed for forestry work, extracting resin." I rushed to their office and in the heat of the moment signed on for 3 months. And I signed Genya up too, since he wanted to go with me. We went looking for adventure, to experience the poetry of labor in the resin forests.

11/13. It's November, straight out of Pushkin, when "the wolf goes on the prowl with his ravenous she-wolf," but it's still warm. Yesterday I went down to the Tura, it was so warm, you could even go for a swim. Or go out and do some plowing in Pushkin's stubble fields, if there had been any to plow. In general, it was like being at a resort, the Crimea or somewhere. Reconstruction [*Perestroika*]! *I went to see Yevdokimov, who used to guard the barns at Tavdinsk.* He lives alone with his old lady, they have a 200–pound hog. They're doing all right, they've managed to maintain their old way of life. Signs of prosperity everywhere, a coat lined with expensive fur, two new pairs of felt boots, good grub, etc. People like them have no reason to be dissatisfied. The two of them occupy an entire estate, complete with outbuildings. And in fact there are a lot of people like that. Life for them indeed has gotten better and happier; the radio blares right into your ear, keeping you posted about the latest events in the world. I saw my brother Misha. The old guy actually seems to be getting younger. And indeed, he is full of energy, though he does look tired and has bags under his eyes. There's some tension in the family: Liza's developed a habit of moaning and groaning like some peasant woman, but there's less and less justification for it. Sure, she has to work, she has to get up early, etc., we have seven people to feed and no food to do it with. But still there are ways of coping, and there's no reason for her to carry on like that, appealing to fate to let her die. One minute her hands are in terrible pain, the next she's got a splitting headache, or she's "aching all over," but then when you take a close look there's nothing really wrong with her, and the whole melodrama was for nothing. At her age she ought to know what's wrong with her, and how to take care of it. But just to moan and groan so people will feel sorry for you and look after you is naive and, in fact, counterproductive: it just gets on other people's nerves. It's an old habit of hers: seeking out reasons to feel sorry for herself, to indulge in tearful scenes, to rant and rave. She lets herself go, sleeps in her jacket, she hardly ever combs her hair or washes, etc., and she behaves that way on purpose. She walks around with a half-crazed, martyred look on her face. Don't we have enough to deal with as it is? We live worse than others, that's true: but autosuggestion is a terrible thing. She thinks I should court her, like in the old days, but you'd think she'd know when enough is enough. It's too bad we have to spend time ridding ourselves of this kind of nonsense: life would be a lot easier without it. And what's wrong with just coming right out and saying: I need this or that, I'm having this or that problem. But no, you see, people have to try and guess. And it's always too cold for her! Eighteen degrees [Celsius] inside, but she's freezing cold. It's not some kind of fever, it's just a bad habit. The woman just doesn't make the slightest effort for herself. I feel sorry for her, but it's irritating too. After battling our way through the ticket line, we finally set off for the Komissarovsky forestry station. We had been told that there would be a car to meet us at Novaya Naimka, but that turned out to be the usual lies. There was no car, and Genya and I set off down the unfamiliar road on foot. There hadn't been any food at the station, even bread; we picked and ate half-withered strawberries along the way. A car came by and we tried to get a ride, but the driver wanted four rubles. No way. We arrived at the forestry office late in the afternoon, and we were given a note to take to Ryzhkov, the foreman: "Give these men some work."

11/17. Some weather. No sign of winter; it's warm, with an occasional drizzle, just go on out and plow your field, you'll be done in no time. By the way, that's the way it was back in 1911, too. Nature starts to shar off and play tricks on us. Life goes on as usual. I did something stupid at work: I wrote something for the wall newspaper. No written response yet, but there are already repercussions: Toiba, my short-skirted boss, is already sputtering with indignation, and it looks as though she might even try to get me fired. Just what you need, you old devil: don't stick your neck out, don't write things. After years of working together the people here have all sniffed each other out; in this environment, the "crony" system has infiltrated their lives like a cat curling up at the fire; you'd have to be stark raving mad to expose their abscesses to the light. But so far it's all taking place behind the scenes. We'll wait for things to come out into the open. Our journal is alive and well. There was an announcement in the newspaper about a literary contest in honor of the twenty-year anniversary. I'm working on a few little things, why not give it a try? Who knows? Ryzhkov, the foreman, a cross-eyed, red-haired man with a convict's face, who is rumored to have been a Red partisan, took a look at the note and mumbled, "We'll find something for you. Do you have any money?" "No, we don't." "That's too bad; what do you intend to live on?" "But we came to work?!" "There will be something eventually." Well, all right, we'll manage somehow. The tool we were given, a solid steel "gouger," was dull, and I started to sharpen it on a whetstone. My quiet Genya was depressed—it was an obvious scam; in the city they'd talked this up to the skies, but when we got here, it turned out there was nothing to it. Instead of a cafeteria, we just go hungry; instead of a dormitory, there's just the open air of the yard of Aunt Stepanida from the Collective Farm—and sit out in the yard in the open air. The same old pattern, as always: a mountain of words, and nothing to show for it. We picked some grass to make our beds and spent the night in a cart. The next day Ryzhkov took us out to the "works." Our job was to extract soft resin from pine trees for turpentine etc.

11/18. It turned very cold today and there's a fierce wind blowing. We labor mightily over the stove, but it's still not as warm as we'd like in the hut. Ominous-looking clouds are rolling in from the north and it's trying to snow, but it still doesn't seem like winter. I'm writing something that would be good for the *Peasant Gazette* and I'm thinking about sending it in. I started in 1906 with the *Country Herald*. That's not the point. I'm not making literature my goal in life; though perhaps I could achieve more in this walk of life than in any other. We'll see. We're always hungry, but we still manage to get by. The next day we went out to the "works." Ryzhkov assigned us a section and showed us what to do; there wasn't much to it: The tree was already ready for extraction: they'd cut a groove down the trunk and started another cut going crosswise; all we had to do was to continue making horizontal grooves and use the gouger to cut down into the tree and drain off the resin. It took 4000 of these grooves to make 5 or 6 rubles. For a strong man with a good gouger it would be an easy job, but I had no strength and I couldn't sharpen the blade properly. Genya's job was difficult and dirty: he had to use funnels to collect the sticky resin in a bucket. The only thing that would get the resin off your hands was kerosene; and that made Genya's hands hurt. But we still managed to get by somehow: we had our fill of low-grade meat and all the bread we could eat. We slept on soft beds in a makeshift cabin and indulged ourselves with plenty of fresh berries. We spent a little over a month working there. I ran myself ragged, and by the time we were done I was a wreck. And even now I'm still just skin and bones, I can't seem to bounce back. One time we were almost burned alive in the cabin. The nights had turned cold, and we had to start building our fire closer to the cabin. That night some dried moss caught fire and our wonderful cabin burned to the ground. Genya was sound asleep, and I just barely managed to push him out of the cabin in the nick of time, before it was completely engulfed in flames. We lost the provisions we'd had there, some berries that we'd gathered to take home to the family, and my shirt. In short, we were hit pretty hard and…the next day we built ourselves a new cabin. At the end of August we came back out of the woods and went to the village to get our wages before returning home. But…that's easy enough to say….

11/19. Apparently winter is upon us: the wind is coming from the east and it's snowing. I suppose tomorrow they'll get the sleighs out. I'm sick and tired of the mud, though I did enjoy walking across the grass to get firewood. Well, we'll make our adjustments for winter. The office got the idea of setting up the wall newspaper; the more critical comments were replaced by clippings from the press. A good response from readers. We'll have to do more, or people will get upset. What a great play could be written based on the lives of these "drones." We'll just wait and see. Genya and I spent ten days in Chashchina waiting for our wages. We went around doing odd jobs: first we gathered berries and sold them for five rubles a bowl; then we did carpentry work, repaired shoes, fixed stoves, sawed firewood. In short, we got by; we lived on potatoes, fresh rye bread and milk. We stayed the whole time at Stepanida Fyodorovna's. She cooked us a meal now and then, and we helped her out in various ways. After ten agonizing days of suspense, we finally got paid; in fact we even got more than we'd expected. Filthy, in rags, we set out for Zavodoukovskaya Station at last, carrying the flour we'd earned on our shoulders. At some point I have to say a little more about Aunt Stepanida….

11/20. There was a lot of snow last night, but some melted during the day, since it was warm and we even had a light drizzle. It's a little hard to walk, and there's some danger that the rest of the snow will melt by morning. And we were all ready to get out the sledges. The river is frozen over in places. Today was an eventful day: an artist drowned—he was a drunkard; a teacher shot himself; some manager hanged himself. By the way, the newspapers pay very little attention to current events; you get the impression that life is just going on according to schedule, without any incidents whatsoever. That's not the way things are in reality, of course. In general, ever since the revolution the daily press has given very little attention to real life, or it just shows one side of things…. She's an old woman, a sixty-seven-year-old widow; since she and her husband had made a decent living in the past, they tried to get her classed as a kulak, and had even confiscated a few things. But she pulled herself together; she came to the village council and gave the "presidium" a piece of her mind, using the most atrocious language, thereby proving that she was a genuine Soviet woman! As a result they accepted her into the Collective Farm, where she became a Stakhanovite: she was very diligent, and worked in good conscience, getting as many working days under her belt as she could. She baked bread to sell and healed the sick using incantations. I saw old women come to her to get "fixed" and to get her to "outline" their boils with her finger to cure them. She even had a woman who was a Party member come to her for treatment. Naturally these sessions brought in some extra income. In general, a resourceful old woman. It made a strange picture: everywhere you look, the new, modern way of life, tractors rumbling past, cumbersome combines crossing the fields, automobiles racing by lickety split, and right in the middle of it, this old woman, chanting for all to hear: "On the sea, on the ocean, on the island, on Buyan," etc. right out where everyone can hear. And evidently it works! The feisty old woman would get up early in the morning and start praying loudly. And each time she would finish up with the insistent demand: "And remember, O Lord, my man Matvei Vasilievich…." A rich topic for a satire; the only problem is that the citizens who are in charge of the press are in general afraid of satires that are too much to the point: what if it should lead to something? We got our money and started home. We ate well along the way, making up for all those hungry days out in the woods. Finally we appeared on our doorstep looking like vagrants, with our ragged clothes barely hanging on our backs.

11/23. It's freezing cold—winter in the truest sense of the word. I don't have time to write a lot, it's time to go to work. I've started reading Jack London. A smart man and an enemy of the capitalists. My kids and Liza show the signs of the wrongs done them, of exile and hunger. It's only natural, the sorry shape they're in….

11/26. As of 11/21, winter has set in. This time the snow melted just a little, most of it stayed, and the rivers have frozen over: all the normal signs of winter. At home I wage an ongoing battle with the family about the way things are done: I'm trying to get the kids to keep diaries, and to put things where they belong. But I'm getting nowhere on either front. Fierce resistence! It must be really hard on them. And maybe I shouldn't get all worked about it; things aren't really that bad. But I think we can do better. Genya works more than anyone else on the journal—he's a wonderful boy, though he does sometimes get a little sulky. It will be a long time before we have enough to go around, and it will take a lot of grease to wash that downtrodden look off their faces. I mean that literally: give children good food, a clean, soft bed, comfortable and attractive clothing—and everything would be different. And when will that be? Maybe never. So should I give up? Sulk and pout? Of course not! Yesterday was the first day of the Extraordinary Congress of the Soviets.[8] It's too bad I didn't get to hear Stalin's speech. At work the reactions are mixed. Toiba, the pseudo–Young Communist, a fanatical careerist, and a greedy, malicious person, was the first one to speak up, "Nothing special. He talks like a Tatar and doesn't command respect. I didn't like it and I stopped listening somewhere in the middle." So much for the changing of the guard! Lenya had a completely different reaction, he's got a malicious side to him: "Quite a speech! Both the ideas and the form of expression. The way he put down the foreign critics—it was simply wonderful! He was even a little free-and-easy with his language, like for example, when he said, gobble them up. And he didn't stick to the time limit; he talked sixteen minutes longer than he was supposed to." Will the new Constitution have anything to offer us? The fat bureaucrats and their henchmen have quite a different opinion. Yesterday Stroshkov, the chairman of the local artel,[9] blabbed out, "The Constitution is one thing, but local authority is something else. Everything will be at someone's discretion: who can be hired and who cannot." And he may be right, the red-faced thug. They can find subversive meaning in the most well-intentioned criticism. Myself, I'm not expecting any real change, I'm content just to keep on the way we're going. They sent my writings to the editorial board of *Peasant Gazette*. Might there be a breath of hope on that front? The kids are starting to gravitate toward supper. We still do have supper; we are finishing the last of the rabbits, alternating with pigs' heads. Well, Moscow wasn't built in a day. Everything will wind up all the same....

11/27. A strong wind, it blows you right off your feet. I lit the stove and brought in some firewood, and now I'm sitting here with my diary. It's warm here, but during the years I was in exile Liza and the kids suffered so much from the cold that they just can't get warm anymore, and they huddle around the stove. "Once bitten, etc." Yesterday I was in the factory cafeteria. Workers without any extra mouths to feed earn 300 rubles each; they live tolerably well and get plenty to eat. You can get a good meal for three rubles. The cafeteria does a fairly good job. My legs are itching again from the dust and from insufficient bathing, it's like eczema. I rubbed them with liquid ammonia. It's a good thing I managed to stock up on firewood: it's not so bad now. I'll pick up where I left off: Genya and I arrived at home, both of us in rags, filthy, with homemade bast sandals on our feet. I immediately noticed an announcement: Wanted: Watchmen. "That's for me," I decided. And so it was. I spent two or three days going from one place to another, with no luck: I looked too desperate and my clothes gave me away. I went to see Yevdokimov, who gave me a reference: "Have known for a long time as a modest, honest man. His conviction was the result of a political error." I set off with this paper to Omtorg, a large trading organization, to ask for a position as a watchman. I presented myself before the fearsome, piercing gaze of the triumvirate for my formal interview. These three men, the general manager, the personnel manager and the Party Organizer are smug, well-fed people who've mastered the authoritative mannerisms and tone of voice. Ultimately they took me on. I was grateful to get a watchman's job with 90–ruble salary; at last I'm an accepted member of the Soviet family and will be getting my own crust of bread. The work turned out to be interesting and easy: sit by the gate for 12 hours, take 24 off, etc. I liked it and even found I could turn a profit: one day you go home with some rope, another day you come across something just lying around, and you just can't help stealing it.

11/28. An unusually cold wind. A cold, full moon in the sky. We're eating some kind of greens that Liza brings home from the dairy; in between the bread and potatoes it passes as food. But we do try to eat better dinners: we cook rabbits and pigs' heads. Of course it's not real food and all of it is revolting, but it would cost us at least 20 rubles a day to eat decently and the two of us together make only 8. Well, that's all right, later on we'll eat better. Yesterday I was accepted into the union. But I'm terrified around all these people who've grown gray at their jobs; they're honest, dedicated workers, and we're enemies and crooks. I had a dream today about meat; I started to chop it, and it turned out to be a head: this one has a brain, I think, but the ones they sell at the market don't. They clear out all every-thing, the brain, the intestines. I'm tutoring Arseny; he doesn't know any-thing: he misspelled the word "above." Really dumb, though he's got a quick tongue. Meanwhile his mother is already casting grim glances this way—a silent threat. It warmed up toward evening. I went to town, and my felt boots got heavy with moisture. Again some hold up with the bread: huge lines, and naturally, people got into fights. What if they lower the ration to 100 grams a head? Then again, no, it's just some commercial maneuver of theirs. All kinds of red tape with my passport, I should have gotten a new one long ago, and they've run out of forms. But if anything happens, it's my fault. Oh, life just keeps throwing stumbling blocks in my way! It's just terrible. The same old thing at the factory office: a lot of talk but none of it makes sense; they can't tell Pavlograd from Pavlodar. Total confusion. And then everyone tears around, trying to catch up to yesterday. In short, a confusion of tongues. Here's the family, all together—we'll get a half meal's worth each.

11/30. A good frost set in after the thaw. Instead of taking the day off, I spent today in the office too. I'm so tired of these godawful numbers. But if you look at it from the standpoint of warmth and energy expenditure, you can only be grateful. Just sit back and enjoy it: I'm right here next to the stove, with thick camp jacket spread under me on the chair for comfort. There's so much noise in the office during working hours, it's like being at the market. It's interesting, the ones who make the most noise are our ladies. They're a kind of uncontrolled, raucous, gang. People get into fistfights in the bread lines. What's interesting is that the ones who make the most noise are the people who have squirreled away two or three days' worth of bread. How greedy can you get! The other day I had a dream about some grouse out in the snow, engaging in some kind of freakish, premature courtship ritual. Are we going to go to war? Germany and Japan have concluded some kind of holy alliance. I don't read much these days and I've fallen behind on political events: I'm just a stoker of the stoves, a bringer of firewood, an editor of a small family journal. I'll write down everything I know, in hopes that the kids will avoid making the mistakes I did. Though young people don't pay any attention to such things, still, it would be useful for them to commit something to memory. Some girl came to see Liza, and they're involved in their own private conversation, along with Arseny; someone keeps saying "Aha?" This "aha" has entered our into daily conversation and is used both appropriately and inappropriately. There's a sign at the gate that says "Night Watchman," but I don't feel like "watching": the worthless bums steal it and toss it way across several yards. So we'll react. Our factory tried to carry on a horse-breeding business on the side, but it was too much for them; today they sold the horses off cheap, they're just glad they could find people to buy them. Some managers!

12/1. December has come, bringing with it a steady, windless frost. I spent 12 full hours in the office and wrote an entire bible there; even Toiba called me a Stakhanovite. I rushed home with three stolen logs, made two trips to get water, chopped and brought in some more firewood and lit the stove. In short, all the gymnastic exercise you could possibly want. Liza has a stomach ache; she walks around tripping over the rugs. She's not as much tired as sulky. It really annoys me: from the look on her face you'd think she'd just given birth or was just about to go into labor. Like a spoiled little girl just waiting for someone to take pity on her. In general I understand and appreciate what she's going through, but at a certain point all that whimpering just nauseates me. Just one look at the factory reveals a mass of abuse, sloppiness and negligence, in general all the things that people get sent to the camps for; from force of habit I want to shout "Help! Thief!" I'd like to write a satire exposing all these dear friends who've grown fat on the wealth of the people; but...bitter experience has taught me that every time some abuse is exposed, it ends badly for the person who has brought it to light. "The lockup is as far as you can go," and they're quick to give out the "wolf's ticket."[10] Let's recall the wise Tatar saying: "Find something—hold your tongue. Lose something—hold your tongue." It's better that way. The kids have come home, Liza shuffles in in her deer-fur boots, dishes start clattering; it's dinnertime. In the morning I fried potatoes in fish oil and that held me for the whole day, plus a roll. Oh, damn this ink, it's bubbling up. All our achievements....

12/4. I came home at 12 yesterday—they've started us working nights; I got up at 5 as usual; naturally, a little shell-shocked. But maybe I'll get used to it. We'll sleep it off on our feet. The bread shortage has just added to all the usual hassles. People stand in line for six or eight hours at a time and talk about the possibility of war. War or no war, the expensive varieties of bread going stale on the shelves will ultimately be sold, and that's a fact. Commerce! But somehow the people manage to get by: just when you think you can't take any more, you give it some more thought and you realize you can.

12/6. Fine winter weather. My night work takes up a lot of time, but the eating afterwards is pretty good: white rolls, butter, sausage, sugar. I eat like a pig. No wonder: I'm starving, after all; I've come in on an empty stomach. But what's interesting is that the others are stuffing themselves to the gills too, just shoveling it in. And meanwhile spouting all this nonsense about how well we live. Meaning they're obviously not getting enough to eat either. "I ate so much today, that, as they say, I'm stuffed to the gills," announced Toiba. But when we sat down for tea, she starts packing it away. In short, quite a hungry bunch of people. It's a happy country, but still a lot of people don't have enough to eat. The war in Spain is going full steam, beautiful Madrid is being destroyed. The rebels will win, apparently, since the Germans are backing them. I went to the bathhouse yesterday. A huge bath, communal in the truest sense of the word. The barber shop there has wonderful mirrors and the barbers have smocks of the finest quality. Just think how much attention went into manufacturing the outfits alone.

12/8. Still freezing cold. With proper attention to the stoves and good quality firewood, our life is bearable; it's warm in the hut. Yesterday the city celebrated the ratification of Stalin's Constitution. Naturally it was approved unanimously, by direct, secret voting. Everyone, no matter what his past, has the right to vote and to run for office. For the first time I took part in a big public rally. Of course there's more idiocy and herd behavior than enthusiasm. The new songs are sung over and over, with great enthusiasm: "He who Strides Through Life with a Song on His Lips" and "I Know no Other Such Land Where a Man Can Breathe so Free." But another question comes up: can it be that people under a different regime don't sing or breathe? I suppose things are even happier in Warsaw or Berlin. But then maybe it's all just spite on my part. In any case, at least the finger pointing has ended. We will continue to stride through life: it's not that far to the grave.

12/11. Time is marching on, just try and keep up. It warmed up a little after the cold spell. Yesterday I stood in line for "bellies," but they ran out before I got there; the workers picked them clean. A man breathes free in our country, but he also starves for free—no one prevents him. Starves and freezes.

12/13. It's warm. We've had an extra dusting of snow. There's been some hold up with the bread, and we're going a little hungry. I can't manage to get my passport changed: there's a line there too and you have to fight to get anything." "A Fine Land, Our Native Land...." "A Man Breathes Free...." Dmitry Pavlovich, the self-important Sergeant, told me, "Stop by, I'll help you get your passport changed. Room No. 1." I went, but it's not that easy to get in: you need a pass. And I didn't manage to get one. What important people! Guards, passes.... I went to see my old friend Yevdokimov yesterday.... I wanted him to help me get some sugar: the man works in the Kingdom of Bread. Everywhere you turn, another stumbling block in your way. Everyone is just worried about saving his own skin, everyone clinging onto his own crust of bread. They're doing a national census.[12] I've been entrusted with 15 households. The little ones are asleep, Liza is at the dairy, the older ones are at school. It's after seven; both my stoves are blazing brightly, and I'm making some soup from cows' feet. I'm sitting under the kerosene lamp, writing with this awful ink. The eczema on my feet is really bothering me.

12/15. Today the family came home with bread from three different shops: you take what you get, when you can get it. I'm reading Dickens. Wonderful! And the kids have gotten engrossed in Hugo; they have to be dragged from the book by force. Today I dreamed about the Dolgovo fields; most likely because I'm writing my memoirs about that period of my life for our little journal. We're doing without bread — we threw together various scraps and made patties out of them, and they gave me cramps. I'm getting to know the masses at the factory. There are a lot of strong, healthy people working there. They've still got some powder in their kegs! And of course they spout all kinds of nonsense about our country. Yesterday I ran into Deacon Sazhin, a former derelict and drunkard. He felt sorry for me and gave me six rubles cash. "This is for what you did for me before." And I took his charity. I think he must be the first man to go out of his way for me. Yes, I did help him get on his feet once. And as far as food goes, we certainly didn't keep track of what we gave him. Still the phantom of religion is still alive, even the clergy can make a living. The spark keeps on flickering....

12/18. You may call it nonsense, but still, dreams are a fact of life. I want to write down an interesting dream I had. Someone told me I could see Stalin. A historical figure, it would be interesting to get to see him. And so...A small room, simple and ordinary. Stalin is drunk as a skunk, as they say. There are only men in the room, and just two of us peasants, me and one other guy with a black beard. Without a word, Vissarionovich[13] knocks the guy with the black beard down, covers him with a sheet and rapes him brutally. "I'm next," I think in despair, recalling the way he used to carry on in Tiflis,[14] and I'm thinking, how can I escape, but after his session Stalin seems to come to his senses somewhat, and he starts up a conversation, "Why were you so eager to see me personally?" "Well, why wouldn't I be? Portraits are just portraits, but a living man, and a great one at that, is something else altogether," said I. Overall, things worked out fairly well for me and they even gave me some dinner.... I've had two dreams about Stalin: once before my release and now this time. And in fact, before the revolution I dreamed about Nicholas II. At the time I thought: what is this all about? I had never seen him and wasn't really interested in him. But then during the revolution and after his execution, I found myself often recalling this strange, doomed man, the last and weakest of his kind. I suppose there is some reason for my Stalin dream. One way or another, this huge comet is destined to leave an especially bright trail across the universe, but it will do so as a comet, not a planet. In any case, I didn't make it up, I'm just writing down facts, demented though they may seem.... I'm sitting here with the boys, picking on Arseny, who just can't seem to get the hang of written Russian. His alphabet has a trillion letters, instead of just 35. Maybe I'm wasting my time, but it is irritating. The older children went to school for an evening of Pushkin's poetry.[15] They're such silent, skittish creatures. Of course I can't really blame them; to a certain degree they're just neglected little strays, hungry outcasts.

12/21. Quite a blizzard. One for the books. Last night I was on my way back from work, loaded down with firewood as usual. I slipped on a bump on the frozen ground and fell, hitting my right side on one of the beams I was carrying. I hit really hard and rebounded into a hollow. It really hurt, but no ribs were broken. I don't know yet whether I'll be all right. The pain kept me from sleeping. The compress didn't do any good. I don't want to die, but it would be terrible to be crippled. Maybe I'll get over it. I spent the whole day on St. Nicholas' Day on "standing duty" to get my passport. From seven to seven. After I got my place in line in the morning, I went into a church. A tiny little church with a cemetery. A scrawny little priest lisping out the funeral service for the people who had died over the past five days. The church is crammed with old women, and more old women are milling about at the gate. Begging. All of them look pathetic, but they remind me of the past. A deacon, wearing a coat instead of the usual robes, coughs uneasily, the priests whisper among themselves. The worshippers cast anxious looks around the church — Is someone going to inform on them?

12/23. The storm is still raging, the snow has piled up in huge drifts, and there's no end in sight. It's warm outside though. My side really hurts, I must have cracked a rib. The doctor at the factory didn't give a precise diagnosis and reassured me: these things do happen. It's not only my rib, my stomach hurts too. From shock, or the blow itself. Everything else is fine and dandy. When we work at night they feed us pretty well. I pick on the kids for not being tough enough, but in fact they're not bad kids.... I had a dream about a narrow-gauge railway, with the train speeding up a mountain.

12/24. My day off. It's still snowing. My side hurts. I went to the flea market. Life goes on. Some of the workers throw money around like it grows on trees; they seem to be doing all right. But we're still not as bad off as some people: we don't eat much bread, but on the other hand we have good soup every day, though it is made of pig or cow heads. Yes, I had been about to draw a parallel between the church and...the passport office. I didn't spend much time in the church: it was boring, and I was in a hurry anyway; but I did notice some people throwing their money around. They buy candles and tiny communion wafers, they write prayer requests asking for health and repose. Then they get into arguments about getting the wrong ones back. On the whole, die-hard adherents to the private property system — my paper, my deceased. The ritual side of religion, stripped of any poetry or beauty, is pretty uninteresting, but on the other hand it is completely voluntary. If you want, go, if you don't, don't. But a passport is part of your everyday life, and it can cause all kinds of trouble. Every citizen is required to have a passport, but in order to get one you have to go through a whole series of ordeals. I tried several times, and finally got my passport only after stubborn and prolonged struggle and many long hours spent in line. I came at 7 a.m. and signed on eighth in line. The office opened at 10, and the official in charge of the passport desk announced: "We will issue passports between 1 and 2." I got my passport at exactly 7 p.m. All that tense waiting, all that time spent in line getting pushed and shoved. And I kept thinking: they'll close the window, they'll stop issuing passports, and I'll have to waste another whole day. Paying obeisance to earthly law costs us dearly, but the passport system makes no more sense than, for example, funeral rituals for old ladies. And they charge you three rubles, too. But then, render unto Caesar that which is Caesar's, render unto God that which is God's. We won't argue about it. The counterrevolutionary revolt in Spain has been dragging on for six months now. So far neither side is getting the upper hand. The Germans give aid, the Italians give aid, and the government of the Spanish republic still hangs on. There's a rebellion going on in China too: Chang Hsueh Liang against Chiang Kai Shek. They'll go on fighting for another hundred years, the devils. And it's a good thing, too; under normal conditions the Chinese hordes would multiply and make things bad for the white races. From that point of view any war is useful: less crowding.

12/31. Well, 1936 is over now. The storm lasted several days and covered everything in a thick layer of snow. Now it's just quiet, clear, and cold. The kids' winter vacation has started. The pain in my side is terrible. When I turn, it feels like all the ribs on my right side are broken. Just rattling around in there. And apparently it affected my heart muscle too: I find myself gasping for breath whenever I try to walk. My heart bounces around like a frozen cucumber in a bucket. The bread our "masters" sell is very expensive, and our budget is coming apart at the seams. Liza is sick most of the time, she doesn't have any felt boots and of course there's nothing good about that. I went out on my census round. Some people live fairly well; they've gotten acclimated. The contusion in my side could do me in once and for all, but I do want to live, in spite of all the hardships. You just have to keep on going somehow. We've got ourselves a real winter here, and all the stories about the climate changing have been proven wrong. Everything just goes on just the same as it did 100 years ago.

1937. January 1. Happy New Year! We had roast meat; no matter what comes our way, we celebrate. Life has gotten better, after all. We'll look forward to even better days to come. It would be nice to celebrate Orthodox Christmas too, as we used to. It got extremely cold yesterday; I went into town and on the way back my nose and fingers got frost-bitten. This house was just thrown together, and the frost hovers over the floor. The firewood isn't much good, but we can still get by. As I make the rounds of the 15 households on my census list, I see that a lot of people live worse than we do; it's a bitter consolation. In spite of 20 years of reeducation, some people are still religious, and when they come to the question on the census form about religion they give a straightforward answer: believer. Old allegiances, old habits.... I fiddle with my little journal, my side still hurts, though it seems to be getting a little better, or is it just habit—maybe I've just gotten used to it?

1/6. Christmas Eve.[16] I sit here all by myself, exhausted; I desperately need to sleep. I spent all last night working on the national census. The kids are asleep, Liza has curled up for the night, too, Genya went to the club to see *Chapaev*.[17] In an hour I have to make my rounds and report to my supervisor. Of course I won't actually go around to the houses, everything is clear as it is. Everyone has been counted; I finished the work long ago. By the way, during the census I discovered that sometimes I make bad grammar mistakes: I thought that you had to write the "non" in the word "nonbeliever" as a separate word. But you have to write them together. The Tatar commandant and my own kids proved it to me with their "Rules of Grammar." Live and learn. I'd do anything not to have to go out. But I have to. It was warm during the day; now the wind is blowing. Tamara is not feeling well. Well, Christmas Eve. In the old days things were different. But what can you do? Still, we have enough meat for tomorrow, though we're short of bread. An empty stomach is better for your health. Well, I guess I'd better start getting ready....

1/7. Merry Christmas, Orthodox believers! I slept well. I carried out my civic duty and did it without bothering people at night too. Morning. The stoves are already lit. The kids are asleep. The rooster is making a racket, soothing us and his one hen. It's amazing how little the kids have to say to me. Yesterday Gennady left without a word and came back without a word. Is that good or bad? What's on their minds? What makes them tick? I can't get them to write in their diaries, and they resist writing for the journal too. They do a lot of reading, but nothing seems to be sinking in. Will they retain any of it? My side still hurts, and there's no end in sight.

1/9. I'm completely overburdened by my night work, I can't manage to give my writings the time they deserve: I go from 7 to 4 and from 6 to 12. That's a lot for me. On the other hand I'm eating well. I sat down to write my Christmas prayers, but I've already started to forget them:

> "Thy birth, O Christ our God, the light of your reason has shown forth unto the world! For those who serve the stars in the heavens bow to you, O Sun of truth, and see you in the East on high, O Lord, glory unto Thee!"

Good words, I can't imagine any that would be better. And here we are trying to rid ourselves of all this, to destroy the very memory of that distant, sublime beauty. We destroyed the churches, took a red-hot iron to the idea and burned it away. But…did things get any better as a result? I have my doubts. Today is papa's name day. How I miss the dear old man! And it would seem to be such a simple thing, the human mechanism.

1/12. It's amazing how quickly time passes. Here it is almost the middle of January already. The intensive work in the office wears me out, I'm not getting enough sleep, but on the other hand I eat well. The factory bureaucrats come to the office for supper. They are all remarkably healthy, well fed people. Soviet power does have people it can count on. The salt of the earth, with ample self-confidence, and a reserve layer of fat too. The people were given a simple technology to master, and now they press confidently onward, though clumsily, one step at a time. I went to the flea market today looking for some felt boots for Tamara, but came back empty-handed. Because of the town's concern about our progress toward Socialism, the flea market was moved out to the outskirts of town, and the private property system is now living out its last days there. People go out there, dragging with them anything that could possibly be sold. If you have money you can buy whatever you want. Life is free there, there are no lines. No matter how you look at it, this market is good both for supply and demand. My side is healing, but there's some internal damage and it still hurts to lie on my right side. It's warm, and there are some snow flurries. From the looks of it we should have a lot of rain in June. So far life is tolerable: it's still possible to get by. The kids are playing draughts; Muza is taking a bath. The whole family bathes at home, the bathhouse is a luxury for us now. "He who was nothing, etc." I ought to read, but I can't find the time. Besides cooking and keeping the stove going, I spend a lot of time with the journal: I want to get the kids involved. They are gradually beginning to show some interest. Not bad for a start.

1/15. The weather: it's warm and snowing. My injury is bothering me less, but a fact is a fact; there's been some internal damage, and I still can't move as freely as before. The kids are getting up; the rooster is making an awful racket. Something happened yesterday that made me think: I pick on my daughter Galina a lot, trying to correct her obstinacy and roughness. She had gone out for bread. When I was out I saw her in the long, noisy line, all blue from the cold, and pressing up against the back of the old man in front of her. And I felt so sorry for my little girl! How can I expect her to cultivate contentment and mental harmony? Where is she supposed to find it? Beaten down by poverty, by her life in exile, how can she be expected to develop a relaxed, optimistic outlook on life? And isn't it perfectly natural that the child should feel awkward around me after seven long years? And is it any wonder that she should recoil when some skeleton of a man shows up out of the blue and starts picking on her? No, I have to stop trying to re-educate them: they'll find out for themselves what is bad and what is good. I'll re-educate myself and just try to set the kids on the right path. The balance of power will have to change: soon I will be the one in need of help and I will have to turn to them.

1/17. I tried to go out for water; I'm still a little sore, but at least I can bear the pain now. I had a dream about some staircase; I was climbing it, carry-ing a bag of grain that didn't seem heavy at all. There's never been a time in my life when I've been without enemies. One way or another, Toiba will destroy me. The little Jew bitch doesn't notice me, she just shouts: "Arzhilovsky!" I'm afraid someday I won't be able to help myself and will give her a piece of my mind, and then it will be all over: as a Young Com-munist, she may be cynical and insincere, but does have a lot of power in the office. You have to be ready for anything. I won't say a word until vic-tory. Apparently things are coming to some kind of resolution in Spain, it looks like they're going to lose. Meanwhile we're getting by.

1/18. Today for some reason the kids got up early: most likely they were cold. Or maybe it was Jules Verne got Gennady up: he's gotten engrossed in his reading. Good fantasies can make a rough life easier to bear. Yester-day I had an interesting conversation with a women who works as a guard. She criticized the way things are and her ultimate conclusion was: "They'll just plunder everything, nothing will come of it; they had Soviet power in America too, and they got rid of it there too." Those women who work as guards are as knowledgeable now as they ever were. Meanwhile fortune telling is all the rage among the young people—so much for their consciousness. All that glamour and excitement. It's gotten a little colder, but the weather is fine and stable.

1/19. I wake up with my dream still fresh in my mind. I was someplace I'd never been before, riding my old chestnut mare down a road. The road ended at a steep drop-off leading down to the dark waters of the Tavda. I could see a village on the other side. The mare hesitated a moment, then plunged into the water and started swimming across, carrying me on her back. Someone else was swimming there too. We were naked. We made it across easily and quickly, but we had left our clothes on the other shore. Should we go back? A woman appears with a basket and she gives me something to wear, apparently she had come across on a bridge somewhere, bringing our linen with her. Then it was spring and I was out gathering last year's berries. That is a bad omen—I dream about berries when something bad is going to happen. The night before Epiphany—freezing cold but calm. The kids have stoked the stove well, and the hut is nice and warm for sleeping. I've completely forgotten the camp now: it all seems like some dream I had long ago.... But think of all the strength, all the thoughts I left there. What an awful captivity that was! Well I was there, but I made it through and here I am; we'll live differently from now on.

1/21. Today it's warmer again, after a light frost. There's rime on the bushes. Yesterday I went to the office of the local artel Progress, they're offering work. For some reason I don't trust them, I have to take a closer look. I thought about how quickly life passes, about all the people won't manage to get tickets. What is literature, for example? A kind of station, a resort area. A lot of people could get on board, but not everyone will manage to buy their tickets in time. Gorky walked up and got his ticket. And he was off to the races. Everyone says, "Look at him go! He's so interesting!" Meanwhile tens and hundreds of Gorkys are left standing at the ticket windows with all their words and thoughts stored up, simply because there aren't any tickets. Life is a speeding train. The ones who have a ticket ride, the others stand by and watch them pass by. I used to have a ticket and I was speeding through life on that train. But now here we are—walking. The line goes on and on, and they're out of tickets.

1/28. I wake up at 4. Liza leaves for the dairy before five; I light the stove. I took the long toboggan out to get water. I made it to the gate without incident, but at the gate the toboggan capsized and the tub tipped over the side. It's a good thing I was carrying an extra bucket of water; at least I had something to show for my labor. Genya went out to get in line for bread; there is some hold up with the bread supply again: huge lines, pushing and shoving. They do have the expensive varieties of bread, which is of no use to the proletariat. My side is healing, it's practically back to normal; but now there's something else: I bought myself some hard felt boots that were a little tight and chafed my toe, and now it's bothering me. "When it rains, it pours." But I wanted to write down a strange dream I had last night. Early in the evening I dozed off and dreamed I was on some construction site. For some reason I'm stoking a stove and I'm all worried: what if the buildings catch fire? Suddenly I hear the sound of an airplane. An enormous, low-flying ship appears, it's loaded with huge bundles of dry firewood which, I assume, will burst into flame at any moment. I think "The moment the airplane comes even with the buildings, fire will break out and everything will be destroyed, including the plane." But the airplane didn't get as far as the buildings; I woke up just as the ship was flying over my head, with its tail just missing the roofs. What a strange dream! I forgot some of the second one, but in general it was about some newspaper article whose last three lines detailed an insult suffered by some Russian citizen. I even heard the phrase: "You there, just shut up!" Sleepy thoughts, arising in a man's head against his will.... The weather is calm and stable.

2/1. Snow again. As I was out shoveling the walkway, I found myself thinking: the fall evidently did something to my kidneys, specifically the right one. It feels all heavy and painful down there. But what's surprising in that? In the camp I had nephritis—inflamation of the kidneys: with this happy life of ours what is there left not to hurt? I'll just have to get used to it. I had the dream during the snowstorm: Tamara has slept in; it's 10, and I can't get her up. I pull down the covers and her whole face is covered with oatmeal. Does it mean she's going to get sick? She goes around in the snow in just her ordinary shoes. And then Genya is handing me a rewritten balance sheet and explaining something; maybe we'll get to work together in the summer, that's been my dream for a long time now. I pick on Galina for being erratic and getting into fights, but actually I feel profoundly sorry for her: sometimes she reminds me of a pathetic little bedraggled, stray creature. What she's been through—all the hunger and cold, the burden of exile—has taken its toll on her. Those years have left an oppressive, permanent mark on the family—the mark of injury, poverty, oppression. I'm still hanging on at work. *It's an obvious fact that socialism is just talk: the only thing anyone around here talks about is eating; their interests revolve around getting hold of things, raises, etc. People have only the most narrow, selfish interests. All of this is begging to be written down in a satire.* But life in all its wisdom has taught me that it's not worth dwelling on the ugliness of life if you have a large family, if you consider soup made of cow lips the height of happiness. The swindlers and various marauders of the Soviet rear guard are so united, so well armed with everything they need, that it makes no sense for an unarmed and solitary man to take a stab at them, they'll devour him. To hell with it, with the editorial pages. They'll run themselves aground without my help. I was thinking about the new Constitution that the whole world is so excited about. But what's all the fuss about? What real difference will it make? It's just for show. Things will just go on the way they always have; the voting process they're setting up may be secret, but it's still unanimous. We're living among so-called "kulaks," in quotes, who have been exiled. No change whatsoever: they're treated almost like serfs, the commandant gives orders, the educator rants and raves, the chairman considers it within his rights to intimidate people, threatening them with exile to the far North. No, comrades, no Constitution can plaster over the great fissure in the Russian land, and the conquerors will not let power slip from their hands. Words and conversations—that's not the solution.

2/2. Last night winter unleashed all its elements: there was a terrible wind and it got freezing cold inside the hut. Everything on the floor froze stiff. We started up both stoves, but it's hard to get the place warm. The kids are huddled around the stove. Toward morning things settled down; it's not so bad now. Our factory whistle hoots hoarsely, marking the beginning of a new, happy life in our country. It was especially pleasant to stand in line for bread and peas today. Yes, you might suspect that it's the people who talk most about socialism who are actually the ones laughing at it the most. Time passes quickly. It often seems to me now that I never was in the camp, that it was all just a dream: but then again.... I picture in my mind all the happy inmates assembled for roll call. Sometimes I try to read, but it can be rather hard to swallow: Soviet literature shows only the good side of life, the part that is for show, and it just doesn't grab me.

2/3. My footsteps crunch loudly in the hard crust of the snow, but the frosty air does not feel too terribly cold against my face. I dreamed that I was flying through the air with some stranger on a special sleigh and I asked, "Are cars even faster than this?" "Yes, just a little," answered my companion. Let's hope Toiba won't kick me out at the plant; she can't stand the sight of me. I read the prosecutor's indictment in the case of the Trotsky Center,[18] it was wonderful! Vyshinsky[19] is pretty smart. But there's one problem! Today Vyshinsky calls all the defendants bandits and swindlers, not sparing his brush, but when they were in power, when the swindler Arnold was in charge of the Main Chemical Industry Bureau, when Radek[20] was writing articles in Soviet newspapers, Vyshinsky didn't breathe a word about the "bandits" arming themselves under his nose. Isn't it dangerous to let criminals get that close? All these discoveries are giving me the impression that if hundreds of sincerely dedicated, battle-scarred Communists, after decades spent working at Vyshinsky's side, ultimately turn out to be scoundrels and spies, then who can guarantee that we're not completely surrounded by swindlers? Who can guarantee that the greatest and dearest of them won't be sitting down there on the defendants' bench tomorrow? And finally, how many swindlers must be swelling the ranks of the Party out in the provinces, if Arnolds have pene-trated to its very center? Help! What kind of place are we living in, and what do we have to look forward to tomorrow? It reminds me of when I first learned about microbes and bacteria; I was reading some science book, and it said that everything, even the air, was made up of living crea-tures. And after that I kept seeing little creatures everywhere, and I could-n't even stand to take a drink of water. That's the way it is now: you look at a man and suddenly he turns into a swindler or a traitor before your very eyes. Arseny snickered over his newspaper and complained, "It's all about the same thing: just the Trotskyite center and you can't make any sense of it." Yes there's a lot being said, only it's too late.

2/4. It's gotten a little warmer. A southwest wind. The food I'm getting is not too bad and I'm sleeping very well. Yesterday I was in town in quest of peas and I stopped in for a minute to see my sister Masha. She's living like an orphan in her own little house, battling poverty. She has a cow. A per-manent expression of grief has settled on her face: the loss of her son and husband have left their mark. For some reason I dreamed about a reli-gious procession with people carrying icons. Old women carrying the icon of our Savior of Zyryanka and not knowing where to set it down. I took the icon from them and placed it on the corner facing Ivan Ignatye-vich's hut. People gathered around as though for a prayer service, but there was no one to start. Suddenly the children, Soviet children, began singing quietly, but in harmony, "Thy immaculate image." I joined in. Then Sazhin, the deacon, appeared in his robes, carrying an enormous Gospel. He beckoned to me to come over to him, and I understood: there was no altar and he needed someone to hold the book. I held up both my hands, the weighty book settled heavily into them. But the deacon had forgotten the Gospel to the Saints (for some reason it was dedicated to

Nicholas, Servant of God) and spent a long time trying to find it. Andrei Strakhov appeared from somewhere. Somehow everything worked out all right. But I was the only one singing, and my voice sounded strange to me, I was dragging out the ends of the notes. Then I dreamed about some new place where I had moved with my whole family. The land lay before us, splendid black earth, just waiting for someone to plow it. "Are we really going to plant here?" asked one of the children. "Of course we are!" I answered and began to pick up some rubbish that was was scattered on the ground around us....

2/8. I've just come back from the cattle yard of the Progress artel, where Liza works making butter and keeping the books; I split firewood and shoveled snow on the walkway. The people at the artel are ambitious, but they are sloppy in how they do things. Everything is done somehow irresponsibly, not the way it should be done. They built an expensive hut for the dairy—the doors don't close, and as a result it's damp and cold inside. The firewood is scattered all around the yard and is all covered with snow, no one bothered to stack it up in a shelter somewhere. Everything is depressing and somehow false. Tamara is under the weather; she has a temperature. The flu or a cold. Rumor has it that there are cases of typhus in town. Of course the newspapers don't have anything to say about such "trivia." Why dampen people's enthusiasm and get them all worried? The frost is holding firm. A friend of Arseny's came by and they're mumbling to each other about their childish concerns. Today at work they had scheduled a public reading of the newspapers. They'd come up with the idea of reading the newspapers out loud for the office workers. What utter balderdash! What the hell do they need a public reading for when every literate employee can get through all the hogwash in the paper in five minutes? Fortunately the crowd started to break up, and the "educator" let us go. Still to come is the "study" of the Constitution. As if there wasn't enough to be depressed about. What would take a normal human being 10 minutes, for us requires prolonged study. Just blabbering on and on. It's tedious and disgusting. They go on writing year in and year out, they spend decades studying, without the slightest progress. Just now Arseny was telling the story of how the peasant Arefey got stuck in the snow (it was in their assignment). He asked me, "Why are you writing all that down, Papa?" "So it won't be forgotten," I answered. It's probably going to snow, I can feel it in my bones. Sometimes it seems as though you haven't been living in the world very long, but when you recall you're 50 years old, it's frightening: it'll all be over before long. And I still have such a will to live, there's so much I'd like to accomplish. Recently for some reason I often recall Dolgovo and the wonderful life we had there. Liza agrees, she says she'd go out to live in the middle of nowhere and leave this culture behind without the slightest regret. True, but nowadays you have to think seriously about such things: you'd be a goner, stuck out empty-handed on some remote farmstead. It looks as though we'll have to stay here for a long time to come, spending more time standing in lines than people do at an all-night mass.

2/10. Just before 6 I went out and got in line for bread. My happy fellow countrymen were already standing there, getting used to socialism. I stole some firewood. It's become part of my routine. I made breakfast: slightly frozen potatoes and 100 grams of bread per person. What can you do? I know we need to eat better, but our finances won't allow it. Still we're not going hungry. And with this kind of life, if you're fired from work or get sick, you're kaput; there's nothing left to keep you going. You can't help thinking about having your own hut, a cow, a pig. We waste so much time on trivial, boring problems! Meanwhile life just goes on as usual; the kids have gotten so comfortable on skis and skates, they just might forget how to walk on their own two feet. Will they keep it up or will it pass, like the winter? So what if they do, there's nothing wrong with it, and it doesn't do any harm. Any time spent out in the open air is good for you.

2/11. It snowed and I had to clean up. And then: the stove, the bread line, I stole two long poles for firewood from someone who had already stolen them for himself. And I got to thinking: a good two kilometers to the bread line and back just to pick up your starvation rations: to commit a criminal offense (theft of socialist property, for even though it's just rubbish, still every scrap is government property). Just to get warm, you have to take risks every single day, wear yourself out. So it is now and so it will be, from now until the end of time. Yesterday I heard from a lady at the office that she and her husband together make 1500 rubles a month, there are only three of them, but still they can't make ends meet. He's an engineer and she's a bookkeeper, but they have to steal, too; he picks up things here and there, and she has to commit criminal acts to get good linen, silk stockings, get her hair done, buy purfume, go to the theater, etc. Criminals everywhere! Though they're in the Party, though they go on and on about Stakhanovite work methods (And what a cruel, predatory system! The strongest people work as hard as they can so as to get as much as they can, so as to have the right to look down on people who are weak or unhealthy!), though they're studying the new Constitution, etc. Let's take some ordinary guy living in Golyakovo, Yegor Bykov. In the summer, working at a steady pace, he stores up food for himself and his livestock, prepares bark for sandals, linen, bast. By wintertime he's all set and can sit back and relax: the firewood's right outside the door, he's got all the hay he needs, and it doesn't cost him anything. He does it all steadily and calmly, without straining himself. And the most important thing: without a single criminal act! In fact it's the other way around, it's the socialist state that is committing a criminal act. It slaps a burdensome tax on Yegor Bykov, who's done nothing wrong, to cover its own waste and plunder, it appropriates a huge amount of bread as a form of taxation, assessing it at an incredibly low rate, so that it then can turn around and sell it at a hugely inflated price. Yegor Bykov is paid 90 kopecks for his grain. For 16 kilograms. Then they sell the worst quality rye bread for 90 kopecks a kilogram, getting their capital back 16 times over. These monstrous crimes force Yegor Bykov to the only possible course of action: somehow to conceal some part of his cropland from the vigilant eyes of various overseers so he can have his own bread. But Yegor Bykov doesn't have any more bread. He takes his young pig—before it's fully grown—, his bast, his linen (if there's any left after the tax) into town and waits in long lines waiting to buy bread, stamping his frozen feet. That's how life is in our happy country these days, where man breathes so free, without even having to pay for the air.

2/13. A real February frost, it just whips at your face. Yesterday I went to see Masha. She's my god daughter, grown up now and already a teacher, and though she is set in her old country ways, it's not to her disadvantage. She remembered Vasya, who was so quiet and nice, and who wound up tossed into a communal grave in prison.... The brightest flowers of the Socialist revolution. A criminal! The orphans stay alive thanks to the modesty of their tastes and their endurance. We talked about Pushkin. I told them about my time in the prison and the camp. I had a memorable dream: A young woman was giving birth somewhere out in public. I was there. The baby was huge. The mother rather cheerfully cut the umbilical cord and started to remove the so-called caul from the baby. The caul was brown and tough. When she finished, the baby started wriggling, all smiles, squinting from the light. Joyfully, the mother announced to someone, "It's a boy." Another unusual thing about the baby was that his brain was on top of his skull, and looked like a hat, covering the top of his head. An ugly cat came up to the baby, and, smiling, he started playing with it. A strange dream. Can you imagine thinking up something like that? Could something like that happen in our happy country? Maybe because I've been eating better, or because I've managed to get some rest, I've dreamed about women two nights in a row. I'm just a sinner, that's all there is to it! We're sitting around the table, eating breakfast. The older children went to a Pushkin program last night and now are reluctantly sharing their impressions. It's rather depressing around here, there's nothing interesting to do. The kids have something on their minds that is theirs alone; it's closed to me. Give them time to grow and develop: some day each of them will have a distinct character and style that's all their own.

2/15. Winter is doing itself proud: we often come home with frostbitten cheeks. No end of hassles with the firewood. This year is the centennial of Pushkin's death. Soviet power has adopted Pushkin as one of its own.... True, the man loved freedom, but he loved his native country as well, he was a true Russian patriot. The late poet was not fond of serfdom. Dostoevsky also adopted Pushkin for his own, but Soviet power is not fond of Dostoevsky. Today I sent a short commentary to the local paper about the outrageous things going on at the factory; I couldn't help myself, the scoundrels are just so blatant about it. Maybe I shouldn't have done it, because I've been known to steal a thing or two myself, but that's just my nature. It's stupid to write down your dreams, but what if there's nothing else to write about? I dreamed about a church, with my brother serving as deacon. He's conducting the service, mumbling something, and what he's saying is far from the sort of thing you normally hear in church. Someone is offering to donate some things to the church, and he answers, "I'm not here just to take in people's trash." He goes into the altar room behind the iconostasis, closes and locks the doors, and keeps repeating, "It's more secure this way, otherwise people will swipe something." An obvious mistrust of laymen. Why would I dream something like that? Just try to figure it out! Today even I felt cold in the hut. We can look forward to forty more days of freezing weather. They're still squabbling in Spain. It does seem as though the "government" won't be able to hold out much longer, though they keep on boasting and bragging. We knock ourselves out giving donations to the Spanish workers. I wonder who is going to get my 1 ruble 50 kopecks?

2/18. We have a unique way of relaxing on our day off: I got up at 4:00 and went out for firewood in 30 degrees of frost—I made five trips and covered 10 kilometers, all told. I spent two hours in the bread line. You'd think that would be enough. Sannikov, the resettled kulak, and I reminisced about how wonderful things were in Tavda. Will it ever be like that here? Late frosts. One good thing—at least the wind has died down. I got into a fight with Arseny yesterday; he'd gone out to play without asking permission, and he tore one of his felt boots, and it can't be repaired. The kids are too absorbed in their reading and they don't like to talk. Maybe it's better that way. A woman in the line today said that the Collective farmers are dropping like flies.

2/19. Another big event: Ordzhonikidze died.[21] The details haven't been made public yet. There was an assembly at the factory. It's interesting how they organize them. An assembly for public mourning, given our level of consciousness, should have been dramatic and memorable, but in fact it was deadly dull, it dragged on and on, and the speakers had to be forced to go onstage. They elect the Presidium for the meeting. The audience is restless and noisy, and at first you can't hear the speaker. He grimaces, trying to find the right words, but then warms up to the task and gives a fairly coherent speech. The speech ends. The director addresses the audience: "Who will be speaking next, comrades?" Dead silence. "No volunteers?" the director insists, and a threatening tone creeps into his voice. Eventually one Party member, then another force out a few words proposing that the factory, to commemorate the death of the staunch Bolshevik, should increase its productivity, etc. They speak without emotion, without inspiration, following a memorized formula. Seshukov, the cultural director, a special settler, also says a few words about taking care of the Socialist Kopeck, the Socialist Board. This particular speaker would have gone and on, right up to the Socialist Nail. All of them talked about our "obligation." Why so? Why didn't anyone think of saying that to commemorate the death of one of the "great" Georgians[22] we ought to propose…cutting the pay of the factory management? That would really make a difference and I'm sure it would improve the overall state of affairs. Not a word about that…. It came down to concrete proposals. The director solicited specific suggestions and zeroed in on Kulikov, a framer. He gets all flustered, and answers, "I've heard everything, there's nothing to add. Let's use that as our basic proposal." Ultimately the specific details were dragged out of us by force: in January we gave 113.4%, in February we need to give no less than 15. Someone yelled out, "Eliminate waste!" But that wasn't accepted, since the higher the quantitative indicators, the more waste. Well, what of it! Ordzhonikidze, in my view, was not such a big shot, and they'll find someone to replace him. In this case the country hasn't lost much, though it hasn't gained much either: one more, one less—the overall picture doesn't change. My dearest better-half just keeps on groaning and complaining about the cold; it irritates me, and I'm losing my respect for her. Maybe it is crude to say it, but what can you do about it? I just don't like it when people moan and groan.

2/21. Yesterday it tried to warm up: the snow on the sidewalks melted a little, and patches of land appeared on the hills. When I find the time I read from Sholokhov's *And Quiet Flows the Don*.[23] He writes well enough, but I wonder how he's going to manage to tie it all together at the end to conclude with the "happy life?" It's hardly likely he'll be able to be honest right up to the end. Given the amount of pressure the writer was under, it must have been impossible for him to be objective and impartial. But once he starts hopping around on one foot, there's nothing in it any more for the reader; it feels forced and unnatural. Yesterday Tamara had a fit of depression and didn't join us for supper. In general she's afflicted with an unsociable and erratic character. The kids' silence, their withdrawal into themselves weighs heavily on me: do we really have nothing at all to talk about? When you're living together with other people, silence is an oppressive thing. On the other hand, you can't force people to talk. If they're not ready to.

2/23. It warmed up, and some of the snow thawed during the afternoon. A full moon. Everyone likes a full moon, but it does make it hard to steal firewood: you can be seen from far away and you lose your nerve in spite of yourself. I just can't shake my thoughts about running my own farm: two or three years of work, and you can kiss hunger good-bye. But for now, of course, we're stuck here. You have to think it through and weigh everything carefully ten times over. "Bread fever" is still going strong in town, it's hard to make ends meet, but people are used to it. They get in line beginning at 2 a.m. Here indeed, "senseless nights, sleepless nights." Still, Sholokhov is a great talent; every character in his novel is a hero, each one has his own separate, distinct life. And after all, that's the way it is! I wonder what he thinks about our "happy life"? Or rather, how he would depict it as it is now?

2/26. A cold morning after a cold night. Signs of life: the sirens are blaring; there's been an accident somewhere. Ultimately something was bound to happen, all good things come to an end. Yesterday Strakhov stopped by, he's an old friend of mine, an unfrocked priest. He's dreaming about going on a fishing trip. The time is nigh: people will be out fishing. Maybe we'll give it a try ourselves.... Life goes on at the same old pace: Today I dreamed — in my sleep, this time — about getting bread without waiting in line. When will that time come?

2/27. I just had this thought: what if there's no point to any of this? i.e. the diaries, the home journal. Maybe it would be better just to stop everything right here and now and just live a life of contemplation? But first of all, it would be boring and meaningless, and secondly, everything would be forgotten and my thoughts wouldn't get any exercise. So be it, especially considering it doesn't cost anything. The rooster is crowing. The rabbits are out preening themselves. I meant to write that it's warmed up. My *valenki*[24] are starting to accumulate moisture; they feel heavy. There was a big incident yesterday in the settlement: one resident had his cow stolen and it was slaughtered in the bushes nearby. But they caught the thief, and he gave away his whole artel; he didn't manage to cover his trail. In general there are more robberies these days. It's strange; people live so well, but crime is not decreasing. Today as I was walking past the factory dump (I was out at 4, going to get my place in line) I heard a young woman, a worker, "speaking her mind." She used the same filthy language that men are prone to use. The other women were laughing at her outbursts. And in fact, all the women are constantly exposed to coarse language; they know the hidden meanings to all the words, so why not use them themselves? Equality in all things. And it just adds to the others' entertainment.

3/1. It's so terribly cold that even I am starting to freeze. In spite of all my efforts with the stoves, it's still cold inside and the sleeping shelf above the stove is the center of activity in the hut. I went to the flea market. If you have a lot of money, you can find anything you need there. And there are people who have money: they take their time and pick out expensive, high-quality things. Tough there's more trash these days. I started writing for the wall newspaper at the factory; I'm can't help wanting to stir up this stagnant swamp. Writing things down does not always lead to bad results: at least you feel better when you speak your mind. Mama broke her arm. The old woman has had a string of bad luck lately. And things are so tight for me that I can't help her. There was a fight in a line at the factory; people were hurt and a couple of policemen showed up. People just can't seem to appreciate how happy their lives are.

3/5. Time rushes on like a fast car. The frosts seem to have ended, at least it was warm this morning. I made three trips for firewood. I keep getting self-destructive thoughts about how you just have to live this way; it's so easy to swipe things anyway. I wanted to write down my dream. It's summer. I'm on my way to visit my sister Fiza. I see Nina coming toward me, she's wearing a pink dress. A little boy is leaning up against the bank under the hut, sucking his thumb, it must be their boy. "You'll be sent off on the 11-th," said Fiza. I seem to know about this already: I'm being mobilized, or exiled, or something. Then I'm at some station somewhere, most likely waiting for a train. I'm wearing a light, nice looking jacket. I walk along the rails, and suddenly an empty platcar without a locomotive comes bearing down on me, full speed ahead, and there's some young man standing on it. I move aside, but the platcar comes down off the rails and takes off across the soft earth, and I'm a little startled. It's stupid, of course, but still it's strange. Such strange images appear out of nowhere! Soon it will be 7:00. I woke up Genya to chop wood; Muza is guzzling down a cup of boiling water, she's on the first shift. Tamara and Galina are asleep. In general they spend a lot of time sleeping. It bothers me a little; they're behind in their development. Arseny is up already, bustling around. Like a lot of children, he has a huge appetite. We don't eat much, but what we eat is not bad, and it's enough for us. I'm doing most of the writing for the journal myself. But maybe it's better for the kids that way, if they will read what I write. Things are still all right at work.

3/6. It was so nice early in the evening, I got my two trips for firewood over with in no time, but a storm blew in overnight and it's still snowing today. I had a dream about the countryside, a place I'd never seen before, with a herd of cattle and some elk walking by a big river. I spent some time reading Furmanov's *Rebellion*.[25] The man spends a lot of time admiring himself and his revolutionary successes. But still, he knows what he's doing. You have to agree with him; people really did take to the revolution. Meanwhile we are enjoying the blessings of revolution and are about to go out to get in line for peas, which the state sells for 1 r. 30 k. a kilogram, i.e. at least 20 times more expensive than "kulak" prices. And this in the twentieth year of our marvellous revolution! You have to assume that the peas will be really delicious. Liza has come running home from the dairy; she's frozen through and through, poor thing, and it's freezing cold in the hut, too. She's beaten down and exhausted, one foot in the grave, and it's partly her fault: going around the way she does in a torn jacket that she doesn't bother to button, etc. She's just let herself go, it's the power of autosuggestion at work. But you have to take yourself in hand: we can still get by and there is hope that things will be better in the future. Gennady is doing some oil painting. He has talent, that can't be denied, and an artistic sense, too. He also reads a lot. I don't know how much of it he's taking in and how much of it will stick. He doesn't talk much. That's good and bad at the same time.

3/8. A cruel frost. The February moon, apparently the whole month will be just as cold. What if March is just as bad? I spent my day off wandering around town. I saw good cuts of meat and expensive gingerbread. I stopped in to see Marfa; Mama is living with her. The old woman has a broken arm: she fell in a bread line. It had a serious effect on her, and she's really gone downhill. She seems to be just hanging onto life by a thread. She talks a lot about death, and about Papa, "He's taken his place with God, let him lie there in peace...." Yes, ultimately all of us will find our place there. I went to see Misha. He had an operation: cancer of the lip. He gets terribly tired. Poor Zina does the laundry herself and she has to put up with her husband's weakness; he's living openly with some girl he picked up. And she comes to see him at home, too. They've dreamed about having their own house for years and years, but I don't think they'll ever get it. An unusual family. Each one of us has his own eccentricities; each of us rows the boat of life in his own unique way. Ultimately we'll all row ourselves to the same shore, we'll "find our place." I feel sorry for my brother, because he's going to have a hard time when he gets old: he'll have to give up some of his habits.

Just now I was caught with stolen firewood by a mounted patrolman. Maybe he just wanted to scare me and there won't be any formal repercussions, but any day now I could get in serious trouble, because people are stealing more nowadays than they ever have before. "They'll give you ten years!" said someone who happened to be there at the time, to scare me. And of course they will, and I'll be an enemy of the people again. Nothing but trouble: I don't want to freeze to death, but there's not much to rejoice about in a ten-year sentence either. The big-time thieves get away with murder, and meanwhile one little "Socialist" log is enough to get a man blindfolded and stood up against a wall. They put up my comments on the wall newspaper, and naturally there will be an uproar.... They'll kick me out, and I'll go out to a farmstead on the Tavda and make my dreams come true. The kids have gathered for supper, it's time to eat.

3/10. Yesterday we had a welcome respite from the cold, but at night it started snowing, and the storm is still going on. Everyone is sick and tired of it, but there's nothing you can do. Genya's paintings are turning out well, and he has a small diary he writes in now and then. But even that is a lot. No question about it, he's making progress. But the girls are in some kind of hibernation. I'm not getting through to them. Either they have some special thoughts of their own, their own private lives, or they are just following in their mother's footsteps — and she isn't going anywhere, just putting one foot in front of the other. I don't condemn her, I sympathize. There's not much between you and a dead end if the burden you're carrying is too heavy for you. And her burden is more than anyone could bear. The cold chases the kids up onto the stove shelf and interferes with their work.

3/11. A couple of words before supper. Galina cleaned up the dining room, and Tamara is in the kitchen, scrubbing the kitchen floor with all her might. Any minute now quiet Genya will show up with his book and sit down at the table without saying a word. The little twins are asleep. Liza is out at the dairy pressing butter for the Collective Farm. I agonize about the shortage of firewood in this cruel cold spell, and about my fruitless trip into town — I'd wanted to make bliny tomorrow, but there wasn't any wheat or oat flour. The blizzard has been raging two days now. Snowdrifts have blocked my wonderful path, and my work as a draught animal hauling in firewood has ground to a halt. I'm sick and tired of the snowstorm, and I wish I could make it stop. But how? With something like this you can't just issue a decree. I don't do anything in my free time, I just lie around on the bunk by the stove. Evidently nothing will come of the writings I sent to Moscow, and I suppose it's about time for me to leave well enough alone. Wrong time, wrong place. We won't say a word.

3/13. Somehow I made it home with the firewood. This is a real blizzard, in places it's hard just hauling your feet up out of the snow. Tomorrow is Yevdokiya's Day; often the snow has started to melt by then, but now we're in the middle of the cruelest of winters, and we need more and more firewood. I'm exhausted, but still I've managed to keep both stoves going. I've been having trouble with Arseny today. I've been angry at him recently; he doesn't want to read and he's completely given up writing, but what really sets me off is his insolent attitude. He counts on his mother to bail him out. Today he went out at 4:30 to see his friend without asking my permission and stayed out till 8. I locked the door and made him stand outside on the porch for 20 minutes. He stood out there whimpering, but didn't break down and ask to be let in. He huddled up under the overhang like some stray wolf cub. I didn't say anything to him. Most likely he was frozen through and through, it took him a lot of time to get his warm things off, and he huffed and puffed the whole time. He's quite stubborn child, though he looks innocent enough. He's got a will of his own. And I suppose he'll stay that way. Or maybe it just seems that way to me. Anyway, the kids have grown away from me, and Arseny has no feeling for me at all. Well, all right. I'll stand aside. Let him grow up without my help. Maybe he'll turn out all right anyway. It's still too early to come to any conclusions.

3/17. Finally it's warmed up a little. I was so sick and tired of the cold. I'm doing without sleep again: I'm working nights at the Trust. They're still putting together the annual report. It's an enormous bureaucratic organization that's taken over a huge, hulking mansion that used to be a merchant's private residence. Socialism has found a use for the merchant's spacious quarters…. The thick-walled churches have come in handy too. Everything that the comrades didn't manage to destroy has proved useful to the Socialist State. The Central Executive Committee issued an order to close and discontinue the cases of all *lishentsy.*[26] But there are no signs of improvement in our life: the true Soviet believers just keep on snarling: "I'll show you!" This salt of the Soviet land never comes down from their platforms where they run everything by command and oppress people; they will always be seeing "class enemies" everywhere. *When will they realize that the problem is not social class, but individuals, and there will be plenty of scoundrels under Communism as well?* Recently I had a dream about three dogs who came up to me to be petted: the next day I ran into three of my good friends. I'm fishing for a job with a good salary; maybe I'll catch one.

3/20. We are freezing, literally. I tried to write, but my hands were all stiff. 30 degrees of frost. Unprecedented cold. I can't believe that in another month it will be warm, and the starlings and ducks will come flying back. But they will. I work in the Trust, and I'm becoming more and more convinced that there's no such thing as Socialism; there are aristocrats, bureaucrats, and then there are people like me to do the dirty work. The accountants, for example, are utterly convinced that the filing clerk is some kind of fallen being who is to be ordered about, browbeaten and run into the ground for 150 r. a month. Some comrades! Tyrants and thieves!

3/22. It's as cold as ever. Today I just about fell into the clutches of the guard watching over the firewood. He chased after me, cursing and yelling hoarsely, "Next time you won't get away with it!" My second warning, and a serious one: there's a real danger I could earn myself a new sentence. Damned if you do, damned if you don't; I don't want to freeze to death either. You have to maneuver your way through somehow. Woe to us, sinners! I'm in a bad mood, I snap at the kids for not being tough enough. And whose fault is it, if not mine?

3/23. We had a slight thaw today. To solve the firewood problem, I've switched over to rose willow. We'll manage to make ends meet. And soon warm weather will be upon us for sure. Because of the high price of bread, we aren't getting much to eat, though you really need it when you're out chopping down trees. You feel the effects immediately, your knees shake. For chopping trees you need a minimum of two kilograms a day. And that's on the low side. We're not starving, but we sure are hungry.

3/27. It's finally gotten warm: yesterday the streams started flowing down from the mountains and there's a "smell of starlings" in the air, as Fiza says. I went to town and thought about how awful it is when your boots are no good. It's been warm all day, and we can expect some slush. Yesterday the snow turned black in a single day. I had a dream about harrowing through deep layers of dirt and being surprised at how easily the earth yielded to the teeth of the harrow. I went out to get in line and got into a conversation with a peasant woman from Guseva. I asked her how things were out in the country. "They took down Nikisha's barn, they're picking up the wheat that they find under the floorboards, kernel by kernel." Nikishka was Nikifor Grigoryevich Yerdakov, a successful, wealthy farmer who lived in Guseva, an excellent craftsman and a literate man. Naturally they shook him out of his warm nest during collectivization, they confiscated it and used it to create a happy life for themselves, and now, for lack of anything better to do, are taking down his barns and looking for ten-year-old grain. So this is our happy life?! At one time Guseva was a prosperous village, and people used to count wheat not by the grain, but by the barrel. Well what of it! They were pretty strange back then. The Trust paid me for my extracurricular hours, and I can spoil myself a little. Yesterday, for example, I bought a kilo of sweet pies for 3r. 40k a kilo. In general, we are managing to get by, taking one day at a time. Our only hen is laying eggs with soft shells. The rooster turned out to be a good boyfriend. I keep thinking: if people reproduced as rapidly as birds, the world would have collapsed long ago, or we would simply have run out of food to eat.

3/28. The thaw continues. At night it freezes up a little, but more and more of it melts during the course of the day. Today people have even put the sleighs away and are trying to use their wagons. There are hold ups with the bread, and we have to expend twice as much energy, and also money, as usual. Most likely things will be tight right up to August. But all is well with us. And who would dare to say that our life is not happy? Though it's possible there will be more lay offs. But there's no point in getting all depressed. We've seen worse. We'll make it through somehow. All the trouble just making ends meet at home, not to mention the distances, makes it hard to do anything for the rest of the family. The people are expecting a lot of rain and a good harvest. The hungry chicken can't stop dreaming of wheat. Though best of all would be a good harvest. Let's just hope the Collective farmer will get his bread to market. Though that's hardly likely.

3/29. The snow is turning to water. I yelled at the kids today. As usual I got up early: 2:30. I went out and got in line for bread. Then I brought in the firewood. The kids were still asleep. Last night we'd agreed that Galina would go out for dough. But in the morning she started making excuses not to go. Genya is huddled gloomily over his book, he's completely forgotten about the firewood. I yelled at them both and said a lot more than I should have. I hadn't had enough sleep, you can understand why I was so irritable, but still it was inexcusable. And then, when Genya, duly submissive, spelled Galina in line, when she had to miss class because of the dough, and I saw how puffy her face was, I felt ashamed of myself, and sorry for the kids. They've been through the torments and pain of exile, their bellies are swollen from hunger, they've frozen through and through because of the rags they have to wear, — and in fact, they're still going hungry, — and on top of it all, here I am yelling at them. I'm ashamed and miserable: why didn't I think before hurting these gentle children like that? Tomorrow I'll apologize. Tomorrow should be a good day for us: we have enough bread for three days and a bottle of oil. Maybe we'll have some real bliny tomorrow.

They're about to shut down the factory; they've run out of wood. What if I get laid off? After all, I don't fit in among all the "Ivan Petroviches." Well, all right. A new phrase has appeared in our lexicon: "Carelessness — the Disease of Idiots." The newspapers are getting more critical. A completely new, unusual campaign in the spirit of the latest Constitution. What it will all lead to, I don't know. You can "smell the starlings," but I don't think this warmth is the real thing. We'll see on Annunciation Day; it's a lucky day. I'm little tired from puttering around in the wet snow. It doesn't take much for an old man like me. Though I feel all the passion of youth in my soul, and I want to live, I believe in a better life....

4/4. Spring is following its usual course: mud, water, warm days, and snow. For example, there was a good frost today. I'm a little worried. Yesterday Toiba started a campaign against me, they're just waiting for the right opportunity to get rid of me. On the other hand maybe I'm making it all up, from lack of sleep. Bad weather is hard on the poor. When will the road lie clear before us? When will life actually become happy? In the meantime you notice with sorrow that one of the kids is wearing pants that are ragged and torn, another's boots flap open hungrily at the toe. The thing that is really frightening is the possibility of starving. We'll eat our cheap meat and then just kick the bucket. Woe to the living!

4/6. The night before Annunciation Day. It snowed all day yesterday. It was below freezing today, but all day it's felt like warm weather is just around the corner. I have to write down two dreams I had. We're living in a small apartment, apparently Fiza is with us and it's a little cramped. A spotted cow comes into the room and lies down on the floor. She squeezes herself in, completely filling up the room from one corner to the other, and makes herself right at home. I think: this place was made for her. And we can milk her right here. Can you make any sense out of it? The second one has more of a bite to it. Genya and I are together someplace, I don't know where. Mountains, woods, you can hear a balalaika playing down below. Genya apparently went down to listen, and I'm left alone. Evening. Twilight. Some sort of barrier made from fresh timber. I see a huge wolf creeping up on me from the other side of the barrier. I'm holding a thin stick. The wolf comes closer and puts his paws up on the barrier. I start fighting him and I sense that I won't be able to kill him with the stick. And the wolf is huge and mean. I glance around and see a long, bare skull with a hefty jawbone lying on the ground. I grab it and start beating the wolf on the head with it. The skull is heavy and solid. The wolf's head suddenly gives way and in a few minutes he's dead. The battle took a lot out of me, but I won. The kids have a week off from school. Let them take it easy. They have a hard time at school: it's a long way away and it's hard for them to learn anything on an empty stomach. If they had enough to eat, things would be completely different. There's no decent meat or butter, and I'm starting to lose my strength again. I think things are working themselves out at the factory. Toiba has started showing me some respect. If they don't lay me off now, it means my job is guaranteed through the summer. I'd like to do something nice for the family tomorrow, but I don't have any money. We'll get by on reminiscences. For the meantime I'll work on the family journal. There are a lot of interesting things in it already.

4/7. Annunciation Day. In the old days we used to go through a solemn chorus of "The Archangel's Voice"; after the service we'd eat fish pies, we'd go out visiting and in general live it up. Those were the days of religious prejudices and "obscurantism." But today I just got up and brought in some firewood — we had run out. I ate 5o gr. of bread, and all day long between the 7 of us we'll eat no more than 3oo. Not much, but it will keep us alive. Welcome, happy life! There's a hard frost and a north wind, and the snow is coming down in big flakes. It means Yevdokiya was right: it's going to be a cold spring. And the signs promise even more: first, 4o degree cold morning frosts, secondly, Easter (May 2) ought to be the same kind of day. We'll see. Yesterday we were talking about how, in spite of our poverty there are other people even worse off than we are, people who are sick, crippled, deformed, etc. It is possible to get by, even living the way we do. *And can we really hope for any better? We can and we must, because there's always a calm after the storm. It's true! There's no point in pouting and moaning. Now a lot depends on what we do ourselves. Onward! Be brave!*

4/9. After Annunciation it froze up again; people wear their felt boots for 3 hours in the morning. The puddles have frozen over. The kids skate on the ice. It got quite warm toward the end of the day. A starling came. He took a look at his bird house, chirped and flew away. I had two surprises today. The prosecutor, Fofanov, gave a true bureaucrat's answer to my official complaint about the illegal eviction of my family: "You may address yourself to the Onokhinsk Village Council to find out the reasons for the dekulakization of your family." An interesting answer! A man shouts "Help! Robbery!" And the guardian of law and order answers pompously,

"I recommend you address yourself to the thieves, and then you will find out all the details." I also got an answer from the editors of *Peasant Gazette*. They rejected my writings, they didn't pass the ideological test. I write about what everyone has known for a long time, I idealize the strong manager, etc. A complete failure. Their literary editor gave me a very detailed answer that filled two full printed pages. *Is there no place for me? By the way, it's a good lesson. Wanting to make sure former people like me won't be coming up with things, nothing we do will be acceptable, everywhere they look they'll see intent to discredit the innocent communists. They are not building a classless society in the broad sense of the word; they are simply pulling the wool over people's eyes. And they know how to do it. For no matter what I say, it will all be twisted to mean something bad, everything will be interpreted as an attempt to discredit the party, an assault by a class enemy. They will never allow us to be equal, and they never will believe that we've forgotten and forgiven everything. We are damned, from now until the end of our lives.*

4/12. It's warm. April weather. No starlings; that means more frost. I started to dig up roots. I can work now, but my boots take a beating. The kids are depressed for no evident reason, and I can sympathize. I went through a phase like that when I was young too. It will pass, but you have to fight it. It's a transitional age, when a man hasn't yet found his feet. I'm thinking about quitting the factory and moving into an artel in the settlement. We'll try to work here: 100 extra rubles. That'll buy you a hill of beans. I'm sick and tired of going hungry. In a couple of days I'll know what I'm going to do. It is frightening to leave a state enterprise, but the artel isn't private business either. I'll try to be brave.

4/14. We've had a real cold spell for two days now; it feels like winter. At night the temperature goes all the way down to 15–20 degrees of frost. I can't recall when it's been this bad. It's really incredible. The ice hasn't budged. The starlings have disappeared. I went out to get firewood, and my hands froze stiff. Yesterday I got some time off, and today I'm going to work at the Collective Farm office, which is all smoky from makhorka. We'll see how things are there. Here's what I'm thinking: *The state is messing around with State Farms and Collective Farms, some plunder the treasury, others are go hungry and curse their lot. And in general, things just aren't working. But what if it were like this: an agricultural country, the government uses its money to buy bread from citizens at the market and then sells it as it sees fit. Instead of merchants and their managers it would be Soviet officials going to market. There would be plenty of bread. And people's lives would be easier and more economical, there wouldn't be as many expenses and hassles, and we would be free of the bondage of the collective system. They'll come around in another 100 years. Right now they're enjoying trying to run things themselves. Meanwhile the farmers take the whole harvest into town, then, cursing and complaining, they turn and go back home with their 500 grams a head. Starving and suffering the whole way.*

4/17. Snow flurries; a chill in the air. Though yesterday felt just like spring and the starlings were chirping gaily by their nests. So Yevdokiya was right: the cold weather has dragged on and on; we've had frost every morning since Annunciation Day. Thirty more days of frost. I've started working in the Collective Farm office. I'm not used to working this way, and I don't enjoy it: people sit around smoking and shooting the breeze, and we wind up not getting anything done. The work falls by the wayside. Saburov is a good man, but he drags it out for days. I'd gotten used to the factory whistle, and it's annoying to sit there all day long and then have to come in in the evening as well. I'm still hesitating. We'll see. Yesterday I took the belt to Arseny for playing with coins. They have this game called "chika." He screamed and yelled, "I'm sorry Papa, I won't do it any more." I must have really hurt him, because he wet himself. I did feel sorry for him, but you have to fight it.

4/19. The frost is hanging on. I had a dream about travelling somewhere; I can see mountains and a river. *On the right is a beautiful church. Could it be a prison? I'm afraid of it.*

5/1. Those dreams were starting to frighten me so much that I hid all my literature from myself and held out till the First of May. Apparently there was nothing seriously wrong; they were just ordinary dreams after all. The First of May. Great Saturday: cold, frost. The starlings are making their nests; the hunters are bringing ducks home, but it's an unusually cold spring. There's still some danger of flooding. It's gotten dry. People are decorating for the holiday, etc. Today the workers set their achievements out on display. Yesterday I saw the artillery; everything is perfect, in fine shape. The Red Army is mighty indeed, and maybe indefeatable. Liza is cooking bliny and has gotten herself all worked up: everything gets on her nerves. I slept well last night and I feel all right. *I borrowed Gladkov's book,*[27] *but it turns out I'd already read it once. What nonsense.* I joined the artel. It's all smoky from that makhorka, but it's no worse than at the factory. We'll give the Collective Farm a try. Easter. A fine, warm, dry day. We had a delicious dinner, and everyone got enough to eat. Liza and I visited practically everyone in the family. Misha played two waltzes by Chopin, and I broke down in tears. The sounds of the immortal composer just scraped my soul. His waltz no. 7 is full of tender sadness, full of deep tenderness for the irretrievable past. I long to put this into words, every note is so dear to me, so much a part of my long-suffering soul. I started sobbing and just barely pulled myself together. An overwhelming, almost shocking impression. I had heard this waltz before, but I was young then and my soul had not yet experienced all this grief; at the time I couldn't understand everything the composer had put into the music. Chopin understood the human soul and he spoke eloquently in the language of music. My brother does play well and he has a profound understanding of music. *I kept wanting to speak in time to the music, using words. Wonderful words about the past. My soul longs for it so; the present is so disgustingly crude and false!*...We talked about the Germans. A coarse nation, but think of all the remarkable people it gave to the world: Beethoven, Chopin, Goethe, Wagner, and so many others. They were all geniuses in the true sense of the word, and geniuses are not born into the lower races.

5/5. A cold, gloomy spring. Though the frost is gone, the leaves still haven't started coming out. I did some digging in the garden. I tire so easily: I am 50 after all, not 25, and starvation rations are bad fuel. Not everyone these days is strong and well fed. Life is terribly empty and boring, judging from the newspapers: not a peep about any other way of life, not the slightest glimmer of hope. The military commissars are throwing their weight around, and not entirely without basis. But on the other hand, we always have done a lot of bragging in the past, and a lot of losing, too. Long live great men! And many thanks for our happy life. *The newspapers are going on and on about how people abroad are celebrating the First of May, but not a word about all the charming things going on at home. An insidious and tenacious machine.*

5/9. Last night we had a fairly heavy snowfall, the wind stirred up the snow all day long. There's a snowdrift a meter thick up against our fence. In general, it has ruined the whole scene. The ducks and geese have come back because of the extreme cold up north. Today the starlings disappeared, the chirping of our winged friends has fallen silent. All the warmth has left our hut. I sent some more harsh criticism about our factory to the editors. Some day I'll really get myself in trouble: they'll get me for slandering decent people. The wisest thing would seem to be just to avoid saying anything at all. But it's like an itch — you just can't resist. What can you do? I'm beginning to get used to my new job. I may have been right to leave the factory. What we're going through here is somehow not like real life: it's as though we're constantly waiting for something. Though the power of the earth seizes hold of you; Genya and I have made a lot of progress turning over the soil; we've covered half the lot already.

5/12. The sun gives warmth, but the wind takes it away. We're digging in the garden. It's not so bad after all: a good family can feed itself with just a spade. I've been feeling especially run-down recently; I feel like a broken man. The weather could still turn bad on us: I've gotten so I can tell in advance. Things are going on as usual. The smoke bothers me, but otherwise it's not bad. The "bosses" stop in, have a smoke or maybe two, they stink up the place, spit on the floor and leave content. What can you do?!

5/26. I wore myself out in the garden: Genya and I dug up the whole lot twice over. I don't sleep much, I'm not getting enough to eat, and so I'm irritable and I pick on Liza and the kids, who have enough to deal with already, with exams going on. It's gotten hot. We could really use some rain, but instead we get powerful winds, and the rain just can't seem to get through. Right now it's blowing so hard that the sawdust is sprinkling down from the ceiling, and I keep thinking the window is about to get blown right out of its frame. In the evenings I go down to the river to get firewood ready for winter; it's not too early to start stocking up. Yesterday the first drawing of the latest bond lottery went through in Moscow. If only just one of our tickets would hit! But what are the chances of that happening? This happiness somehow keeps passing us by…Dream on.

6/6. Stifling heat. My day off. Instead of taking it easy, I wore myself out, I went to the bazaar and wandered around the flea market. What a life! The people gorge themselves and drink. Everything is as it should be. Our pilots have landed at the North Pole, and now we are making a great show of our pride. *They'll slide around on the ice up there, pocket their extra travel money, run up an incredible expense account and fly on home, where the fools will shower them with flowers, and as a result the state will have to increase its budgeted expenses for scientific discoveries and add a kopeck or two to what they charge the poor slobs who don't go up in airplanes. What is there to gain from sliding around on the thick polar ice? If you ask me, not a thing. But bragging, portraits, the names of great men in the newspapers, no shortages here. Well, let them amuse themselves.*

6/19. At last we've gotten our rain. The land, which had gotten so parched, now makes squelching noises under my feet. All nature rejoices at the rain: the seeds are well rested and all they need now is a few sunny days to bring them up out of the ground and make them bloom. The birds have fallen silent, but at the first sign of sun they'll come to life and start their joyful chirping and singing. The kids have finished their exams. They got good marks. Now we want to pile up some working days. Oh Lordy. I started corresponding with Labuta. There is already some possibility of getting sent there. We'll wait and see, we'll think it over. Today I dreamed I went fishing and caught a carp with silver scales and a bird's tail. *An interesting dream. The GPU[28] has uncovered a whole group of high-ranking secret agents, including Marshall Tukhachevsky. The usual executions. A replay of the French Revolution. More suspicion than fact. They have learned from the French how to kill one's own.*

6/30. Summer is really upon us now, hot and stuffy. The rain brought out the grass and the crops. Life goes on as before; we still don't have enough to eat. But we haven't given up yet. I even spoil myself a little: I've gone in to town, I treat myself to something extra to eat now and then. I'm stealing from the family. That's what it amounts to. If we are to eat normally, we need no less than 35 rubles a day, and we're spending 5–10 rubles per person.... Is that really so much? Meat is 3 rubles for 400 grams. 100 grams of butter: 1.50. What about groats? Sugar? Milk? Why bother calculating? No wonder I look like the living dead. Thank God, we're used to it; it's been going on for over two decades now. And how long will it go on? Everything is fine, everything is as it should be.... *No wonder the pilots work so hard: they don't care about conquering the North Pole, they just want get something to eat. In addition to their regular salary with all those extra zeroes, they got a bonus of 25,000 rubles. They can make it through a whole year without hunger! One of Gorbunov's[29] characters hit the nail on the head: "You can't fly away from the good life."* They do their flying, get what's coming to them, get kissed. They flew across the Pole non stop all the way to San Francisco. *They carried out Stalin's itinerary. Conquerors!* The flight is all over the latest newspapers. *In addition to their main specialty, all the pilots have made valiant efforts in the writ-*

ing profession as well: Vodopyanov even wrote a play, A Pilot's Dream. Yes, they do have something to tell about. In any case, these aren't coachmen we're talking about here. For some reason the latest edition has nothing about the heroes. They went to a reception given by the President. They'll get a good solid meal and give some speeches through an interpreter. Most likely I'm not writing purely from envy: this kind of success doesn't appeal to me. That's the kind of man I am; without "flights" of fancy and ecstasy.

7/8. Time flies so quickly! Sometimes it even scares me. But it's really true; we're always in the air, flying somewhere. We fly and we live. Butterflies and insects even manage to make love on the wing. We've had some rain and thunder. Haymaking has started to the music of the rain. Things are going on as they should. Even here I've found the magic cap of invisibility. Will it make things better for me or not? Our meager bread rations lie in front of me on the table. The kids are sleeping to the sound of the rain, after their hard day of weeding. The samovar is starting to gurgle. A disgruntled sparrow is chirping outside the window: he doesn't like rain. We continue our conjugal life. It turns out everything is as it should be. But if it should bear fruit, then we're in real trouble. But then God gives us the day, he will feed us too. We'll get something, at least. After all, we are still alive! We've been through worse, and we can get by on what we have. I need to get ready for work, it does put food on the table. Everything is calm at Shipka. The happy citizens of the USSR are signing up for defense bonds with unprecedented enthusiasm. *They peeled me for 100 rubles too.* And the rain just keeps pouring down. Some of the crop may rot out in the fields. Well, we'll eat what we get, even if it's rotten. We have enough enthusiasm for that.

7/22. The heat is gone; it's cold again, almost freezing. In the morning we had to wear mittens. The wind has been blowing from the north for several days now. We spend a lot of time working in the field, and there's no time for writing. I can't remember another summer when it was so cold in July we had to sleep in our fur coats.

7/27. Finally it's warm again, after the unusual cold spell; a warm rain just passed through, and now the sun is peeking through the clouds. I pile up working days and pick on the kids for not being tough enough. Of course, there's no point in picking on them, I prefer them reserved and quiet to what they would be like if they were tough. *But won't the mongrels just peck such gentle children to pieces?! We continue to live hand to mouth.*

NOTES

[1] Aleksandr Vasilevich Kolchak, 1874–1920, Arctic explorer and naval officer, flag captain of the Baltic fleet at the outbreak of World War I, then vice admiral of the Black Sea fleet. In 1918, a military coup d'état in Omsk brought him absolute power in this region. In 1919–20, he was regarded by the Whites as supreme ruler of Russia. After his overthrow in January 1920, he was executed by the Bolsheviks.

[2] Ukrainian Cossack leader of the seventeenth century, who betrayed Peter the Great when he joined Charles XII at the battle of Poltava. The author refers certainly to Pushkin's poem "Poltava," in the double context of the preparation of the 1937 Pushkin commemorative celebrations and the image of Mazepa as a national traitor.

[3] Young Pioneer. Member of the Pioneer organization, a youth movement founded in 1922 as a junior branch of the Komsomol. The movement was guided by the Communist Party and was open to children aged ten to fifteen. Although membership was not officially compulsory, almost all children of these ages were members. The organization had adopted some features of the Scout movement: it held camps, festivals, sport gatherings, and so forth. The red neckerchief was used by young pioneers as part of their uniform.

[4] Famous Russian utopian novel of 1863 which became a "classic" in the Soviet period.

[5] Russian traditional dance song of humorous character.

[6] Reference to Anton Pavlovich Chekhov's 1898 story "The Man in a Case," which became the paradigmatic illustration of retreat and concealment.

[7] Article 58 of the Penal Code for "Counterrevolutionary Agitation."

[8] The Eighth (Extraordinary) Congress of the Soviets which adopted the new constitution on 5 December 1936.

[9] See "Chronicle of the Year 1937," note 14.

[10] The expression "wolf's ticket" refers to a document (or passport) of the Tsarist times indicating the unrealiability of its bearer, preventing access to state service, learning institutions, etc.

[11] See "Chronicle of the Year 1937," note 27.

[12] Enacted in 1936, realized on 5 January 1937, this census was never made public. The reasons were, among others, the high number of citizens who declared themselves to be religious believers. The Soviet government voided the census by the decree of 27 September 1937, under the pretext that "it had been realized in profound violation of elementary statistical rules and of governmental instructions."

[13] Joseph Stalin's patronymic.

[14] Stalin's involvement in plotting a spectacular holdup in Tiflis (Tbilisi) on 25 June 1907, in order to "expropriate" funds for the Party.

[15] Reference to the Pushkin Centennial. See "Chronicle of the Year 1937," note 16.

[16] Orthodox Christmas.

[17] Film by the Vasiliev brothers of 1934, after the novel of the same title by Dmitry Furmanov. It emphasized the "class essence" of the civil war and the organizing and leading role of the Party during the struggle. *Chapaev* became the first experiment with totalized state demand, as marked by the well-known lead story in *Pravda* of 21 November 1934: "The Whole Country is Watching *Chapaev*."

[18] The Second Moscow Trial ("Trial of the Seventeen") of 23–30 January 1937.

[19] See "Chronicle of the Year 1937," note 13.

[20] Karl Bernhardovich Radek (Karl Sobelsohn), 1885–1939? Communist propagandist and revolutionary, early leader of the Communist International (Comintern), expelled from the Party in 1927 as a Trotskyite, readmitted in 1929, he adopted a pro-Stalin position and was made member of the newspaper *Izvestiya*, where he wrote extensively on foreign events. He was also appointed in 1935 to the commission that prepared the 1936 Soviet constitution. In October 1936 he was arrested and accused of Trotskyite conspiracy. In January 1937, at the second Moscow trial, he confessed his guilt to the fabricated charge and was sentenced to 10 years in prison. Despite rumors of his release in 1941, it is commonly assumed that he died in 1939 in prison or a labor camp.

[21] See "Chronicle of the Year 1937," note 20.

[22] The other "great Georgian" was Joseph Stalin.

[23] The great Don Cossack epic for which Mikhail Sholokhov (1905–1984) received the Nobel Prize in 1965. The authorship of the novel (published between 1928 and 1940) was questioned, however.

[24] Felt boots worn during great chills, which become useless when the snow starts to melt or when it rains.

[25] The novel *The Rebellion* (1925), by Dmitry Furmanov, is devoted to the struggle of Soviet power against a rebellion in Central Asia.

[26] The *lishentsy* (people deprived of civil rights) were "class aliens" who belonged to the former priveleged classes before the revolution. Targeted since 1918, the category of *lishentsy* was abolished in 1935.

[27] Fyodor Vasilievch Gladkov, 1883–1958, famous for his *Cement*, one of the first "production novels" of the Soviet era. First published in 1925, the novel was constantly rewritten by its author over thirty-three years and was one of the most often printed books of the Soviet Union. Arzhilovsky probably refers to Gladkov's second novel *Energy* (1932–38), dealing with the construction of the Dneproges hydroelectric plant.

[28] Acronym for "State Political Administration," that is, the security police organ, which replaced the Extraordinary Commission (Cheka) in February 1922 and was transformed into the United State Political Administration (OGPU) in 1923.

[29] Ivan Fyodorovich Gorbunov, 1831–1895, writer and actor. Master of oral storytelling on popular themes.

PHOTOGRAPH OF SHTANGE'S HUSBAND AND NEWSPAPER ARTICLES ABOUT HIM

GALINA VLADIMIROVNA
SHTANGE

Galina Shtange's diary, entitled "Remembrances," spans the years 1932 to 1936. The excerpts here are from her 1936 diary, which also includes her autobiography, "G.V. Shtange, wife of a professor of the Moscow Electromechanical Institute of Railroad Engineers (MEMIIT)," provided at the request of the All-Union Conference of the wives of the Commanders in the transportation field of the People's Commissariat of Communication and Transportation.

Galina Vladimirovna Shtange was born in 1885 in Leningrad. Her father was an engineer. Describing her education, Galina Shtange cites two classes of institute, followed by the entire curriculum of the gymnasium with an additional course in pedagogy. In 1903 she married Dmitry Aleksandrovich Shtange, who, at the time of writing is a professor at the Moscow Electromechanical Institute of Railroad Engineers. During the period covered by the diary, she was the mother of three sons and one daughter, and she had a twelve-year-old granddaughter and two grandsons (one, two and a half years old, and the other eight months).[1]

Under the special heading of "community work" Shtange mentions a series of personal contributions to society that she had made since 1905, including the organization of amateur performances for school children and warm meals for students of the railway school, as well as nursing in a hospital during World War I. She had to give up her social activities during the troubled period of the postwar era. Having on her hands "a sick mother, four children, a kitchen garden and a cow," she was forced to "concentrate all her strength on feeding and raising her children." The difficulties she experiences in pursuing her "community work" and other social activities due to the worries of every day life is one of the main themes of both Shtange's diary and her "autobiography." In 1919 Galina Shtange worked as an accountant in the Administration of the Northern Railways but had to quit her work again because of the illness and death of her mother. In 1922, while living in the settlement of Udelnaya, she was elected member of the settlement Soviet, member of the jury, and then judge of the

People's Court. In 1922 she took care of a girl rescued from the Volga region during the famine, gave her an education, and sent the girl back to her older brother after three years. Then, once again, Shtange was obliged to abandon her social work because she had to take care of a family of fourteen people.

In 1933 she resumed her community work by organizing amateur theater performances in the settlement of Udelnaya. In 1934 she moved to Moscow. On 13 May 1936 she joined the women's movement with the wives of the Commanders in the Transportation Field of the People's Commissariat of Communication and Transportation. She was present during the first organizational meeting, where the women were given their first directives as to what kind of work was appropriate for them. Shtange started with planting trees and bushes in her courtyard. There followed a number of activities within the organization, such as presentations on the women's movement for recruiting purposes and missions to collect information about women's work. In October 1936 Shtange was member of the presidium at a meeting devoted to the struggle of the Spanish people, organized by the wives of the workers of the Moscow section of the People's Commissariat of Communication and Transportation. In December of the same year, she was a participant "by invitation" at the All-Union Conference of the Wives of Red Army Commanders. On 24 December 1936 she was present at a banquet for "Lazar Moiseevich" [Kaganovich]. On 7 December 1936 she had partial charge of the kindergarten of the Moscow Electromechanical Institute of Railroad Engineers, where she worked "until the present day." Galina Shtange's autobiography does not mention that her husband was in prison in 1928, probably in relation to Stalin's persecutions of the technical intelligentsia at the end of the 1920s. The diary does.

Shtange's diary is a perfect example of what Philippe Lejeune has called the "diary-herbarium," where elements of every day life enter into a dynamic with the thread of the handwritten text[2]: parallel to the chronicle of her daily life, Galina Shtange pastes *onto the pages of her diary invitation cards for a banquet at the Kremlin, published photographs (for example, a snapshot of her husband with Kaganovich), letters from her relatives, newspaper articles. Shtange's "diary-herbarium" magnificently illustrates some recent interpretations of the theory of text. To use Roland Barthes's formulation, the text is like a woven cloth (this is its etymology); previous criticism put its emphasis on the finished product, the text being considered as "a veil behind which the truth has to be found, the real message, in other words, its* meaning...." *Now the very texture of the cloth has come to the forefront of reading, and meaning is born out of the materiality of discourse, out of an interlacing of codes in which the subject moves forward and unravels, like a spider that dissolves itself in its own web.*

DIARY OF GALINA VLADIMIROVNA SHTANGE

Remembrances

May 2, 1936. After a full day's work, Mitya and I decided to take a walk and enjoy the sights of Moscow celebrating the holiday. It's not that simple these days just to go out for an evening stroll! All Moscow has turned out to celebrate, and the streets and squares are clogged with cheerful people in their holiday best. Decorative lights illuminate the streets and there's music everywhere. All the streets have been decorated, some more than others, but the center of the city is simply indescribable. In the central squares the artists tapped deep into their imaginations to illustrate the theme of this year's celebration: "A happy Childhood." Stalin loves children dearly and does absolutely everything he can to make their lives happy. By the way, they've recently opened a children's theater in the building of the former Second Moscow Art Theater. The company of this theater was sent out into the provinces, since it was of inferior quality, and the facility was promptly made over to accommodate the children's theater.

The organizer of the theater is Natalia Sats.[3] Our young artists Irina and her husband helped paint the murals.

May 5. Today I went to the Academy of Sciences to see if any progress has been made on the dachas. We got on the list in the fall of 1935, when Mitya became a member of the Academy of Sciences' dacha-building cooperative. As a member of the presidium of the transportation commission of the Academy of Sciences, Mitya had the right to join. Now we can look forward to having, at some point in the future, our own house and garden — small though they may be — outside Moscow, at the "42-nd Kilometer" Station of the Kazan Railway line.

May 13, 1936. Over the last few days the whole Soviet Union has been eagerly following the reports in the newspapers about a wonderful new women's movement. The initiators, wives of the Commanders of the People's Commissariat of Heavy Industry, called upon all the women in the country to join the movement, and there was an immediate response from the wives of the Commanders in the transportation field—the People's Commissariats of Communication and Transportation (PCCT) and of Roads.

And to my surprise I find myself a member of the organizational group representing the wives of the Commanders of the PCCT.

I was sitting at home, preoccupied with my own narrow little family affairs, when Zabelina came over and invited me to take part in an informal meeting with several other ladies from the PCCT who wanted to join the movement. Naturally I agreed.

After a very brief discussion of our intentions, we wrote a letter to Comrade Zimin, Head of the Political Division of the PCCT, expressing our desire to join in the overall effort to improve the lives of workers in the transport sector. We asked Zimin to meet with us as soon as possible, since we wanted to deliver our letter to him personally. It was already 11 in the evening by the time we met with his secretary. The late hour didn't stop us, since we all knew that the PCCT leadership works until 2 or 3 in the morning.

[...]

As I think back over the past, I recall that I always used to enjoy community activities, but that was way back before the Revolution, and I'll be writing about that later. After the revolution things were hard for my large family, and all my energy was spent on the struggle to protect them from adversity. But still I did try several times during those years to get involved in community work. Most notably, when we were living in Udelnaya, I was elected to the Village Council. I didn't last there for long; there was a blatant campaign to rid the Council of an "aristocrat," which was how they viewed me at the time. It was very insulting, and I turned in my resignation.

[...]

Afterwards people kept trying to get me involved in club activities, but I had to turn them down because I had absolutely no free time. Still, in 1932 I managed to put together some excellent plans for the Woman's Day celebration on March 8 in the Udelnaya Club. Unfortunately there was a huge snowstorm and all my efforts came to nothing—the celebration fell through. The storm brought down the electric wires, the performers couldn't make it, and practically no one showed up.

After that we moved to Moscow. We moved into the PCCT building on Novaya Basmannaya Street. This apartment building had been assigned a

wonderful activities manager, a much-decorated Party member. He immediately got to work organizing the housewives and set aside an excellent
room for the "Red Corner."

The "Red Corner" is something like a club, a place where people living
in a particular area—in our case, the apartment building—can get
together for work or entertainment. All kinds of special activity circles
were organized for the housewives to raise their political consciousness
or study music, singing, and needlework: a circle called OSOAVIAKhIM,[4]
for training Voroshilov[5] sharpshooters and cadres for chemical weapons
defense; a circle for the regional branch of the Red Cross, one for literacy,
one for protecting childhood, etc. Of these, I went through the civil medical defense and chemical weapons defense training, and at present I have
two badges certifying my completion of that training. I wanted to join the
permanent medical defense squad of our building, but unfortunately my
age (51) and the state of my health (a bad heart) won't allow me to sustain
such physically demanding work. Still, I consider myself obliged to be
ready for any encounter with enemies, which we have plenty of and therefore I plan to enroll in a nursing course in the fall.

May 14, morning. Last night, caught up in the enthusiasm of the people
around me, I boldly joined the women's movement. But this morning I
woke up in fear that my physical strength will be inadequate and that I
won't be able to do as much as I should or would like to.

Evening[…] We were all in the meeting hall by 8. It is a wonderful room,
very modestly furnished. Pogrebinsky from the Political Division was
already there, he was in charge of our meetings. Fourteen people were
selected to work as an executive organizational subgroup for liason with
the Political Division and the Local Committee. Then Pogrebinsky gave
us a list of potential areas of work. It turns out that the PCCT has dormitories for workers and young people, 3 kindergartens, nurseries for children, Pioneer Camps, cafeterias, buffets, literacy circles, a children's
wilderness sanitarium in Malakhovka, PCCT and branch clinics, amateur
theatricals, cultural improvements in the workplace environment, flowers, ornamental gardens, installation of banners and slogans in PCCT
buildings, Red Cross, OSOVIAKhIM, libraries, workers' projects, such as
a mechanical accounting office, motor transport depots, a newspaper—
Gudok (The Whistle)—, schools, gymnasiums, and a children's resort near
Anapa-Belimag. After he finished his list, I asked whether the PCCT had

a rest home for invalids and elderly retired people, former workers in the transportation field who don't have any families. He answered that, though he was ashamed to admit it, he didn't know. Then we started figuring out who wanted to work in what area. I gave my name and said I'd like to work with the dormitories. He says, "But Shtange! You really have to make a contribution, since your husband is such an important person." I felt a sudden hot wave of joy come over me when I heard these words that characterize my dear Papanechka so well. On the other hand I was terrified: would I be able to do as much as I should? "Noblesse oblige!" Tomorrow I'll get down to work, I'll try to measure up to those expectations that Pogrebinsky talked about. I've gotten together with Grozdova, an activist from our building, and I'll go see her tomorrow at 10 a.m. for a meeting to discuss the details of how we're going to proceed.

May 17. Yesterday I was called to our institute for a preliminary meeting with the party organizer of the Institute to discuss the progress of the women's movement, and they asked me to give a speech at the general meeting on the significance of the movement.

I'm afraid that I won't be able to do it—I've never spoken in front of a large number of people, except maybe in an amateur theater production.

Right now I'll try to write down all the different thoughts that are taking shape in my mind.

"Comrades, my fellow women, allow me to express my views about the women's movement that came into being gradually in various corners of our country and has now manifested itself as a powerful surge of energy.... You see, I'm already quite old, but this wonderful movement has taken such hold of me that I just can't sit idly by. I feel, I am aware that I must bring my life, small as it may be, and place it on the alter of our fatherland. Let us begin modestly, for it is out of small streams that great currents emerge...."

There was an eclipse of the sun on June 19, Aleksei Maksimovich Gorky died[6].

[...]

August 27. So much for my community work! To tell the truth, I assumed that it would come to this, but still I had no idea it would happen so soon. I was completely engrossed in my work for two months. I found my element and felt wonderful, in spite of being so tired. I managed to get some things done; and I could have done a lot more, but such was not my fate! Circumstances will not let me be distracted, even for a moment, from what's going on at home. Borya had a son on August 15 and neither of us has a maid, in fact they don't even have an adequate place to live. Just a single ten-meter room and of course there's absolutely no way for him and Dinochka and the newborn baby to fit into it, along with their furniture, all the baby things and the little bathtub. He was told he'd get an apartment by around September 15, but for now they will have to live out at the dacha.

And I just can't leave them to their own devices. I feel awfully sorry for them, the poor things, and I have to come to their aid at this difficult time. So I decided to give up the work that I love so much, and take up cooking, dishwashing, and diapers agian.

It's hard enough for me to take care of even my own personal affairs.

Right now there's a possibility of exchanging our apartment for a better one, but I'm afraid I might have missed my chance because of the baby. I feel so awful when I think about my darling children, I'm in such despair, I could just cry.

Here they are, in order:

Boris, a marvelous person, smart, gifted, and an extremely conscientious worker, but things just haven't worked out for him in life.

He married for the first time when he was only 20, to Irina's friend Olga Baeva. They had a daughter, Ninochka, a charming girl. Olga is a very decent person — a wonderful mother, a beautiful woman, a hard worker, and outgoing, but she's got an evil streak, just like her mother. The two of them together tormented Boris for seven years until finally they got divorced. After a year and a half in the doldrums he married again, even less happily. His second wife was a young woman who was interesting and not unintelligent, but neither of them had a speck of love for the other. Plus she turned out to be quite sickly and didn't have the slightest inclination to start a family. So it was that they came together without love, and so too, without discord, they went their separate ways.

Again he pined away in solitude for some time, until he met Dina and married her.

They're into their second year of marriage, and apparently they love each other, but their life is not happy. To begin with, Borya has worked in out-of-the-way places, in unhealthy conditions; it really ruined his health, and he even started to lose his hearing. He keeps going for treatment, but it doesn't do much good. Because of his bad hearing, in spite his many wonderful qualities and all his knowledge, he hasn't been able to advance in his career.

Right now he's an acting sector chief in the Stations Department with a salary of 700 rubles, and for now that looks like about as far as he's going to go. He's held back at work, and it causes him no end of suffering. Naturally they're always short of money; he has to set aside 200 rubles for his daughter Ninochka. He's constantly on the lookout for piecework, which is very hard to come by these days. In general money is a constant struggle for them. He has a hard life, the poor thing, and I can't do anything to help; it's hard on me too.

They named their son Andrei. A wonderful boy, he's growing and developing marvelously. Dina takes excellent care of him; she's patient and loving.

August 28, 1936. Irunechka has a hard life too. She's an artist. She married Boris Shatilov, a classmate from art school. They got married when Mitya was in prison and we were in desperate straits, materially speaking, so I couldn't set her up properly with the things she needed, and I had no money to give her either.

They moved in with Boris's parents in a room that was so small that you could only sit or stand in it, there was no question of taking a step in any direction.

They lived in that tiny little room for two years, I'm amazed that they managed to keep their sanity. Utter destitution. They decorated handkerchiefs for pocket money, but they were too proud to ask their parents for anything. Gradually they adjusted and managed to go out and find work for themselves. After two years they got a fairly good room. But it's just one room for the two of them, along with their easels and all the things they use for their painting. In short, they really get in each other's way. Plus they have to do everything themselves; there's no room for a maid, though they could afford one.

My poor little girl has to cook, clean, mend and fix things, wash dishes, and do all the other little things that have to be done around the house, earn enough to live on, and, most importantly, to develop as an artist, which is everything to her. She's exhausted and her nerves are worn ragged. Plus Boris has a difficult personality—he's coarse, selfish and inclined to jealousy.

Irunechka is already a recognized artist who gets good reviews in the press. Her work is included in all the exhibits, and she has a 500 ruble a month contract with the state. She got a state commission—a large painting to commemorate the 20th anniversary of the October Revolu-

tion — and she's already done the scenery for several stage productions.
[...]

October 5, 1936. Today is the long-awaited day! Today our dear Vov arrived with his family from the Far East.

Vov, my own adored darling son, dear, quiet Valyusha, and wonderful little Sanechka!

I love you all so dearly, Papa and I are so happy that you're back, we'll help you so much, we'll take such good care of you!

My only regret is that we can't arrange decent living conditions for you.

What joy to be all together again! It weighed on us like a heavy stone to have Vov out living out there in the Far East with his education incomplete, and now that stone is gone at last!
[...]

October 15, 1936. Well I've just been to Rostov, and now I'm on my way home, thinking back on the four and a half days I spent there.

On the morning of the 10th Perfilyeva, the chairman of the Women's Council came from the Administration to pick me up. She took me to the Political Department to see the women's affairs coordinator, Com. Perepetailo, who gave me a warm welcome.
[...]

We went first to the Lenin Locomotive Works. The women had been given advance notice about our visit; they met us at the factory entrance and took us to a room that the factory had put at their disposal. The room was fairly large, and it had been decorated with flowers and slogans. In the middle of the room stood a large table, covered with a red tablecloth. The whole Wives' Council, plus stenographers, was already there waiting for us.
[...]

They seemed just delighted to see me. They seated me at the center of the table, and we had our picture taken. I also told them about the purpose of my visit, and then the activists from each brigade reported on their work.

I listened and took notes for five hours. Without a break, so I got terribly tired. Then they took me around the shops in the factory so I could see with my own eyes the improvements they had made there and on the factory grounds. As I went around and looked at everything, I was very moved at how concerned the women are for the worker and his workplace. The workers gave us a warm welcome. Nowadays workers are no longer surprised when women show up in the shops; they have come to see us as their most solicitous helpmates. Between the reports and the tour of the shops we went to the cafeteria where we were served a good, delicious lunch. The cafeteria is large and clean, with small tables covered with white oil cloth, curtains, flowers, and large white towels hanging by the washstand. All the staff wear white smocks. Everything was remarkably neat and well organized.

Upstairs there's a wonderful café where they have accordion-playing in the evenings. It was already dark when we left the factory, and the entire Council came all the way out to the car to see us off. As we were crossing the factory courtyard, the women picked a bouquet of flowers for me from the flower beds that they had planted themselves all over the factory grounds, in places where there used to be mountains of scrap and rubbish lying around. There was no end to their delight at my visit. "We're so glad, so glad," they said, "that someone has taken an interest in our work. Now we will go back to our work with renewed enthusiasm."

"Give our greetings to Comrade Sypacheva and tell her that we wish she would come see us more often." The next morning we went back to the Lenin Factory and were taken around the children's nurseries, the dormitory for workers coming in from the line, the construction site for the kindergarden that would accomodate 100 children, and the store in the huge apartment building. This store had been planned, built and furnished exclusively by women, and they continually monitor the delivery of goods and make sure that there are no violations. The women have put so much energy and love into all this work (I attach my notes, which give a more detailed description of the work of these women). From there we went straight back into town to see Administration's children's home and the Red Corners in the railroad workers' apartment buildings, where women work with the children. In both places the children made a presentation first, and then we heard reports by activists from the women's volunteer groups. I sat through 6 hours of speeches without getting up, taking notes almost the whole time. Very impressive. The children in the children's home are healthy and happy—they sang and danced. They're polite, clean, and affectionate. They just adore Perfilyeva, they call her "our Mamochka."

[...]

When I left, they asked me to pass on their greetings to Comrade Stalin and L. M. Kaganovich.[7] I laughed and cried at the sight of these children, who had been brought in off the street, and are now so happy, healthy and decently dressed. The Red Corners were decorated with beautiful artwork

by the children, so neat and carefully done. From there, straight to the theater. The theater is huge and luxurious. The outside is perhaps a little
too daring in design, but the interior, though not lavishly decorated, still
has extremely tasteful forms and colors. The performers were good too.

I stayed up half the night writing. The next day, more nurseries, dormitories and a sanatorium for 400 children. The nurseries and dormitories are
beautiful. The children are much better off in these nurseries than at home,
all their needs are taken care of. The sanatorium simply amazed me. In a
dacha district outside town there's a beautiful garden with nice, clean little
houses in it. Charming little outfits and pajamas and masses of toys. You
simply can't believe you're in a medical institution. Bedrooms, playrooms,
dining rooms, each better than the one before, all of them furnished with
great care. They have doctors of all different specialities on their staff, and
once a month professors come and make rounds. There is a nurse too. The
children are from two to four years old, they gain up to three kilos. The windows are fitted with netting to keep the flies out, and they are all open, but
still it's quite warm, since they heat the rooms well. A beautifully equipped
shower room. There I learned that children who have the measles are being
given a new treatment that is the last word in medical science: intravenous
infusions of antimeasles serum (human). And one more thing—every day
the children are given juice made from fresh vegetables and fruits: cranber-
ries and other berries, fruits, carrots and cabbage. One glass a day. I'm
going to start giving juice to my grandchildren.

From the sanatorium we went directly to the Administration to see
Perepetailo and worked there until 11 p.m.

When I got home I sat in bed and spent the whole night writing. I was
so tired that I can't even remember going to sleep. I woke up early, before
sunrise; the light was on, all my papers and materials were scattered all
over the bed, and I was still holding the pencil. I immediately sat up and
started writing again. Then it was off to the Administration to type everything out, organize my materials and pack for the trip home. I worked
right up to the last minute, then the director of the Political Division
invited me to come see him. It's a good thing I can hold up my end of a
conversation, since I had to talk with him. He was so gracious, he regretted I hadn't seen the Caucasus Station and insisted I come back in the
spring and visit the Caucasus St., since the women there are doing wonderful work. "Thank you," I say, "but it's out of my hands. If they send me,
I'll be glad to come." "Well," he says, "we'll ask for you by name." Judging
from that, I guess I made a good impression.

I went straight from there to the train. There were no more seats in the express train, and I barely managed to catch a regular passenger train, and now here we are, taking our own sweet time. Fortunately the passengers are nice.

October 25. Today is Vanyusha's birthday, and I was out all day long. The whole family is terribly hurt because I'm away for days at a time. They laugh at me and want to draw cartoons of me. Vova is especially hurt. "We'll just have to pack our suitcases," he says, "and go on back to Khabarovsk." I simply don't know what to do — I can't give up my work, and I can't give up my family either. Tomorrow I was supposed to apply to the Local Committee to get Sashenka accepted into the nursery. Valya really wants him to go there, it's hard for her to take care of him, but I can't understand how you can entrust your own child to strangers, unless you absolutely have to, just so you can have some more free time.

October 31. I couldn't get Sanechka into the nursery. I'll just have to divide my time between family and work, which is what I'm doing at the present time. It's putting a lot of stress on me, I'm becoming exhausted and irritable.

November 1. I went to the first performance of the amateur theatrical circle organized by the Council of Wives of the PCCT Commanders. The show wasn't anything special — just the usual amateur performances. Some of them were interesting.
[...]
The women's jazz ensemble was pretty good.
Valya is upset at me because I don't help her enough — I see that and feel for her, but what can I do if I simply don't have the time?

11/11/36. To the "artists" Irina Dmitrievna Shtange and Boris Alekseevich Shatilov:

> Honorable spouses, where are you
> Irina Shtange and Boris?
> Neighbors write you, friends do too,
> Yevgeny Mister and Mistress.
> You, dear friends, may have forgot
> That Uncle Misha passed away,
> But as for us, we grieve a lot,

And we've got some words to say.

[...]

This poem was written by Irina's husband's brother, Yevgeny Shatilov, to commemorate the anniversary of the death of Uncle Misha, the husband of my aunt, my father's elder sister. They used to live in Warsaw, where Uncle Misha had spent his whole life. Then, during the war with Germany, they moved to Moscow with their two daughters, Tanya and Lida. The daughters married and moved away, my aunt died in 1920, and Uncle Misha was left all by himself in his old age. First he worked at some minor jobs, then he retired and his daughters sent him what money they could.

He was an intelligent, educated man, a real Warsaw nobleman, in general a very interesting man, but with an nasty personality. His only pleasure was to visit us at our dacha, and he took advantage of every opportunity to do so. He would come, get some relief from his solitude in a comfortable, family atmosphere and have a home-cooked meal, which he never got at home. All our children loved him dearly, since he would play cards with them and always had some interesting story to tell.

When Irina got married, she and her husband moved into a building just across the street from where Uncle Misha lived. And he started spending an awful lot of time at their place.

Ultimately his health started going rapidly downhill and on November 9, 1935 he died completely unexpectedly, after just a few days' illness. All his property went to the State, since his daughters couldn't get there in time to claim it. We took a few little things to remember him by.

When his condition became serious, Irina's husband called me to come over and stay with him. By the time I got there he was already semiconscious, but he recognized me and tried to tell me something, which I couldn't understand. He lay there on his deathbed in his room (which was more like a dump than a place where someone lived) in the early morning hours, with me sitting beside him, pitying him with all my heart, but unable to help.

The death pangs began at 4:00, his last breath rattled in his throat, and he died in my arms.

November 13. In the evening there was a meeting in our building to discuss Civil Defense planning and I was elected to the Committee of the All-Russian Red Cross Society. I pledged...rubles to help the women and children of Spain.[8]

December 4, 1936. I came back from a trip today and Vovik was gone, he'd left for Yalta.

The PCCT wants to publish a book about the work women have been doing in the transportation industry. A lot of material has been gathered, but it's still not enough. That's what my trip was for; I was sent to Vladikavkaz (now Ordzhonikidze), Makhachkala, Grozny, and Prokhladnaya. The Women's Organizer of the Northern Caucasus Railroad accompanied me everywhere. I brought back a lot of material, but I don't know whether we can use it or not. All this has caused me a lot of anxiety. It would be a real shame if I couldn't complete my task, even though it's out of my control. I mean, how could I bring what doesn't exist, what I wasn't given....

I didn't find anything to cheer me up at home either. My sons Borya and Zhenya are all worn out, they look terrible; we haven't gotten any letters from Vova, and meanwhile Olya sends bad news — Tolya nearly died of furuncular angina, and they're utterly destitute. And I don't know what I can do to help. Money is awfully tight. Mitya works terribly hard. Their wives are throwing fits. Valya says, "I've decided to take Sasha to Khabarovsk, let Vladimir stay here to finish his studies and get his degree. This way of living isn't enough for me. I want to work. I can do it in Khabarovsk, since my Mama's there and she can take care of Sasha."

In my day mothers didn't think that way, and they weren't in such a big hurry to put their babies in nurseries and dump them into the hands of strangers; they brought them up themselves. When you tell her, "But a child could very easily catch some infection in the nursery and die," she says, "Well, that's natural selection. If he makes it, that's fine, if he doesn't, there's nothing to be done about it." That's how today's young mothers think, and just imagine what it's like for me to listen to it, when I was always ready at any moment, and still am, to this very day, to give up my life for that of any one of my children.

And Tatyana is simply insufferable. She has an offensive, rude, insolent way of talking. And acting, too. I find out that Zhenya has been working every day until four or five in the morning. It turns out that she's pushing him to finish his studies at the Institute as soon as possible. I got terribly upset. What can you do with dear ones who behave like that? Patience, patience and more patience, but I don't have any. Tatyana has been working on them both, Zhenya and Valya, turning them against me. And Zhenya has been developing a bad attitude. Well, God bless them, they'll regret it someday.

My life has become somehow empty. No, not empty, it's full, but what it's full of is not mine; it belongs to others, and meanwhile what is dear to me, what is truly my own, is getting away from me, leaving me further and further behind. I gave birth to them, I brought them up, and now I'm in the way. I've got to pull myself together somehow and just make myself ignore them.

Irunechka is my pride and joy. She's good, affectionate, caring. True, I don't see her life up close, maybe I wouldn't get along with her either if we lived together. My one happiness is my Mityaechka. With him everything is reliable, stable, permanent. He won't betray me, he won't stop loving me. I am the only one in the world for him, just as he is for me.... The only thing is, we have no time to be together; our work is always coming between us, and we see and talk to each other only sporadically, both of us are tired....

I think Valya and Tanya are upset at me because I have so many interesting things to do, while they spend all their time sitting around at home. Valya because of the baby, and Tatyana because she's so lazy, she just doesn't want to get involved in anything; all she cares about is clothes, having a good time, and flirting.

December 6, 1936. Last night Stalin's new Constitution was adopted. I won't say anything about it; I feel the same way as the rest of the country, i.e., absolute, infinite delight.

Today there's been a Demonstration going on since morning, with a Parade. Everyone is cheerful, there's music and singing everywhere, the streets are full of people. Booths have been been set up with various delicacies, and there are even tables with white tablecloths, loaded with all kinds of refreshments for sale at reasonable prices. I saw with my own eyes a samovar with hot tea at the "Red Gate."

I didn't go to the demonstration, since I had given the maid the day off, and I have my hands full at home; all kinds of things have been piling up that need to be taken care of.

[...]

December 25, 1936. Today I'll write about what I've been through over the past week.

On December 18 I was invited to the PCCT to a meeting with Comrade Kabluchko, who is the Chairman of the People's Commissariat Commission for Issues related to the Women's Movement. There were 200 of us there, and they announced that the PCCT would send a delegation of women to the National Conference of Wives of Commanders of the Red Army, set to begin on December 20 in the Kremlin.

We were told that the delegation of 100 women and 50 children would include us, and in particular, me, as the chairman of the Moscow Electromechanical Institute of Railroad Engineers (MEMIIT).

[...]

Our program was decided: we would enter singing "A Spacious Land, My Native Land," then the wife of the locomotive engineer Krivonos would give a speech, then we would present our gifts, an armored train and a railway medical car, and then we would go out, singing a brand new march specially written for railway workers that's not even been printed yet, called "The Transport Sector and the Army — the Dearest of Brothers." Our whole performance was aimed at proving that indeed the Transport Sector and the Army are dear brothers.

The armored train would be presented by Krivonos and Troitskaya, wearing their medals, and people who have the "Ready for Medical Defense" badge[9] and the Red Cross sash would present the medical car. Since I have both the Medical Defense and the Air and Chemical Defense badges, I was offered the honor of presenting the car. Naturally I was very glad, since this would give me the chance to see our whole Government up close, especially Stalin, whom I love so dearly.

Rehearsals began the next day. I had already attended two rehearsals and had arrived for the third when Kabluchko called me out of the ranks and told me that I would not present the car, and would not be participating in the delegation, but would receive a guest pass into the Kremlin, for seats toward the front.

Of course that is a lot in itself, that too is a great honor and sign of trust, but still I was hurt that they could do that to me, to remove me from the delegation right in front of all the other women. I felt very embarrassed and hurt. When I went to pick up the tickets, they explained that it was just because they had severely cut the size of the delegation, and because I represent not the PCCT, but the MEMIIT. It took me a long time to calm down, but eventually some very urgent business having to do with the kindergarten took my mind off it. I'd been spending my mornings running around taking care of things at the k/garten and hadn't been attending the morning meetings. I just showed up for the evening meetings at 6:00, and the only time I spent the whole day there was the closing day of the Conference.

Since I obviously will have to tell about what I heard at MEMIIT, and most likely will have to write a report too, I won't write about that now, I'll just give my impressions.

On my way to the Kremlin I thought that when I went into the meeting hall and saw the whole Leadership, I would be more in awe, but in fact that didn't happen, since I was so far from the rostrum and the hall was so huge, that, being nearsighted anyway, I couldn't see anyone or anything clearly. All I could see were the outlines of a group of people, but I couldn't make out their faces at all.

My main reaction was a feeling of intense pride in being in the Kremlin, in this historic hall.

I listened very carefully and wrote down everything I could. The most memorable impressions for me were when the delegation of children of the commanders of the Moscow Garrison came up and Stalin reached out to them, pulled them up to the rostrum where he was standing, and enfolded two of them in his arms in a warm, fatherly embrace. It was so touching to watch that tears welled up in my eyes. The procession of children's delegates, all dressed in white sailor suits, was a beautiful sight to see. The column was led by a beautiful, radiant girl of fourteen; she was followed by a soldier and an imposing-looking woman, both of them wearing badges of distinction. Then came the flag-bearers, then a whole mass of children, the biggest ones first, then progressively on down to the smallest ones. They brought him a gift, a homemade model training aeroplane, then flowers and all kinds of toys, even a Teddy bear and a doll. It was very beautiful and touching. In general all the processions turned out well, and they brought all kinds of gifts. The Heavy Industry Delegation presented a model aeroplane and the title to a real training aeroplane. The Water-Transport Workers' Delegation presented a beautiful model steamship. A whole sea of flowers, ribbons, banners, etc. Music, singing and prolonged cheering.

On the last night of the Conference I was hurt again. I'd already left the hall when I heard that a meeting of the PCCT had been called and that everyone was going, even the people who were in the Kremlin. I was terribly worried—why hadn't I been invited? I asked everyone at home whether there had been any calls for me, but no one knew anything, and the maid was asleep. I'd concluded that for some reason I wasn't considered worthy of attending, and then in the morning the maid says, "Galina Vladimirovna, someone called yesterday about a conference at the PCCT, and I told them that you weren't here."

I was very upset at everyone at home; they couldn't care less about what

I do, and I was upset at the women, too, who apparently simply don't want me to show up at such events. And it really was an extraordinary occasion. Lazar Moiseevich Kaganovich received the women without ceremony and spoke with them very simply and directly and gave them instructions for their work in the future.

I was terribly annoyed and hurt, I even quarrelled with my friend, who hadn't bothered to think of me.

The Conference of the Wives of Red Army Commanders closed on the evening of the 23d, and on December 24 Kaganovich gave a banquet in the club for all of us, which he attended himself. He was right there with us, he talked and behaved very simply. He listened to the singing and watched the dances, and even took a turn on the dance floor himself, and afterwards even asked how he had done. Just like one of us.

I sat to Lazar Moiseevich's left and, since I was seeing him for the first time in my life, I studied his face carefully. He is rather handsome, and

Here a large, three-column clipping from the newspaper Gudok *(The Whistle) is attached to the diary page. It tells about Kaganovich's talk with the leaders and delegates of the PCCT, on the occasion of the National Confer-ence of Wives of the RKKA (Workers and Peasants Red Army).*

his eyes are simply wonderful, so expressive! Above all, enormous seren-ity and intelligence, then firmness of purpose and an unyielding will, but when he smiles, his basic goodness shows through.

He spoke a few words about what a modern woman should be like, about her place in the family and in the community, about how all women ought to work and how we need to be aware of the international situation and be ready at any moment to take the places of our husbands, brothers and sons if they go off to war. Then we went over to the big hall and the dancing started. Lazar Moiseevich was right there with us and even took a turn on the dance floor, and his wife danced some fox trots with Postnikova.

After this reception, everyone went back and started to set up meetings everywhere in the transportation sector to report on the instructions Lazar Moiseevich had given.

December 22, 1936. What Lazar Moiseevich Kaganovich said at the recep-tion for the wives of commanders in the Transport Sector.

I didn't get to go to that reception so I just noted down what Zabelina told me about it.

1. Concern for our husbands: cook good food for them, don't cause them any stress, create a comfortable home and a good relaxing family atmosphere.

2. In our movement, as in the movement of trains along the railways, there is a main route and then there are supplementary routes, and the two are not to be confused. Our primary concerns are children's institutions, community issues, literacy programs, and promoting culture. If we have any strength left over, (as when train cars carry an overload), we can join in production work as well. He will not stand in our way if we do, but that's not what's important.

3. We should not be allowed to be used as supplementary nonparty workers, or to do what paid workers ought to be doing themselves. I want you to be interest added on to our capital and not an extra force used to meet production targets. If that is the case, your movement will not be making a real contribution for me, it will just cover for what the men were unable to do themselves. I want to see you as something like inspectors, whose job it is to reveal sore spots and sound the alarm about them.

4. You yourselves are the most important thing in your movement. Your cultural, political and overall development. Study, acquire a skill, strive to be ready, in case of need, to take over your husbands' work.

5. About creating a core of activists. He will consider our movement truly significant only when all women have gotten involved.

We need to create all kinds of circles to help ourselves learn and teach others. The work should be happy and joyful.

You men will understand that it is to your advantage when your wife is active—you will feel more stable yourselves.

Of course I noted down very briefly only the most essential points.

December 27, 1936. The year is drawing to a close. It was a painful one for me. The family is upset that I spend so little time at home. I'm sorry for them, but what can I do? I'm not old yet, I still want to have a personal life. I did bring up my children, after all, and I did a good job of it too. Now that I've fulfilled my obligations to my family, in the few years that remain to me I want to live for myself; I will always be sincerely glad to help them.

My Report at the MEMIIT
on L.M. Kaganovich's reception

Comrades, our beloved People's Commissar Lazar Moiseevich Kaganovich has taken great interest in us women; he has received us and warmly encouraged us in our work. L. M. attaches great significance to our work, but he will consider our movement truly valuable only when it encompasses all women, only when every woman is uplifted, every woman who, for whatever reason, or for no reason at all, has not yet actively joined with us in the task of building a better life.

But at the same time L. M. reminds us and emphasizes that our first thoughts and concerns must always be for our husbands. The work our husbands are doing is difficult and crucial, and we must make our homes into a place where they can truly rest from their labors, we must create peace, comfort and joy for our families.

L. M. compares our movement with the movement of a railway — both have a main route and supplementary routes.

The main route of our work is the children's institutions, community issues, literacy programs, and promoting culture. And if we have any energy left over, then we can join in production work as well; he won't stand in our way, but he doesn't believe that is our main route. Then he says that we shouldn't allow ourselves to be used as unpaid reserve workers, that we shouldn't do jobs that other people who are assigned to a particular task are supposed to be doing themselves. If that happens, our work won't do anyone any good, it will all just be something extra added on to what the men have already achieved. L. M. wants to see us as something like inspectors whose job it is to reveal sore spots and sound the alarm about them.

Our work should be joyful, it's only natural; man is a social animal. He can be happy and joyful only in a collective. Leave a man alone, even in a golden palace, and his joy for living will just fade and die. Only an awareness of his usefulness to society can bring joy and satisfaction. We must not only work, but also enjoy ourselves as well. The most important thing in our work is ourselves, our cultural, political and overall development, and this is what we organize all these different activity circles for.

We must study, comrades, study and teach others, learn a skill. There are no women in our country, and there cannot be any, who would not be able to find some application for their talents.

We must also be aware of the international situation. If we are drawn into a war and our husbands, sons and brothers have to leave, we must be able to take their places at a moment's notice. Now take me for example. I won't live to see the day I could take my husband's place — he's a professor — but when I was at the Conference in the Kremlin, and when I heard Lazar Moiseevich, I decided on a course of action I would take in such a case.

And now our brigade of 4 people — Comrades Neimaier, Shumskaya, Bove and myself — is working in the kindergarten of our institutes. I started my work

*there after Com. Brodovskaya left, i.e. December 7, and in these 20 days we
have achieved the following:*

*1. We have expended the entire 35 thousand that was budgeted to the
k/garten for equipment, that is, for acquiring linen, furniture, dishes and other
necessary items. We gave the children good perennial plants and will teach
them how to take care of them. We gave them a radiola* [radio with a record
player] *and now we will have good music for our New Year's party.*

*2. Most of the material we bought has been marked and cut, and the sewing
has begun. An order has been put into the workshop for mattresses for the children's beds, based on the number of children, a total of 105.*

*3. We have conducted several conferences; at one of them we made a list of
small repair jobs that need to be done immediately, and the work has begun.*

*4. We accelerated and completed the work registering the k/garten for the
Dzerzhinsky Railroad.*

*5. We have taken action to improve the appearance of the k/garten and to
bring the playground up to standard. The poles for the canopy are in place and
electric lighting has been installed.*

6. We have begun the search for a dacha for the k/garten.

*7. We have resolved to conclude a socialist emulation agreement with
K/garten No. 1.*

*The work is being conducted with the full cooperation of the k/garten
administration. We hope that by April, when Lazar Moiseevich calls us in for a
conference, we will be able to hold our heads high before our Great, Mighty
Leader Com. Stalin and our beloved People's Commissar Lazar Moiseevich
Kaganovich.*

January 1, 1937. The New Year got off to a bad start. Mitya got the flu. Today
Dina suddenly fell ill, she either caught cold or got the flu from Mitya. A
sudden high fever and chills. It gave Borya a real scare, and he called me.
When I went over there I was shocked; she's just lying there, crying:

"I'm so tired," she says, "I just can't go on." And how could it be otherwise, there she is all alone, having to do everything all by herself. The baby,
washing the diapers, taking the baby out, the cooking and cleaning. All
they have is 10 meters; they can't take on a nanny, there's no room for one.

Now Dina's sick, so Borya has no place to sleep. They have a folding cot,
but there's no place to put it, there's no room. Borya decided to put three
sofa cushions on the floor and sleep on them. It's just horrible when you
think about how people live these days, and engineers in particular.

I heard about one engineer, who lives with his wife in a 9-meter room.
When his mother came to visit, there was absolutely no place for him to
do his work. So he put the lamp on the floor and lay down (on his stom-

ach under the table) and worked that way, he couldn't put it off, he had a deadline.

I wrote down this example so that those who come after us will read it and get a sense for what we went through.

January 8. At last Borya got a 20-meter room and they're moving today. Though there was an ugly scene when they turned in the old room.
[...]

[A fragment of a letter from Olga, Shtange's sister, who lives in Leningrad, is attached here.]

After all, you just can't keep stringing night onto day the way you do, without making up for it somehow. I mean, judging from what Vera writes me, and even from what you write yourself, you're working constantly without a break, for 22–23 hours on end, and then what? In my case, I don't have anyone depending on me except for my sons, but you have Mitya, who really needs you, you mustn't trade in the joy of life with such a man for a problematic career as a "professional wife."

April 15, 1937. We've just taken Zhenya to the station; he's being sent off to work on the Tashkent Railroad. I'm just crushed; this trip ruins all his careful plans; now he won't be able to take his exams. It's some urgent assignment from the PCCT, and his exams were scheduled for two weeks from now, and he was supposed to work on his thesis after that. Now everything is down the drain.

The trip is supposed to last a month, but who knows whether he'll be back a month from now?

And we were so looking forward to these exams, the culmination of all his hard work. All the strain and sacrifice, all the efforts he put into attaining this goal. We were so happy—in fact we were even afraid to let ourselves be happy—that Zhenya would be graduating at last.

And look what happens: two weeks before the end they take him away from his studies and send him away. I can't find the words to express all the pain in my soul right now. This is the worst I've felt in a long time. And it's painful for me even to look at Vladimir. We worked so hard persuading him to come back from the Far East and finish his education, and now 6 months later we have to admit that it was all for nothing. He doesn't want to, and he cannot live the life of a student, dependent on his father. Spending all his time with his nose in a book, all that intensive studying, living without a source of income of his own, it's so hard for him; he's just literally wasting away before our eyes. He's thin, pale, moody, it's obviously causing him unbearable suffering, and I gave up trying to persuade him not to go back to Khabarovsk a long time ago. That's obviously his one and only dream. He keeps sending telegrams there, but there's no answer, and he's suffering terribly, both from regret that he ever left there and from desire to go back.

He doesn't want to finish his education, he doesn't seem to care about the future, which can offer him nothing but a job at the technician's level, since in spite of all his knowledge and experience, he doesn't have a degree.

I feel so sorry for him, I'm all torn to pieces. I don't know how to help him. Now I regret that I ever persuaded him to give everything up and come back here. Here, of course, he can't count on finding the kind of position he had there.

If only he had an intelligent wife who understood the importance of a higher education. If she had the desire and the ability, she could create a calm, peaceful family atmosphere and support her man, but Valya is just a frivolous girl who's sick and tired of sitting at home with the baby and sees a return to Khabarovsk as an opportunity for a freer life for herself.

She spends all her time here moaning and groaning, and that just depresses Vladimir even more.

Lord! So much misery. How can I help my darling, beloved son?

Today in one of those conversations we just keep repeating over and over, he said something horrible:

"I'm just being destroyed, I'm dying. I'm deprived of any possibility of living a real life. After all, in life you need to have lots of different experiences and impressions, but I have absolutely no impressions at all."

This attitude of his is so terrible! What can I do to make things easier for him? I look at him and suffer more with every passing day. I think that maybe if I gave up my community work to take care of Sasha and free Valya from having to look after him, maybe things would be different.

Of course that would be an enormous sacrifice!

Why should I, after bringing up four children and after going through so many hard times, in the declining years of my life, at the age of 53, have to give up my personal life just so my son's wife can live the way she pleases. This would be such a great sacrifice for me that I'm not even sure that I could find the strength in myself to suppress my desire for a personal life one more time, and of course this would be the last time. The main result would be to make Valya's life easier, but my beloved

Vov would still go on suffering, and who knows how it all would end.

No,...better just let him go off and live his life the way he pleases. He doesn't work, he just sits at home studying, and he's doing it all on his own, since he couldn't get into the institute right away.

A life like that, without any external impressions, is of course difficult for a young man, and he doesn't know how to get any relief. And Valya is no help — all she does is whine and add to his suffering.

My dear boy, go if you want to. It will make Papa and me terribly sad, but still, your happiness is our happiness. It is just awful for me to see you in this state.

[...]

May 8, 1937. It's been almost a month since I've written anything in my notebook, I just haven't had a minute to spare. I went to bed every night at 2 or 3 a.m., and in the days leading up to the First of May I didn't get to bed until 4 or 5, and the last day I worked through the night at the k/garten and didn't get home until 8 o'clock the next morning. We had to decorate the building for the holiday and there was a lot of painting to do. We painted a panel with a flower pattern for the assembly hall, and I did a Ukrainian hut that filled a whole sheet of plywood, and two car wheels and I thought everything up and directed all the work myself. I made sunflowers out of wood shavings. It all turned out rather well and all the guests liked it, but I lost my enthusiasm for the work because of the disgusting atmosphere of careerism that surrounds us. This desire people have to steal each other's achievements and take all the credit themselves is so disgusting that I even decided to give up the work altogether and just settle down at home with my dear family.

But I won't get to do that — they've just announced that the Congress of Wives of Transportation Commanders will go ahead on June 30 as planned, and everything has started up again, and again the pressure is on to speed up the work. I reviewed our obligations under the socialist emulation agreement, and I see that I still have a few things to finish up, or else I will ruin things for the whole collective. Then I thought that my proposal to present Lazar Moiseevich a set of china, hand-painted by all of us women, had fallen through, but it turned out I was wrong. Yesterday Zayonchkovskaya called me and told me that everything was still on and that we had to go to the Dulyovo china factory for preliminary negotiations. We got our preliminary designs together and went out there today. The administration gave us a nice welcome and approved our designs, after making a few comments, of course. We agreed on all the details and then we were taken around to all the shops where the china is painted, and they showed us where it is made. I listened and observed with great interest and I'm sure that we will manage and that our china will turn out just fine.

[...]

Of course all this is very interesting and nice, but what about the family? Everything at home is in a state of total collapse. First of all, there's absolutely no money; nothing is getting done, and the very sight of Vova just makes me feel awful. He is so unhappy and so oppressed by his dependence on us, that I've stopped trying to keep him here. But what makes it so terrible is that his trip to Khabarovsk fell through; someone else got the position, and nothing else appropriate has opened up.

The poor boy is just crushed, and there's no improvement in his health either. None of the doctors can figure out what is wrong with him. Tomorrow they'll do some more tests, we'll see if we learn anything.

I'm just sick at heart and we're completely out of money. I think I'll sell my fur coat (it's all worn out anyway) and my dress tomorrow, otherwise I'll never make it till payday.

Our life isn't a whole lot of fun, in spite of all the indicators saying how happy we should be. And how could it be otherwise, with such wonderful children? But still, they all have troubles of their own that make their lives difficult.

With Borya it's his bad hearing, he's so talented, but it keeps him from advancing in his career. And they're hurting for money too.

Irunka has made a lot of progress in her painting. She worked with Pimenov and Vasiliev[10] (both of them major artists) on a panel for the Paris Exhibition.[11] The panel is being sent to Paris tomorrow. You'd think how wonderful that must be for her, but she's very depressed, she and her husband are constantly fighting, apparently he's envious and he thinks there's something going on between her and Pimenov too.

They tore Zhenya away from his exams and sent him to Tashkent to check on the progress of the work going on out there. At least he'll be back soon, maybe it won't have too serious an effect on his studies or his thesis. He'll probably come back with a lot of interesting stories to tell. I haven't heard any news from my sister in a long time and I'm terribly worried. My poor, poor Olyunechka, it's awful just thinking about what a hard life she has. If only she were in good health, but she's very ill, and she doesn't have the time or money to get treatment.

I, or rather Mitya, help her all we can; we send a little money now and then, but we don't have that much ourselves, and there are a lot of us,

Papanechka, me, Vova, his wife and little boy, and Zhenya and his wife. Each son gets 100 rubles for his expenses, plus room and board. Not to mention the dacha we're building, which we have to pay installments on, and they're not small, either. So that's how things are.

[A letter from Olga [Olya], Shtange's sister, is attached here.]

My dear Galinochka,

First of all, thank you so much for the money you sent, both times. Though I'm ashamed to accept it, I have no choice, and now I'll move on and tell my sad saga.

While Simonov was gone his mama caused me all kinds of trouble, through [illeg.]*, she started up a campaign against him, and I turned in my notice, though I did have some prospects, both for advancement at work and for getting a room.*

Yesterday at the infirmary they ordered me to sign in immediately (between May 10 and 15) at the clinic (the neurology division of the Bekhterev Research Institute Hospital, that's where his wife works) and also yesterday Simonov signed an order for my dismissal.

Once I sign into the clinic I lose both my room and my job, and I don't have any choice because, to tell the truth, I do feel quite unwell, so here I am, sick and without a job, too. My whole life is shattered, everything that I was working for is now in ruins. Tolya will be in the camps now at Volodya's, with [illeg.]*, of course. Things have gone so badly. On May 10 Vova is going to the camp, he can't stay here, and Zhenya is going to be on leave beginning the 15th, he can't stay either, and I'm being put in the clinic, and I myself know that I have to go, my head won't stop spinning, and I can barely walk.*

Galochka, you know what this is? It's something we inherited from Mama's father, the alcoholic, all of us and the Sipoviches too, we have bad "cardio-vascular systems," especially Marianna, Antonina , and me. I don't know whether the treatment will do any good; in any case I don't mind dying but I'd do anything not to wind up the way Marianna did.

When I sign into the clinic I'll send you my address (It'll be between May 11 and 15). If you are going to send anything, send it to Vladimir, I don't know his summer address yet, but I'll send it to you soon. Overall, everything is just awful. How things will go for Tolya from now on, I don't know myself, it looks as though I don't have much time left myself.

Well, so long. Hugs and kisses, with all my love to everyone. Love,

Olya

[...]

May 16, 1937. Last night I left for Leningrad; I'm going to see Olya. The poor thing is seriously ill, and Zhenya (our cousin) signed her into the neurological division of the Bekhterev Research Institute Hospital. I was terribly worried about her: there she was, all alone without any money, and without a job too. She needs money and moral support.

I didn't have any money of my own, but Seryozha brought some and I sold my fur collar and silk blouse, and we managed to scrape some together. I'll go and stay with Olya for a day or two, and I'm very concerned about what shape I'm going to find her in. I feel so terribly sorry for her, the poor thing. I just dropped everything and left, and I have so many urgent things to attend to, both in my community work and at home. In a couple of weeks we should finally get our dacha, after all this time and all our hard work.

Two years ago I found out that the Academy of Sciences was building dachas for its employees on a cooperative basis. Mitya happened to be leaving that very day on business and he said sadly that he just wouldn't be able to get anything done in time to be included in the cooperative. At the time I got him to sign a blank piece of paper and to give me proxy to act in his behalf.

The next day I started going around the offices, trying to get Mitya included in the cooperative, since he is a member of the Transportation Commission and the Transportation Terminology Commission under the Academy of Sciences.

While I was at it I borrowed some money from a friend, and by the time Mitya came back everything had been taken care of.

Now our life's dream is about to come true, — by June 1 we ought to get a little dacha 42 kilometers from Moscow on the Kazan rail line.

Like all these cooperatives, ours, the "Academic," turned out to be not the best quality and the dachas are not quite what we were promised. They're not equipped for winter, there's no stove, no fence, no icebox, no shed. But still we're glad and we hope that with our sons' help, and also with the money that Mitya will get when he publishes his course materials, we'll manage to bring the dacha up to standard, and we'll feel an enormous sense of relief, knowing that we have our own little corner to go to in our old age, and that no one can take it away.

Now I'm dreaming about the garden we'll have, and I'm trying to free myself from all my other commitments so I can concentrate all my energy and attention on our own little corner.

And I do have an awful lot I'm working on right now, — June 3o is the Conference of Wives of Commanders in the Transport Sector, and we're frantically getting ready. At the Institute, I have to make sure we meet all our obligations under the Socialist emulation agreement between our Wives' Council and the Wives' Council of the Leningrad Institute; then, at the PCCT, Zayonchkovskaya and I have to finish the china set to present to Lazar Moiseevich. Zayonchkovskaya will go to the factory at Dulevo on the 2oth, whereas I won't get to go until the 25th. On the one hand I'm scared to take on such an important project, on the other I'm eager to get down to work.

[...]

Here I am at the hospital. I got a pass for the 7th Section, where Olya is. I'm sitting in the hall, waiting for the doctor to come. Just now one of the patients had a fit, right in front of me. It was terrible! I was so scared! Then I go down the hall, and I hear Olya calling me: "Galina." I turn and there she is, lying in bed. I talked to the doctor and he let me go in to see her, but he couldn't tell me anything definite about her illness, since she's undergoing tests. It'll be five days before they know anything definite. Then Zhenya came and we went to see Olya together. In the morning they took some spinal fluid and so she has to lie on her stomach, face down.

So I did get to talk with her, and we were very glad we got to see each other. Olya doesn't feel bad, but she's still dizzy. The headaches are not as bad as before. Zhenya will write me on the 2oth to tell me what the doctors decide, and Olya will spend a month and a half or so in the hospital.

I started back for Moscow in the evening. I'm in the train right now. I've caught up on my sleep and now I'm eager to get back to work. After breakfast at home I'll go to the k/garten again, I have to finish up the inventory. Now I'm looking out the window and admiring the lovely countryside around Tver. Lots and lots of cherry trees in bloom and wild apple trees. Now I know that cherry trees like it damp, that's why there aren't very many where we live.

May 17. When I saw Tver (now Kalinin), the memories came rushing back. I recalled two periods in my life. The first was when I was still very young and I came to visit the Belotserkovtsys. They were friends of ours. We were very attached to each other and missed each other a great deal when we were apart. They moved to Tver from Polotsk, where B. P. was working. He was transferred. I arrived there in high spirits, all dressed up, we danced and had a wonderful time in their marvellous apartment, we took walks in their enormous garden.

At the time B. P. was in charge of a the Tver Railway district and Mitya was a special assignments engineer for the chief of the Polessie Railroads in Vilno.

The second period was after the Revolution, beginning in the famine year of 1920. In early spring Mitya travelled on assignment to the Caucasus and brought back some salt, which was impossible to come by anywhere at the time. We had to plant potatoes, but we didn't have any seeds. So I went to Tver to do some bartering and exchange salt for potatoes. At the time you could get anything you wanted in exchange for salt.

I took Borya, the salt, and some bags. Borya stood in one place at the market guarding the bags, while I ran around exchanging salt for potatoes. I'd get some, drag them to where Borya was waiting, and then run back for more. We spent the whole day this way and got ourselves five bags of potatoes. With enormous difficulty we managed to load them onto the train ourselves (Borya was 15 at the time), and we brought them triumphantly home. A couple of days later we started the planting, all completely by hand, except we used a horse for the actual plowing, since our plot at the dacha was large, almost 1 1/2 acres.

At that time a lot of people were going specially to Tver to get apples, but we couldn't be bothered with apples—we were barely able to feed our large family and were in fact close to starving. All those years of famine I had to go around from place to place looking for bread, but I'll write about that later, since the train is arriving in Moscow now.

In the same car with me is a family on their way to Sevastopol—the husband and wife, a nanny and three children, one is three and the other are twins, 9 months old. They're screaming and acting up, and the parents are literally going to pieces, especially the papa. Of the three of them, he's the best with the children. It's strange to see, but nowadays the majority of fathers have gotten so they do a good job with their children.

May 13, 1937. Zhenya has just come back from his trip. He's tanned and happy. He's telling us about what he saw out there.

As far as the region in general goes, he says that Central Asia is not what it used to be when we were there. New buildings, trams, they're taking down the old buildings, but there are still a lot of yashmaks.[12] Zhenya helped some people take a yashmak off one of the women. The workers have bicycles, and most of them have a gramophone. They have a lot of money, more than they know what do do with, they ignore their law prohibiting alcohol and have started drinking like crazy.

I've gotten involved in community work in our Dacha Building Cooperative, the "Academician." I'll help out, anything to get our dacha as soon as possible. They're promising to have it ready by June 1.

Will our dream really come true?

On the 25th I have to go out to the Dulyovo factory to paint the china for Lazar Moiseevich's present and then it's straight on to Leningrad to settle things for Olya with the hospital, with money and an apartment.

Where will I find the time to do it all?

[...]

May 14, 1937. Today I heard about a terrible thing that happened to one of our most popular professors, S. P. Syromyatnikov.

He's a wonderful man, but has a terrible drinking problem. It's like a disease with him, it's incurable. But still, he does have a medal of merit.

Well the other day, some gang jumped him at the Yauza Bridge while he was drunk and they stole everything, his passport, his annual travel pass, and his medal certificate, and they stripped him of his medal and took it too. It was a terrible scandal.

[...]

July 15. Today I decided to make myself sit down and write down some important things that have been happening in my life, both at home and in my community work. Recently I've been running around like a pot aboil, working on all my projects, I haven't had a moment to myself during the day, and in the evening I simply haven't had any energy—first there were all the preparations for the Congress, ours, and then, after it was postponed indefinitely, all kinds of family difficulties came up.

Assuming that the Congress would take place on June 30, I had to work twice as hard at the k/garten, so I would have something to report. Then there was the struggle to get a winter dacha for the k/garten from the Institute. We got a wonderful one, but then we had to fix it up for the special needs of the kindergarden and move the children out there. I also had to coordinate our wives' needlework for the exhibit that was being planned for the Congress and help finish up the work on our gift to People's Commissar L. M. Kaganovich.

Here I attach the report I wrote for the newspaper about the gift:

"A Picture in Needlework"

[...]

On the occasion of the Conference of the Wives of Transportation Workers and Party and Government Leaders, a gift was presented to L. M. Kaganovich from the Wives' Council of our MEMIIT. It is an embroidered copy of a drawing by the artist Kupriyanov, entitled The Railways, *which is located at the present time in the Tretyakov Gallery. The original drawing was done in Italian pencil on ivory-colored paper; it depicts a railroad bridge with a locomotive rushing out from underneath, full speed ahead; a freight train is crossing the bridge, leaving a light trail of smoke across the sky. The drawing was transferred by applying different thicknesses of black and white gauze and chiffon; the finer lines were stitched on with different lengths of black, gray and white silk.*

The picture is mounted in a frame of Karelian birchwood.

The most difficult part of our work for us was the selection of the theme.

After long discussion the Wives' Council settled on the Kupriyanov drawing, which offers a combination of a transportation-related theme with a wonderful artistic execution; its dramatic representation of our era of great forward advances in the field of transportation reflects the message our collective sought to convey.

The copy was made to commemorate a particular moment in the life history of the transportation field and has assumed the identity of an artistic embodiment of a topical theme.

Sixteen people were involved in the project. Agnessa Markovna Shabad acted as artistic advisor.

G. Shtange

July 8, 1937. At the organizational meeting at the PCCT to discuss the preparation of gifts and needlework for the exhibit we had a terrible time coming to a decision on what exactly we would make for a gift. At the very beginning the Political Division proposed that we embroider a map of the Railroads of the Soviet Union, and then I proposed that we paint a set of china, based on a transportation-related subject. My proposal was accepted unanimously. A brigade of three people was formed to design the china—brigade leader Zayonchkovskaya, myself, and Lapina. But the Political Division declared that I represent the Council of Wives of the MEMIIT, not the PCCT, and so I was not accepted as a member of the brigade.

The china was painted at the china factory in Dulyovo, under the direction of expert craftsmen. Now the china set is done, though I was not able to be a part of this beautiful project. But still, the idea was mine, and if

it hadn't been for me, there wouldn't have been any china set either.
[...]

August 24, 1937. As of August 22, L. M. Kaganovich is no longer our People's Commissar; he's become the People's Commissar of Heavy Industry. We'll just wait and see what will become of us and our Wives' Councils, that Lazar Moiseevich paid so much attention to.

Will the Conference take place and what will be the fate of our wonderful embroidery? How will we be treated by our new People's Commissar Com. Bakulin.

The little note that I wrote about the embroidery done by our activists, called "A Picture in Needlework," appeared in the newspaper, and I was even given an honorarium for it — 10 rubles.
[...]

September 2, 1937. Today the Central Executive Committee[13] came out with a resolution to intensify the struggle with espionage, sabotage, and wrecking by stipulating a maximum prison sentence of up to 25 years for those guilty of the above-mentioned crimes.
[...]

September 24, 1937. In June of this year construction work was completed on the canal joining the Moscow River with the Volga. Now steamships and barges pass by where people used to plow the land, where they gathered mushrooms and berries. Today we went out to see the canal. Borya got us all tickets for the expedition boat of the Union-Trans-Project (the office where he works), and off we went. Everyone had a good time on the trip, our only regret was that the weather took a turn for the worse today and it was cold. What a joy it was to look at that beautiful, magnificent structure; it is particularly pleasant to note all the taste that went into its exterior appearance. The river station at Khimki is very beautiful, — from a distance it looks like lace. There is a whole sea of flowers in front of the station building, and in general there are flower gardens everywhere at all the sluices and piers, and their arrangement is very tasteful.
[...]

Conversations Overheard

I didn't hear the beginning of the conversation...
Then he says, "Well I go to the church, do what I'm supposed to during

those hours, receive my pay and leave. In short, what I do there is just a job, no different from yours. Anyway, the archdeacon has a wonderful voice and he can really put away the liquor. You go there, he takes a few drinks and asks, 'What would you like to hear?' and once he gets started, he can sing circles around anyone else. What a voice."

"But why didn't he put his talent to some other use?"

"Because his family was clergy, and he was educated in a religious conservatory. They didn't know any better."

"Well there are some old women living near us: they have a priest who goes to see them, he speaks twelve languages, and writes books in twelve languages. He's registered as a resident here in Moscow. You think he just goes there to pass the time of day? No he's spreading his propaganda. He'll tell some people, 'Let me marry you'; to others he'll say, 'Let me christen your children.' And it works. Just recently he christened two children, four and eight years old."

"The children are big enough to understand, and they report on everything they see. 'He,' they'll say, 'annointed our heels,' etc. Just think, he christened a young pioneer." "Well, you know that church called 'Unexpected Joy' on Mariinskaya Steet? Well, that church donated 25 thousand rubles to the Spaniards. I wonder where they got their hands on that kind of money?"

"What do you mean? People go to church, and there's your money. And of course they have to prove that they are not against Soviet power, so they make these donations."

At those words I left the train car and I don't know what they said after that. Too bad.

[...]

October 5, 1937. Evening. Tonight there was a meeting in the MEMIIT to report about the year's work at the Institute.

The head of the Institute gave a detailed report on the political, scientific, educational and financial status of the Institute. He divided all the departments into three categories: excellent: of which there are three; satisfactory; and the rest—unsatisfactory. Then he announced that the "foremost and best department in the institute is the department of locomotive management headed by Professor Dmitry Aleksandrovich Shtange." These words were followed by thunderous applause, the likes of which I had never heard within the walls of our Institute—the auditorium was literally shaking. I was sitting in the second row watching the stage, where my dear Mityaechka was sitting on the presidium, and my heart ached and nearly burst with pride and joy. Reporting on the social activities of the Institute, he said that the Council of Wives of our professors and instructors had contributed a great deal and had been very helpful, especially Comrades Syromyatnikova, Korneeva, Bogdanova, Shtange, and Privalova. And so it turned out that the work done by Mitya and me has produced wonderful results and has been publicly recognized in front of the whole Institute. It was so nice, I was overjoyed, but Mitya didn't look good at all; he just sat there looking miserable. When the official part was over I asked Mitya why he was so sad on such a joyful occasion. "I," he says, "am too tired to feel happy." We didn't stay for the concert and just went home.

[...]

October 5, 1937

[...]

Back at home we put Papanechka to bed and called the doctor immediately. The doctor diagnosed a weakened heart due to overstrain. He prescribed complete peace and quiet and five days or so of bed rest, then a long leave from work.

I was so upset, I suffered so for Mityaechka, it was so awful to think that the demands of his work were considerably shortening his life. Just think, he didn't have a vacation this year or go to a resort, and he worked nearly 20 hours a day all summer long, without any days off. The reason for all this work is the publication of his course materials, which are coming out in two parts. The first part was written by Mitya when he was in prison, beginning in October of 1928; it was finished in 1930, and is called *Calculating Pulling Capacity*. Any day now two more books are due to come out, the first and second parts of his course: *Depot Management and Locomotive Use*. Mitya began the 1st part of this book in prison, too, and worked on it in bits and pieces when he could find the time. He really sat down to work beginning in fall of '35. The 2nd part was written by him in '36/37, with several co-authors, one of whom is our Borya. He wrote the part on supply routes. How proud I am of raising a son who at the age of 32 can be a coauthor with his father, a professor.

Well it was the writing and editing of these books that overstrained him so much, since L. M. Kaganovich, our People's Commissar, had set such a firm date for its publication.

When Glavlit (the Censor)[14] read Mitya's course book, he said, "Your book, Professor, is a golden book."

[...]

[A letter from Shtange to her husband Dmitry (Mityaechka) is attached here.]

My dear, beloved Mityaechka,

It's the 28th, and I still haven't gotten a letter from you. I'm very concerned. So far I only have one bit of news: I have to give up my community work.

I just can't go on like this, — I can't just go and sign in without doing any work, and it's simply impossible for me to work. Sashenka is constantly sick and it looks as though it's going to go on for a long time, since before he didn't have a fever, but now he does and he has a bad cough too. And what would you expect, running around naked like he does for several hours every morning.

The worst thing is having to abandon my comrades at such a difficult time. I ought to be spending the whole day taking care of things at the nursery school and k/garten, but I don't even show up at all. I thought and thought, and I decided just to submit to fate. I'll have to just be patient and wait until Sasha gets a little bigger.

Otherwise nothing has changed. The doctor came to look at Sasha and he said that he has bronchitis.

I'm going out to try to get some money, mine is gone already.

I kiss you, my dear, warmly, with all my love.

Galina
10/28/97

[...]

[Two letters by Dmitry Shtange to his wife.]

My dear, darling Galyushka.

This is my 5th day here, but it seems like I've been here a whole month. Not a single letter from you. Everyone else gets letters, but each time I ask I get the answer: "Don't worry, they'll write." Naturally I'm worried. I shared a room with another man for four days, today they moved me into a room of my own. It's not very big, but it's quite comfortable. It's furnished with a good bed, a wardrobe, a wash stand with running water, a desk, a night stand, a desk chair and an armchair, a frosted-glass ceiling light, and a table lamp with a shade. There's a balcony facing south west. The sun shines and warms the room from morning until 2 in the afternoon. The weather has been good. It's chilly at night, and in the early morning there's even some frost here and there. The sun

starts shining at seven and it warms up quickly, it's already quite warm by
9:00, you can go out without a coat, some wear white suits. Beginning at about
3 in the afternoon a cool wind blows in and it starts to cool down. The routine
is—eat, bathe, walk. I mainly take walks with Anna Moiseevna and her many
acquaintances, Chikhachev came down with something and has been sick in
bed for several days.

My dear Galyushka, make sure to write, otherwise I'll be worried and
instead of helping me, coming here will make me feel worse.

I kiss you all, warmly.

Mitya
10/30/1937

[...]

My dear, darling Galyushka.

Yesterday, today and tomorrow we celebrate the 20th Anniversary of the
October Revolution. Yesterday was the formal celebration, during which your
husband was elected to the presidium, and then supper, dances, and entertain-
ment. The evening festivities were a great success. Today I went to the demon-
stration and now there's a band playing outside on the square, and people are
dancing; in the evening there will be a movie. It almost feels like summer, the
sky is clear and the sun is shining, it's warm and there's no wind. I can just
imagine how Moscow is celebrating the October anniversary this year.

I spend my days the same way as before, it seems to me that I've been here
for several months already, while in fact it's only been 12 days. I haven't lost
much weight, just 1 kg, but I feel good.

Goodbye for now. I kiss you all warmly.

Mitya
November 7, 1937

[...]

November 28, 1937. The election campaign has been going on for two
months now. Everywhere there are rallies, educational sessions, campaign
meetings, and agitation centers; canvassers are going around door-to-
door, and the radio is broadcasting poems and songs about the election.

[Almost the whole page is taken up by a newspaper clipping with the
slogan: "Glory to the creator of the Constitution of the USSR the great
Stalin!"]

Something interesting happened to us in the middle of all this. Tanya
was talking with Zhenya, and she says that she can't make head or tail
about who to vote for, and so she doesn't care who gets elected. Zhenya

got up right then and there and called our precinct and asked them to tell us whether they have some kind of newspaper or brochure about the upcoming election, since we have this citizen here who is having trouble figuring it out and there's nowhere she can read about it. They promised to let us know when they got the newspapers back. The very next morning a canvasser showed up at our door and gave Tanya and our maid Frosya a detailed explanation of the election procedures. I was struck by such promptness and readiness to go wherever they're called.

[...]

December 6. I'm sitting in the train writing; I'm on my way to Udelnaya again. This time I'm going to look for an apartment for Olya. If they don't extend Aunt Tanya's residence permit, she will have absolutely nowhere to go—just out onto the street, period. I know that what I have in mind is practically impossible, but still I'll give it a try. Then I would move Olya over to Moscow and I would be a thousand times happier and more relaxed, and Tolyasha would be able to study here just as well, of course. Certainly we aren't in any position to pay rent out of our salary, so I will have to start making some money myself.

I can do different kinds of cloth painting, you can make pretty good money doing that, but somehow I haven't been able to get myself set up. I went around looking, but no luck anywhere. Undoubtedly you need "pull," and I don't have any. They told me at the "Artist": "We're not taking anyone on until January." Another place gives you all the work you could want, but you have to use your own paints, and they're extremely difficult to come by these days. So here I sit without any money coming in. The manager of our k/garten is planning to go on leave and can't find herself a good substitute. She really wants me to fill in for her for two months. If I agree, I'll earn 600 rubles during that time, but I'm terribly afraid,—after all I know practically nothing about teaching. I guess I'll have to go to the teaching center and do some studying.

Recently I've been busy working on a very serious, urgent project, organizing a children's nursery for our Institute. A fair amount of the work has already been done, but there's still a lot left to do. For two days now I've been spending all my free time putting together cost estimates for equipment. It's a hard job and you have to be meticulous. That's why I haven't written anything at all during the last few days, but today I want to write about the way things are going with Zhenyurka.

About Zhenya [one of Shtange's sons]

Things are going well with him—in three months he should graduate from the institute, and he's working on his thesis now. He sits working on it literally day and night, resting only on the weekends, and even then not entirely—he spends part of the day working. In general over the last few years Zhenya has been working terribly hard; after all he only got a stipend in January of this year, and other than that he got nothing the whole time. Except for the 100 rubles he got from Papa. So he had to work and study at the same time. Both he and Tanya like to wear nice clothes and have a good time, and all that takes money. So he had to work hard.

[...]

And in spite of that, he did wonderfully, both in his studies and in his military service. He has two letters of thanks and two books that the commander of his regiment gave him at the end of basic training, and in the Institute the Head of the Institute himself said that he is a "wonderful student."

This fall he did some work for the "BAM,"[15] and he discovered a major error in the work he'd been assigned. He reported it, and they disputed it, but he managed to prove he was right, even though he was just a student, and was up against engineers.

In general Zhenya is not only capable, but even talented, and he has a very kind heart, add to that his good looks and kind personality, and anyone would have to agree that the worth of my Zhenya is very high indeed.

Now Tanya, that's a completely different story. Like Zhenya, she's beautiful and good-humored, but she's a terribly shallow person. All she cares about is clothes and entertainment, and absolutely nothing else. She has a lot of ability, she could do anything she wanted if she took her mind to it, but she is only willing to work enough to gratify her immediate desires. For example, the whole winter of '35, she worked day and night knitting ladies' wool collars to order. You couldn't buy wool then, so she would pick up old knitted things at the market, unravel them, wash and dye the wool, and knit collars and sweaters out of it. She earned enough money in a single winter to buy herself a 750-ruble bicycle, a 350-ruble silk coat, and some other things too. But in general she's just unbelievably lazy. This fall she enrolled in the Institute for the fourth time, to finish her education. That really surprised me. She lived in Moscow for five years without the slightest desire to study, and all of a sudden, right when Zhenya is finishing up and most likely will be sent to work in some remote place, she's come up with this

burning desire to study. I figured that she had gotten her mind set on staying in Moscow at any price. Three months went by, her scholarly ardor vanished and she's turned terribly lazy, she does absolutely nothing at all. I
don't think she has the strength of character to graduate.

[...]

the 11th, evening. I tried to listen to Stalin's speech on the radio just now.
He was speaking to voters about the election for the Supreme Soviet.
Unfortunately Sashenka wouldn't let me hear the whole speech and I
only caught individual phrases, which I wrote down:

> ...I would like to assure you, comrades, that you may most confidently place
> your trust in Com. Stalin.... You can count on Com. Stalin fulfilling his mission
> before the working class...for the intelligentsia.... You yourselves know, every
> family has a black sheep.... Uncommitted people are of no use to anyone....
> People need to instill in their deputies the idea of emulating the Great Lenin...
> [...]

Stalin speaks very slowly and distinctly — extremely simply, so simply that
each word penetrates into your consciousness and I think the man cannot be found who would not be able to understand what he says.

I really love that, I don't like highfaluting, bombastic speeches that are
aimed at creating an acoustic effect.

December 12, 1937, 6:30 a.m. I've just come back from voting and I want to
write about what it was like.

Mitya, Vova, I, and our maid Frosya agreed last night that we would go
out early to vote and would be at the polling place right when it opened,
i.e. by 6:00 a.m. Mitya woke us up; we dressed quickly and went down-
stairs thinking that we would be among the first people outside, but it
turned out that there were already a lot of people on the streets heading
for the polling places. Our precinct polling place was on our street, in No.
14, Novobasmannaya, in the club section of the PCCT, in the very rooms
where L. M. Kaganovich received us last year. The room had been decorated nicely with slogans and flowers. Literature and newspapers relating
to the occasion had been set out on the chairs and tables.

When we went in ten minutes before the beginning of the election,
there were some 25 of us in the room. I wanted to get in line first, but for
some reason was too shy to, and instead sat at a table together with Mitya,
Vova, and Frosya. The minute we sat down, a man came up to Mitya and

told him that he was taking down the names of the first voters for the newspaper *Izvestiya*. Apparently it was Mitya's three stars[16] that attracted his attention. He asked his name, his profession and where he worked, and how long he'd been there. After that Mitya and I went and stood by the doors into the next room. The doors were closed but the moment the clock started striking 6, they flew open and the voters began to file in. I went in with Vova, and Mitya went with Frosya; she had named him her proxy, since she herself is illiterate.

There were poll workers everywhere, showing people where to go. In the second room was a table where the ballots were being given out: envelopes and two sheets of paper (a white one and a blue one) on which the names of our precinct's candidates were printed: Bulganin[17] and Kabanov. Booths had been set up in the next room where people put their ballots in the envelopes and sealed them, and there were two ballot-boxes.

[A small drawing by the author is attached here, representing a room with booths and a portrait of Stalin.]

After we deposited our ballots we went out and congratulated each other.

I felt a kind of excitement in my soul, I don't know why, and there was even a lump in my throat. Maybe because I had only slept two hours last night? but more likely because we were the very first of the first voters at the first such election in the world. In the same building a special room had been set up with a New Year's tree and toys for children whose mothers could leave them there while they got their ballots and voted.

When we got home, we spent a long time comparing notes.

[...]

[A letter from Olga, Shtange's sister, is attached here.]

My dear Galinochka, I meant to write you every day beginning December 8, but on that very day I received my residence permit and from then until the 11th I was running around trying to get myself registered to vote in the Petrograd Region. This morning at 8:00 I went to vote and with a clear conscience I turned in my ballot for Litvinov[18] and Kalinin.[19] As I dropped my envelope into the ballot box I felt with my whole being the truth of the Arabic saying "The tiniest little fish can stir the depths of the ocean."

You worry about me too much, my dear, I don't have anything to rejoice about, but there's no cause for alarm either. I can't boast about my life, but I get by all right. Aunt Tanya has gotten so mired down in filth, nastiness, and greed that it is stifling her innate goodness. Here's an example for you: she goes to the dump and drags home bottles, tin cans, corks, rags, etc. "They'll come in handy, I'll turn them in for salvage and get money back for them," and at home she offered to make Tolya a jacket out of a fine black cloth coat with woolen wadding that had been so completely eaten away by moths that you couldn't find a single vershok [approx. 2 inches] *intact, much less enough for a jacket.*

Here's what our relations have been like: when I moved in with her, she welcomed us with open arms. For three days she was an angel incarnate. In those 3 days I cleaned up without the slightest harm to her. She let me clean up somewhat and then, on the 4th day, she really let me have it for daring to move the books from the floor to the "bookcase" without her permission. This "bookcase" is just a plain box, placed upright, but she won't let me put the books in my table, the one with the shelves. When I moved the books onto the bookcase, it turns out I destroyed all the papers she needed to get her pension and on these grounds, in spite of all my assurances that I had never touched them and had never even seen them, she just kept on making scenes about it, right up to the 21st, old style. On that day she went to church and came back all refreshed and affectionate, cordial, and kind. After a couple of days I got up my nerve and brought a bucket and a couple of other things of mine (I'd left my belongings with a friend of Aunt Tanya's). After that she levelled the charge that when I had gone around cleaning the room without her authorization I had thrown into the garbage one of the dessert spoons of the set of six she had bought once for 5 rubles at an auction. I assured her that when I was cleaning I had found a spoon behind a trunk and had put it in the cupboard, to which I got the answer that there ought to have been not one spoon there, but two, and since I had found only one, that means I had thrown out the other one. "Yes it's true, I'm a no-good scoundrel, and I threw your jewelry in the garbage." And on and on like that. She is extremely sensitive about me bringing over any of my things; she'll say "go ahead, bring it, put it here," but the minute I bring something and put it somewhere, she flies off the handle. She collects bottles from the drugstore and turns them in for money. She keeps them in a cracked clay pot. When she comes home, she immediately counts them to see if they're all there and make sure I didn't steal any.

I have to tell you that the whole time I lived out of a suitcase, no bed, no dresser, no table, no nothing. Finally Aunt Tanya herself understood that you can't live that way, everything gets dirty and ragged, things get scattered and lost, so when I got my money, she says, bring your dresser over here today or tomorrow. We discussed the project in great detail, how to go about it, who would bring it, how much to pay for the delivery, and she left for work. We brought the dresser, put my things in it, and arranged everything neatly in the room and made it look perfectly acceptable. Everything worked out just fine. She came back in the evening calm and content. Then yesterday morning I went out to take care of some things. Tolya stayed home, he had to study. When

I got back Tolya was in the kitchen and he informed me that he hadn't gotten any studying done because there was nowhere for him to work. I went into the room, everything is topsy turvy, all the things are still scattered all over the room, she's been through everything. She asked whether I had taken the brown material she was going to use for a skirt, etc. She's furious and won't talk to me, she doesn't believe me. It's just unbearable. My health is the same, I've been having headaches recently. In spite of all my suffering I really do want to stay here. I think that the length of my letter will compensate for the delay

I kiss you and yours warmly

Olga

December 24, 1937. The other day Borya stopped by and said that his work, "A Station Plan Designed for the New Stakhanovite Work Methods in the Area of Transportation," which he had turned in to the All-Union Scientific Society of Engineers and Technicians, had been awarded a prize: a certificate and 1500 rubles. Borya is pleased, and I am downright happy for him.

Poor Seryozha finds himself in a very difficult position. He left Vera and the baby here for the time being, intending to send her money for the trip as soon as he arrived and got his travel reimbursement.

It turns out that the people there haven't been paid for 2 months now and he's sitting there without a kopeck to his name, he can't get any money anywhere to send Vera for the trip. And she's completely insensitive, she keeps writing him letters moaning and complaining about how bad things are for her here.

Of course she's not doing that well here, but so far she's not really bad off, meanwhile all this has turned Seryozha into a nervous wreck, he's not sleeping at all and just can't take himself in hand. Today Vera got a postcard from his coworkers, telling her get hold of some money somehow and leave immediately, since Sergei is in really bad shape. They are afraid that he might come down with nervous fever. The whole situation is just terrible. Tomorrow I'll take the letter to Seryozha's main office and demand that they give Vera some money for travel.

After all, they could destroy an entire family, with Seryozha out there and Vera and the baby here. I feel so terribly sorry for Sergushka. And I can't give Vera any real help either, I'm having terrible money troubles myself.

I've already decided not to go out for New Year's, I'll take the money I'd been saving for that and lend it to Vera for the trip.

My sons are dreaming about Stalin. Borya dreamed that he came to visit us and had a friendly, intimate conversation with us.

And the same day Zhenya dreamed that he was defending Stalin from an attack by a bandit.

I wonder what these dreams mean?

[...]

December 19, 1937. For several days now I've been wanting to write down what I've been doing and thinking, but I just haven't been able to find the time. The maid just had two days off in a row and I had to do absolutely everything myself: the cooking, the cleaning, the food shopping. I must say that we have really magnificent stores now, both in design and contents.

The meat, fish, vegetable, and delicatessen departments are stocked with a wide assortment of high-quality goods. The meat can be a bit off, but even then only occasionally. But there's plenty of poultry, mutton and fish, with a lot of variety. Lots and lots of canned goods of all kinds, the likes of which we had never heard of before. All kinds of very high-quality convenience foods. I use them constantly to save time. You can even buy hot boullion for 40 kopecks a cup. It's only in the last month that there's been a shortage of dairy products, especially butter, but I hope that won't last long.

Of course I wouldn't want to say that the stores in Moscow look luxurious, of course not, except for the so-called model stores, but in any case over the past 20 years the stores have completely changed and are now unrecognizable. All of them without exception, especially food stores, are clean and orderly, and all the clerks wear white smocks. The majority of food stores are open until 11. There even are some that are open until 3:00 A.M.

Things are a lot worse when it comes to shoes, clothing, linen, and cloth. Last year, even as late as last summer, there was plenty of everything, but since fall it's gotten hard to find what you need. I don't know what the explanation is for this, I hope it's just a temporary hitch. In general people do buy a lot and literally all the stores are full. There are even stores especially for glass and crystal dishes, for plastic goods like buttons, buckles, bracelets, combs, and even for things like tea cups. When you recall the first years after the revolution and the way things were back then, it's just exhilarating to think that all this has been achieved in just 20 years.

Take for example our cinema. I also compare the movies today with what we had before the revolution. The majority of the movie theaters in Moscow are luxurious. They have buffets, there's jazz playing. The content and superb execution of our films arouse admiration even abroad. If you take such pictures as *Chapaev*,[20] *Peter the First*,[21] and especially the most recent film, *Lenin in October*,[22] you simply forget that you're sitting in a movie theater, and not actually participating in what you are seeing. I saw that picture with Mitya. He had seen Lenin up close and he says that the external resemblance is perfect.

About Borya [one of Shtange's sons]

I already wrote that Borya is specializing in stations and junctions. That work involves security matters, but for some reason Borya has not been given a clearance. This situation severely restricts what Borya can do at work, since you can't solve problems properly without knowing every-thing, and also, it has a terrible effect on his morale. He feels slighted for no reason, surrounded by mistrust, and with his character the way it is he suffers so much, that he decided to write to Stalin. I'm very concerned, since I don't know how it all will end.

[...]

December 27. Today Mitya was formally granted the title of Doctor of Technical Sciences. The secretary comes out of the meeting, starts to con-gratulate him, and says, "If you could have heard how they praised you!" Then one of the newer professors comes out and says, "They love you so much here! And so do I!"

How wonderful it is for me to hear this.

[...]

December 30, 1937. The New Year is almost upon us. Every office, every family is finishing up their business for the year 1937 and getting ready to celebrate the holiday. Everyone has a New Year's tree now, though there was a time when they were completely banned. I remember a time in Udelnaya when I wanted so much to decorate a tree, but we didn't dare. But now people do everything they can to make su re every child has the chance to enjoy a New Year's tree. Everywhere, in all the offices, k/gartens, families, even in the parks and squares, trees have been decorated beauti-fully and the stores have started selling tree ornaments, which have been significantly improved both in quality and in quantity. Last year it was hard to get hold of ornaments — they were few and far between and very bad quality, and Zhenya and Tanya made their own toys themselves. But this year I bought a lot of charming little things and I'll decorate a tree and have a party for my grandchildren on January 1.

[...]

December 31, night. Mitya and I welcomed the New Year very modestly at home with Valya and Vova.

We wished each other a happy new year, lit the lights on the tree, had dinner and everything. Zhenya and Tanya came back at 3:00, they had been at a New Year's party with some friends of theirs. Zhenya was terribly drunk, I have never seen him that way before. Pale as death, cold and with a barely detectable pulse. I was so scared that I still can't get to sleep and I keep checking on him. After all, you can die that way.

Today's youth simply doesn't know how to drink, all they can do is drink themselves into a stupor, they have no idea how to carouse tastefully.

I don't know how I can get Zhenya to stop drinking that way!

[...]

January 15, 1938. Our students are in the middle of their exams. Tanya has failed two exams, she came down with angina and gave up studying. Valya has passed all her exams with a "satisfactory," and today she even got an "excellent." Vova has gotten all "excellents." They are all serious people and they'll certainly make it through. They work literally day and night, they've gotten terribly thin and pale; you just feel awful for them. I place all my hopes on the two weeks' break that comes after exams. They really need to get a good rest.

Irunechka is leaving for Leningrad tomorrow, where she'll be working with the artist Pimenov and her husband Boris on a curtain for a production in the Mikhailovsky Theater. They'll be gone about a week and a half. Irunka has promised to visit Olya. Zhenyurka works on his thesis day and night. Borya has been invited to consult with them at the Institute. Zhenya is already working on getting himself a job on the BAM — after graduation he wants to go do surveying work for the BAM. Tanya wants to go with him too.

I already wrote about how Mitya is at one and the same time both a Doctor of Technical Sciences and a student in the upper-level course at the Marx-Lenin Institute. Yesterday he took a test and got the following note from his instructor: "Very intelligent performance." I consider it unbelievable impudence on the part of an instructor to comment on the intelligence of a Doctor of Technical Sciences. Well I won't let it bother me, I'll just assume he's a fool.

Things are going badly for me, both my community work and my affairs at home are in a state of disarray. I have to pull myself together, but I just don't have the strength for it. Fortunately the cold has eased up a little, it's gotten a lot easier to do errands and pick up Sasha at the k/garten. All that freezing cold weather over the last month had really gotten to me. Lately I've noticed that our wives have started going their separate ways, one after the other, not without reason of course — it's because of the departure of their husbands from our Institute. I'm afraid that soon there won't be anyone left there to work anymore. My health isn't too good. I'm getting more and more headaches and dizzy spells, but I just don't have the time to get treatment.

[...]

January 24, 1938. The regional committee of the upper school is requiring our Wives' Council to work on a performance with the children for presentation at the Children's Olympiad, set for the beginning of March.

We didn't want to put on some old standard at the Olympiad, so we came up with the idea of staging a musical version of the fairy tale "Limpopo."[23] It's never been performed before and is the property of the radio station.

I went to the radio committee today, to the children's broadcasting section, and asked them to give me the score for the fairy tale. I'm still working on it, but it looks as though things will work out. I got the composer's agreement.

[...]

January 28, 1938. Last night we were at a meeting of our dacha-building cooperative, Mitya and I. They finally assigned us the 18th lot and have promised to finish the dacha by May. Now there's hope that our three years of efforts will come to fruition. Will our dream really come true, will we really have a corner of our own in our old age? On our way home I started trying to persuade Mitya to spend less time working during the school vacation. And suddenly he blew up and started yelling at me right there in the middle of the street, using the rudest and most improper language. I was just shocked. What's gotten into him? If it's his nerves, he has to get treatment. If he's losing control, he has to take himself in hand, but this is no way to behave. I was very hurt, but a feeling of anxiety is stirring in the depths of my soul. This sort of thing has never happened with him before.

[...]

February 17, 1938. These are remarkable times we are living in. There was a formal ceremony at the Institute this evening to discuss the work done

during the first semester. To stormy applause and cheers, Mitya was presented with this year's "Transitional Red Banner," which he accepted on
behalf of his department. Now the title of honor, "Red Banner," will be
added to the name of his department (He's the department chairman).

I was awarded a shock-worker[24] certificate for my community work. All
this is so nice, I can't find the right words to express it.

Zhenyurka is finishing up his project, and I'm retyping his explanatory
notes.

My long-suffering Olyunya will move to Udelnaya from Leningrad on
the 25th or 26th. There's absolutely no place there for her and Tolya to
live; they did manage to find something here, though it's not perfect.
Volodya sent his mother some money for moving expenses and for their
own travel, so that eases their money troubles.

I don't feel at all well, and I'm afraid that I will have to give up my work,
though I would really be sorry to do that.

I'll give it some more thought.

February 24, 1938. Today I made scenery in the k/garten for the performance we're putting on to commemorate the twentieth anniversary of the
Red Army: a sea scene with a ship and an airplane flying overhead. The
scenery was very difficult to make, but it came out well.

I feel terrible: I'm nauseated and my head is spinning.

March 1, 1938. I gave up my community work today, not completely, as I
had meant to, but for a long leave. My health keeps getting worse and
worse, and I have more and more to do at home. Sashenka has been home
from k/garten for two weeks now; he's been sick with bronchitis. Valya
spends the whole day at the Institute and I have to stay home with him.

On the 26th my long-suffering Olyunya and Tolya came and they need
help getting settled.

Spring is coming and the workers have to be pushed to finish the dacha.

And I am the one who has to do all this, but when? I have so much work
to do at the Institute too.

So I had to leave my community work, which I did with an aching
heart. I'm terribly depressed and I keep worrying about the things I left
unfinished.

On February 25 we celebrated the twentieth anniversary of the Red
Army at the k/garten. The celebration turned out very well, and my
scenery was especially good, it was a great success.

After the children's performances and refreshments, a tea was organized for the teachers and invited senior officials from the leadership. The head of the pedagogy section asked to be introduced to me and praised my scenery, noting its artistry, taste, and the overall realistic impression it made on the children, which should reflect on their artistic development. In general everyone in attendance admired it and told me so.

[Several newspaper clippings are attached here. They all mention the celebration at the kindergarten and Shtange's role in it.]

At the tea our brigade was honored and thanked and each one of us—Shumskaya, Neimaier and I—was presented with a bouquet of flowers. It was all very moving and I was deeply touched.

I've taken my final leave of the k/garten, since if I do return to work it won't be to the k/garten, but to a children's nursery and I won't be doing theater there, since they have more serious problems to deal with here. The children's performance for March 6 didn't work out; we didn't get beyond rehearsal. The children were poorly prepared and I got quite sick and couldn't put enough energy into it.

If I feel better and if Sashenka goes to k/garten, I will devote myself to children's theater again and prepare several numbers for the Olympiad.

Nothing at all is happening with the nurseries.

March 2, 1938. Today the first day of the right Trotskyist bloc.[25] I won't write about it since I'm saving the papers and it all can be read there. [...]

March 28, 1938[...]I have two more important things to do—to set Zhenya up with what he needs for his apartment and to get some high boots for Mitya, Vova, and Zhenya. There's a shortage of manufactured goods right now and it's difficult to get your hands on anything of any kind; I have to get up very early in the mornings to get in line at the big stores. For 4 days now I've been going to the military department store, trying to get hold of some canvas boots and galoshes. The line starts forming outside the store at about 2 in the morning and by the time the store opens, there's a crowd of a hundred thousand (or almost that many), 2/3 of which are people who've come in from the collective farms. Quite a few of them are from the Ukraine, but they come from everywhere, mostly for manufactured goods. There usually aren't very many saucepans and other household goods put out for sale, so when I realized that there were no saucepans and no boots or galoshes, I rushed over to the housewares department.

And after 4 days I finally managed to get two saucepans, but for young people just starting out you need to get absolutely everything. I simply don't know how I'm going to manage. Tomorrow I'll get up early again, and I'll head out early to hunt for more things, though my sides still hurt from all the elbowing today.

[...]

NOTES

¹ In the text she refers to her family using various affectionate diminutives. Her daughter Irina (Irunechka, Irunka) is married to Boris (Borya); her three sons are: Boris (Borya), married to Dina (Dinochka), with one son, Andrei (Andriusha); Vladimir (Vov, Vova, Vovik), married to Valya with one child, Sasha (Sanechka); and Evgeny (Zhenya, Zhenyurka), married to Tatyana (Tanya). Shtange calls her husband (Dmitry) Mitya, Mityaechka, or Papanechka. Her sister Olga (Olya, Olyunya) has one child, Tolya (Tolyasha). Shtange herself is referred to as Galina, Galochka, Galinochka, and Galyushka.

² Philippe Lejeune, "L'intime et l'étranger" (The Intimate and the Extraneous), *Nouvelle Revue de psychanalyse* 40 (fall 1989): 47.

³ Natalia Ilynichna Sats, 1903–? Soviet theater director and actor, one of the initiators of the first theater for children. Wrote plays, opera and ballet libretti for children. She was arrested in the late 1930s and spent long years in the labor camps.

⁴ Acronym for "Society for Cooperation in Defense and in the Aviation-Chemical Development of the USSR," created in 1927 for supervising the military training of civilians. Its activities eventually spread to most aspects of Soviet life. By 1939, some twelve million people were members of it.

⁵ Kliment Voroshilov, 1881–1969, Marshal of the Soviet Union, vice president of the Coucil of Ministers of the USSR from 1946 to 1953, president of the Presidium of the Supreme Soviet of the USSR from 1953 to 1960.

⁶ Maxim Gorky is the pseudonym of Aleksei Maksimovich Peshkov, 1868–1936. Shtange uses here the "real" first name and patronymic of the writer.

⁷ See "Chronicle of the Year 1937," note 51.

⁸ Ibid., note 23.

⁹ Slogan that served as the name of a movement launched in 1934 with the aim of providing the general public with a basic knowledge of medicine and first aid.

¹⁰ Yury Pimenov, 1903–1977, People's Artist of the RSFSR, Lenin Prize laureate, for whom art had to "assert the emerging beauty of the new," which he illustrated in one of his most famous paintings *The New Moscow* (1937); Vladimir Vasiliev, 1895–1967, Soviet artist, former student (like Pimenov) of the VKhUTEMAS during the early 1920s.

¹¹ Reference to the Universal Exhibition of 1937. The panel, created by a whole brigade of artists, was entitled *The Stakhanovite Movement*.

¹² A veil worn by Moslem women to cover the face in public.

¹³ The executive organ of the Congresses of Soviets until 1936, until replaced by the Supreme Soviet, as a result of the 1936 constitution.

¹⁴ Glavlit, acronym for Chief Administration for Literary Affairs and Publishing.

[15] Acronym for Baikal-Amur Mainline. The BAM was the so-called second Trans-Siberian railway, designed to link Siberia with the Soviet Far East. Its construction, which started in the 1930s within the labor camp system, was realized only in the 1970s.

[16] A decoration.

[17] Nikolai Aleksandrovich Bulganin, 1895–1975, Soviet statesman and top administrator. Chairman of the Moscow Soviet in 1931, premier of the Russian Republic (1937–38), chairman of the Soviet Union's state bank (1938–41), deputy premier of the Soviet Union (1938–41), etc. He eventually became premier of the Soviet Union from 1955 to 1958.

[18] Maksim Maksimovich Litvinov (Meir Walach), 1876–1951, Soviet diplomat and commissar of foreign affairs (1930–39), advocate of world disarmament and collective security against Nazi Germany before World War II.

[19] Mikhail Ivanovich Kalinin, 1875–1946. Formal head of the Soviet state from 1919 to 1946. As chairman of Central Executive Committee of the All-Russian Congress of the Soviets, Kalinin supported Stalin, survived the purges and retained his high party and government offices until shortly before his death.

[20] 1934, film by the Vasiliev brothers. See Arzhilovsky's diary, note 17.

[21] 1937, film by Vladimir Petrov, after the novel of Aleksei Tolstoi.

[22] 1937, film directed by Mikhail Romm.

[23] African river, mentioned in a well-known poem by Kornei Chukovsky, that served as a model for a musical comedy of the 1930s.

[24] See "Chronicle of the Year 1937," note 6.

[25] Third Moscow Trial ("Trial of the Twenty-One").

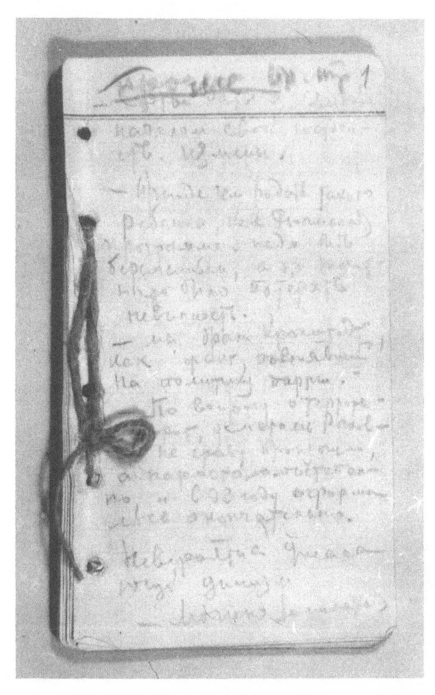

VLADIMIR PETROVICH STAVSKY

In 1937 Vladimir Petrovich Stavsky (Pseudonym. Born V. P. Kirpichnikov) was thirty-seven years old, and the general secretary of the Union of Soviet Writers as well as chief editor of the journal Novy mir.

Born in 1900 in Penza in a workers' family, he became a member of the Communist Party in 1918. He served as a commissar during the civil war and was an active participant in the grain confiscation units during collectivization in the Kuban region. This last activity is "documented" in his novellas "The Cossack Village," "The Run Up," and "On the Crest." He died in 1943 during World War II at the front, where he was serving as a war correspondent.

Stavsky entered history as the "executioner of Soviet literature," because he authorized the arrests of numerous members of the Writers' Union. His denunciation of Osip Mandelshtam, which led to the poet's arrest and eventual death in a labor camp, was published in the newspaper Izvestiya *in 1992.[1]*

Stavsky's "exemplary" career, from modest origin to the highest literary honors, which one could only maintain through compromise with the ever-shifting power structure, his alcoholism, the tormented handwriting of his notes, which were deciphered only with great difficulty, the abundance of illegible passages in them: all this testifies to an illegibility of history in which the boundaries between black and white are blurred.

DIARY OF VLADIMIR PETROVICH STAVSKY

January 1, 1938. The dacha at Skhodnya. Morning, gray and monotonous, peeked in through the cracks of the shutters. The spruce trees stood tall, forming a gray wall outside the house. Snow was falling, light, dry, crumbly.

The paths were dusted with a thick layer of snow. I went outside—it was warm, and the clouds lay low in the sky. The powdery snow gave off an air of virginal purity.

I wonder if our hunters have gotten any wolves. The real hunting is just beginning! I imagine I'll get a telegram from them.

I take a walk in the garden. Day dawns quickly. The snow just keeps coming down. The outstretched arms of the spruces are weighted down with snow. And the air is so fresh!

After breakfast we went out for a a walk. Following the roadway down to the streams. With all that snow it was tough going. You walk, looking all around you, And it's so quiet! A titmouse chirps far away, the sound resonates across the distance like a plucked string, and lingers in the air so long like a caress.

The snow on the river has started to melt and it's got a greenish tint to it, like wax. We make our way down to the dam.

[…]

We hear the noise of the sluice long before we reach the dam. There's a big window in the ice and snow and the water flows through, pure and cheerful, not a care in the world. A feast for the eyes.

We crossed over the dam, went up into the woods and started off to the right, crossing the clearing.

The snow keeps pouring down, covering our tracks. A fox has crossed by, quilting a delicate trail across the snow.

And here's a rabbit standing right in our path, he's not afraid of anything! He leaps to one side, 4 whole meters. Must be his lair. And how about that fox? Even in the middle of winter this forest that seems so dead is teeming with life.

The fine pattern of a mouse's footsteps under a bush. Further off, a squirrel leaps from one spruce to another. And it's so quiet now in the woods, just a light breeze stirring the air; the light, pliant branches of the birches ring out to each other. The birches can be quite striking: you'll see some that look so dazzlingly white, arrogant and saucy, but they'll have a pink blush infusing their bark, as though the tree was embarrassed about something. A tree like that fills your heart with joy, like one of the family. I saw some blushing ones like that last March, across the stream outside of Dmitrovo. And the stream was singing then, too, in its silvery voices….

On our way home it stopped snowing. Right before our eyes the clouds lifted and started to disperse, giving a hint of the blue sky behind them.

The sky cleared completely by evening. There was a brilliant sunset, but I don't know what got into me, I fell asleep and missed the whole thing.

Then after dinner I looked out the window: a half moon over the birches. The powdery snow in all its glory.

After five the stars appeared in the sky and a frost set in; the snow squeaks underfoot, and the sound carries far off into the distance.

The armfuls of snow on the spruces sparkle and shine, the snowy foot-prints on the swept pathway are like patches of sunlight on a July day.

The trees cast dense, dark blue shadows. In the garden, a blue darkness fills the space between the ground and the branches of the trees. Pinkish lines of smoke climb into the air above the house.

Strips of light shine through the thin shutters, and the house gives off such a feeling of warmth, comfort and refuge. Before going out I looked at the wood burning in the stove, at the golden heat of the coals. And the moon the snow the stove and smoke the pale blue glow of the stars aroused an overwhelming feeling in me, my distant, irretrievable and eternally beloved childhood....

I wander around the dacha, the trees—spruce, birch, oak—press in close to the house like a wall. My favorites, three big oak trees growing from a single root. Standing on the lawn outside my windows like [illeg.]. The spruce trees in the distance across the road are so tall and luxuri-ant—they tower into the sky and call to mind those sleepy, broad-shoul-dered mountains out in Chechnya or Dagestan somewhere that rise up and block half the sky.

Night strides across the country, New Year's night, exuberant and gay. To the right of the North Star, Ursa Major, the overturned dipper, like a round dance of stars or something.

And the whole sky is covered with stars and it's like spring sounding in the air.

Moscow, March 29. 12:00. The sun is already high in the sky.

The cars rush by, and flashes of light speed across the roofs. The sharp silhouettes of passers-by, sharp shadows on the asphalt of the square.

The big lilac tinged bulk of an apartment building. In front of it, a little, low-lying house; its roof shines in the sunlight and a blue gray line of smoke curls upwards.

The racket of the car horns. The silhouette of Pushkin, lost in thought.

Behind him the jagged outlines of the new buildings under construc-tion cut across the sky.

Moscow, 3/31. Morning, still at Skhodnya. I open the shutter as usual, and the thick greenery of the spruces fills my eyes, and over the serrated row of their peaks, the resonant blue of the sky.

Nelka is scampering around in the garden, with Uncle, our cat, chasing after her. Suddenly Nelka gives a shout and waves her arms, and the cat disappears. I didn't notice which way he went. Now Alma, the sheepdog,

appears next to Nelka, wagging her tail. Then all of them are gone....Th
Nelka comes running back, shinnies up a tree, extracts the cat from t
branches and tucks him her against her chest, covering him with the fl
of her jacket. The cat's eyes are full of terror.

We started off again, Olga in the lead. With Lyusya tagging along.

We stop on the bridge across the Skhodnya. A harsh wind whips acrc
the valley. A severe frost set in overnight. And the water level is down
centimeters from where it was yesterday. Yesterday a chunk of ice g
stuck between two broken bridge supports. Now it's suspended the
with its fantastical patterns sparkling.

But there's still a lot of water in the river and streams, the angry, turb
lent current beats against the shores, first one, then the other. And t
aspen grove on the other side seems wrapped in a tender, greenish fog.

On the other bridge, the one over the main road, we wait for the c
Looking down from there you get a clearer view of the flow of the spri
waters. A family of ducks, with their flashy, colorful drake, swims arour
for awhile in the water, then comes out onto the ice.

The ice gives a cracking noise, krrr—, it sounds like shooting som
where, far off.

On the way back to Moscow I read Ketlinskaya's "Courage."[2] She has
much material. And her disposition is so bold. She introduces dozens
heroes all at once. And still manages to individualize them.

Tanya, so childlike, in her dressing room, is very good. Andrei Krugl
too, the Communist who falls in love a week before he has to leave....

In general she gives so much material in 60 pages that in the hands
another one of us writers would fill three novels!

What can we expect from her in the future?

At the editorial office of *Novy mir*.[3]

2:00. What crazy weather! At 12:00 it was clear. Then a cold gray stoi
cloud moved in and the air over the square turned white with snow. T
passers-by raise their collars against the storm. And then the sun com
out again. And the sky is blue. But then it turns gray and murky again.

August 13, 1938. This morning there was a joint meeting of the Soviet of t
Union and the Soviet of Nationalities.[4] Then back to the editorial office
Novy mir. And in the evening, the Soviet of Nationalities again. The issue
an enormous one: the judicial system. But the speaker—People's Comm

sar Rychkov, though he included a lot of interesting material, couldn't hold the attention of his audience. People had to force themselves to listen.

After the speech there were informal meetings in the corridor. Tandit.[5] My conversations with him were most interesting.

He's preparing a speech on "Organizational Principles of Bolshevism."

"Volodya, give me some examples from real life, examples of self-sacrifice. You know how easy it is to tell stories about heroism during times of war or armed struggle, or about the heroic exploits of the Bolshevik underground. I'll take examples from the lives of the leaders. I'll tell about [illeg.]. Do you know that story…?"

"About how he held his hand in the flame and burned it?"

"That's the one! I don't know if it was actually him or not. But that image of a man created by reason, it's a majestic image. Such force of mind and will—to take and burn his own hand. It's a striking, exceptional example. But what I need is an example of self-sacrifice from our own lives, one that would make a house painter or some other ordinary worker say, "That's something I can do myself!""

"I've got it, listen to this! It was in 1934, as I recall, and things were going badly in my group. People weren't asking questions. And the Party Control Committee Plenary was going on at the same time. I send a note up to LMK,[6]

"I urgently need to talk to you."

He read the note and gave a barely perceptible grin. Then he looked over at me and nodded. I stayed behind after the meeting—which lasted until after midnight. He walks by and takes me by the shoulder, "Let's go!"

We went to his office in the Central Committee. Several members of the commission were there, how many of them are now [illeg.]?

"All right comrades, let's finish up the resolution."

And we got down to work. LMK put so much care into choosing and deepening the language!

Around 4 or 5 a.m. the phone rings, the Kremlin line. LMK picks up the receiver,

"Valerian? Hello! To the *troika*[7] on the bread problem? You go ahead and get started, I'll be there by morning."

Everyone exchanges smiles. The fresh Moscow morning is bursting in through the big windows. Sparrows are making a racket outside in the trees near the "clock." I can hear the sound of water spraying from the fire hydrant; they're washing down the street.

"He'll be there by morning!"

LMK continues his work. Then he gives instructions. Says good-bye.

"You carry on, I have to be moving on."

We all troop out after him into his assistants' office. On the American table there are some leftover sandwiches and glasses of tea that has gone cold. LMK grabs a sandwich and wolfs it down greedily. Then another, then a third. Then he bursts out laughing, flashing his white teeth.

"And here I was wondering where I got such a bad headache. It's because I forgot to have dinner today!"

"Can you use that example?" I ask Tandit.

"I've seen that so many times!" he laughs, "but I can't say it myself. You write it down, and I'll use it and quote you. Damn you writers. Why do I have to go looking in history for examples? I need an example of self-sacrifice, I need to show a Bolshevik at work, and I take the Bolshevik Pavel from Maxim Gorky's novel, *Mother*."[8]

"As far as writers go, you're right. But now about self-sacrifice. What you need to do is broaden the question. Why limit yourself to self-sacrifice? A creative outlook, that's what our life is based on, creativity. It's everywhere, everywhere you look you see brilliant, intoxicating examples. Though in general the question you've brought up is an enormous one. Wait, I just remembered something else,

Spring, 1931. May. The "Farmstead" State Farm. I was working with a Communist from the cooperative in a tractor brigade. We were helping out and learning about how things were done. And it was freezing outside, we were having a cold spell. The tractor drivers were doing a wonderful job. One night the two of us were sitting outside, passing time. A full moon. You could hear the rumble of tractors out on the steppe, and the drivers singing as they worked. A fine night.

Suddenly my Communist says,

'What makes them work so hard? They're hungry, cold. It's so hard for them.'

'Maybe so. But you told me yourself about your work in the Kolchak[9] underground, and about the time the Kolchak counterespionage caught you and punished you.'

'True. But after all, I dedicated my whole life to the revolution. I made a conscious choice.'

'So how can you deny those young tractor drivers the same right?'"

"And you know what, Lev," I said to Tandit, "I knew he wasn't one of us, I could sense the enemy in him even then. And sure enough, a couple of years later, it turned out I was right!"

"Great! That's a really convincing example. You ought to sit down, Vladimir, and do some writing."

"I've got as many examples as you could ask for. Listen to this, I had this conversation…Wait. You see that thin, round-shouldered guy over there, that pilot? Take a look at his throat."

Balanov,'" a Hero of the Soviet Union," was walking past. He was thin and stoop-shouldered; his face was long, with a thick nose, a large chin, and a small mouth with a thick lower lip. He had a high forehead and he combed his hair straight back. His eyes were light blue, with a touch of gray. On his chest he was wearing the Order of Lenin, also the order of the Red Banner and some medal.

I'd exchanged greetings with him before.

"Hey there, nice to see someone from home!"

"Hello."

He's missing the index and middle fingers on his right hand, and there's a deep scar on his throat: an opening on either side of his Adam's apple, one going in, the other going out.

"Do you know his story? He was wounded in the air, but still kept on fighting and shot down several Fascist planes. He waited until the battle was over to land, and when he did finally make it down safely, he was all covered with blood, and nearly unconscious."

"That's some story! But these are all extraordinary examples that took place under special conditions. But what I need are examples from our own lives, striking examples of heroism and self-sacrifice."

"But neither heroism not self-sacrifice are possible in our everyday lives without a creative outlook! That's what I'm trying to say. And I'll lay it on the line: what we're talking about here are the most fundamental questions of our life! You know, I bet the Master will have something to say about them sometime soon."

"Yes! He's a philosopher. He's interested in the role of personality. And that's extremely important right now, you know. Now that the problems of our material welfare have been solved."

"I can tell you, the machinists have more money than they know what to do with."

"Well there you are! And the legal questions are taken care of in the Stalin Constitution. That's all quite clear. But say a man has put in his 6 or 7 hours of work in the factory. What then?"

"Well, that's just it! He has to study! And you know, art is going to play an enormous role in all this. We can't even imagine what an enormous role art will have in our new society."

I go out to see him off, and the two of us walk through the Kremlin. The hot sun beats down on us. But suddenly there's a fresh, gentle breath of cool wind [...]. And the sky is a special kind of blue today! The houses over in Zamoskvorechye shine in the sun. The whole Kremlin is shining.

The wise, thick greenery of the spruce trees lining the parapet in front of the Great Kremlin Palace.

My darling motherland, my own!

August 14, 1938. Moscow. Today was the beginning of a new stage in my life. And it was all so unexpected, so simple, and at the same time, complicated.

I was at Pospelov's[12] yesterday. I was completely frank with him, "I'm feeling terribly uneasy. There's something wrong with the way I'm being treated in the Writers' Union. Believe me, Petro, and remember what I'm saying now. A year or two will go by, and sooner or later it will all be clear, how they planned to ruin me, a good Stalinist and Bolshevik. It will be clear who it was that wanted to do me in. And if the Writers' Union supported me, things would be completely different."

He listened sympathetically. He didn't say anything, that's just his character, to be reserved and cautious.

Then,

"You have to write, Volodya! You can write, and you do it well. You can tell by, say, your article about Gorky—everyone read it, and they all praised it. Just carry on with your editorial work at *Novy mir* and write."

He doesn't name any names. But I can see by his eyes that P. N. knows what's going on and what people have been saying, he's very well informed.

The textbook on the history of the Party is being edited by Comrade Stalin.[13] It will be out by fall.

At last we'll have a real textbook!

I call Nikitin from Peter's office on the Kremlin line.

Nik, "Where have you been?"

Me, "Around and about."

Nik, "Come on over. I'll be at the Secretariat of the Session."

*

In the evening I went down to see him in the meeting room under the corridor in the Great Kremlin Palace.

He's sitting there looking exhausted. He's all sweaty, and he keeps trying to straighten out his fine white silk shirt.

"How are you feeling?"

"Not bad. I managed to get some rest."

"Write! You have to get down to your writing."

"I don't feel like going to the Union. Do I have to?"

"Don't bother! Let the six of them run things themselves."

"How are they doing? Can they manage?"

"They do all right. They show up, take turns."

"When is the Central Committee going to make its decision about the Writers' Union?"

"Soon, any day now, maybe during the Session."

"What changes did they make in the draft?"

"They increased it to 5 pages. Zhdanov[14] said we have to appeal to a broader audience; everything was turned over to him."

"What did they decide about the leadership?"

"There will be a 15-member Presidium. The permanent Secretary of the Presidium…"

"Will be who?"

"Fadeev."[15]

"I see. Who else?"

"He will have a permanent board."

"So I guess my work in the Writers' Union is finished?"

"Yes. Write."

"What about *Novy mir*?"

"Keep on with your editing work! We're not considering any changes. You'll need to increase the editorial board."

"All right. So those of us on the editorial board will come up with our own proposals and present them ?"

"Fine, go ahead."

"I'd like to do some travelling, to Gorky or Kuban!"

"Hit the road! You're a free man now…We decided to let you take a rest."

"Well thank you."

"You see, we're helping you out!" He laughs. He's up to something. How I miss Mekhlis.[16] He would have come to a decision and just told me straight out, without all this snickering and chuckling.

Then we talked about the journals. Yermilov has been removed from *Red Virgin Soil* for publishing Shaginyan's novel *The History Exam*.[17]

We had that novel in *Novy mir*; Krupskaya[18] and Dmitry Ulyanov[19] had given it positive reviews. It was only on Fadeev's insistence that I turned it over to *Red Virgin Soil*. Shaginyan had promised it to them before.

It gives a distorted picture of Lenin, (he doesn't seem Russian at all). The Central Committee proposed to:

—confiscate the novel.

—issue Sh[aginyan] a stern censure through the Writers' Union.

—show Kr[upskaya] her errors.

—remove Yermilov.

The guys in the Writers' Union said that the speaker on the Presidium of the Writers' Union was none other than Fadeev.

And they made some changes: Shaginyan was just given a severe reprimand. And not only Yermilov, but Fadeev himself, too, were censured.

When I heard from N. that F. was to be on the permanent staff of the Soviet Writers' Union, I felt a twinge of pity somewhere in the depths of my soul for him. After all, for him as a writer things are really bad, just about as bad as they can be.

I went from Nikitin's to the Session meeting. A huge hall, bathed in gentle sunlight reflecting off the frosted-glass chandeliers.

Way up in front, in a niche behind the presidium, stands a full-length statue of Ilyich.[20]

The Soviet of Nationalities is in session.

So many new people have been raised up by the Party! Bilya [Misostishokhova][21] from Kabarda is sitting in the back. Her face is dark and dusky, and her hair is pinned up in braids around her head. The slightly slanted eyes and characteristic thin lips—all the signs of her nationality. But she's wearing a fashionable gray European suit, with the Order of Lenin and a Deputy's badge displayed on her chest.

Sitting next to me is Shura Artamonova from the Grozny petroleum refineries. Suleimanov[22] from an aul[23] in the Caucasus is behind her. [illeg.] is a famous brigade leader, he has the Order of Lenin too. In the morning I saw Aleksei Stakhanov[24] [...] A simple, calm, freckled face. He has a calm, alert demeanor that ever so subtly commands respect. His well-developed shoulders are so powerful that his back stoops slightly forward. Nikita Izotov[25] is bigger than Stakhanov. But I think that Aleksei Stakhanov could give him a run for his money.

But how calm and sure of themselves they are—Stakhanov, N. Izotov, Bilya, Shura, all of them!

They are confident in their power, courage, their bravery. It's hard to find the right words to express this confidence, but I'll try. It's a feeling of power, might and serenity that comes from the realization that the mighty Soviet people, a hundred seventy million strong, is behind you.

Everyone is closely following the events in the Far East.[26] But there's no panic; people are calm.

"Our guys sure showed them and they can do it again."

The topic of discussion at the Session was the budget. Somehow here, in the Soviet of Nationalities, the victories resound more vividly and clearly through the columns of figures.

The delegates from the Ukraine, Turkmenia, and Azerbaijan support the budget. And they tell of the struggles and triumphs in their own republics. These stories fascinate the other delegates.

Through it all, a constant refrain rings out loud and clear: "If 27 billion out of a 125-billion ruble budget for defense is not enough, we'll give as much as necessary!"

In the evening after the session I went to the Central Committee. The first question was about the Far East.

"We're being modest when we write that we killed 400 men. According to my own modest count we did away with a whole division, at least. And the heroism of our men!"

One of our wounded men is ordered to go to the field hospital. He answers, "I can't!" "But you've been commanded by your superior officer!" He stands at attention and snaps, "As a citizen of the USSR I cannot leave the field of battle! I feel just fine. I serve the Revolution." There's your story, all ready to go. I'll write a story about that fighter. And one about that observer in Madrid too! This will be the beginning of my new life as a writer.

And really, it's surprising; it's hard to believe that everything is turning out so well!

When I was at Nikitin's I had asked him,

"Have there been any complaints about me?"

"No! Just write. We decided to let you take a rest and do some writing."

"What then?"

"It didn't come up. Zhdanov said he'd talk it over with Comrade Stalin."

Well that simply took my breath away. What more could I ask? But still, there's a kind of murky doubt in the depths of my soul, a feeling that I've been wronged. And I told Pospelov and Tandit about it. Both of them reproached me, and justifiably. Especially Tandit:

"Things are going just great for you. They wanted to hunt you down, to destroy you and throw you out. But nothing came of it. You left with dignity. Keep on with your editing, but the main thing is to write."

"You made such a brilliant debut. Your books were a resounding success. No one cares about the Writers' Union, but everyone is wondering why Stavsky isn't doing any writing. Why is he silent? Doesn't he have anything to write about?"

At that point the phone rang. It was Epshtein, the Secretary of the Party Committee of the Chief Administration of State Security,[27] asking him to give a speech on the organizational principles of Bolshevism.

"There will be a total of 390 people."

"Though even 20 or 30 would be enough. What more does a Communist really need? It's the ultimate happiness just to be able to go out and tell people about Lenin and Stalin."

"I'd love to hear it as soon as possible."

"I'd better wait until after the Session. I need to get ready. I don't want people to fall asleep during my speech."

Then he says, "I could give a speech about the organizational principles of Bolshevism at any time, day or night. It's my element. But I really should prepare. Pick out the most striking and clever examples. So people will enjoy it."

And he's so strong and calm, so sure of himself. What a great guy, that Tandit!

One of the arguments he used to reassure me, "What's the matter with you, Vladimir! I had a harder time of it when I left the Central Committee of the Party. They made me out to be a Trotskyite, but I fought hard and was vindicated on every point. Now look at you. What's your problem? It's perfectly clear. What you have to do now is sit down and write something really powerful!"

He's in the [illeg.] right now, an assistant to Chairman L. M. Kaganovich.

"I don't know where he gets his energy! Just two hours of sleep and he's back at it again, like a pot aboil. Where does it come from?"

"From the Master!"

"You're right. It's so inspiring. You see the country as a whole, how it's governed, how the masses live. You feel it all, the very pulse of life. It's so interesting, Vladimir."

"I can only envy you and be glad for you!"

And I truly am glad for him, from the depths of my soul!

Then we went on to other things, we talked about everything. Including Fadeev.

"What's he writing? Nothing at all!"

"Though his sketches on Czechoslovakia are interesting!" I say.

"You're right there. But there's more to write about right here at home.

Any journalist can do something like those sketches. Though I have a very high opinion of Koltsov, his Spanish diaries."[28] I take out the galley proofs and read about Dolores [Ibarruri] and José Dias,[29] their conversation about Comrade Stalin. And out of this spare, impetuous and explosive dialogue a vivid picture emerges, portraits of two people, the expression of the feelings of love for Stalin that we share.

How marvellous and wise were the words of the message he sent to the sick José Dias.

"Your main battlefield now is your health." And these words reveal all the tenderness that the greatest genius of humanity felt for a fighter for Communism, a companion-in-arms, a dear comrade! And these words convey all the wisdom of the leader. You are a Communist, history has placed great tasks before you. Your health is also a front in the battle. You must struggle and triumph here as well.

"You are to consider this a matter of vital importance to you!"

I am reminded of a story Fyodor Bykov[30] tells:

"In a conversation with me, Lazar Moiseevich [Kaganovich], advised me to take care of my health. He stood up and pulled his belt out, away from his waist, 'See how trim I am? If I can tell from my belt that I'm starting to put on weight, I immediately get down to work on my gymnastics. The Party needs my health, my organism — I have to keep them in ideal working condition.'"

Matvei Nikiforov also brought it up with me.

"You have to be a little more careful about your drinking. I'm not opposed to a glass of cognac every once in a while. I enjoy a drink myself. But I know when to stop. Look at you — you've just let yourself go. I'm older than you, and look at me!" He stands up and pulls out his belt. He's not skin and bones, by any means, but there's no extra fat to him, no belly. You can see he works at it:

"You ought to do gymnastics too. The way I do. That's what you should do, my friend!"

Dear comrades! I can say with pride that I have banished alcohol completely from my life. Nicotine too. And I am pulling myself together, for real. [...]

August 19, 1938. Moscow. I have so many impressions stored up!

I have to really take myself in hand, to increase my daily work load and write more. All I've done during all this time is jot down some notes in my notebook, but I still haven't gotten down to the main thing, that is, the outline for my major work. And how to go about it? I just can't put my mind to it. Everything is so difficult and complicated. And what's the point in doing things carelessly?

Today the Session finished its work on the fourth question—Soviet citizenship. They've already passed a law. What an exciting, fascinating subject for a story! Just start with the words, "I, a citizen of the Soviet Union..." But no, that's too much like Kataev's "I am a son of the working people."[31] But that's not the main thing. What's important is the title itself—Citizen of the USSR—how incredibly sublime it is. How passionately Maxim Gorky would have responded to it! So what's our excuse? What are we waiting for—some other subject?...Meanwhile here's a perfect story, all ready to go! The Far Eastern border, battle, the Red Army soldier, wounded, but refusing to quit the field of battle; he's ordered to leave, but he won't go. His reason: "I am a citizen of the Soviet Union."

I read Baidukov's remarkable "Fantasy" in today's *Pravda*. Soviet super-long-range bombers are destroying an enemy naval squadron during a storm. One bomber is hit, and its high-spirited Ukrainian crew makes a quick decision as they come down: they choose a target, an enemy cruiser, and crash their plane right into it. Baidukov is very knowledgeable about his subject; I'm sure that this sketch of his will take the world by storm. It's sure to arouse all kinds of commentary abroad! But there's just one thing: why doesn't he give any way to rescue the flight crew when the plane is shot down? I mean, while it's still in the air. And there is a way: just make sure they all know how to pilot the plane. There was a report about "flights" in America. Why didn't we hear any more about it?

Yesterday was "Aviation Day." I can't find the words to express my emotions; a poignant, gentle ache somewhere in the depths of my soul speaks to me, repeating over and over, why am I getting old? Why didn't I try earlier to get in shape and improve my health? And how many precious hours did I waste, just drinking them away? Suddenly a memory flashes across my mind: I'm lying on a bed of pine twigs, the needles poke my cheek. The infinite depths of the March sky, with the stars sparkling overhead. And then? Then a wild ride, the city. That moment, there under the sky, on a crystal-clear spring night—a moment of bitter, excruciating reproach....

But those days are gone forever. And I have to do something right now, to preserve and try to restore my health. Something is wrong with my eyes...I can just barely make out the faces of the people on the Presidium with my right eye...What torment!

But now about Aviation Day. In the morning a dark blue storm cloud formed above the spruce and birch trees to the East. A gentle wind was blowing. Each individual leaf on the trees was quivering.

The first loud raindrop breaks through, then a second, they scorch my skin. I run back to the house from the volleyball court. The rain comes down like a thick net, it pours down the window panes in torrents. Would they really call off the show? The storm passes on, moving in the direction of Moscow. It's overcast, but the clouds are very high in the sky. Maybe it will clear up.

Fedya and I drive in together. The line of cars starts at the Nagornoye turnoff. It's only 1:00, but the highway is already crowded with traffic. We counted a couple hundred cars, then gave up:

"If I had the gas from all those cars, It'd last me a whole year."

We turn onto Volokolamsk Highway. And the sun comes out! The freshly washed leaves glisten. The city has come to life. Policemen and agents from the Cheka line the highway. Here the traffic is bumper-to-bumper: no passing, you couldn't squeeze in even one more car!

A hollow, echoing tunnel. Two rows of round lights lining the walls fill it with a gentle, pleasant light. This is the famous Volokolamsk junction; the river runs through a conduit underneath the tunnel. The Volga-Moscow Canal runs above the tunnel. To one side there's a railroad bridge crossing over the canal. On the canal embankment above the tunnel, flower beds form portraits of Lenin and Stalin. Now we're at the airfield. A policeman up ahead is waving his arms, directing traffic through the gate. I leave the car and head for the "right stand." The crowd builds up quickly.

What a view! A lot of care went into choosing the site for this building. It stands on a hill to the right of the Volokolamsk Highway. The site forms a semicircle. Beyond the highway, on the other side of the village of Tushino, a steep slope runs down to an open plain. This is the flood plain of the Moscow River. It forms a smooth, flat lowland, enclosed on the other side by the Moscow river and low hills this side of the village of Strogino. The embankment of the Kalinin Railroad runs along to the left. All this creates a huge natural amphitheater. The crowd has gathered as far as the eye can see, filling the plain to the right and the low hills on the other side of the Moscow River. The tops of hundreds, no, thousands of cars shine in the sun. The crowds blend into a shifting, multicolored blur. Farther off, the airplanes stand in stern rows on the grassland, with the miniature airplane hangars on the left. Trucks mounted with antiaircraft weapons and antiaircraft machine guns, four to a truck, are standing near the hill.

The air is filled with the rumble of car engines, and a fresh breeze is blowing. Banners flap in the wind. A gray blue rain cloud hovers in the sky, and the sun comes in and out of the clouds. The entire sky is cheerful, powerful and in continual motion.

My old friend [Koshits][32] starts talking, and they're off to the races. There's a lot of double entendre, and it makes me feel queasy.

A lot of people I know. There's Betal in a thick fur hat (astrakhan); he's fit and muscular. He makes fun of my belly.

"So we've agreed: give me a year and I'll lose 40 pounds."

"All right. We'll go on a couple of bear hunts together, and before you know it the weight will be gone."

I look him right in the eyes — Is he really inviting me to visit him in Kabarda?

"I'm writing it down, Betal!" (I take out my notebook and write down what he said.)

Betal: (seriously?) "No! It'll be good for you to do some travelling. You'll see a lot of the country. And you'll write about it."

"My dream is coming true, Betal!"

Some of his comrades come up, Betal introduces them to me; "Bilya, Bilya [Misostishokhova]." She's imposing and tall. The slightly slanting eyes, the cheekbones a little high in her face, there they are, all the signs of her nationality. She's wearing a short jacket and a long, loosely-fitting black dress made of thin silk. And what a figure! Her legs are a little too big, but they're strong and sturdy though. Bilya has sure spent a lot of time on horseback. She's wearing the Order of Lenin and a deputy's badge on her chest.

"There's half a million people here, I'd stake my life on it!" I say. "Half a million?" Betal flares up immediately. "Why there's a million here, for sure. Take a look, will you Vladimir? Such power, such strength! The people!" And he chops the air after every word with his hairy, powerful fist. He laughs, flashing his big, white teeth, spaced far apart in his mouth.

"We really smashed the Mikados in the mug, the Germans are next."

"Have they taken off?"

"[illeg.] They sure have, they're on their way!"

The balloons rise up into the sky and disappear. Way off in the distance the portrait of Comrade Stalin appears against the blue of the sky.

The amateur air brigade takes off. The pilots are young. They only fly in their free time, without taking any time off their regular work. But up they go in perfect harmony. And that's the whole point: "keep out of each other's way," is how [Koshits] put it. And this "keep out of the way" is what prevents accidents.

What really impressed me was the "flying wing" figure. You just can't believe it's an airplane. It's like some big huge, and for some reason, shaggy, butterfly, that's what comes to mind. And the planes just keep rushing through the sky.

One of them is red. [Koshits] announces: "Katya [Mednikova][33] protesting against male domination in the sky."

We get used to things so quickly, you watch the planes and their flight doesn't surprise you any more. But that one simple act—flying an airplane across the sky in a straight line—comes only as the result of enormous training.

September 14, 1938. The dacha at Skhodnya. I took out my previous notes and gasped. The last one is from August 19. Almost a whole month ago. And what have I gotten down on paper in all that time? If you don't count the 10 pages about Dmitry Ivanovich Martynov from the Kaganovich Factory, and a couple of reviews and an editorial on the results of the Session, I didn't write anything at all. I guess I just have to say right out, how hard it is to be a writer. Today at tea Olga told me something that made an immense impression on me.

Here's her story:

It was about a conversation she had in a taxi. She had felt sick and decided not to try to economize on the 3-ruble cab fare. She's on Myasnitskaya Street and a taxi comes by. She calls out to the driver,

"Comrade, give me a lift!"

"I can't do it, comrade, you have to go to the taxi stand."

"I'm in a hurry, and I'm feeling sick. Just give me a lift."

"Well, all right."

They got to talking. Olga asks,

"Why aren't you working as someone's personal chauffeur? You can make more money that way, and the work is better."

At this point the driver lit into her. "Better, you say?"

Olga actually recoiled: the guy's face was furious, his lips twisted back.

"I made myself a vow, never to work as a personal chauffeur again!"

"Why, what happened to you?"

That broke the ice. It happens sometimes: a man lets something build up inside, and the moment someone asks what's wrong, he completely bares his soul and tells everything, right down to the last detail.

"I used to work for an engineer from one of the People's Commissariats of Industry. The pay was good—seven hundred thirty rubles a month. When I started I was making five hundred. But when I saw how they carried on, I decided the hell with it; I said something to my boss, and he immediately offered me a raise. So I stayed. That went on for a while. I'm all ready to quit once and for all, but they break me down with those raises of theirs. I sure saw my share of filth there. Apparently my boss was originally a worker himself, but he had left all that behind. He wore one of those jackets with the huge shoulders. The minute he got a car, he turned into a pig. It happens so quickly, I just can't make sense of it: it's obvious that he used to be a worker, but now look at him. He knew how to drive, and sometimes he would go out by himself. I figured it out: if he went out alone it meant he was on the prowl. You'd go up to the car after he was done with it, and the mudguards would be all crumpled, the engine would be all messed up, the finish all scratched up. And inside, what a mess! Not a car, but a brothel on wheels. You just feel like hosing the whole thing down good with a fire hose before getting in. His wife was no better. She got herself a German lover, and I'm supposed to drive them around. Then she learned to drive herself. She'd take the car and it's off to her German, and devil knows who else. They'd try to outdo each other. He's living there in his own house with his secretary, with a typist, I wouldn't doubt it if he was involved with the courier, too. He didn't let a single skirt get past him; obviously he figured that if someone worked for him, then she owed him. What a pig, I couldn't stand the sight of him. And he'd grill me about his wife: where's she been, who was she with, was she by herself? Then she'd start in: was he by himself? She had ugly peeling skin on her face that she covered with make-up, and she had dyed her hair blond, but it started to fade and the dark roots showed underneath what a sight, like a mangy old sheepskin coat.

"She'd send me here, send me there. Take a note, go to the market! Once I found a note in the car, Comrade chauffeur, tell me who your master's been carousing with. Call me at this number, and she'd written the number on the note. I'll make it worth your while....

"How do people manage to befoul themselves like that, just imagine! I was so desperate to get away from them, but they kept on giving me raises.

"Just looking at them made me sick. But when they were together, they were so tender and affectionate with each other....

"So what if they were originally workers? Shooting's too good for people like that, they foul the air for the rest of us. I just can't understand how it happens: a guy, just a regular guy, one of us. But he crosses some dividing line, and he's like a pig with his whole mug covered in filth. A regular worker doesn't get into that much filth in his whole lifetime. Maybe he takes a drink or gets a little rowdy now and then, but nothing like that!"

That story really bothered me. And just yesterday [Doronin][34] was telling me about his own experiences:

"Back when they were building the dachas in Peredelkino,[35] I worked there as a truck driver. The manager would come over in the evening and say, 'Could you deliver some boards for me?' 'All right.' 'How much will you charge?' 'How about ten?' 'All right, go ahead.' So you deliver the boards. Make ten or so trips. In a month I managed to earn over two thousand. And he'd credit me with overtime on top of it—3 rubles an hour."

"And you didn't feel guilty?"

"What was there to feel guilty about? Everyone there was doing it! [illeg.] anyone with an ounce of energy."

"Lyashkevich too?"

"So what if he did?"

"Tell me, what about his dacha, did he do it honestly? Can you really build a stone house on a five-hundred ruble salary?"

"Oh come on. Of course not! He did his share of scrounging. A brick here, a log there, and the delivery is free. He's his own boss, and well, he built himself a dacha! What blind fools the secretaries of the Writers' Union were, Shcherbakov,[36] Stavsky and the others...."

We must wage a fierce struggle against swindlers and thieves! I'll make sure to bring up this important subject in my new work. But where to begin?

A factory? But I don't know enough about factory life. Very well.

Kuban? But there's no one to leave in charge of *Novy mir* right now.

Grozny? Here, too, I'd have to start from the ground up.

More plans:

—write a quick play about Spain, and about the Far East, about the battles, about the heroism of the fighters on the Bezymyannaya Heights.

And I just can't get my personal life in order!

And I'd like to write something about hunting!

It makes your head spin!

But first of all, let's start by establishing a strict, disciplined work routine. Write down something every day, observations, meditations, everything I see that is striking or interesting. It's amazing: I found the strength to rid myself of alcohol and nicotine—I just put my mind to it and broke the habit, just like that, but this time it's not working. But it will.

I'll start today.

The day before yesterday it started to feel like autumn. It was early evening, and we had started off for the Pyatnitskoye Highway via Kryukovo. A storm cloud filled the whole horizon in front of us. Little drops start falling on the windshield. Maybe it will pass us by? After Kryukovo the road turns off to the left and runs between two rows of old birch trees, forming a dark, pleasant avenue. The road is rough and gouged with deep ruts. We cross the bridge over the railway embankment, but the road doesn't get any better. Dusk is moving in rapidly. It's completely dark in the woods. The drops come down faster and faster. Then it starts to pour. We stop in a clearing. There's no point in trying to make it to the Pyatnitskoye highway. Suddenly a pale blue bolt of lightning splits the clouds, followed by a thunderclap. We turn back. It couldn't have been that long, but the road is already soaked through and through. The car lurches from one side to the other. How am I ever going to make it back through that nice little avenue from the bridge to the highway?

There are ditches on both sides of the road this side of the bridge. The car starts to slide off to one side, but by jerking the steering wheel back the other way I manage to steady it and get back on the road. Now there's a rise and we're driving through wet sand. To the left is a steep drop-off, to the right, stones. The wheels lock, and the car skids first to the right, then to the left. And finally we make it to the bridge!

I ease the wheels into a deep rut. I'm worried, I've already scraped the bottom of the car against the ground a couple of times. I open the door wide and lean out; the rain beats against my face, but I can see better this way. I keep the car in first, riding the brakes, but that turns out to be a mistake. We lurch suddenly off to the left, and I brake at the last minute, turning off the engine. The wheels are hanging right over the ditch. I shift into reverse and back up carefully, keeping the wheel in the rut. I can hardly believe it when the little house by the highway comes into view. And here's the highway itself. What a great feeling. I step on the gas. And suddenly there's such a flash of lightning that I'm completely blinded. I hit the brake. And for a long time I can't see anything at all.... On the highway we're driving behind a truck carrying a load of hay, and I can see all of it, down to the last detail, reflected in the asphalt.

Then we pass the sign and turn left into the "Wings of the Soviets" hunting preserve. [...]

We didn't get home until late into the night, and it rained the whole way.

We arrived at Skhodnya yesterday at about 10 o'clock. The clouds broke, and the stars were so pleasant and bright against the dark blue of the sky.

A little later the moon came out. When I went out to see [Doronin] it was bright outside from the moonlight. There was a sharp edge to the air, and a musty smell of autumn, a light song somewhere in the night. Autumn is here. I woke up in the middle of the night. The moon shone through the window. It was so bright, you could see each individual twig on the spruce trees. And the trees here are so tall!

In the morning, it's overcast outside my window. Some blue sky peeps through, but it clouds over again. Fog. Magpies hop and cackle in the garden, looks like a whole brood. Titmice are chirping right above the window. Autumn is here.

I'd give anything not to have to do my gymnastics. I just barely managed to drag myself out of the house. And I couldn't get any energy up the whole time I was exercising. The wind rustles. The birches are covered with yellow leaves. The oaks are still at their peak. These are my favorites: three of them, triplets, that grew from a single acorn. Of all the places I've lived, this one is closest to my heart. There are three sets of "triplets" on the lot, these oaks here, then there's a set of birches, and one of spruces: three birch trunks and three spruce trunks, growing from a single root. Both the birches and the spruces are old—they're very tall, and if you stand close to them, you have to lean your head way back to see the tops. In the evening, looking out from the porch or my window, I see the spruce tree against the background of the evening sky, and all around it, the birches, just like a copper engraving.

The clouds blew over by noon; the sky shone bright, with a clear, ringing blue color. Outside the window, long, slanting shadows lie across the ground, the sun has started moving down in the sky, not like in the summer, when it's right overhead. Autumn is here. My thirty-eighth autumn. I need to get down to my writing, to write more forcefully!

It's been a whole month, I have to finish what I started about "Aviation Day."

What I remember is the immense cupola of the sky, the sun coming in and out of the clouds, it's better that way, you can see better. The hangar buildings showed black against the flat ground of the airfield. What struck me most that day was the raid by "enemy aircraft" and the defense of the airfield. It was an incredible, emotional experience for us all. First, the three-toned blare of the air raid sirens. Then the fighter planes on alert take off into the sky. The attacking planes come speeding over from behind the hills on the right, flying low to the ground. They're invincible. The defending fighter planes swoop down at them from the depths of the sky. But the enemy planes have already broken through. Then comes the rattle of the truck-mounted machine guns. The antiaircraft guns, also mounted on trucks, fire, sending flames up high into the sky [...].

The attacking planes speed over the hangars, and a broad flame flares up. The earth shakes from the blast, and black smoke swirls up and gathers into a cloud that covers the entire hangar complex.

The siren blares out again; the fighter planes fly off toward the distant hills, heading straight for a new fleet of bombers that have appeared to the left of the church, just like a flock of birds in the pale azure of the sky. And suddenly they're right overhead. The antiaircraft artillery roars, the shots are distinct, somehow resilient. And then the bombers are gone, the hangers are gone too, in their place are black clouds of smoke, the bright flames of the fires, and logs and boards falling onto the ground. The noise from the explosions hurts my ears....

That was the air raid. Right after it came the air battle. The fighters take off with a roar, rising nearly vertically into the sky; they turn sharply and dive, then soar up again. Their mission is to fly around to the rear of the enemy, catch him in their sights and press the triggers of the machine guns. No, these are no longer machines, they're people up there in the sky, who have subdued the metal and made it into a part of their body; it serves them, diving down from one side, as quick as a thought.... I'm standing next to Pumpur,[37] a Hero of the Soviet Union. He keeps turning around, scanning the sky. He's wearing sun glasses. I bought some just like that in Valencia. Pumpur is smiling; he's cheerful, satisfied. Looking at him, I recall Baidukov's article again, more vividly than before. Those brave, cheerful Ukrainians....

The show ends at 5:00. I don't feel like leaving. There's a crowd at the edge of the field.

1/1/1939. 12 midnight.

       oo   -".   Skhodnya. The vacation home.

What happiness!

To celebrate the New Year with the people nearest and dearest to my heart!

My dear, darling Lyulya! We've been through so much suffering, so much sorrow! But now the path to happiness is before us! The path of heroism and triumph! It's all up to us.

You are so dear to me! A fellow human being, in the best sense of the word. The snow is pouring down from the spruces and pines, I know. The night is darkest blue, and there's not a star in the sky. But in our hearts, yours and mine, we have stars, and sky, and happiness!

Do you remember? Our vacation in Kislovodsk, the sea of lights below us, the silence, so quiet that every sigh, every movement resounded in the air. The two of us together.

And do you remember? Moscow, twilight, and we're swimming. The sound of an old Russian song coming from somewhere. And the feeling in my soul is so free, so easy. It's because of you, my beloved, my darling!

And do you remember? The night, the moon, the tree trunks gleaming in the moonlight, the two of us together.

My darling! The whole richness of life appears before my eyes, all of life beats in my heart, my beloved!

And I want to live, together with the epoch, together with Stalin, together with you, my beloved, my darling!

And we will triumph!

And we will be happy!

I love you! My darling!

[...]

Skhodnya, March 30, 1939. Well it's starting to look like spring. I woke up after 9, opened the shutter, looked out and gasped. The sky above the green wall of spruce trees was so clear and blue, there was a magnificent white cloud with the sun shining so brightly at its edge that I felt a thrill in my soul.

After 10, Olga and I went out for a walk. We went down into the Skhodnya river valley.

"Look, look, what's happened to the woods? Everything has just burst out in bloom!" babbles Olga. But there's a simple explanation. Last weekend there was thick fog and the woods looked like one solid, massive wall, but now we can see each individual twig. Over there on the hill is a cluster of aspens, with a tender green blush on the bark of their branches. Behind them a mighty line of spruce trees stands at attention. The sunlight brings out the bright greenery of their dense, sturdy needles.

Quietly, gently, we make our way to the "Wings of the Soviet." In Rzhavki a herd of young girls comes toward us. One of them, all freckled with flaxen forelocks opens her little green eyes wide.

She walks alongside, and in a bass voice: "Oh, what an impressive couple! Oh, ho, ho!" She throws open her coat and parades forth in her yellow hair-band, blue blouse and red skirt, like the flag of some foreign country.

The waters from the spring thaw swirl and churn under the bridge, singing loudly as they rush past. The thin ice cracks noisily.

On the other side of Rzhavki we turn to the right and soon find ourselves in the woods.

We're surrounded by dense birch forest. Up ahead is a low, gently sloping hill. A frozen, well-travelled road crosses over from left to right, holding the water like a dam. We tried going to the left across the snow, but couldn't, and there was also water to the right. We turned back, carefully stepping in our old tracks; in a couple of places I had to pick Olga up and carry her across the water on my own long-suffering back.

Wispy white clouds have been moving across the sky. Then all of a sudden gray storm clouds move in from the north. The air fills with snow flurries. Some spring!

[...]

It is late and blue twilight is beginning to set in when we arrive home. We walk slowly along the highway, dragging one foot after the other.

In the west, over the dark line of the woods, a pure azure sky shows through a break in the clouds, with a small, wispy pink cloud floating in it, the kind we get in midsummer. Green water rushes noisily through the ditches. The alder and birch copses on the nearby hills are lilac-colored in the twilight. Flocks of raucous gray rooks circle over the village. Spring is here.

April 6. What a fine spring it's turning out to be. The day before yesterday we had a nip of frost, and there were even some snow flurries. Then today storm clouds blew in and covered the sun, and there was a light, warm rain. The first April shower. The snow in the fields is nearly all gone, though there's still a lot in the woods. It stuck there and settled in, spongy, grainy, and tinged with blue. Though there's no snow in the fields, water rushes through all the gullies. The streams sing a melodious and passionate song, and on the bare, blackened branches of the trees and around the starling houses, starlings sing in an undertone — they've not yet found their voices.

All day long images have been coming back to me from my dear, unforgettable childhood. A yellow bunting near the road warbles out its little song. I picture the song as being green. Gray rooks are poking around on the lowlands, in the reddish grass left over from last year. In the villages, in Yelino, in Rzhavki, in Chernaya Gryaz, multicolored linen hangs, swaying in the breeze, on fences that the rains have faded. Blue and red shirts, fiery jerseys, yellow blouses. The woods are still mute. Snowdrifts line the road. A green willow dangles its gray velvet catkins above the snowdrifts.

I recall a March day, just like this one, when I was about six. My grandmother was taking me from the village to visit my mother, who was in Penza at the time. Then, as now, gray clouds were hanging low in the sky, right above the shaft-bow. Water had collected in yellow puddles on the roads. Someone broke off a big willow branch for me, it was all covered with catkins. In the evening my mother talked with my grandmother, and I felt terribly sad. It was chilly in the house, the corners of the unplastered log walls were damp. A wet April storm droned outside the windows. Suddenly two sirens blared out, filling my childlike soul with confusion and a terrible melancholy. Their strange harmony made a sad and frightening impression on me at the time. I recall that harmony to this very day....

There's a lot of water in the woods, too, and puddles have formed there in the depressions in the icy crust of the snow, and the white trunks of the birch trees are reflected in them, just like the pictures you see on medallions.

Kuzmich didn't seem too glad to see us when we got to the lodge. He's sitting there writing out hunting permits for local hunters. The little girl Emiliya is by the doors, she's just come out from behind the curtain, her brother German is even smaller, he's playing and talking to himself on the bed behind the partition. And that's it, the entire living space of the family of Kuzmich's son Victor.

Olga asked, "Who thought up those names Emiliya and German?"

"Who thought them up, their parents," I say. Kuzmich tears himself away from his papers.

"I was opposed to it, but do kids listen to their parents in this day and age? They really do sound like Fascist names, not ours, not Russian at all...."

Moscow, April 11. Zuyev called this morning.

"You didn't go out anywhere yesterday? I was really scared. I tried calling you once, then again, then a third time, but you weren't there, my god![38] And do you know what it's like out in the country? All the branches are bowed down to the ground, there's so much snow. We had a terrible storm — so much for spring."

"I didn't know. Well, should we go or not? I mean, to Zavidovo."

"To Zavidovo?" Zuyev asks, without the slightest interest. Of course I'm glad that Zuyev has gotten back on his feet. Anyway, we arrange to start off at 3:00. Maybe we'll go to Zavidovo. Zuyev says he's sure that the black grouse will be mating in the birch trees in the fields there and then blurts out,

"It's important to observe what's going on in nature."

"What, are you going to write about it?"

"Not at all, why should I write anything out there? I just want to observe."

Zuyev called back in fifteen minutes.

"Vladimir Petrovich! Keep in mind that I've bought some fresh pike-perch, and then a fine big cut of meat, and I also have some smoked kutum,[39] so don't go out and buy a lot of food. I'll pack everything carefully and we'll take it with us."

"What's the matter with you, Dmitry Pavlovich?"

"This one's on me! Remember how you made me eat? 'Eat your fill! Have some more!' But I'm back on my feet now!"

And there was such pride, such dignity in his voice. I was downright glad for him.

4/17/1939. Last night Sasha Mironov came over. He said that E's wife had poisoned herself with veronal. They pumped her stomach but they couldn't save her. The doctors still don't know how veronal works. [...]

About Sholokhov:[40]

"During the conference he went off into the archive, and he stayed in there the whole time. The delegates wore all worried,

"Where is he? Where's Sholokhov?" He came out and apologized. He said that he'd been working on some important materials!

And he told me: "As for you, you should be glad that you made such an easy landing, with a parachute. The Order is your parachute. Be glad and proud. Problems with your nerves? Get some rest! Work every minute, read, go to lectures, don't miss a single one! Absorb everything, and then, as Hegel said, release your reflexes into the world around you, i.e. write your book!

"Though the best cure for nerve problems is sleep and fresh air. Go out hunting, take walks. And that will restore your nerves."

He's cheerful, good-humored. It's a joy just to look at him. "So how are you? Have things gotten any easier? Looks like it!"

And indeed I do feel a lot more relaxed.

[...]

I don't know, maybe I'm wrong, but if I am, I am cruelly and intolerably wrong. But yesterday I got the impression that N. is desperate and will do anything to gain a position with the leadership. She let it slip when we met to select the staff.

"You don't need a secretary! I'm leaving!"

And then the sentence: "Whoever controls the staff is the one who is really in charge."

Well, what choice did I have? Should I have fought it out with her? When the main thing in my life is to write, just to write!

And that's what I'm doing, writing, day in and day out.

And what riches I discover in myself! Mironov was right yesterday, when he said I didn't need to go anywhere: "Just sit, write, assimilate all your experience."

Sometimes an oppressive mood takes over me, a feeling that something is going away and leaving, leaving me behind....

But really, what a wonderful life! What magnificent triumphs! And what a magnificent struggle still lies ahead!

Today's papers carried Kalinin's response to Roosevelt's message to Hitler and Mussolini.[4] It was downright touching:

"I consider it my pleasant duty to express my deep sympathy, together with sincere congratulations...."

This brings me such pride, such joy!

NOTES

[1] E. Polyanovsky, "Smert Osipa Mandelshtama" (The Death of Osip Mandelshtam), *Izvestiya* 25, 26, 27, and 29 May 1992.

[2] Reference to a 1938 novel by Vera Ketlinskaya (1906–1976), devoted to the construction of Komsomolsk-on-Amur.

[3] See "Chronicle of the Year 1937," note 44.

[4] The two equal chambers of the Supreme Soviet of the USSR.

[5] Lev Borisovich Tandit's identity could not be clarified, except that he was the author of the pamphlet *Triumf ucheniya Lenina-Stalina o diktature proletariata* [The Triumph of the Teaching of Lenin-Stalin about the Dictatorship of the Proletariat] (Moscow: OGIZ, Molodaya Gvardiya, 1934) and the editor of *Ustav Partii — nerushimaya osnova partiynoi zhizni: Sbornik statei* [The Rules of the Party — The Indissoluble Foundation of Party Life: A Collection of Articles] (Moscow: Politizdat, 1936). We are grateful to Orest Pelech, Slavic bibliographer at Duke University, for having provided this information.

[6] Lazar Moiseevich Kaganovich. See "Chronicle of the Year 1937," note 51.

[7] Possibly a reference to the Committees of "Three Officials" (*Troika*), which were created in February 1930 to supervise the dekulakization operations.

[8] Maxim Gorky's famous novel of 1906, which eventually became a "classic" of socialist realism.

[9] See Arzhilovsky's diary, note 1.

[10] Nikifor Fedotovich Balanov, 1909–1981, war pilot, participant of the Spanish civil war of 1936–39. On January 12, 1937 he was severely wounded but managed to land his plane on his airfield. In June 1937, he was awarded the title of Hero of the Soviet Union. He also received the order of Lenin, of the Red Banner, and other medals.

[11] Highest honorific title of the USSR. Introduced in 1934, it was awarded for distinguished services to the state, both personal and collective, and involved an act of heroism. The first recipient of the title was a Soviet pilot who, in 1934, saved the crew of a ship in distress.

[12] Pyotr Nikolaevich Pospelov, 1898–1979, chief editor of the review *Bolshevik* since 1931 and member of the editorial board of *Pravda*. Pospelov was also a member of the Central Committee. Eventually, he became the chief editor of *Pravda*.

[13] Stavsky has in mind the *History of the All-Union Communist Party: Short Course*, published on October 1, 1938, determining for years to come the Stalinist dogma and sanctioning the rewriting "by Stalin" of the country's history. On the history of the *Short Course*, see Robert C. Tucker, *Stalin in Power: The Revolution from Above, 1928–1941* (New York: Norton, 1990), 530–550.

[14] See "Chronicle of the Year 1937," note 25.

[15] See "Chronicle of the Year 1937," note 11.

[16] Lev Mekhlis, 1889–1953, one of Stalin's assistants. Secretary of the editorial board of *Pravda* after Bukharin's removal in 1929, candidate member of the Central Committee after the Seventeenth Congress of the Party (1934), chief editor of *Pravda*, head of the Main Political Administration of the Armed Forces after Yan Gamarnik's suicide on May 31, 1937 (see "Chronicle of the Year 1937," note 36). From 1938 through 1952 he was member of the Orgburo of the Central Committee.

[17] *The History Exam (Bilet po istorii)* was an early part (and version) of Marietta Shaginyan's Lenin cycle, eventually published in the 1960s. The special resolution of the Central Committee of the Communist Party in August 1938 (provoked by the publication of the novel), and the circumstances of which are depicted here, are characteristic of the difficulties undergone by the Lenin cult during the Stalin era, during which the leader of the revolution could only be mentioned together with his "best pupil." See Evgeny Dobrenko, *Metafora vlasti. Literatura stalinskoi epokhi v istoricheskom osveshchenii* (Metaphors of Authority: The Literature of the Stalin Era in Historical Context), (Munich: Otto Sagner, 1993), 86. The specific problem of Shaginyan's novel was that it mentioned, for the first time, Lenin's Kalmuck origins.

[18] Nadezhda Konstantinovna Krupskaya, 1869–1939, Lenin's widow. Beyond purely nominal and secondary posts, Krupskaya devoted herself to her passion, that is, pedagogical research, to her book on Lenin, and to the publication of his works. Despite the fact that she espoused the views of the opposition in 1925–26, Stalin obtained her moral backing. She was the helpless witness of the liquidation of the entire Bolshevik old guard.

[19] Dmitry Ulyanov, 1874–1943, Lenin's younger brother.

[20] See "Chronicle of the Year 1937," note 45.

[21] Spelling unclear.

[22] Perhaps Abdul-Bagab Bekbulatovich Suleimanov, poet from the Daghestan Autonomous Republic, or Ozorbai Suleimanov, Kirghizian poet.

[23] Mountain village.

[24] See "Chronicle of the Year 1937," note 6.

[25] Stakhanovite model miner.

[26] The Soviet-Japanese border incident at Lake Khasan, 29 July–11 August 1938.

[27] Security Police organ existing within the NKVD.

[28] Mikhail Efimovich Koltsov, 1898–1942? writer and journalist, author of *Spanish Diaries* (1938) about the civil war in Spain. He was arrested shortly after the publication of this work, as were many other participants in the Spanish war.

[29] See "Chronicle of the Year 1937," notes 32 and 33.

[30] Fyodor Petrovich Bykov is mentioned several times in the RGALI archive, but his identity could not be established.

[31] Title of Valentin Kataev's novella of 1937, devoted to the civil war.

[32] Spelling unclear.

[33] Spelling unclear.

[34] Spelling unclear. Probably Ivan Ivanovich Doronin, 1900–1978, Soviet poet who has written on the unification of the peasantry and the proletariat.

[35] Famous writers' colony on the outskirts of Moscow, opened in 1935 on the initiative of the Union of Soviet Writers, who attributed dachas to second-rate writers (but belonging to the Union's power structure), as well as to the flower of Russian writers (Isaac Babel, Boris Pilnyak, etc.). Boris Pasternak found there a haven to write his *Doctor Zhivago*.

[36] Aleksandr Sergeevich Shcherbakov, 1901–1945, Soviet literary bureaucrat. Member of the Presidium of the Writers' Union after 1934, he was elected first secretary of the Writers' Union Secretariat during the first plenum after the First Writers' Congress on 2 September 1934.

[37] Pyotr Ivanovich Pumpur, 1900–1942, war pilot, participant in the Spanish civil war in which he commanded the airforce operations on the Madrid front. He received the title of Hero of the Soviet Union in April 1937, as well as other distinctions, such as the Order of Lenin and the Red Banner. In 1940–41 he commanded the Airforce of the Moscow Military Region. In 1941 he was repressed and died in 1942. He was rehabilitated in 1955.

[38] Stavsky spells this word with a small letter, following the official Soviet use.

[39] Variety of fish without scales from the Caspian Sea.

[40] See Arzhilovsky's diary, note 23.

[41] Reference to Roosevelt's attempt in April 1939 to get Hitler and Mussolini not to attack any of a list of thirty-one nations.

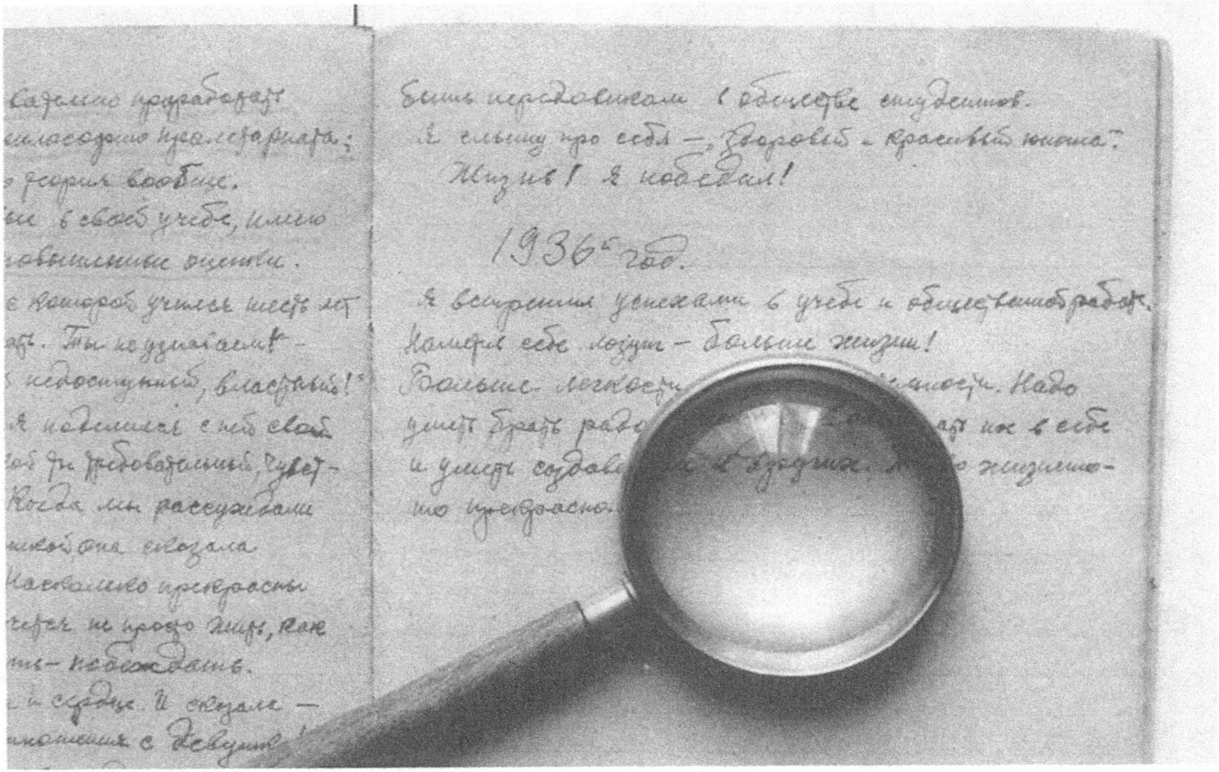

Page from Potyomkin's diary (1936)

LEONID ALEKSEYEVICH
POTYOMKIN

Leonid Alekseyevich Potyomkin was born in 1914 in the village of Poisava, Kama basin; his father was a postal employee. He left school before being able to attend the higher grades because he had to earn his living. He dreamed about entering the Moscow Institute of Philosophy and Literature (IFLI), but his application was rejected. Many institutions of higher learning at that time accepted only graduates from workers' faculties (Rabfak), which existed in the USSR from 1919 to 1940 and prepared students who had no high school education. Mining institutes did not require the certificate of a workers' faculty, so Potyomkin applied to the Sverdlovsk Mining Institute, and was accepted. In 1937 he graduated with a major in engineering and geology. He started his career as a borehole sampling worker and eventually became the vice minister of geology of the USSR (1965–1975).

He spent the years of 1941–45 in the Transcaucasus, where "he prospected and supplied copper for a copper-smelting factory." He became a member of the Communist Party in 1941. From 1945 to 1948 he served as the commander of a geological expedition on the Kola Peninsula, Pechenga region. After the discovery of an important deposit of nickel in this location, which had not been considered promising, Potyomkin received the diploma of discoverer (of which he is still very proud today) and was transferred to Moscow. There, he held very high posts in the administrative organs of the metallurgical mining industry.

Potyomkin is also the author of two books: On the Northern Frontier *(1965),* The Protection of Mineral Wealth and of the Environment *(1977). Since 1975 he has been a "personal retiree of All-Union significance." He received this status for having been, as he says, "an explorer of mineral wealth and a labor veteran with forty-four years of work experience."*

DIARY OF
LEONID ALEKSEYEVICH POTYOMKIN[1]

10/4/34. To Astakhov's lecture on literature.

Over 500 people fill the Assembly Hall of the Chemical Engineering Department. The professor limps up onto the stage and starts his survey lecture on the arts. I take notes greedily on a scrap of paper. I run out of paper. I ask my neighbor, a stranger, for a piece. He gives me one. The lecture nourished me with food that was sincerely desired, not primitive, but deeply thirsted for. Fresh, nourishing food. I envisioned the problem of the arts, an evaluation of a number of figures in the art field and I assessed my own feelings and thoughts comparing their examples. I got all stirred up, I was enabled by my thoughts and perceptions being fresh, valuable and just the thing for our topical problems today. Hearing all about Esenism[2] and the others infected me with optimism and artistic potentiality. The next day I hear a lecture on the history of the countries of the ancient East. Then on philosophy about Democrites. Greek philosophy, as philosophy per se, is of enormous interest to me. It's so very alive, realistic and relevant, not at all extincted. Its thoughts and conclusions can be felt and sensed inside oneself and checked.

Our institute is organizing a University of Culture too. I am signing up people in my groups. Myself, I'm interested in all the series. World history, Russian history, history of literature, history of science, history and sociology of the arts, the culture of labor, imparting experience from old to young, history of dialectics, current politics, and geography.

I'm amazed at the cold and indifferent reaction of the students, the majority including academically stronger guys didn't even sign up at all. Limiting my interest to 4 series but it turns out you have to sign up for just one, since they will be going on simultaneously. That annoyed me. I signed up for two series anyway: history and sociology of the arts and history of literature. It was nice to hear one of the students say: sign up for a series that will have music you need to learn to appreciate music. I'm glad. My reward is the challenge to master culture, understand art, to love the beautiful. In my military class I confidently heed with a clear gaze. Once the instructor the chief of the educational section, in whose speeches I had noted a somewhat cultured, generalizing type of thought, was cornered by some "argumentative" students. I saw clearly where the students were in error. I took the floor and presented my thought so powerfully and clearly that he was just ecstatic — that's absolutely right. What wisdom. You really bailed me out.

"That's right, that's right," repeated the guys in the class.

We are not plagued by dying shudders of desperation or seized by melancholy spiritual quivering fear of living real life. No Esenin types here.

[...] Our institute had a special celebration to commemorate the opening of the University of Culture. I stop in at my sister's put on a necktie and go to the celebration. The formal part was a speech about the University of Culture given by the rector of the university, a professor of social sciences of our institute.

These words stuck with me: What we need is people who will easily bear the enormous treasures of knowledge.

Then there was dancing. The hall filled to overflowing with dancing couples. And the music, the music it companies my thoughts, engenders them, or I feel sensations in it, thoughts and even the ideology of healthy, strong youth; the ideal, mighty energy of the simple powerful enrapturing beauty of a human man, a member of humanity.

[...]

I signed up for a literary circle at our institute. They invited me to the editorial offices of *Gorniatsky Shturm* (The Miners' Storm). I go there, the student editor gives me such a warm friendly welcome. We had a heart to heart conversation about the literary calling. He ordered me to bring my diary.

The next day I brought the diary. I didn't feel much like reading my diary out loud in front of people and I did a lousy job of it. My enthusiasm about the city did not arouse any interest. He pointed out some inaccuracies here and there. He asked me to read him the part where I enrolled in the Higher Technical Educational Establishment (VTUZ), but all I have there is just a dry listing of the facts. "You're no good at reading aloud," he said and took the diary. I showed him where to read: about that time I met the actress. He reads it to himself. I suggest he read the description of my trip to the Caucasus.

"Wait, stop there, I'll be damned, this is interesting," he answers. Then closing the diary he raised his eyes to look at me and said, "You can write, Potyomkin. My first impression of you based on those excerpts was pretty bad. But this here is a different matter. You write about the most ordinary thing, a simple encounter with an actress, and manage to engage the reader's attention, which is not something even writers who have mastered the form can always do. In your conversation you raise interesting questions and you are correct in your thinking. The dialogue is interesting. You've got yourself a story there. But what are the consequences of this conversation this encounter? Write that part out separately rework it and we'll take another look at the defects. But your style, is just atrocious, so many mistakes, both orthographical and syntactical. Write, study."

He read me a sketch out of *Gorniatsky Shturm* and turned to his assistant, "Let's give him a topic to write on." The assistant came up with a topic, the new recruitment. But I didn't have an organic, spiritual understanding of it. Then the editor said, "We need people from the VTUZ, so why don't you write a description of a typical student? If you need help, stop by and we'll talk it over."

I was very pleased with this first evaluation of my artistic endeavor. Not understanding up to this time the forms of literary production. For the first time I came to understand and sense the structure and composition of a short story. The task of polishing my theme, idea, and plot had settled in my mind. The second main part came to me: what happened after the meeting I had already described and this second part is an actually existing consequence of the meeting, it is reality, just like the first one was in itself. And with this consequence an idea was expressed. From that time on, no matter where or when I happened to have a free minute, even if it was just on a tram somewhere, an idea would take shape in my mind, the major, profound, original idea of depicting the new man with his extraordinary rich spiritual world and his new, noble attitude toward love. The philosophically entertaining consequence of my meeting with the actress gladdened me with its convexity, clarity distinctness and lifelike versimilitude.

That judgment of the editor opened up my eyes to construction, enlightened me about the essence of the literary art. I recognize myself as an incipient writer. I know what I am to do. The plan and project are finished, all that's left is to carry it out, to correct, revise, study thoroughly and complete the project.

[...]

November 4. The Party Organizer suggested that I apply to the Komsomol, while we were in the cafeteria having supper and informed me about the next meeting of the Komsomol group.

5th. I stayed after class to attend the Komsomol meeting. After the Komsomol organizer's speech summarizing the work completed by the Komsomol group and our tasks for the future, I took the floor and calmly and concisely noted the absence of an active role on the part of the Komsomol in promoting socialist competition and set us the goal of supporting and actively conducting the work of the leadership triangle of the group. The party organizer who had spoken quoted my statement and mainly just developed some individual points I'd made further

They considered my application. They discussed about the possibility of reinstating the membership of people who had been excluded from the Komsomol. The group applauded my application.

I told about my life. There was a proposal to accept me as a member, with worker status. They took a vote several people raised both hands.

At the age of twenty I celebrated the seventeenth anniversary of the October Revolution for the first time satisfied with a certain degree of personal worthiness. In the first place as a self-respecting trade-union organizer (social activist), then as a shock worker confirmed by the Trade Union Committee, one of 2 out of a total of 60 students and finally a pure, solid and committed member of the Komsomol.

I spent those days of the October holiday engrossed in my literary effort, which as was determined in the hands of the head of the literary section of the Institute newspaper dashed all the elaborate aspirations and showy flights of fancy of my premature judgment. And I was left with just the modest assessment: "You can write." With my work load at in the institute I missed my chance to attend the lecture series of the U. of Culture of the Industrial Institute except for the literature series. But that did not increase my capacity for work at the institute and for the institute, as I note with regret. What happened was the time I had freed up that way slipped through the cracks and wound up being not work and not time off either, which is something I just can't stand. The lack of the company of a respected woman which so disciplines and enlightens us burdened me at times with a kind of dull indifference, a superfluity at a given moment a lack of knowledge as to what to do or rather what to undertake.

You burn with desire, with a certain shade of longing for tender sincere contact with Her. And I know they are simple, prosaic and often even coarse and petty, and they don't have that tender, theatrical, sincere, aroma that people say they do. And you cast a simple and perhaps rude glance over the people around you. But you don't see her, the one upon whom you would bestow that high sincere concord, that tender sincere feeling that they induce.

12/20. [...] One of the concierges in our dormitory is favorably disposed toward me. There are three of them. They are 20–25 years old, at the present time not married. Not bad looking. They're perfect "Marusyas" and "Nyuras," in the free, popularly established signification of those names. It is no big deal for me to respond to their cheerful casual mood in kind.

Here I saw natural living simplicity.

Desiring to reconnoiter along these lines I said in passing to the brunette with the big hazel eyes and the clear face,

"Come see me, I'm all alone."

"If you're not lying, I'll come," she answered but for some reason she didn't. I saw the happy, complacent, kind, warm constantly shining enlightenment of the smile of the other one, who goes out with all kinds of people without giving it a moment's thought. She is quite contented and happy with her life.

The above mentioned state that comes upon me every now and then is replaced by a sensation of satisfaction and moral uplift when I'm working and when something goes right at work.

12/6. The funeral of Kirov.[3] The funeral procession floods the streets with a sea of people. I'm studying the personality of Kirov as a revolutionary a leader, and a speaker. An image that I consider my ideal.

I'm confirmed at the plenary meeting of the Komsomol Committee and I receive a membership card in the Lenin Communist Union of Youth. [...]

I went to the industrial institute for a celebration devoted to Heinrich Heine. A large, fat, imposing woman entered the packed assembly hall. Manifesting an intimacy and familiarity with the audience, speaking so simply and enthusiastically she urged everyone to move up toward the front and gather closer together. As I listened I found myself reliving the life and activities of Heine. His captivating, tender, free, expansive artistic nature impressed me. It is only an artistic fabric of that nature that is truly artistic, aesthetic and stands in poetry on an equal level with the poetry of genius. But I didn't like his romantic songs. "I cried in my sleep." This is indeed the sobbing of a sick soul, one that is familiar to me. Her crying is tender, dainty and high-pitched, but that made me dislike it even more. I felt my face burning and I couldn't stand it. Nevertheless I left the lecture wrapt in an irrepressible, frenzied, self-indignant impulse to demand, to summon up from within myself a large scale of activity equal to that of the great people of the past. I sensed with a feeling of shame that we in our great time are petty and small against the background of the giants of the past. We are still as Pushkin put it: "We all had a bit of schooling, joking about it, somehow or other."[4] They learned foreign languages in a matter of months, they knew 30 languages, whereas we spend years in language classes and can't even master one. They studied languages and read foreign literature, whereas we haven't even read what is absolutely necessary, what comprises the precious crystals of our literature's treasure-house of culture.

In a conversation along these lines I had a student object to me, with a grin on his face: "Who are you basing that on!?"

No! In order not to drag yourself along in the footsteps of history in order to go forth joyfully, worthy of our time and role in history, you have to be ahead of the leaders of the past. We need to be greater than the great people of the past.

Welcome to the year 1935 in the country of Socialism!

I've just come back from a Komsomol meeting we worked on the resolution of the IX Plenary Meeting of the Central Committee of the Komsomol on political education, and the Komsomol's work promoting education among the masses. I spoke out in the debates voiced the enormous purport and meaning of the resolution and linked it with the goals of our work toward becoming worthy bearers of the calling of advanced, politically active and committed youth.

Tirelessly working to raise my cultural-theoretical level, embodying absorbing in myself the ideal of a social activist and theoretician, a revolutionary, a party worker of the great school of Lenin. But I was dissatisfied with my speech. I didn't talk in freely developed instantaneously formulated thoughts, my thought couldn't come up with clear and emphatic enough words to keep pace with my headlong enthusiasm. Imprecision of thought made the precision of words lose its meaning. The words dragged the meaning along and formed into sentences in the air. This is speech without preparation that's that I was drawing attention to just now.

A new years toast to the great successes in the cultural and scientific enrichment of culture, and science and the potentialities of life. To precision, intensity of work, to the culture of speech. To self-confidence, high spirits, and good cheer.

[...]

After class I go to a lecture: "The Low-life Scum of the Zinoviev Group[5] and the City Administrative Committee Decision about the Party Meeting at the Mining Institute." The speaker is a charming young woman, a student in our institute's graduating class. She is a good speaker and her Party spirit is enchanting to watch and listen to. You get the impression of a serious, active party worker with a well-educated and cultured appearance and a gentle, kind feminine face that stirs the affections. It's an image no one healthy in body and spirit could resist. She said: the State and Party expect the Institutes to produce not just specialists in their fields, but Bolsheviks, Komsomol activists, and upstanding members of society, plus good specialists. She also noted—"Man is a vectored value"—what's important is not just the quantity of knowledge, but where that knowledge is directed.

Our institute's party organization got another lesson. The first was about the Volfson-Nechunev group which, under cover of drunken jokes and one-liners composed a letter to Com. Stalin called "To Mr. MacDonald," which demanded that he change his policies and threatening him if he didn't. Anyway, the second lesson was the party meeting of December 26, which betrayed carelessness and indifference and a lack of revolutionary vigilance. The lecture about the low-life scum of the Zinoviev group was given by Professor Grebenev, chairman of the department of Social Sciences, a former Deborin[6] follower who has not recanted or admitted his errors. By the way. He did not interest me at all and I didn't even like him. He spoke in a monotone and just gave all the facts in chronological order. There was no sense of Party spirit or revolutionary clarity; he lacked motivation and zeal. He was cold and distant, he wasn't simple and direct like a real Party man should be and he sounded stuck-up too. I remember how he cut me down at the Political Economy exam for pronouncing a word wrong. He crushed any desire I might have had to answer normally. And also it made me doubt my own abilities in social sciences, my favorite subject. And I did worse than I ever had and I couldn't have done any worse.

So anyway on the 26th of course he couldn't come up with any practical measures for protecting against the depraved thugs who take cover behind the Party banner. He didn't mobilize the audience to revolutionary vigilance either and he didn't see any need to and didn't find anything to confess about even though he had political blunders in his own works. The Party committee had not required the different groups to report at the meeting about their practical experience in the struggle against anti-Party elements. And so the city committee expelled the double-dealer Grebenev from the Party and dismissed him from his job and gave the

Party committee secretary a severe reprimand. The Party committee expelled Yarudin, the director of the institute, and also is asking the regional Party committee to fire him from his job.

And listening to the young communist girl's lecture I had this passionate impulse: in spite of the impossibility of it to study hard for my exam in Theoretical Mathematics, study hard enough to pass T. Math on January 11. To celebrate my birthday on January 12 with a victory over the most difficult obstacle standing in my way at the end of my 3d semester at the institute, on the 8th I went to the opera *Faust*, we had it reserved. It's so depressing I have to pass TM and am in no condition to study. With a real irritable feeling, I just eagerly drink in the music. And Charles Gounod's music expresses my feelings. I find in it the expression of my feelings. Because the composer's expression of his feelings and ideas is so rich, deep, and beautiful, my own feelings are ennobled, my personality develops. I dream about the ideal of my personality and I burn with a selfless, irrepressible passion for perfection for the "onward to the future!" that is so distant. I thirst, I demand gigantic capabilities of myself. I sense that human life is interrupted at the end. How quickly the lives of individualities blossom and are extinguished before my eyes. I need to muster all my potentialities, all my abilities so as not to smoulder, but to blaze up, to inflame illuminate and warm people this alone is the vindication, joy and great happiness of life.

We need to create ever more, ever better for mankind, in this we find the self-satisfaction of the personality, the eternity limitlessness of the blooming of life, like the eternal flow of matter.

[...]

January 12. I celebrate my 22-nd birthday in the festive mood that comes upon me during each quizzes, examinations, and tests. When the results and successes of my work are chalked up. And plus also the success achieved specially with my own personal holiday in mind. After classes I went to see my Mama and sister at the Ural Heavy Machine-Building Plant (UZTM). I had a bath in the bathhouse without having to wait because of my student identification.

On the 12th I wrote in my diary. In the evening I saw the film *Happy Fellows*,[7] which got first prize at the world film festival in Venice. Its cheerfulness and musicality make for a pleasant spectacle, arousing cheerfulness in the spectator.

[...]

1/26. The film *Kirov*[8] makes an extraordinarily valuable and strong impression. The enormous thirst of our leaders to study, live, and work is reflected in the enormous interest with which everyone in the auditorium holds their breath as they follow every action and movement of their beloved leaders. I want to study as comprehensively as possible the turbulent, multifaceted life of S. M. Kirov, who was so selflessly devoted to the cause of the world communist revolution. The documentaries did not encompass all of his colossal activity in its entirety, but in each individual incident, insignificant though it may be in size, the seething energy of Mironych[9] blazes forth. It is a graphic, living example of the work, leadership, and managerial concern of the Bolsheviks.

And the joyful, fervent speech of Sergei Mironovich is an example of genuinely revolutionary, emotionally enrapturing speech, whose profound sincerity and precision, which enrich the meaning of the words and reveal the enormous significance of the sentences, captivate the listener. It convinces you that the oratorical art of the school of Lenin and Stalin is the most paramount, mighty, and delightful of all the arts. In this film, together with our dear, beloved government, you reexperience the enormous loss that inflames the columns of intrepid workers, millions strong, and their unquenchable hatred toward class enemies.

You leave the auditorium wrapt in an irrepressible, impetuous headlong drive to work with Kirov's managerial solicitude, initiative, and energy.

[...]

1/30. I read Gleb Uspensky's "New Times, New Concerns" and "Kisses."[10] With what a miserable morass of blood and filth shedding by vampires and irreparable hopeless sufferings did capitalism poison the relations between people and rot their souls as it developed in Russia.

You too Gleb when you saw the *Venus de Milo*, an art work by normal children of the Greeks, you too were enlightened by the lofty thought that there would come a time when people would be just as beautiful and fresh as the *Venus de Milo*, and noble, bright and clear as crystal would be the relations between people. I feel so stirred that there's a rumbling in my heart and tears in my eyes, how wisely this thought is confirmed in my life, in the great experience and nobility of our society that is being created.

I have before me the speech on the government's work that Com. Molotov[11] gave at the 7-th Congress of Soviets of the USSR. How clear, just, reasonable and noble are the policies of the dictatorship of the proletariat. How majestic and grand are the successes of the policies of the wisest party of all mankind as it creates a joyful, bright, beautiful life for all men. And the overwhelming majority of the population (millions) of our country building a socialist society consciously and actively are new men in the prehistory of mankind. Men of the true history of mankind. It's those people about whom Uspensky dreamed with his noble bright reason surrounded by gloominess.

Right outside my window is a skating rink with slides made of wood and painted with the colors of joyfulness cheerfulness and health; the dexterity and beauty of the youth, both workers and students and adults too, right up to aged workers regaining the youth they never experienced. And above the skating rink the marvellous, tender elegant melodies of the best music ever created by mankind and the charmingly beautiful sounds of the voices of Soviet singers flow out of an enormous loudspeaker and billow in the air. How I would love to spend time in the theater in the company of an interesting girl, a pleasant person to talk to, a friend to whom I would express my whole soul and ennoble with the seething feelings of a tender refined love.

I don't want to turn to grisettes, though some of the guys do sometimes when they're drunk. I want a kind of ideal friendship the lofty kind that my masterful dreaminess depicts for me.

Left with my romantic, ineffective reveries, cut off from a realistic more simple, vital and much more beautiful state of affairs I turned to books. I read some revolutionary satires, sarcasms and ironies that were light and "entertaining" but saturated with socially ideological class content, and also the antireligious and erotic songs of Béranger, French writer (1780–1857), exposés that shocked the hypocritical morality of the petty bourgeoisie, expressing the strong traditions of the Great French Revolution and the stubborn ferment of the Republican, the firm positions of the hard-working petty bourgeois craftsman in the prehistory of proletarian revolutionary ideology. But Béranger burst the bounds of petty bourgeois socialism. To the precursor of revolutionary, proletarian communism — a socialism that was critically utopian during the period of its revolutionary essence. And he pays attention to the working class and the incipient proletarian revolutionary ideology. His positive view — his idyllic petty bourgeois utopianism is an advocacy of modesty, virtue, universal love, small intimate joys, and the labor of farmer and craftsman. Such is the historical significance of the poetry of Béranger.

I read Heine and about Heine I noted his connection to K. Marx and the unique resedimentation in him of the ideology of one class into the ideology of another, right on up to the revolutionary proletariat. I was especially thrilled by G. Serebryakova's *The Youth of Marx*. It is both an artistic embodiment of the history of the proletarian revolutionary movement, and a valuable edifying material in the sphere of Marx. In this work I found the expression of a lot of my own views and opinions.

[...]

In the tram, on the street and in the reading room I looked people over seeking among them a friend primarily from their exterior appearance and well on February 4 I was sitting in the reading room of the Belinsky Library and I noticed a brunette with elegant facial features wearing a blue dress enrobing her plump but not fat figure of average height sitting at the next table. I looked at her and caught her eye a couple of times. The guy sitting next to her got up and left and I moved over and sat down by her, and she glanced at me. Contemplating her, I was enraptured and overcome with tender feeling. I couldn't read I was too excited to. Looking at her gave me a pleasant, ticklish stir of pleasure. The thought came to me: "There she is, the one I've been looking for, I mustn't miss my chance!" In my thoughts I expressed tenderness, words of love to her. And at the same time figuring nothing would come of it. She won't even talk to me. She must have lots of admirers. Though I would give up my soul to her.

She's reading a chemistry textbook and taking notes. Finally I ask her, "Are you studying something in particular?"

"Not necessarily," she answers, bestowing a clear calm look on me with her hazel eyes.

"People here mainly study what they like best."

"I work on all my subjects here."

"You are from the chemical engineering department?"

"Yes. What about you?"

"Am I bothering you?" I ask.

"Yes, a little."

"I'm sorry."

But I can't concentrate. I just read the same line over and over, ten times. Then I talk with her some more. Then we read and finally I tell her that our institute has bought up a block of tickets to a show at the Theater of Musical Comedy, would she like to go? We happen to be talking about

Opera and Musical Comedy. And she answers, "I might as well."

I ask, "When are you leaving?"

"I'm just finishing up now."

"I'm already done. I'll wait, I can walk you home."

"Don't wait for me. I live nearby, so you won't have far to go."

"Will you be here tomorrow at five o'clock?" I ask.

She thinks for a minute and answers, "Yes, I will."

I wish her all the best and leave the library a happy man. When I go to the cafeteria my roommates are there and I tell them about it.

"That's awfully hard to believe," they comment.

"What do you mean? I sat next to her all day long."

All the way home I was wrapt in stimulating feelings and thoughts. And thinking it over I decide to go out tomorrow morning and buy a new suit and get all dressed up.

[...]

2/5. I bought myself a suit at the arcade for 109 rubles using money I'd saved up in the bank when I was working. I arrive at the reading room, all dressed up, and there she is. I say hello and bring up the theater.

"By the way, I told my sister and she wants to come too. She's so interesting," she said with a smile.

I tell her that the institute hadn't bought the tickets after all.

"You can't get ahold of them just like that."

"Yes I can, I can get some, but two or three?"

"Two, then."

After some more small talk I sit down at a different table. She goes out for lunch. When I come back I catch her eye. She smiles. She brings over a journal to show me, laughs, and points out something funny for me to read. I read it with restrained calm almost indifferently. And then we go to the theater.

During the intermissions we stroll around the foyer, arm in arm. During the first intermission when we were standing at the railings, a young man came up to her, he was somewhat older than me, and well dressed. He had a lively, cheerful conversation with her. When he left she told me that he was a student from the Construction Institute. I was constrained with self-dissatisfaction. The conversation didn't get off the ground it was stuck in a seriously crumpled philosophical genre.

What I liked in *The Bride Market* was Jacobi's music and the ballet part. As I walked the brunette home I asked her her name.

"You mean you'd really like to know?" she asked. "Zina." I noticed a sincere gleam of moisture in her eyes. "I'll see you in the reading room; the next special event we have in the institute I'll invite you," she said. We didn't have far to go just across the street.

[...]

Classes start tomorrow. There's a lot of hard work ahead before our next vacation. Getting down to work, playfully and enthusiastically. The intensive, culminating military training course in the 2nd year of the Universal Military Training (VVP), ending with exams. With the living image of my brunette constantly on my mind, I was overcome with an even more powerful drive to be a grown man in all senses to act firmly and confidently for her sake, to be a commander in the broad sense of the word, morally and physically. To speak beautifully and forcefully, not losing my dignity in any situation or conditions. I've become even more enamored of physical exercise, I've decided to learn to dance and have come to sense the beautifulness and success of life in a joyful energetic mood.

For her sake I fervently review in my mind the joyful times in my life and wonder where I found the strength that ensured the success of my actions during these days. Most likely it came from an aspiration and desire to be worthy of her love that was reflected in my actions, imperceptibly for me.

[...]

I got down to work organizing ballroom dance classes for my two groups. The club mgr. stipulated a minimum enrollment of 40. Only 15 signed up from my group. I signed up 8 people from the second group of our class and asked one particularly energetic student to recruit from outside our groups.

[...]

On days when I had no classes I went to the reading room and waited for the brunette to show up. Vain were my hopes to see her. Her inimitable visage, confident and in control of life, appeared in my imagination. So many tender, sensitive feelings rumbled in my sensations if I were a composer or a poet I would caress people's hearing and ignite their hearts with them. Not seeing her, the sad melodies from the radio were perceived by me with painful bitterness. I felt myself to be a lonely man. But I know that you have to look at things simply, enthusiastically maturely calmly and confidently. So many times did I vow not to analyze life, just to live it. "He who lives does not analyze life." I picture in my mind how she, who has grasped the practical side of life grasped society, would break into peals of laughter over all my analysis. And sometimes I too can laugh.

3/6. [...] In the evening I went to a lecture about Beethoven at the institute and a demonstration of the artistry of Beethoven which turned out to be the best concert. Beethoven infects the listener with his mighty will by means of music. With his beautiful, cheerful and rousing music he tuned my nerves and made of me a victorious warrior on the battlefield of life. Concentrating his will he creates a most delightful state, where there is no hardship, no self-doubt, where the whole organism is on alert, striving to act and able to act with lightning speed. His optimistic revolutionary overture, his inflaming chamber symphony and miraculous vocal compositions. I left Beethoven with life seething up inside me. If I saw my brunette right now I would enchant her with the flame of my tempestuous cheerfulness.
[...]

3/12. I'm back in the reading room, hoping to see the brunette. Fleeting encounters with beautiful girls are momentary, like marvellous, rapturous dreams and for some reason are just as irretrievable and induplicable, each one individual. Only a new "dream," no less beautiful, and an even more increasing feeling can banish without the slightest trace all those torments that linger from preceeding "dreams." But I don't know whether even one newly encountered enchantress from among those who pass me by would be able to pull me out of my state of inner complacency. To other no less interesting ones, without especially noticing them, I am indifferent. But the others, you yourself are charmed by your own limitless feelings. And the more tender feeling you nurture for them in yourself, the more tenderness you seek in them, the more they captivate you.
[...]

I arrived at the first meeting of the ballroom dance class organized by me in a bad mood. I had gotten a group together. Students from other courses flocked to me asking to be included. I signed everyone up and called the roll. The group had grown to a total of 70 students from all over the institute.

If last year I had showered reprimands on the guys for every single violation of discipline and people called me a little dictator, and also sensing a certain friction, and alienated from the interests of the masses. Well, now I have imparted a living, comradely character to mass education. My cultural initiatives have coalesced the interests of the group around me. My tactical instructions have not had a single nonfulfillment. Not a single formal reprimand from the leadership triangle, my comments have great expedience in meaning. Relating to each individual member sensitively, with comradely warmth, I enjoy the respect not only of each student in my group, but also of everyone who knows me.

What a broad, multifaceted school this is. Here I'm not only learning the sciences, I'm also learning how to live and work. And best of all, I'm being molded into a worker for society. Only the strict discipline of an academic program can make us into capable workers. I can only hope for success in my studies and greater self-confidence and enthusiasm in my community activities.

3/24. It's been a month and a half since I've written anything beyond a few lines in my notebook now and then in between my work. And I don't have any time to write now either exams are in five days, but feeling myself overflowing with content I've taken up my pen anyway. I timidly allow myself to be distracted from the sociology of the arts. And suddenly a rush of artistic, emotional generalizing thinking elevates me above my petty, everyday cares into the heights of an optimistic, joyful life in its eternity, commonality and unity of the great and the beautiful. The more I look into philosophy, the more I sense the lack of a fundamental, general understanding in me, a system of specific knowledge and the need to master, to possess Marxism in all its limitlessness, which illuminates everything, both in its theory and the practice of the Communist Party and the history of human societies, as well as in its understanding of science and the arts.

In Joffe's *Synthetic History of the Arts* I encountered a certain coincidence with my own approval of Beethoven, but I go beyond that I elevate Beethoven to an ideal both as a personality and as a composer. His all-subjugating will in music is akin to my own undisciplined will, rising to the attack.

I knew the words already and the first time I heard the opera; I was disappointed in the vocal weakness of expression of the great enormous meaning in the arias. I had imagined and I had wanted to hear an expression of that grandeur of meaning with particular emphasis a complete

correspondence to the all subjugating, all stifling might of the sound.
[...]

*

I came home from dance class in an elevated, joyful mood and a little irritated too. I felt wonderful today, as the organizer and brigade leader[12] of the ballroom dance class. Only people who had passes or my permission were allowed into the hall. Thanks to that the class was orderly. I was burning with energy and enthusiasm. If in the previous class I had lost my temper and behaved rudely with a couple of girl comrades and had gotten off to a bad start with them. And instead of 70 people the class had 100 or so.

But today I responded sensitively, energetically, and warmly to every comment or question addressed to me. With my energy, enthusiasm, and inner warmth I engaged and consolidated everyone's respect and even reforged my bad relations with the two students from last time merging them into the general current of respect. If at the first class I had felt covered by a veil of a certain shyness. At the second one my embarrassment was replaced by anger. But today overcoming my shyness and awkward severity, enthusiasm and energy bloomed forth. I see that those outbursts of love that create and heat up my inner warmth, not accepted by the guilty parties, poured out into love for the whole group and were enriched by mutuality. And with that powerful force of respect of the group I can confidently, boldly force those guilty parties to love me.

Yesterday I saw the opera "Boris Godunov,"[13] as part of our series. Sitting in the special box for shock workers, surrounded by strangers, I learned from their conversation that they are fifth-year students. I asked the girl sitting next to me what institute they're from.

"The Mining Institute. I know you well, too. I see you a lot in the institute, especially in dance class."

Talking about dance class and the opera I felt how behind they were in their development, and how some of them in fact are only just beginning to develop thanks to us.

[...]

4/4 [...] Dance class fell through twice because of a misunderstanding with the dance mgr. and because of my transfer of authority to my assistant, who was careless in fulfilling my request to make arrangements. Having made a note of this, I stated to the dance mgr., "Why am I wasting my time making arrangements with you if you don't coordinate them with the club mgr. I can do a better job of working with the club mgr. and scheduling the dances myself." The dance mgr. agreed. In this way I took on the responsibility for making arrangements for the dance classes myself. To the satisfaction of my groups my assistant proclaimed me dance mgr. When I make arrangements with the club mgr. I let the dance teachers and the people in charge of music know, and my assistant posts the announcement.

The last six hours — two three-hour classes — I danced with my sister. The first time I couldn't get the waltz right at all but I did get some pleasure and inspiration in the other dances, the Mennon, the Two-step, the Chardash, and the Ku-ka-pu. When I relaxed and concentrated on the music instead of artificial memorized, rote-learned steps I had natural movements expressing musicality. And the music in combination with my own movements provided me with an as yet unexperienced feeling of delight, satisfaction and tempestuous pleasure.

At the last dance class today (4/24) I started to get the hang of the waltz too. And in the other dances including the Krokovyak and Podispan I felt even more pleasure and the need for artistic, musical movement, as in a musical exercise session. And so I persistently brought myself into closer contact with the dance music. I overcame an inborn musical deafness of mine in this form. The guys were very satisfied with the dance school. It introduced us to the basics, but most important, brought us into contact with a field of entertainment that had been inaccessibly distant before. [...]

This academic year, as never before, I absorbed everything that the institute has to offer outside of academics. That aroused a certain apprehension, but I emerged triumphant. The very next day after exams ended we went out for geodesic field work. The weather was bad we were out working in the rain and mud.

I experienced a challenge to my pride due to a barely sensed awareness of the secondary nature of my role in the brigade created by the smug and divisive character of the brigade leader.[14] In measuring the relief of the terrain using a plane table and a tachymetrical polygon, we came up with contradictory results, the first produced by me the second by the brigade leader. The brigade leader insisted on the correctness of his results based on theory. We had to compare our results and make them agree. Using data to prove my point I vehemently refuted his results. He objected that his results had been conform to the actual terrain. I went to the site and again proved the correctness of my contour lines. The brigade leader stood by his opinion. He went to the site and convinced the instructor that his results were correct. Opening the plane table, I stood at the observation point and commenced to disprove his results. The instructor changed his mind and agreed with me. I suggested taking the measure of the observation point. They had taken it as a given. Even then the brigade leader gave in only a little, he still insisted on some of his results. I refused to yield. And after my new refutations the brigage leader ordered me to correct his plan myself, using my own method. With the instructor there I subordinated his results to mine with completeness, standing on principle, and invited the author to refute me. "I can't disprove it," he gave in.

We worked in the field or in the lab from 7 a.m. to 10 p.m. And we still hadn't been given a test in Dynamics from the previous session the instructor had scheduled a test during geodesic field work. I suggested to the brigade leader that he demand that the instructor post our grades in Dynamics anyway, without a test, since the semester was over. The brigade leader got all riled up and stated,

"I want him to give us a test."

"The triangle[15] can't function in its present form," I concluded.

A few days later the instructor himself did what I had proposed. Up to then the brigade leader hadn't paid any attention to my objection and he'd included a "strong" student in a strong brigade and furthermore one who wasn't a construction student, at his request, and in that way had skewed the membership of the brigades that followed.

Anyway, one time I was working on the tachymeter and the brigade leader ran up to me and yelled:

"How long is this going to go on, Potyomkin!"

"What do you mean," I asked, intentionally calm.

"This slander about me supposedly not working but just loafing around. You are going to keep this up?"

"I don't know. It depends on you," I answer, still cool and composed.

"No it can't go on this way. I've laid hands on Fomichev. Am I going to put up with everyone asking why weren't you at work."

And he asked me to put a triangle together. Having informed the Party organizer and the Komsomol organizer they accepted my proposal. And at the next meeting, together with the whole brigade, the investigation confirmed my information, I presented an accusation with which the triangle agreed. They voted. To exclude the brigade leader from the union. To strip him of his status as a shock worker. To remove him as brigade leader.

[...]

*

O life! I feel you so impulsively, efficaciously (vitally) for the first time in my life. Now, for the first time in my life I have squared my shoulders freely, boldly, fervently and maybe even audaciously and can look at people with triumphant self-confidence. I am in the front ranks of those who are mastering the technology of production. I am not only a member of a production brigade I am an assistant brigade leader. I am first to grasp new things and pass them on to my comrades. I vehemently reject incorrect tactics and perceptions of production tasks.

It is my fate to take cruel action against those who stand in my way. There is no opposing force of personality that would not be mercilessly destroyed by me. No sooner do I sense the presence of an oppressive force than it is doomed to perish. My view of the world is triumphant. I gain universal respect through both my modesty and my fairness even to those cast down by me.

With multiple emotion and rapture I pronounce the words of S.M. Kirov "Our working class has firmly taken into its own hands the population of our great country, 170–million strong..." In this lies the invincible force of my will destined to triumph. This force is the great fairness, genius and wisdom, the vital might of the class and its brain, the party, whose child I am being cultivated to become. We are free.

The last show in our series is going on now at the Opera Theater. It's *The Demon!*[16] I go to the Reading Room of the Belinsky Library, I'm in a mood to celebrate and would like to see Zina. I go in and there she is. I note a nervous agitation in myself. Suppressing it I go up and greet her. I don't see anything on her face — not surprise or pleasure or annoyance. She answers without interrupting her work. Then with a polite smile she raises her finger to her lips signalling me not to interfere with people's studying. I invite her to the Opera. She thanks me and says that she's seen the opera already and unfortunately she's very busy this time; she's got exams coming up. I left her alone and wrote her a letter expressing the feelings that I've had pent up inside for all this time.

From the crossed-out version:
...the refined exactitude in my attitude toward others but especially toward myself expresses itself in the form of a kind of self-dissatisfied crav-

ing for perfection but the life I have lived (which has been somewhat unique) consists in the gratification of desires. It's true that "nothing contributes so much to success in life as the presence of a high ideal." My comrades have complained to me about my only values being refinement, purity, and beauty but they notice only the external side, but in our socialist society we must demand this from each other too. Gleb Uspensky's luminous thought during socially filthy and parasitical times, arising from his rapt contemplation of the *Venus de Milo*, that there will come a time when people will all be as beautiful as the *Venus de Milo*. And as Marx says, the people's relations between people should be clear and transparent as rock crystal. This is the time of the socialist society. But there must and can be a special aura around social roles, over the significance of work for society. All of this is the apogee of perfection. To attain perfection by serving society and succeeding at it, i.e. at socially useful labor I experience expediency, happiness and the joy of life. I realize I've bored you, but such is my cursory qualitative, and quantitative, too, if you will, analysis of personality. As for my inclination toward the engineering of men's souls, it is inborn in me.

...I picture our friendship as fraternal in the sense of an ideological unity whose goal is to aid in the development of an independent personality through the spiritual cooperation of both parties in their community work. This is the source of its beauty and wholesomeness, the preservation and justification of which is a test of character and heart, as Heinrich Mann put it.

The version she got:

Zina! Your image has kindled in me a mighty new flame of turbulent reveries and an irrepressible upsurge in my community life.

This flame reflects as an aura around the immutable victories of a will destined to triumph. And for that reason I want to share with you only beautiful treasures, the feelings and thoughts of my inner world.

The outlines of your simple and enchanting beauty, charming in their tenderness, are not alien to a sincere sensitivity.

I am most sincere, but believe me only for you. The exactitude I demand in my relations with others, but mostly in myself, has not allowed me to be indulgent of those who have desired sincerity. But do not fear an excessive persistence on my part and do not resort in vain to hypocrisy in your relations with me. I will be satisfied with candor on your part, severe though it may be. Forgive me for my inclination toward the engineering of men's souls, which was inborn in me. But I do not press upon you my canons there is no need for you to talk to me in my own language. I value any progressive tendencies in a person.

I wish you a rapturously joyful life, one that is worthy of you.

with the comradely greeting of a fellow mining student, L. P.

When I was seeing her out, after a few casual words about the end of classes I gave her the note. She hesitated before taking it.

"I'm afraid to take anything. Did you write it?" And she took it with interest and pleasure on her face, "I'll read it, I will."

She asked my last name. With high hopes of seeing her tomorrow and putting it off until then, I didn't tell her. I stopped in at the reading room in the evening she wasn't there. I took my sister to the theater. I sat in the shock workers' box. During intermission I saw another brunette I know. She was in the middle of an animated conversation with a student and I didn't go up to her. When she saw me a serious look came over her face.

During the next intermission she was walking with a girlfriend. I went up to them and joined them. Her friend went off with another girl and we were left by ourselves. She called another girlfriend over and that one left after a couple of minutes too. Another friend of hers, a student, came over. He took both our hands. He was drunk. She expressed her displeasure and turned away from him. I offered to accompany her.

"All right," she said.

After the show I saw her in a crowd of students talking casually among themselves and laughing loudly.

I overheard someone say, "That sure got rid of Lenyok."[17] Wedging myself between them and her I started talking to her. As she answered me she turned back to her friends and continued her conversation with them. I stepped off to one side. And I saw a couple of students holding her hands. She protested, but was laughing at the same time. The next day I stopped in several times at the Belinsky Library. Zina wasn't there.

I throw my coat on over my shoulders like a cloak and run out into the woods in the direction of where the second girl lives. I had never felt so powerful in my life. The awareness of what I lack, or what I am doing without, swelled my will and furrowed my brow with a mighty, destructive force. So what if they don't love me. So what if I suffer rejection at the hands of beautiful girls. All this will arm my gaze with a severe force will fill every nerve with determination. I will not quaver before anyone or anything. Like Grisha Neznamov I will have a will of iron, an invincible character. I feel myself to be an all-powerful demon and I sing, "And you will be queen of all the world! You, my companion for all eternity."[18]

I went to the movies alone and saw the film *Pilots*[19] and heard Com. Stalin's speech. Com. Stalin's speech impressed me deeply with its simplicity and intimacy the familiar accent of his origin mobilizing me to social and political activism.

Today one more victory of my initiative was won by me. The guys changed their minds about going to the Caucasus. But I would not abandon my initiative. After arranging things with the chairman of the All-Union Voluntary Society of Proletarian Tourism and Excursions (OPTE) cell of the institute I went with him to the Regional council of the OPTE. There an elderly OPTE staff worker a talkative man who had done a lot of travelling in his life unfurled an alluring gallery of reminiscences to me. I wrote down all the attractions he listed of a "heaven come down to earth." We discussed the schedule of the trip with the chairman of the Regional Council. He offered to arrange a special excursion just for me—140 km. on foot along the Sukhumi Pass across the crest of the Caucasus Mountains. From Sukhumi to Batum and back to Sochi via the Black Sea by boat. Counting military travel warrants it would come to 300 rubles each.

I told my comrades, they were concerned about the cost. Then I got the idea of taking my plan to the Trade Union Committee, and presenting it personally to the director of the institute. In the morning I presented my proposal to give a subsidy for the trip to the best shock workers, the ones who completed the Universal Military Training (VVP) with the best records. The Trade Union Chairman gave his approval and we went on to the director's office. I passionately expounded my plan to the director. The director approved it with youthful ardor and enterprise. I left his office with the fervor and high spirits of the new men shown in the film *Pilots*.

6/1 at 22:00 we set off for camp.

I set myself a goal: to emerge successfully as a full-fledged middle-rank commander a commander who is morally upright, cheerful, and with a steadfast self-confidence. At the first meeting of the battery I told about the excursion plan, proposing the slogan "Top students travel free! Let's complete training camp with only top evaluations and commendations for exemplary discipline!"

7/10. Training camp is over; it was our last time at the rank of ordinary Red

Army soldiers. I am not not satisfied with my results. I did not achieve the
desired triumphs. I, a man who educates my comrades ideologically
through the print medium, who conducted classes with inspiration, fath-
oming the depths of the essence of knowledge as the best of pedagogues,
in elimination shooting, independently of all my knowledge, I made mistakes in my data preparation and in aiming as a consequence of an
absence of vigilant attentiveness and sharpness of memory in a state of
strained agitation. I was unable to conduct myself in the necessary way,
i.e. the more serious the situation, the more necessary it is to be relaxed
and cheerful. And I was not chosen to be one of the three who are granted
the right to shoot live shells.

[...]

Beginning tomorrow the platoon commanders will go through a special
twenty-day training course. How I longed to become a full-fledged commander. For to be a good commander means to be a full-fledged personality. I consider it a matter of honor to bear the title of commander in our
army. Among our commanders here I have seen the most worthy people
of our heroic time. They are heroic examples of the new men of socialist
society. Men of the Bolshevik tribe.

The perfect speech of the commissar of the regiment serves as an
example of cogency in its presentation of clear thoughts penetrating the
entire depths of the essence of phenomena. In terms of its enthusiasm,
the clarity of its sound structure and the delightful culture of its language.
With a deep awareness of the meaning of the words I uplift my voice with
astounding force and join the chorus as we march to my favorite song, the
march from the film *Happy Fellows*.

[...]

I'm so pleased with the training course. Here I am, a middle-rank commander of the revolutionary, proletarian Army. My heart clenches up with
joy. I am all wrapt in ardor and impatience to work with my platoon. I do
combat drill. My pure, clear, resolute voice turbulently concentrates the
attention of the platoon. I explain. I point out shortcomings. I motivate
people with my mood. With a single glance I cast boldness and daring
into the eyes of a man and I see igniting in them the flames of our shared
joy in his desire to carry out the order better. The candor and warmth of
my attitude. The most advanced and active ones surround me most
closely with respect and amicability. No shouts or cursing. But a strictness

that is inseparable from mutual respect, but at the same time in no way subordinate to it.

I was appointed duty officer for our regiment. Our asst. regmt. commdr. of the student batteries, chief of the training sect. of the military department, met me in the commanders cafeteria gave me his hand with marked attentiveness.

"Well how does it feel Com. Potyomkin, regimental duty officer."

"That's right. Regimental boss," I laugh.

"Yes indeed. Deputy regimental commander," he adds.

The regimental commander and regimental chief of staff were out on the shooting ranges. I had to not only take care of things at my own discretion but also to overcome a certain laxness amongst the petty officers of the divisions, the duty detail went like clockwork. Crossing the front line toward me the duty officer from the student battery ran up to me and reported to me in an agitated voice.

But in my former comradely voice I said, "Let's go have a look at how things are going in the battery." In the same tone, but briskly, I pointed out the shortcomings and let him go. Having saluted he turned and set about carrying out his duties.

With my warm, comradely attitude I earned respect in the student battery as well. But I do have a defect it is that I'm still not always sufficiently cheerful and self-confident. I need to develop my role and my mission and elevate them in the light of consciousness. You must respect your work, yourself and your milieu. Then your activity will be successful and joyful. Your mission will be fulfilled and overfulfilled. You must inspire your role and your work with meaning.

[...]

7/31. We arrived in Sverdlovsk.

The guys changed their minds again about going to the Caucasus. And in fact I'd had about enough of nature myself over these past two months. [...] But an even bigger group of us got together for a trip to Leningrad. And I signed up for a military discount ticket to Leningrad too, experiencing a much greater thirst to see and understand the cultural and historical treasures of that city and Moscow too along the way.

[...]

Leningrad produced a comprehensive, satisfying impression as the treasure house of the cultural-historical heritage of Russia. Among its monumental traces of the past you sense the deeply rooted, majestic, mighty character of the Great Proletarian Socialist Revolution. Here you experience a feeling of satisfaction and gratitude for this gift of scientific content presented to the whole people.

The former Tsarskoe Selo[20] is a neglected park. Abandoned avenues. The barren courtyard. Faded and rusting roofs. The palace facade, once white, now gray. All this gives a strong impression of a time that is long past. A social system that has perished once and for all, never to return, that bears the historical stamp of literal death. The false "light" that tormented geniuses and a righteous love illuminates the Posthumous Pushkin Monument. Entering the palace of Catherine the Great you cross over two centuries and find yourself in the midst of the glittering and shining luxury of architecture and furnishings that created the false greatness of Russian despotism. Peterhof[21] that showy front courtyard of autocracy gladdens the heart with its transformation into a cheerful and beautiful place of rest for the working people. I came home from Leningrad renewed and enriched. I did not regret having to leave Leningrad. I felt completely satisfied with my impressions. I was pleasantly conscious of the exhaustive fulfillment of the purpose of the trip.
[...]

The primary source of my internal life was my experience of poverty in childhood. By the time spring came around every year we would run out of bread. We would go around the cupboards gathering up "mouse crumbs." During the "hungry year" we ate goose-foot plants, crows, and some kind of bluish clay. I went to see a rich peasant on the pretext of wanting to play with his son. When I hear that the son isn't home I just stand there until they give me a piece of bread. But then they stopped giving it to me. So I go to the mill. I stuff my pockets with flour and eat it. Meanwhile my mother is starving at home. So at night I grab a bag and go out. As my mother says goodbye she whispers, "For god's sake, make sure you don't get caught!" I make my way to the mill, using the bushes for cover, and wade through the water to the wheel. I climb up into the mill. Trembling all over I pour some flour into my bag from the bin. Back home, after eating my fill of flat cakes cooked on the cast-iron stove, I climb up above the Russian oven to sleep. I didn't know when my mother slept. She used to stay up all night sewing for people, saving up money to send my sister off to the city to work. Finally we scraped together just enough for a ticket. We walk forty km. to the landing stage. Without a single piece of bread. My mother and sister send me out to beg "in the name of Christ." In the first village I hold my hand out under a window. Just seven years old, I'm bestowed with a dose of cruel ridicule and mocking insults. Having received a piece of bread from a woman I take it tearfully to my mother. The "alms" I gather go to my sister for the road. At the landing stage I get in the ticket line. People guard their pockets, grab me by the scruff of the neck, and throw me out of line. I don't go to school in the winter, I have nothing to wear. From my constant colds I get chronic bronchitis. The usual carefree games of childhood passed me by.

The mockery and scorn I suffered created self-doubt, fearfulness and doubt in my own strength in my young soul. Apprehension before taking any action, a hopeless bitterness grips my heart and it was then that I countered humiliation with pride for the first time.

The material violence committed against mental and moral freedom from generation to generation inculcated spiritual enslavement, feeble-mindedness, and weakness of will in people doomed to material poverty. An inherited loss of the sense of one's own human virtues and of the faith in one's own virtues and their free development. That is what troubled my consciousness. and stirred my will to indignation and protest.

In elementary school I was weak-willed, sickly, physically ugly, and dirty, I dressed worse than everyone else, and I looked at myself with a vexation that tormented my soul, which poisoned my consciousness and wounded my pride. I felt that I was the lowest, most insignificant of all people. Every time I was attracted to a captivating girl I experienced explosions of a crushing torment caused by the awareness of my insignificance and unworthiness. Furrowing my brow, I learned to suppress my desire for immediate reciprocity, and to strive and believe in my dream instead: to be worthy of universal respect and love. I despised and mersilessly rent the outer layer of submissiveness, humiliation and inertia that had covered me and that I had come to accept as a part of myself. To overcome poverty and the spiritual enslavement of personality this has been the essential meaning of my life up to now. The awareness of my own material and spiritual poverty called forth a tremendous thirst for a new superior and strong man. Indignation and scorn are imperfect. So I had to change nature and transform the harmony and beauty of a dream into reality and power. This power made me exclaim: either betray myself or not live. The power of rebelliousness over the course of eight years of my conscious existence set me tasks of struggle and triumph. I not only wanted a lot but also demanded of myself on principle that I be capable of a lot. My consciousness demanded it cruelly and uncondi-

tionally irrespective of the physical possibilities. It set me the task of changing not only my physical nature but also my character and psychology.

Extremely sensitive to my own faults, seeing mostly only the negative
side of myself, I was eternally dissatisfied, and I strove fanatically to
embody enormous standards in my activity. In literature I found and
noted the best traits of the human personality. I studied them with great
rapture in my contemporaries. Plunging into practical life among the
workers, I encountered new human relations in their midst, new men,
free, honest men; simple men of action, with an inexhaustible abundance
of living creative energy and incredible potential for development.
[...]

Proper relaxation is one of the most important ways of raising the productivity of work. Physical exercise, bathing. Normal sleep. Breaks from
work. Indulging in pleasant diversions: dancing, singing, listening to and
studying music playing chess. A new society needs new men, but new
men originate in the ones who came before, just as the new society
replaces the old one not just inevitably, but in struggle and the destruction of the old.

Today at my physical I was excused from physical training because of
my nerves. In the fall I experienced the nightmarish paralyzing effects of a
nervous breakdown. A state of depression caused by overstrain. The nervous upset disorganized my mental activity. And then the Party committee, at which I always spoke brilliantly, started causing me torments each
time due to my awareness of my weakened psychological state. But no I
will not give in to the course of my disease. I have cultivated in myself a
love for physical exercise, harmony in my interrelations with the collective. Defying my medical restrictions I go not only to exercise drill but
also to special physical education classes. The music of the march they
use for exercise drill expresses the joy of health, the happiness of vigor
and the rapture of youth. Every day I do exercises and rub myself down
with a wet towel. How good it feels to be all gathered into a coil of resilient
energy, whose center of gravity is the will, which expresses itself in an all-
seeing, lively gaze that penetrates right through to the essence of things.
Physical exercise is a progressive force, a force that opposes slavish sub-
mission to the weaknesses of the body. One minute I am invincible,
seething with energy, a potentate, the next — trapped in the throes of an
abnormally sensitive and tender soul. Two opposing forces are battling
each other inside me. One that leads to a state of depression, sluggishness

of the spirit, agitation, idleness, and fatigue. A force that negates the life in me and deprives me of the life around me. And an opposing force, one of vigor, energy, and self-confidence. This is the force of life and its triumph. What joy does a sense of physical strength bring. You feel yourself the master of a healthy body, seething with energy. What pleasure do you experience from the awareness of your own life. A wonderful equilibrium of physical and intellectual powers, endowing the consciousness with a keen clairvoyance. Thought and action, they are lightning speed, creative initiative. A sluggish thought swimming on cloudy waves gains bright clarity in concrete activity. Thought knows no obstacles, nor thinking—any delusions. A vigorous, burning, triumphant view of the world. A direct link to people's hearts. I strain my will to regain my health, to restore myself as a full-fledged member in the collective of new men. I sought life: I strove to sense life and only physical exercise gives me the impulse of life, allows me to sense the joy of life. What happiness my propensities bring. What fertile soil do they find in our society.

Four callings are embodied in me: engineering men's souls, philosophy, politics, and leadership. A craving for the most profound understanding of the essence of the world. Draining dry the cup of inquisitiveness and persistence. Pride in a politics based on principle. Turbulent creative leadership. The infinite expanse and depth of the tasks, the limitlessness of the perspectives. This is my life, its success and joy.

Deprived of the joys of childhood, I am now experiencing my only and greatest joy—the creative organization of the work of my student group. I took on all the concern and responsibility for the group myself. I put together a hard working triangle and established complete unity in the group. Through the amicable efforts of the whole triangle, my thought is being transformed into enterprise.

[...]

I set my group the task of transforming itself from one of the lowest-achieving groups in the department into to one of the best, to be first in our class. I took on the obligation in my own individual socialist emulation agreement—to raise the level of fulfillment of the socialist emulation agreement by group from 60% to 90%. This required me to mobilize the group to keep from lagging behind. To make the fulfillment of our obligations the main focus and goal of each student, to struggle against a formalistic, contemptuous attitude toward them.

Our class had an academic meeting with the instructors, the department triangle, representatives of the Party committee, and the trade union committee. All seventy people welcome my candidacy to lead the meeting. My speech in the debates was longer than the dean's report. I harshly and unambiguously blamed the dean's office for the poor performance of our group in particular. Even though I knew how unilateral my strike was. But I destroyed the bad attitude toward our group and the opinion that we will not be able to take our exams. In his concluding remarks the dean confirmed my arguments and agreed.

[...]

Finally the long-awaited time is upon me and with all-stifling passion I have intruded into the labyrinth of philosophy. I expose each question with exhaustive completeness to its primary source and in several works at the same time. I am perturbed and concerned about intensivity and efficiency. I don't have enough attention left over for my other subjects. I had very little time to spare for my Sopromat[22] and was dissatisfied with my preparation, but my grade — superior — caressed me with a bright confidence in my ability. In my Diamat[23] seminar not one of seven people questioned gave a satisfactory answer. The instructor was perturbed. I announce that I will organize group study sessions before the seminar meetings. This means that I will have to really work hard on my own studying since when I got into my in-depth studying I fell behind in the lectures. Tomorrow I need to conduct a session on the latest topic: the philosophy of antiquity, which we don't have a textbook in. My imagination pictures the boundless perspectives of my plan. I see before me the large scope and significance of my initiative. I am all agitated, I burn with a joyful impulse. I rummage in the "histories" of Greece and philosophy. I studied from 3 until 10 but I only got halfway through the subject. I sign out a half-dozen books from the reading room. And I didn't finish my studying in the dormitory until five o'clock in the morning. And then at seven I had to get ready to go to class again.

After class the brigade leader announces that there will be a dialectical materialism class at eight p.m. I go home for a nap. One of the girls wakes me up just before class. We arrive at the institute there are already fifteen students there. They listen with great attention to my exposition of ancient philosophy. I consolidate their understanding with questions and answers. We worked for four hours. A few days later the group asks me to conduct another study session. Some twenty students showed up including a few from other groups. I conduct a "conference." I ask questions about all the material we have covered. I have to summarize or explain practically every single question. And I notice that every time I explain something my understanding gives rise to new thoughts and new meaning is amplified and even discovered anew. I am interested in the process of thinking all of a sudden I say something I didn't know beforehand and that I will know (represent) only after I've said it.

After the "conference" I am bestowed with attentiveness. The girls seize me by the arms. I don't have any gloves on and they won't let me carry my book bag. Cheerful, interesting, ardent, friendly relations seethe up around me. Me, whom no one ever loved and in fact who had nothing to be loved for. The love in me which was not accepted by a single girl flared up in the form of a love for society and the bright joy of a great love of society. Not only will I compel a girl who has infatuated me to love me, but all society will love and respect me too.

"You have enough notes for a whole book," the girls comment. "I am doing a thorough study of the laws and categories of dialectics. What kind of people are we anyway, damn it, if we can't make use of scientific methodology in our own practical activities."

"You philosopher!" One of the girls claps me admiringly on the shoulder.

While determining the monthly progress evaluation in dialectical materialism the instructor calls on the best student in the class, one of my rivals. His answer is not very clear. The instructor gives him a "good" and comments, "You need to justify your grades."

"Now Potyomkin here will make me happy, I'm sure," he turns to me.

"But of course!" the class answers for me.

"Shall I ask you some questions, or not?"

"Of course." And he asks me about Hegel. With the precision and power of a political agitator I reveal the essence of Hegelian philosophy and begin to substantiate and develop it with inspired logic. I'm cut short by the second question. After my first confident sentence, which illuminates the question at a single blow, he asks another question and ponders what grade to give me. After all, he had told the class that he would give the superior mark, a five, only to someone who would "grab stars from the sky," he wouldn't give a five to someone who is merely "god himself." And the students are yelling, "Superior! superior!" "Well all right, we're all human after all," says the instructor, "I'll give just one five in the whole class." At the faculty meeting the instructor tells the commission that I'm the leader in mastery of Marxism. He conducts a second seminar with the group. When he asked the question he said: "a big ship needs a big ocean." I answered loudly, confidently and meticulously since I knew that students had come from other classes to hear me.

The fact that I did so well in Diamat it's not just by sheer chance. It was an absolute necessity. From childhood I fostered in myself the habit of thought and reflection. My capacity for theoretical thought was achieved in my consciousness through suffering. Severe deprivations spurred me on to prevail in abstract thinking (the disadvantageousness of my personal characteristics tormented my senses and disturbed my thought). Superior for me was a minimum. I required of myself ten times the amount of study I needed to get a superior. I am not satisfied with my knowledge. I want to possess at least as much knowledge and speech as the instructor.

For the most part, my fifth semester in the institute was devoted to Diamat, thus attaining my dream — to thoroughly master the only true, philosophy of the proletariat; all-powerful, like its theory in general. And by the way, for the first time in my studies, I have high grades in all my subjects.

I ran into a girl I'd gone to school with six years ago in Naberezhnye Chelny. "I wouldn't recognize you now. You are unrecognizable!" she exclaimed. "So inapproachable, so masterful!" I greeted her like a sister. "How demanding, sensitive and proud you are!" When we discussed about relationships with a girl, she said,

"How interesting life is. How wonderful people can be. How I long not only to live day to day, but to struggle, to live and triumph." She revealed her caresses and her heart to me. And she said, how noble are your relations with a girl! At last my troubled will achieved triumph once unnoticed in the crowd I have now become he who concentrates influence and leadership in his hands. I am he who has forced others to direct their exclusive attention to him as the best student and leader. I fulfilled the imperative I set myself three years before I enrolled in the institute — to be a leader in the society of students. I hear people say that I am "a wholesome and handsome youth."

Life! I have triumphed!

1936. The new year finds me successful in my studies and in my community work. Set myself a motto: more real life! Ease up in my work. I have to be able to take the joys of life, to embody them in myself and to be able to create them in others. What is alive is beautiful.

[...]

I saw my aunt for the first time in ten years. She was amazed at the sight of me, she exclaimed, "What happiness! Who would have thought back then that you would be studying in the institute?" She hadn't seen through the shell of poverty to the potential in me and she hadn't known that personal merit is enslaved by material deprivation.

No, it's not just by sheer chance that I'm in the institute, it's the necessary consequence of the socialist revolution, which raised us up from below and elevated us up above their heads. It is our mission, we children of poverty, to change society for only we can change it and be equal masters in a classless society. Our will is triumphant. What seemed and was impossible, what we only could dream about is becoming a reality. In the society of workers I arrived at the conviction that not only are we not incapable, not deprived of the possibility of being valuable and advanced people, but on the contrary only we children of poverty and incredible hardship must and can create the new society. It is our mission not only to play an active role in building the new society, but to direct the work of construction. Only we are granted the mission of educating all the rest of mankind and giving mankind a chance to really bloom.

The Party organization nominated me as a political agitator. I can't find the words to express my joy. After all it has been my striving my dream to be an agitator. There's no role more meaningful or beautiful. I plunged rapturously into my study of this, the greatest of arts, at the feet of Lenin, Kirov, and other leaders of the Party.

Political agitation was an unintentional manifestation of my life in society. At the age of fourteen I would spend long evenings in the village engaged in serious discussion with the adult peasants and old men and in these everyday conversations without being aware of it myself I elucidated the current policies and decisions of the Party and the government. I recall a conversation I had in the winter of '29 with two peasants, a man and a woman, in response to the widespread belief that the collective farms would not take root I confidently concluded that all the peasants would be in collective farms, or else they would never rid themselves of poverty. The next day that peasant woman shared with her neighbors her firm decision to join the collective farm.

In '31, every night a most lively, comradely, sincere circle of workers would gather around around my bunk in the tar workers' barracks with an ironsmith and a miner at the center. It was this circle that first expressed approval of me — "Just listen to him talk! Slides right into your head like it was oiled."

In '32 being union-certified in Blagodatka thanks to decisive agitation activities I conducted a socialist competition for all the shifts and succeeded in getting the workers awarded the title of shock workers.[24] At a time when the workers generally believed that there was no need for socialist competitions.

And now I take up this art consciously and in a well organized manner. [...]

How wonderful life is. Lovely music caresses my hearing, expressing my mood. How wonderful are the prospects for development, how pleasant the potentials that are being realized. O life you are as beautiful as this music is vibrant and triumphant, stimulating a drive onward to action that is just as triumphant and vibrant.

[...]

April. Everything I had to get done by May is finished now. I have freely entered the ranks of the leaders in my department. The way things are going now, in all probability I will be the union organizer for the department next year. I will lead the department and bring it up out of last place. It is a difficult and honorable task. I've already gotten to know the department and its group leaders and I'm preparing for this task.

May. I listen to Tchaikovsky's 6-th Symphony. How wonderful are those melodies expressing the striving of the human will to freedom. A protest of the rebellious will that deserves to triumph, but is crushed by the despotism of the social order. The superior position of the forces of oppression is reflected in the sadness of the melodrama. In our life the melodrama—a keen perception of the unattained (shortcomings)—mobilizes people for the struggle, but it does contain genuine happiness for it is the attainment of something better, for in its complete conception it is invariably the success and triumph of life. What is so charming in Tchaikovsky is his love for life. Against its background I felt that I must not substitute the primitive force of passion for the beauty of feeling. Feeling must find aesthetic satisfaction. Love must be beautiful like this music. And I must not allow this to make me reject my views.

On my day off a sunny and fresh morning I go out to see an image like unto the charm of an early spring morning, to arouse enchanting feelings like unto the enchanting purity of an azure-crystal sky, the healthy freshness and tenderness of the early rays. This is the beauty of nature; how much more beautiful must be our love. I hasten to the image that I cherish, that charmed my heart. How gently did she touch me, but how generously did she bestow a storm of the most tender of emotions. How beautiful was the melody of feelings that she bestowed upon my heart. How many the story lines she engendered in my consciousness. I seek a lyrical thought in the whole arsenal of imprinted human love. And I pour out my love into the Neapolitan song "O girls tell your friend...I know the Sun still shines you are my darling, my sun." But I find out she's gotten married. Does it mean the sun has set for me? No! The sun of love kindled by her in my heart is triumphant. I am confident of an aesthetic love. And I wish her such a love and genuine happiness with her chosen one.

1. Tender ecstatic love
2. The iron discipline of the mind rejects it as an obstacle to my goal

The sensitivity of an artist is awakening in me. I feel that something beautiful has touched me, the beautiful features of the human character, the perfect actions of the healthy vibrant beauty in the people around me. I experience a pleasant temptation to ponder over life and myself. I feel the proximity and the possibility of beauty, of the ideal. A kind of stream of living joy runs through my body. I want to understand this thing I've been through with furrowed brow, unnoticed, to try to express it with my heart, from life itself. What I went through becomes so wonderful (now) but how annoying that I found no joy in it. How nice I begin to feel when I think back on it. With what a bright love for life do my eyes burn. The joyfulness of the strong, celebrating their triumph, creating happiness for people. Love is the flowers of life.

[...]

June. [...] The circumstance that I received a superior in the most difficult and basic disciplines (Diamat, Sopromat, geology of the USSR) indicates that in the other disciplines, if they had merited more attention from me, I undoubtedly could have gotten a superior. So I earned my award and the increase in my academic stipend. How pleasantly and promisingly do I begin to find social significance in the memoirs of my thoughts and feelings, though I do not attach any greater significance to my diary than just the preliminary jottings of an author. And finally finding and experiencing happiness in life the feelings I have expressed in my diary have spoken up in the words of the Anthem of the Socialist Revolution.

The field work I've just conducted at the coal deposit and what I've learned through passionate study of the methods of organizing work and the deposit have given me all I needed for my report. Resolving to get only superiors next year I set myself the task over the summer of mastering cartography and translating *The Geologist's Reader* from English. To learn the works of Lenin based on the six-volume edition. I have to pay greater attention to my own, my only gift—my passion for social theory and social-political activity. I must study Leninism and the History of the Party with all the depth characteristic of me, I must develop my personality in this area and cultivate the necessary qualities in myself. I must educate myself so as to devote my personality, my mind, and heart to the cause of the Party, but for that I need to polish my mind and heart so as to become one of its motors.

We finished our 3-d year of VVP training and are now lieutenants in the artillery reserves. In commander training the colonel noted my qualities as an instructor and pedagogue. We did parachute jumping from the training tower. It's a wonderful feeling to be in the open air with a parachute. One of my comrades will soon make a jump from a plane with a delayed opening of the parachute. Even before I wanted to be engineer I wanted to become a paratrooper.

[...]

6/1. I met Z. F. while working on my electrical engineering in the Belinsky Library. She attracted my attention with her female charmingness. The passionate dream of making her acquaintance flared up in me. An obstacle to my dream arose right then and there in the form of the student she was talking with. But she noticed my persistent glances and as she later recalled she wanted to catch my eye but couldn't. The moment the student left her side I went over to the newspapers that he had left on her table. She got me into a discussion of the government draft resolution banning abortion.[25] We had a cheerful exchange of opinions. And I invited her to the music hall she refused because of her upcoming exams in anatomy, therapy, midwifery, etc. We left the library together and I invited her to the movies. The film *Seven Brave Men*[26] was an interesting combination of the work of the northern expeditions with the participation of a geologist and a doctor.

[...]

6/6. I met her in the morning with a bouquet of lilacs and we went out into the woods. She read leaning the book on my chest about tuberculosis. And I listened, asked her questions and looked up at the green crowns of the pine trees so beautifully edged with the transparent blue of the sky. I couldn't continually be so indifferent as to keep from interfering with her studying. She lost her temper at my advances. Ultimately I demanded reciprocity for my feelings, so generous, but so firmly restrained by her.

"I'm generally unaffectionate by nature, I've never kissed anyone, not even my own mother."

She wouldn't let me kiss her telling me that her clothes and face were dirty. All this preventive health of hers gets in the way of my feelings.

June 10. [...] My dream to get a job that will offer the most comprehensive practical training has come true. I didn't take advantage of the opportunity to travel away somewhere for my work and I do not believe it expedient to go off to some unfamiliar region to unfamiliar conditions for my practical training when Sverdlovsk itself is surrounded by classic deposits like the one at Beryozovo, the copper mine, etc. And a good half of the students haven't even visited them and don't even know them, to our shame. Well this inertia indifference and absence of curiosity have bothered me for a long time and I've cherished the thirst to study primarily these mines right here outside the city that are among the biggest ones in the Union, to get so I feel at home in these mines and out prospecting. And to follow the development of work in the mines outside the city not only on field work, but during my whole course of study in the institute. To link my particular classes with actual mining practice. In this way to study both in the institute and in the mine simultaneously and indissolubly. Coming to the realization that this is the only expedient and reasonable thing to do I blazed up with an enthusiastic surge of energy. How ideally beautiful was my work. And I could no longer prevent or control myself. After all they were only dreams, but most likely there were no more openings at the mine. I go to the mine, but this time my unrestrained enthusiastic ardor was not forced to agonizingly and painfully dethrone the fascinating plans of human thought and snuff out the flame of rapture kindled by my heart. To block the ray of thought that illuminates my prospects, to dethrone my beautiful dream. In the geological-prospecting bureau of the Beryozovo mine management office I was taken on staff to work drilling in the mines.

A dream founded on a material basis is becoming a real program of creative activity. I encountered the welcome of the leader to workers in the gold industry, while working at a wonderful gold deposit and in the

Geological Prospecting Bureau, whose head, chief engineer, geologist, and senior drilling foreman were given awards, which resulted in the addition of the honorable title "Union Gold" to its name. I feel at home in the mines. I am mastering all the different aspects of mining activity. I am gaining the skills of underground surveying and documentation for gold-prospecting.

To overfulfill the new increased norms and give a Stakhanovite level of productivity is a matter of honor for me.

[...]

July. I spent the whole first month of my practical training familiarizing myself with the deposit and doing geological work. I was enraptured by the fascination and significance of the deposit. I considered ideal beauty to be fulfillment of the norm at two hundred percent. Taking on this endoubled task I aimed at each day and each mine. Running in the heat in my heavy overalls from one mine to the next other and lowering myself all sweaty into the cold bowels of the earth I meticulously and unhurriedly did my surveying and sampling work. But by evening a cold had manifested itself. I felt indisposition and my enthusiasm was replaced by dissatisfaction with my weakness. But I tempered my skin in the battle against the cold. I laid out in the sun and got sunburned, I slept outside with just my shorts on. On my days off I walked through the woods to the river. I made no concessions to my indisposition and it passed unnoticed in the course of my work. Twice every five days I made the rounds of my twelve mines. The prospectors and brigade leaders miscalculating in a tectonic deposit "violation" shower me with questions share their impressions and ask me to help them elucidate the conditions of the bed.... I burn with passion to grasp the secret of nature in the bowels of the earth. Cheerfully, with mischievous pleasure I climb down holes not adapted for climbing. The stony masses resonate my voice.... We are born to turn fairy tale into reality, to overcome space and expanse. The practical data predict a 120% fulfillment of the order, but I consider it absolutely necessary to give 150% using all possible means, in the last days of the month I push fulfillment up to 152%.

August. [...] On my day off I came to Sverdlovsk. I saw the film *Circus*.[27] The ideological-emotional contents of that film are beautiful. It fascinates the viewer and fills him with a sensation of good cheer. The psychological resurrection of Mary Dixon in the country of the new mankind, growing and blooming together with the triumph of rising socialism. Her first free and confident joy in life filled my eyes with tears of sympathy and an excess of our common joy. And at that moment of renewal, living clarity and sincere purity you involuntarily cast a glance at your own life before the image of creative wise simplicity, the charm of sincere purity, persistant energetic creators of a happy world.

Kolya and I share a room in the dormitory. But as before beautiful music flows out of the radio into the empty room and it has plunged me into strong emotion. Not so long ago all of us classmates were a carefree, impetuous horde, but now the face of a worker has begun to appear in each of us.

Youth is happy in that it has a future. And this youth must be spent in such a way that the future should bloom forth like wonderful greenhouses in the present. How beautiful is the life I have lived up to now, but so far I have achieved very little. And I'm sorry that I have experienced so little of the happiness of youth, that at times I have not noticed it. Youth you filled me with an impulse and you, o life lived impetuously and brightly, you did not recognize any difficulties, you pushed me on up the steep peaks of life. You demanded from me everything of which a man can only dream, you gave me great resplendent plans. [...] The mighty joy of mankind in bloom. I rush forth to achieve the unachievable even more forcefully without sparing my energy to turn dream into reality. Life, you must reward me with the flowers of an unexperienced joy. Let my life ascend as a beautiful firework, be it only a momentary flash, at mankind's celebration of its triumph.

NOTES

[1] The entries of this diary do not always follow a strict chronology.

[2] Reference to Sergei Esenin, 1895–1925, famous "peasant" poet of the 1920s, who committed suicide in 1925. The term "Esenism" was a popular negative epithet of the period, related to the bohemian life style of the poet and the group of "Imaginists" he belonged to.

[3] See "Chronicle of the Year 1937," note 24.

[4] Inexact quote from *Eugene Onegin* (1833), chapter one, part five; the verse reads: "We all had a bit of schooling, something or other, somehow or other."

[5] See "Chronicle of the Year 1937," note 29.

[6] Abram Moiseyevich Deborin, 1881–1963, influential professor at the Communist Academy and the Institute of Red Professors during the 1920s. His

interpretation of dialectical materialism, understood as the synthesis of Hegel's dialectics and Feuerbach's materialism, dominated Soviet philosophy during the second half of the 1920s. Deborin and his school came under attack in December 1930, when Stalin called for the struggle against "Menshevizing idealism."

[7] By Grigory Aleksandrov, 1934.

[8] Probably a documentary film. To the best of our knowledge, it is not listened in any official filmography.

[9] Diminutive and "familiar" form of Kirov's patronymic "Mironovich."

[10] Gleb Uspensky, 1843–1902. Russian populist writer who depicted the life of the urban and peasant lower classes.

[11] Vyacheslav Mikhailovich Molotov, 1890–1986. Soviet statesman and diplomat. Since 1921, member and secretary of the Central Committee and candidate member of the Politburo. Supporter of Stalin after Lenin's death, he became the head of the Moscow Party Committee. From 1930 to 1941 he was the chairman of the Council of People's Commissars, i.e., the prime minister of the USSR.

[12] See note 14.

[13] By Modest Mussorgsky.

[14] Brigade leaders: name given to a team of workers constituting the basic production unit in an entreprise. The brigade leaders were usually highly skilled workers and served usually on the managing board of their entreprise; they worked alongside the ordinary members of the brigade.

[15] Three persons, heading an office or an enterprise, along the lines of administration, Party, or trade union.

[16] Opera by Anton Rubinshtein of 1871, after Mikhail Lermontov's narrative poem.

[17] Diminutive of the name Leonid, with a negative connotation.

[18] Verse from Rubinshtein's *Demon*.

[19] By Yuly Raizman, 1935.

[20] See "Chronicle of the Year 1937," note 17.

[21] Peterhof is known as the Russian "Versailles," near St. Petersburg.

[22] Strength of materials class.

[23] Acronym for "dialectical materialism."

[24] See "Chronicle of the Year 1937," note 6.

[25] See "Chronicle of the Year 1937," note 7 (about the "Mothers' Assistance Law" of June 27, 1936).

[26] By Sergei Gerasimov, 1936.

[27] By Grigory Aleksandrov, 1936.

STEPAN FILIPPOVICH PODLUBNY

The following biographical notes are quoted in part from Jochen Hell-beck's article "Fashioning the Stalinist Soul: The Diary of Stepan Pod-lubny (1931–1939)" in Jahrbücher für Geschichte Osteuropas *(forth-coming). Both the editors of the present volume and Jochen Hellbeck have been in contact with Podlubny during the last few years.*

Stepan Filippovich Podlubny was born in 1914 into a family of wealthy peasants living in the Vinnitsa district of Ukraine. After the October Revolu-tion, his father was stripped of all but a modest plot of his previous landhold-ings. On the basis of his class origin, his family was dekulakized in 1929, and his father was deported for a three-year term of administrative exile. Stepan Filippovich and his mother also left the village. They obtained forged docu-ments showing them to be of worker origin and settled in Moscow. His mother worked as a janitor, while Stepan became an apprentice in the fac-tory school of the Pravda printing plant. He entered the Komsomol, headed a shock-worker brigade, edited a wall newspaper, and was a member of the factory board. Between 1933 and 1935 he attended a Komsomol middle school. Upon graduation he was accepted into the Medical Institute. In 1936 the Komsomol learned about Podlubny's concealed kulak origins, but although he was publicly expelled from the Komsomol, this incident did not damage his standing at the institute where he continued to study.

Podlubny kept his diary from 1931 to the present day, with several inter-ruptions. The excerpt here covers 1 January 1936 through 11 January 1938, with an interruption of almost one year (from 31 December to 6 December 1937) "crossed out [from his life] like an unnecessary page," as he writes. Podlubny must have crossed out many pages of his life. A passage from his diary of a previous period reveals to us his "secret": he had become an informer for the State Security in the fall of 1932. When, many years later, Stepan Podlubny deposited his diary at the Central Popular Archives in Moscow, it was, to use his own words, an "act of repentance."

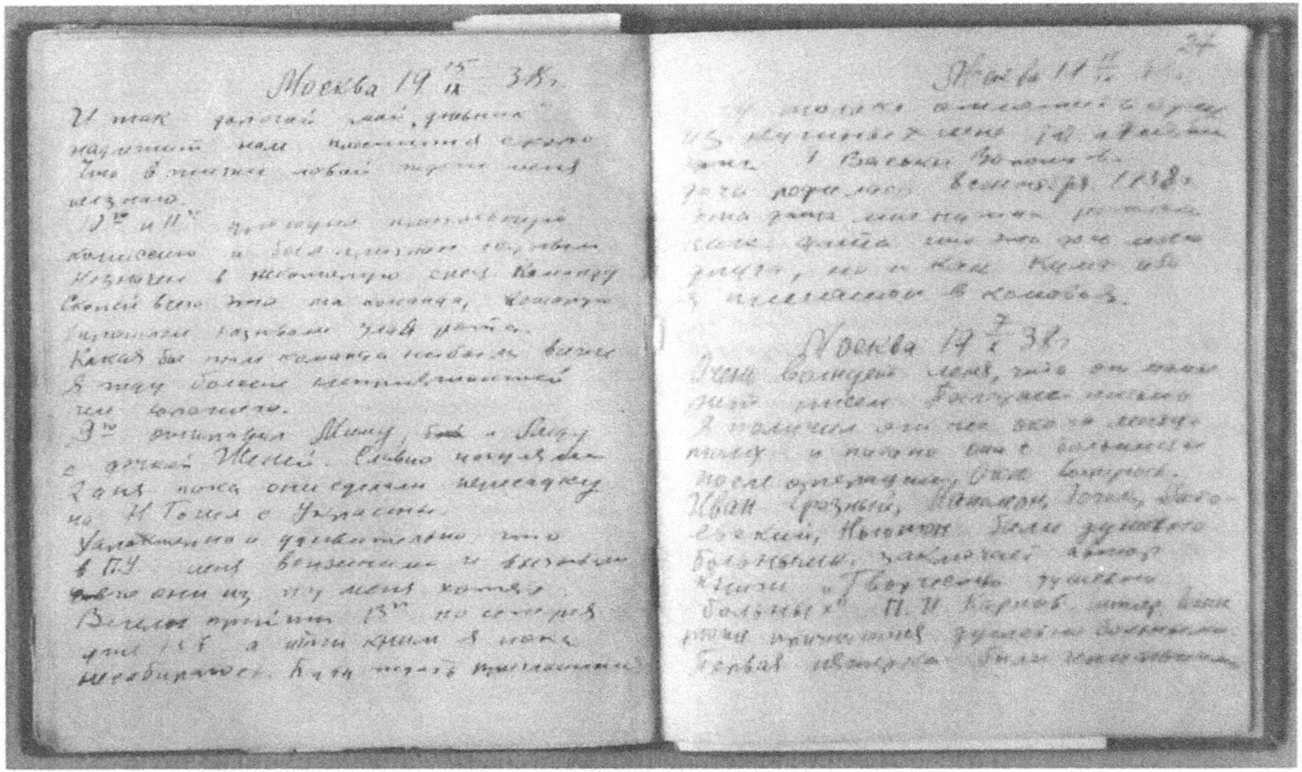

Page from Podlubny's diary (1938)

Diary of Stepan Filippovich Podlubny

January first, Nineteen thirty six. Welcome, 1936. I was so used to writing the number five that I automatically wrote it on the first page of my diary for 1936, too. Welcome, new year! I ushered you in properly yesterday over a glass of wine. Will yesterday's happiness continue through the year. I ask what the new year has in store for me, but it is a different question from the one I asked in years past. I used to ask how I would be punished for my past, and that was all, 100%. Now this is only 40% of my question, the other 60% is what will I achieve, will things go my way in 1936.

January 2, 1936. 12:30. I didn't go to the institute today. Most likely they'll count me absent. It'll be the first time, I've skipped a few times before, but I always brought various kinds of forged excuses. It's overcast, with a light fog and drizzle, the snow is melting. Water runs in little streams along the cracks in the sidewalks. The very picture of spring, though it's only January. Yesterday's new year celebration is still fresh in my memory, I say yesterday because I didn't get home until 4 in the afternoon. Evening. A thick cover of wet snow, trampled and uneven in places, covers the ground. I put on my hat and coat and hurry to the barber's. In spite of the early hour I get on the tram heading for the train station. I can't wait. It's 10 o'clock at the station. I'm too early. I get on another tram and go to Kolya's. At his apartment I exchange my warm hat for a visored cap and at 10:40 we head back for the train station. We meet Katya and Kolya first. Then Mitya. Tanya and Shura Stepanov (T. is Kolya's better half) are in the waiting room. We go up and exchange greetings. The train leaves in 10 minutes. Laughing and joking, we get on and find ourselves a place to sit.

Kuntsevo. It's stopped snowing. We go up to the house. 10 minutes left before 12, i.e. before the new year. We make it into the apartment with five minutes to spare. We throw off our coats and sit around the table. Exactly at 12 we drink to the new year. Then I offer the second toast to the old year 1935. Everyone has a good time. Kolya and I are the life of the party.

Night. We're all just a bit tipsy. The Leika camera keeps clicking, capturing our group in various poses. A warm, quiet night. In the distance, the black silhouette of a pine tree stands out against the white snow. Tanya and I go out for a walk together. It's quiet. Only the Moon watches with a big smile on her blurry face. The road leads out into the field. Unexpectedly we fall and roll around in the snow. Then we go back the way we came.... that's all. A short two-hour nap. We sit around the table again. The clock says 12 noon. The street, a snowball fight. Again the camera clicks, capturing the whole group together. We all head to the station together, two by two. The train car. We nod off, rocking quietly in the train. Moscow....

6/18/36. This year I lost my love for my diary. I believe the reason is I no longer have to deal with those life-or-death questions, the kind you have to hide from the people around you. A lot of what I can't tell people gets lost in the huge volume of things I can tell and share with others.

There are fewer and fewer thoughts that I have to keep hidden now that my friends and acquaintances know the main thing about my past that made me hide my thoughts before and share them with my diary.

Still, I won't deny it, such thoughts do flash through my mind, but I muffle them by talking with my friends about some other topic that's similar, but safer.

The page before last, that strange one that could be entitled "Out on the Town with my Diary," would be incomplete without the latest news that befell me a few hours after I wrote that page.

We left Mamontovka /May 30/, all of us together, to visit Drundin in Klyazma. He wasn't there and neither was his wife. And while I was there I broke my leg in a stupid accident near his dacha. A warm May evening. And it's common knowledge that in the evening, when it gets dark and cool, the May bugs are more temperamental than they are during the day.

I'd never been out in the country before and had never seen May bugs. Suddenly a group of extremely temperamental bugs flew by over my head and one of them caught my eye.

As one who appreciates and adores animals and bugs and loves nature dearly, I started chasing him (I wish he'd never been born, the bastard). It didn't take me too long to catch up to him, but he was flying just a little over my head, I jumped up and took a swipe at him with the bookbag I was carrying at the time and...my bug got away but I landed with a sharp pain in my knee which was preceded by a dry crack just afterwards. When the first sharp pain subsided my friends helped me stand up. In the heat of the moment I managed to walk a kilometer or so with them supporting me, but my leg swelled up fast and convinced my reckless head of the need to start for home.

On the way back which got harder and harder we stopped at Drundin's. This time he was home and she was home all of them were, home, but this time not everything was "at home" in my head because of the pain.

Thanks to Sasha Bolkov, I don't know how I can pay him back for taking care of me, I will never forgive [sic] it, he got a car at the station and, together with Vera and Lyusa, drove me home. I can't describe the feeling that came over me when I was at home in bed for two days and all of the guys and girls my old friends got together and came to see me.

After all I haven't worked at the Pravda Complex for a whole year now, and all of them are from there, but this visit during those difficult minutes when I was in such physical and emotional pain meant a lot to me, looking at them I couldn't help shedding a few tears, especially with the thoughts going on in the back of my mind, about how depressing it was to be all alone here without my father without my mother I was alone, and what's worse injured. But the people who came to see me, who paid attention to me were an inspiration, a spark that stirred my desire to live and dispelled my misery.

7/2/36. The Moscow-Tagil Train N 46. 18:15.

7/28/36. The Urals. Nizhny Tagil. I arrived in Tagil on the evening of July 4. Contrary to my expectations no one met me I had to find the way myself, tromping the streets through dirty mud that came up to my knees at times. No one could give me directions to the right street. Finally, and with great difficulty, we arrived, all worn out and exhausted.

I knocked at the gate. Two pairs of dog muzzles barked loudly.

"Be so kind, we're here to see Andrienko."

"Get out of here, Tuzik, Loza, I can't hear what he's saying.... Where do you know him from? Come on in." Aunt Yugina's dark, wrinkled face. "You sit there I'll call Musya."

I was struck that all the way out here, so far from the Ukraine, people were speaking Ukrainian like it was the most natural thing in the world. [...]

"Hello," a girl with a flustered, unhealthy face with squinting eyes hesitantly gave me her hand. "It's Styopa."

From these words I guessed that this was Galya's sister. I met her husband. Afanasy Viktorovich Komarov.

Her face was all red and pimply and her neck was covered with boils, which was why her head didn't move at all on its axis except sideways and she kept lifting the tall stand-up collar of her shirt to cover her blemishes.

When she wasn't doing this she walked around flirtatiously with her hands on her thighs or stood with one leg sticking out to one side like a statue of some half-wit beaureaucrat.

A small, poorly furnished room and what I liked was there was dumplings on the table.

We knock. "Yes, come in." I enter the apartment. A tall, thin, dark-skinned man with black eyes gets up from the table opposite me. He wasn't expecting us and he's all flustered.

We exchange greetings and I introduce myself.

Styopa. "I see, I see. Please sit down." But there's nowhere to sit. A few rickety stools, a chair, a bed, a chest of drawers. I meet his wife. Lida. She's good-looking, seems nice. Misha is overbearing and demanding, likes to brag. There's nothing wrong with his mind, but his environment doesn't dispose him to improve himself. He lacks refinement.

In spite of his 450–ruble salary he's in financial difficulties. Dusya's family, I'm informal with her because she's the wife of the head of the household, Andrei Yemelyanych Slobodenko. Everyone except Musya and their aunt work. Besides their work at the collective they have their own work at home. They have a half-hectare kitchen garden. If you count the field around it, it's even bigger. They grow potatoes and all kinds of things for cooking.

A horse, a heifer, a milk goat, chickens, etc. It feels more like a country village than a town. And it seems like their work home, their concern about the hay, etc. is more important to them than their work for the collective.

July seventh, evening. We went to Yelizaveta Mikhailovna (actually Milentyevna) Leontyeva's house, she's Moisei's girlfriend.

We got acquainted. As always when I meet someone new, I don't rush to get into a conversation until I've scoped out the circumstances and the people around me. I don't say anything. I just listen while they talk. The next day when the three of us we were out walking, we ran into a snub-nosed girl with a few freckles scattered over her face. Gentle features, short flaxen braids.

We kill time, the four of us, wandering down Volkov street, Moisei and Liza arm-in-arm, me with my hands in my pockets. I just hold my tongue and listen. Then we split up. Moisei went with Nina and I took Liza by the arm and we went down Zayacha Hill. The next day since Liza got jealous of Nina we had to trade back. I walked until nightfall without touching her. Then unexpectedly and unnoticed both by myself and by her I took her by the arm. At two in the morning we were sitting on the bank up under the wall of the hut, and I kissed her "unexpectedly." She got flustered and hung her head. After the first kiss came the 2nd, 3d, 5oth and she wasn't flustered any more and things followed their normal course.

Lipovets in the Ukraine. 8/22/1936. My diary which has come along with me on my journey isn't getting any attention. I rarely open it in view of the absence of boredom and of the necessary time and inclination. I was in Nemirov or rather the village of Talageevka. Since August 4 I haven't even picked it up. And now in the town of Lipovets I haven't picked it up either, not since August 13.

Life on the collective farm among people who were once low-class is hard and is scant in the way of entertainment. Everyone moans and complains about how bad life is.

After making the rounds, paying a diplomatic call on acquaintances, we applied at the local council to get Mama's voting rights restored.

Nothing particularly soul-stimulating has happened which is why there's nothing on the pages of my diary.

Everyone is envious of our way of life. They envy Mama's and my nice clothes, they envy us for living in Moscow they are envious about everything. Some people are envious and downright nasty too. Nadya Antononovykh and Vasya Kh-n came with us on our visits.

Nadya—when I left she was just a little kid now she's already a 19-year old girl—she's a student in a medical training school.

Vasya's all grown up big and tall, he's a man now and works in the mines.

Guys or girls often come up to me, shake my hand and talk and I don't know who I'm talking to or what their names are.

I heard a good Lipovets story.[1] Two Jews are guarding a horse. One's lying on his back he asks, "Moshko you sleeping." "No, Leiba I ain't."

"Well, what're you doing then

"Just thinking"

"What's on your mind"

"I'm thinking that what if everyone in the world turned into one single person, every oak tree turned into one single oak tree, all the ponds turned into one single pond, all the axes turned into one single axe, and what if that one person took that one axe and cut down that one oak tree, and that oak tree fell into that one pond, what a hell of a plop that would be."

"Leiba you sleeping"

"No I ain't"

"Well what're you doing then"

"Just thinking"

"What's on your mind"

"I'm thinking was there a horse here or not?"

The Nemirovskys

This boss goes up to a peasant and asks:

"When are you going to deliver all this grain? Why didn't you deliver until now?"

"Just wait till it dries, then I'll deliver it."

"Why dry it? First deliver it and then it will dry by itself."

This collective farm worker's walking along the field and he runs into another one who's out there working instead of saying hello he says "you're doing a lousy job" the other one answers "ain't that the truth."

This girl from the collective farm is sitting in some tall weeds just counting up all the days she's worked, and a guy from her same farm comes by with a rake and says what good are you with all them working days?

Moscow 8/29/1936. Here I am back in Moscow.

I left Lipovets on the 25th. It was raining, and I couldn't get to Nemirov to pick up my things. I arrived in the same clothes I had on when I was paying my calls.

I hurried not knowing how things were at the institute. I arrived the 27th and really regret getting back so soon. I'm already starving because Mama stayed there and Father you know isn't here anyway. I'm alone. I don't have any money and no matter where I turn in the city I need money everywhere and everywhere the prices are out of reach.

I'm living now on just black bread sugar and cold water for there's nothing to heat the tea with there's no kerosene and there's nothing to put the tea in anyway, there's no teapot.

And I really need money. I owe 3 months rent, my quarterly bill. And to buy notebooks and books: where can I get it and how can I start living on my own. I'm used to leaning on Mama and now I'm getting scared here by myself. I need to do my own laundry that's only half the problem I'd do it myself but I can't afford to buy the soap. If I buy soap I won't have enough money for black bread.

On the 27th I found myself with a group of guys I was with in the 9th grade. All the former students got together. The ones who went to the institute are in their second year now, and the others are out of school. It's too bad that the way things have worked out in my life, I have to repeat my first year at institute.

I did have a good vacation in these two months. It was different from Moscow both in the Urals and in the Ukraine, you need a change every now and then.

10/8/36. As always these days I don't open my diary and I don't unburden my soul i.e. the filth from my soul. Though it's not like there's nothing to write about, there are things that bother me.

The life of a lonely bachelor is boring. I'm alone. Completely alone. Sometimes I get so lonely that I have conversations with myself, especially at night, just sitting alone at the table. Mama is in the Ukraine trying to get her voting rights restored. She sent a parcel, 50 rubles of which I sent 25 back. I sent her a package with fall clothes. Father's in Yaroslavl and we don't write to each other.

My solitude would be terrible if it wasn't for visits from old friends.

Mitya and Polina come almost every day and on the weekends Kolya and Katya come too.

Things are going on as normal at the institute I study but I don't go to class every day, I let things go like last year, putting everything off for good intentions. So far people respect me all right and I can choose the company I keep.

Everyone keeps asking me the same old question, why don't I get married. You have an apartment all the necessary conditions you're not a bad catch. Why should you wash the floors and do your own laundry and cooking when a wife could do all that for you? But I can't imagine myself married and of course I wouldn't dare think of getting married without having Mama approve my wife beforehand. I respect her a lot and I'd hate to hurt her feelings by getting married when she's away.

Maybe I'm joking here and don't really mean it but when I'm with the 4 of them I often think about Zoika. People talk about her so often I have to come up with some way of holding up my end of the conversation, which

makes me think more about Zoika myself. When you add in my solitary
situation, though it doesn't mean necessarily that I'm going to get married soon, still it makes me think more about the need to have a special
girlfriend, especially since I'm always with people who are paired up.

It's gotten to the point that I've started wanting to see her here in my
apartment. After a few conversations about this with Polina in particular, I
finally decided on the 6th to go to the Iskra where she was supposed to be
playing volleyball. Mitya and I were in the Tretyakov Gallery that day. We
stopped on the way and picked up 4 tickets to the movies and were on our
way to the Iskra by 3. And there the meeting I had wanted and waited for
so long took place. Things took an unexpected turn. There was no volleyball game, it turned out she was sick but she was there at the Iskra. She
declined the invitation to the movies claiming she was sick. I don't know
what the expression on my face was while we were talking but when she
left, Polina completely sincerely, judging from her intonation, said, she
turned you down Styopka don't take it too.

I was so broke up by what had happened that once I was alone again I
spent a lot of energy trying to resist the urge to just go on a binge.

Finally considering my own state of mind and wanting to create an
even stronger impression that I was suffering for her I stopped at home
and got a quarter-liter and some sausage. I sat down at the table and
started drinking, all alone. I was a sight for sore eyes. Sitting all by myself
at the table with my quarter-liter, wineglass and kolbasa,[2] with an utterly
forlorn expression on my face which I stretched out to make myself look
even more pathetic. In the evening I got together with the four of them.
We played dominoes. It was entirely possible they noticed I'd had too
much to drink but when I asked Mitya he said I didn't seem any different
to him than usual. Of course I never get drunk and that's why I seemed
just like normal then. As Mitya says it's cheaper to bury you than to get
you drunk.

By the way I'm writing at the present time just for the sake of writing,
I'm not stopping or thinking about how the thoughts fit together. Mitya
and Polina are sitting, or rather reclining, behind me on the sofa. I have to
keep myself busy so as not to interfere with their conversation and their
romantic activities. This is what made me get out my diary. I'm writing just
to make my pen scratch.

I'll put the story of my "romance" in quotes because there actually was
no romance, it began in 1933 when Zoika and I went along with some others to the rabbit-hutch. I got a good look at her there there was a little

attempt to get closer that didn't lead anywhere and that's the way things have been up to now.

Back when I was working at the Pravda Complex I paid more attention to her than to anyone else but I didn't make any special effort to get closer to her. I took every opportunity to observe her whenever I could, I can't say I wasn't attracted to her. But I left the Pravda complex without getting any closer than that. Now when I talk to people about her I try to convince them that Zoika is like a book I didn't read. I mean, a book that I started reading but stopped, I was interrupted or circumstances made me break off at the most interesting part. Like any interesting book in such cases that attracts you and keeps your interest up to the point when you come across some other, more or less interesting book, that draws your attention away.

11/23/1936. Letters keep me from writing my diary. Before, when I wanted to express my feelings in writing, I used to note them down in my diary, but now with all the people I'm corresponding with, I pour out my feelings to them freely, in a different form.

A lot of rather not uninteresting things have happened recently, which ought to be written down, even in some detail. On 10/26 my dear friend Mitya Gorenkov joined the army. And after the 26th I felt a lot of turmoil in my serene head and chest, I poured it all out in letters to Mitya, and to repeat myself i.e. to write it down twice is just as boring as to take a book you've already read and read it all over again.

But something at least about two big incidents like the going-away party at Sashka Bolkov's with Polina and Katya, there was a party at Senka's, too. These 2 days are especially deserving of attention since they concern internal feelings and intimate matters, having in mind Zoya. It's strange that she's still stirring in my reckless head, and it's about time I stopped thinking about her considering that nothing happened between us and three years have gone by since I first started noticing her.

The fact that I'm here without my parents doesn't bother me too much, it isn't as much trouble as I thought it would be. Of course at first glance you'd think a grown man ought to be ashamed to talk about his mommy and daddy being gone, etc., but what I have in mind is not the actual formal presence of parents, their loving parental words etc. that's all nonsense of course, what I mean is my parents help getting things done around the house, things that would seem to be trivial, but that take up a fair amount of time. In any case my experience over the last 3 months proves I can do fine living alone, I can do all that housework, things like washing the floors, laundry etc., by myself, but without material support. Of course out of the 105 rubles I get per month, I can't afford to spend anything on myself.

12/31/1936. Well here it is, the last day of 1936. 4 hours remain till the end of the year. The main thing on my mind is that my mother will be here soon. My nerves have been coiled tight as a spring for two days now, aching in anticipation.

December 6, 1937. No one will ever know how I made it through the year 1937. No one will know because not a single day of my life this year has been illuminated in this so-called diary, I can't even recall the details of my life in this year myself, and if everything turns out all right, and there are only 3 more weeks to go, I'll cross it out like an unnecessary page, I'll cross it out and banish it from my mind though the black spot the massive ugly black spot like a thick blood stain on my clothes, will be with me most likely for the rest of my life.

It will remain because my life during these 341 days of 1937 has been as ugly and disgusting as the clotted blood that oozes out in a thick red mass from under the corpse of a man dead from the plague. The feeling a man has who's not used to the sight of blood and sees a scene like that or recalls it, that's what I experience when I go through my memories of this past year.

A painful and disgusting year. Or rather, my life this year has been painful and disgusting. Maybe it always seems that way, that the unpleasant experience you're going through at the moment is worse than anything you've been through before, but it really does seem to me that this year was if not the very worst of all the years I've ever been through at least it was one of the most painful ones. It leaves a miserable impression. It seems to me that the noose around my neck keeps getting pulled tighter and tighter every year. It feels like it's tightening more and more rapidly, at a regularly increasing rate and that it keeps getting proportionately tighter and tighter at the same time, for example I can't remember a time this year when the noose around my throat was loosened and I was given even a day to breathe freely, filling my chest with air.

Maybe I won't be able to express the intensity of the grief that I experienced this year, but I have to say that I expect the noose to tighten even more in the near future, maybe I won't be able to express it all or I won't have the patience to write it all down, for it's all too disgusting, but if I wondered whether it was worth going on living, I'd have to say there wasn't much pleasant or sweet in my life. Right now I am calm and that's why I can just move the pen across the paper, tracing the curving letters of these not altogether pleasant words. Naming the things I've been through.

Mama hardly worked at all all year and I didn't get a stipend. We lived off Kostya and his money.

I finished the school year with terrible marks and I still haven't dealt with all the consequences.

When I came back from vacation I brought Lyvaveta's Anya with me I went through all kinds of trouble and worry getting her a residence permit and setting her up in school, and when I got everything finally worked out I had to send her back, because of her parents. Her father came to Moscow and tried to establish a place for himself so he could settle here permanently, but he got sick. He spent 2 months in the hospital and left empty-handed.

I lost all my good friends and my friends from the institute and was left all alone. Solitude is no fun. I completely wore out my clothes I had no shoes and nothing to wear for every day much less for special occasions, and there were many days when I didn't eat a single crust of bread and had to walk to the institute because I didn't have the 10 kopecks tram fare.

That's all just the general scheme of things, it doesn't say anything about my feelings, but what I went through each time something happened in the overall scheme of things and my situation in general drove me to despair. If you add in the daily squabbling with my mother for when there's something wrong in a family there's almost always a lot of fighting, that would give a little rough sketch of what my life has been like recently.

Add to everything else the fact that I'm going to have to drop out of the institute with my current situation being what it is, and even someone who's not in the know about what I've been through will understand that things really don't look too great for the guy and little by little the psychologist will agree! I have to get through this, it's not easy, it's not easy at all. Life is not easy, damn it.

Of course I don't care about living for my own personal pleasure for it's nothing but trouble, but I take some comfort in the need to go on with my life just out of curiosity, to find out what will come next. Well why not, live and learn, you can always stop living but you can only do that one time.

12/18/1937. The noose around my neck gets tighter every day. It's getting harder and harder to breathe, the air stinks and the rotten smell gets worse with each passing day. There's a Ukrainian saying that captures a whole philosophy of life's misfortunes in just a few words. "You've got the runs, all you need now is the cough." All I needed for my state of mind to be complete, with things going the way they were in general and at the institute in particular—and I was already completely broke—was the final blow, and it came December 9 of this year.

From conversations with people who live in our apartment building we heard some alarming news that certain people from the Moscow Criminal Investigation Department (MUR) were very interested in the people we've been associating with and that they were gathering information about Mama. There was talk of a search and they said Mama was going to be arrested. Unfortunately we were not able to take complete advantage of the loose tongues among our domestic secret service that is we did not draw the necessary conclusions. Or rather I drew a conclusion I took some preventive measures, but Mama didn't do anything herself. I recommended that for the time being we leave the apartment and sleep in someone else's apartment until the end of the election campaign.[3]

Judging from the way things were done in 1935–36 we knew that such things as exiles from Moscow were done 10–15 days before the October or May holidays, and in this case that meant the elections on December 12 and the voting in May and Mama took comfort in the fact that there was less time left.

Our mistake was that we expected to be exiled but not by any means arrested for there was no basis to assume something that extreme. Well, policies change and it's not my fault that all these decisions are made in secret, I personally hadn't come across such a case before.

Of course I've heard a lot of rumors about various people being arrested, no one is surprised by this any more, but I just couldn't in my wildest dreams imagine my mama a semiliterate woman being called a Trotskyite, since I know her very well, and even in a fit of the worst possible suppositions I couldn't imagine that for old sins and what the newspapers call "former activities," with her living such a clean life now, that for old sins like that she would be arrested. There wasn't any ground for suspecting that. Of course I expected us to be exiled any day.

What happened was on the night of 12/9 at 4:00 the caretaker came over with an armed representative of the Fourth Section of the MUR and conducted a search after showing his personal identification and a search warrant. All indications were, judging by the way he was going about the search, that he was looking for weapons. Naturally he didn't find anything, as he wrote down on his form, and then he invited Mama to put on her coat and come down to the MUR with him for a minute; first he took her passport and put it in his pocket. Mama didn't have time even to get properly dressed for the cold or to pick up any money, even a kopeck, and she just stood there in the room, terrified by the unexpected shock, all pale with wandering, uncomprehending eyes, undoubtedly sensing instinctively that she would never see this beloved room again. She gazed around silently and couldn't find a word to say in parting.

She glanced around again and looked at me with her eyes pleading and inquiring at the same time, she wanted to ask or maybe say something but she didn't say a word and just held out her hand for me to clasp, and holding back her tears, forcing herself, with the last bit of strength she had left, to be brave and not show any weakness in the last parting minute, she turned her head and followed the deputy and the caretaker to the door. I gathered my last strength, trying to keep my spirits up and hers at the same time with a carefree and happy expression on my face and making little joking comments, I said don't stay away too long and be back in time for tea, but in my own soul I knew that we wouldn't see each other for a long time. She knew it too and I saw it in her eyes that she understood that I was just putting on a clever act so as not to play out our parting scene with tears which wouldn't help at all but would just upset our nerves.

I took another look at her bent back, she already had turned from me, at her old coat, I caught a glimpse of the tattered backs of her felt boots before they vanished into the black cavity of the outer door. Since I was barefoot and just had my undershorts on and so as not to get into a tearful scene I didn't go out to see her off.

12/19/1937. Exactly 10 days have passed since Mama was invited to go down "for a minute" to the 4-th Section of the MUR and that was the last I saw of her. Not only did I not see her, I didn't even manage to find out where she was.

In spite of the fact that the information office at 38 Petrovka Street opens at 10:30 when I arrived there this morning at 7:00 to sign up I was already 71st in line. This is where you get information about people under arrest, who is where, that is, whether he's still at Petrovka or whether he's already been sent off to the camps. A small cramped and dirty hall smelling of fresh human sweat. Because people with children don't have to wait in line several had made a point of bringing along their noisy little brats who had no idea of what was going on. It was like being at the market, with all the noise of people getting into arguments with each other or standing around in groups discussing the circumstances of the different arrests: when they occurred and for what. With this general racket in the background no amount of threatening or pleading would settle down the whining kids, they raised such a cacaphony that your heart shuddered for you'd think they were being slaughtered. Outside the windows people stood in a long line along with a crowd of others who had stepped out of line to stretch their legs.

Every day over 1000 people come and stand there in that awful line half of them leave at the end of the day empty-handed without even getting up to the information window, the other half finds out about where their loved one is but can't do anything to help him and just waste their time pointlessly, ruining their health too.

One old man had come from out of town to find out about his son who was arrested here in Moscow, he told me he had stood in line all day yesterday but hadn't made it to the window and he'd spent five freezing cold and sometimes damp and foggy nights out on the street under fences or at train stations, and every morning he'd go and get in line again. Yesterday he was standing in line with an old woman about his age, I'd seen this old woman, all gray and hunched over with a worn-out, sad, wrinkled face. She looked about 70. Her turn didn't come up yesterday either and, when the old man told her that he had no place to stay she invited him to come to her house. He didn't turn down the opportunity to catch up on his sleep for the whole week.

The old woman has 3 living sons, all grown. You'd think what else does an elderly old mother need when she has three grown and also educated sons. But things have gone badly for her. One fine night all three sons were taken away. The old woman's peace and happiness was destroyed. And now chances are she will have to spend the few years she has left to live just sitting all alone and weeping, thinking back on the sons she loves and who love her.

I saw her go up to the window, being of fairly short stature she braced her arm on the sill so as to stand up taller and her toothless old gums mumbled out the names of her sons, the first, the second, the third. It turned out they all had been sent into exile. Two big yellowish drops appeared in the corners of her eyes, trickled down her wrinkled cheeks and fell onto the dirty floor, disappeared in the dust and mud, the next people in line trampled on them and ground them into the floor with their heavy tread. No one paid any attention to the weeping old woman. She's not the first and she's not the last either. Her little bent figure separated from the line and the old woman slowly made her way to the exit, tapping the floor with her cane as she walked.

Naturally the question arises as to why people are being put in prison.

There are various reasons. For robbery, drunkenness, drunken brawling, for previous convictions, for a word spoken at the wrong time and place, but many people just don't know the reason. He was arrested and there he is in prison and I don't know why. Maybe he knows, but if he doesn't well then the person in charge of his case or the one who signed his arrest order ought to. A man is not always in control of his fate.

There used to be a saying, "We are all under the will of god." Now this saying goes "We are all under the will of the NKVD." Oh, what a life! Nothing but trials and tribulations and there's no end in sight.

I've dropped out of the institute. I regret that so much, damn it, I really regret it. What makes me any worse a man than the others who stayed and are going on with their studies. I can't imagine what the future holds for me. I spent 15 years in school but without a degree just grab yourself a shovel and go dig ditches. What am I qualified for?! Of course a citizen of the USSR has the right to an education, but the right and the opportunity, the conditions for it, that's two different things. You also need to have the right to study in addition to the right to an education. If I live I'll see what comes next, I can always find the time to die.

12/20/1937. I can't forget the words, the prophetic words spoken by Veronika Ivanova in her letter to me back then in 1933 after we came back from the rabbit-hutch and used to run into each other occasionally in the Central Park of Culture and Recreation and occasionally would philosophize to each other in letters.

In one of those letters she said "You are secretive, you try to get everything from the other guy without giving anything yourself, if you keep on living that way you'll wind up without any friends." And now here I am, all alone. Whether it's for the reasons Veronika, who I still respect today, predicted or for some other reason, still a fact is a fact, I'm all alone in life. Not only have I lost my friends, I don't even have anyone to talk to.

I can't forget what our philosophy was based on and the stupid reasons we went our separate ways.

She was a well-brought up girl from a well-off, cultured family from a family of the Soviet aristocracy. I'm the son of a grounds keeper. We might have been equals in terms of our level of culture. But we were far from equal in terms of money and the way we dressed. On these grounds I advanced the theory that our seeing each other couldn't lead to anything we are completely different people with a big gulf between us. No matter how she tried to bridge this gulf as she said herself I stubbornly and stupidly rejected all her efforts and ultimately caused us to break up, which I still regret to this very day five years later. I want to see her so bad. I'd explain and ask her forgiveness.

Here I got all carried away by old memories of bygone days and forgot the question I brought up about solitude.

I can't find any explanation for the fact that I'm cut off from the people I used to work with at the Pravda complex some of them joined the army, I've lost track of where others live. And I didn't feel like I belonged at the institute either. I didn't get to know the other guys at the institute, I didn't find fertile soil there and all apparently because of stupid shortcomings like my clothes that were all in rags, for with my sharp mind and my culture I am way above the others, but those others have a whole lot of money. And evidently the old saying "money is everything" is also true under present-day socialism. Socialism is all well and good, but give money its due.

The same goes for girls. I'm not going with anyone in particular, and I haven't had a real girlfriend before, though I've met girls I like. And it all comes down to money. When you can't afford candy, movie and theater tickets, you haven't got anything to wear you can't get anything started.

There is one girl though, Liza. She's completely devoted to me. It would be hard to find someone more devoted to me and I don't know if I will ever meet anyone like her again, but I don't have any special feelings for her. She has pinned her hopes on me, though I have been honest with her and warned her about where I stand. Everyone wonders why I don't marry her, but even though I'm all alone in life I have no desire to take such a step. I don't want to get married, though I wouldn't object to having a son. Things just tend to work out that way in my life, as though all I'm doing is just letting bad things to happen to me. Or maybe it just seems that way, that the bad things stick in my memory more than the good things, but it does seem to me that my life is just one bad thing after another. For some reason I just recalled my trip to the Ukraine last summer.

When I was staying at my aunt's house outside Nemirovo, from sheer boredom and loneliness plus idleness, though I have to admit there was a lot of work to do but I couldn't make myself do anything, I took it into my head to go to Lipovets. For whatever reason, I find myself drawn to the place where I spent my childhood. One fine day I covered the whole 35 km. on foot, and overcome with emotion I entered the village of my childhood.

I spent three days there, enjoying myself, visiting old acquaintances, but everyone was worn-out and short-tempered from the harvest, which was at its peak right then, and naturally there was nothing for me to do because there was no one to spend time with, they were all busy working from dawn to dusk, and sometimes all night long, too.

After just three days there I went back to my aunt's. Before leaving for Moscow, I decided to go back just one more time and bid farewell to my childhood home. Just like the first time, just like the year before last, when I drew near to the outskirts of the town and looked down from above at those familiar houses, gardens and streets criss-crossing the valley below, each time, like this last time, Nekrasov's[4] poetry came to mind and deeply moved, I declaimed some verses out loud. And there they were again, those familiar places where the life of my fathers was sterile and empty etc., but as I walked along the familiar streets, I gazed eagerly into the faces I recognized, but who didn't recognize me (they'd forgotten). I stayed on another day and night in Lipovets.

A bunch of us got together people with time on their hands like Valya Vasilyevskaya, Nadya, and Lyusya Polhazhka Martsina's niece, the grand-daughter of old Martsa, may she rest in peace. As the party broke up late that night we agreed to meet in Nadya's apartment the next morning at 10:00. When I got up in the morning I decided to visit the family graves first, before going to Nadya's. The cemetery was overgrown with weeds and it seemed hostile to me. Dead silence. After searching and searching I finally found the grave of my grandfather who died such a legendary death. It began "Here lies Yevdokim Podlubny died September 16, 1904. Rest in peace dear father. A final gift from his loving sons." The grave was in ruins and all overgrown with thick weeds. Only the marble gravestone itself, which had sunk half-way into the ground, and the inscription, already partly covered by earth, bore witness that here, right in this spot, lay my grandfather, a man I'd never known.

It was 11 when I got to Nadya's. Everyone else was already there. I noticed that Lyusya was preoccupied and upset about something, her eyes wandered about restlessly, she wasn't listening to anyone. I'd already noticed that in my mind but had thought it was nothing—people are always worrying about something. To distract her, I started paying more attention to her, cracked some jokes and then finally recalled what had happened yesterday when we were out swimming. Incidently, that event deserves some attention. The day before was very hot and we decided to go for a swim. We put on our bathing suits and headed out to the swimming spot at Chaisynsky. Tall, rocky cliffs, the shores. Big stones in the shallow water near the shores. The warm green water of the river. On the other side of the broad river, a carpet of yellow and white lilies. We splashed around, playing and frolicking joking like little kids. When we got good and tired we decided to swim over to the other side and get some lilies. Lyusya refused. Saying she was sick and she couldn't swim. Valya had no objection. Nadya categorically refused. I'm a good swimmer but before that I had been carrying Lyusya on my back for a good long time in the shallow water near the shore. Without considering whether I was up to it, I proposed carrying her to the other side. I held her tight against my side under my right arm and started swimming steadily, using my left arm. Valya swam alongside. We had got to within 5 meters of the shallow water on the other side, when I started feeling tired. Without giving Lyusya any warning, I decided to switch hands, i.e., to hold her with my left arm and swim with my right. I let her go for just a second, and she immediately dropped like a stone, straight down to the bottom. I dove down after her. I grabbed her by the legs, stood in the slimy mud of the river bed and hoisted her upwards. There was no more than a half meter of water over my head. Finally I ran out of air and decided to fill my lungs with fresh air and anyway it's pretty stupid to stand under the water like that holding onto someone's legs to keep her from drowning. I surfaced, just for a second. Naturally this time I let go of her legs. I didn't manage to get all the way up, for she grabbed me by the neck and both of us sank back under.

Our struggle under the water continued for several seconds. Those few seconds were enough for me to gulp down a few mouthfuls of warm green slimy water, and I didn't get any fresh air into my lungs at all.

Instinctively I shoved her away from me, surfaced, gasped down a combination of air and water, for she grabbed onto my legs and dragged me down under the water again. The underwater battle resumed. I broke away under the water and ducked over to one side. I surfaced, greedily gasped down a few breaths of fresh air and glanced around. Valya, white-faced, was splashing around above the water. I couldn't see Lyusya on the surface. I dove back down like a stone at the place where she'd gone under. I remembered advice I'd heard about how to rescue people from drowning, not to let them grab you by the neck. I felt around until I found her, thrashing and flailing wildly with her arms and legs. I grabbed her by the neck, pushed off the bottom and kicking my feet and swimming with all my might using my free arm I started swimming toward shore. Valya swam alongside.

Finally I saw Valya stop swimming and stand up in the water. It's only up to her waist, that means I can stop too; the thought flashed through my brain. I stood up with my legs braced wide, swaying and trying not to fall down, and pulled Lyusya up with both hands.

Her face was as white as a sheet, her terrified, uncomprehending eyes rolled wildly in their sockets. I set her down on her feet in the shallow water. Her pale face flushed red and tears started pouring down her cheeks. Slowly, without a word, we walked through the water to the shore and sat down in the grass. Finally we started discussing what had happened. We spent some time picking flowers, without any particular pleasure, and each of us seemed to be thinking the same thing—how to get back to the other shore, which we had to do before we could start home, and where our clothes were, though no one said it out loud.

When we had had a chance to rest we started discussing our predicament. I made her agree not to grab me by the neck and in general to stay perfectly still, and that would guarantee our safe crossing. Valya carried the flowers, and not without trepidation I took hold of Lyusya and started swimming slowly, conserving my strength. We made it across safely and we all swore not to cross the river again. Then, laughing and joking, we discussed the details of what had happened and we all put on a carefree appearance to each other, pretending it was nothing, but I think we all were left with an unpleasant aftertaste, at least I was.

Sitting next to Lyusya, I started up a conversation with her about yesterday, joking a little, but I could tell from her face that she wasn't really listening; she had something on her mind. Valya and Nadya went out for a drink and Lyusya suddenly started, glanced at the door after them and asked nervously.

"You don't know a thing?"

"No," I say.

"No one told you anything."

"No," I answer, trying to keep my voice and expression calm, though inside I'm feeling a little anxious.

"Uncle Vasya told me that there was a meeting of the [local] NKVD last night; he was there since he's the chairman of the Rural Council, and they were talking about you. They want to arrest you."

In spite of the shocking news I maintained my calm exterior and gave the impression that I wasn't expecially concerned, that I had no sins on my soul, but inside I told myself, "Let's talk this out."

"Uncle Vasya said you have to leave immediately, after dark if they find out where you're going to spend the night they'll come and get you."

Lyusya insisted so I agreed to leave town within two hours. We agreed on a place to meet, from there she would take me to a village 7 kilometers from Lipovets where her relatives live, and she would go on to their place.

Exactly two hours later we started up the open road leading out of my home town. From the town where I was born, where I spent the golden years of my childhood, and now I was forced to run from it like a mad dog not knowing why. I did no one any harm, I never hurt anyone in word or deed, it may be true I didn't do anyone any good either, but is that sufficient reason to deny me the right to spend 3–4 days peacefully in this place I know so well?

We took our time, walking arm in arm, but before I knew it we'd already covered 5 km. The road to her village branched off, crossing through the fields. I was to follow the broad, straight high road. The old people said that in the old days horses were used to carry the mail along this road. They recalled seeing the horses all in a lather, racing by at a full gallop along the broad embankments that lined the the road, carrying the mail from one posting station to the next. The road is much narrower now, the farmers plowing the fields have chipped away at it on both sides, though actually the road itself is still pretty wide. But I can still remember cattle grazing on the road, which was twice as wide back then.

As I recall it, the embankment was still smooth-edged and even and so wide that two carts could pass each other without any trouble whatsoever, and all overgrown with weeds and it stretched like a ribbon out into the distance, like a railroad line. The broad plain, covered with a carpet of grass and weeds, stretched from the edges of the embankment in a wide band. The main road that has remained to the present day runs along between the embankments.

We didn't want to part. We sat down by a fork in the road. Then we lay down. Then we kissed, and after the first kiss, the first dozen followed, then the first hundred. The sun was already setting, painting the whole sky red, when we sat up again. She had 2 km. to go, I had 30. She insisted that I go to her village, and she kept after me until I agreed to go and spend the night there. The people there welcomed me because they knew me and hadn't seen me for ten years. We had dinner and sat up on the bank under the house and kissed another couple dozen times, then we parted for the night. In the morning I set out across the fields to Nemirovo. She came along to see me off. The broad expanse of freshly mown fields. The black shapes of haystacks looming up all around us. When we got about three kilometers from the village, we went down into a valley. Not a soul anywhere. Silence. We decided to stop and rest in luxuriant grass of the roadway, two paces from a stack of bound wheat sheaves. We sat, then lay down and kissed until our heads spun. Another man in my place would have taken advantage of the situation for his own personal carnal goals. But I am honorable with the female sex, and I went no further than kisses and close embraces, though if I had tried I doubt I would have encountered any resistance. The circumstances were very conducive, and kisses provide excellent bombardment in a decisive attack.

The sun had disappeared behind the western horizon long before, twilight was moving in, and there we were, still lying in each other's arms and kissing. I rewarded her generously with my kisses for the favor she had done me, and she returned them, perhaps in gratitude to me for saving her life. But we went no further, so as not to ruin a good thing.

This area was as dear to her as it was to me, but now that her vacation was over she was planning to go on to Voskresensk, 80 km. from Moscow. We decided to go to Moscow together. I would go to Vinnitsa on the narrow-gauge railway and buy her a ticket on the way, We would meet in Vinnitsa on a specific day. That's what I did. And we met there and rode on to Moscow together.

It was already completely dark when we got up for the last time kissed and went our separate ways. She had 3 km to go, I had 30 km. With 10 km to go before I reached my destination, the village of Krikivtsi, I made myself a bed out of a sheaf of wheat, spreading it out under a haystack, covered myself with my cloak and another sheaf of wheat, and went to sleep. I was awakened by an aching in my knees. There was a light drizzle coming down. The sheaf of wheat had soaked through but the cloak had prevented the moisture from getting through. My knees were all cramped from the way I'd been curled up. I shook off the tufts of wheat, put on my cloak, kicked off my shoes and, rolling up the cuffs of my trousers, started trudging off down the road, which was all muddy from the rain.

12/21/1937. Today Alla Ivanovna Vorontsova dropped in unexpectedly to complain about Vasily Ivanovich. It's been a month and a half since the wedding,[5] and living with them has been a continual torment. It got so I had to start taking my meals separately, this has been going on for two weeks now and Vaska yelled at me and threatened to kick me out of the apartment altogether. And all from not having enough to get by. I owe everyone money. You say something, and you just get yelled at in return. So I went and told her father when you married her off you promised to help out and now what, have you forgotten?! Vasily heard about it and all hell broke loose. I'm not upset at him, I know he's got a short temper. I put up with his father he's the same way, and him too for the last 23 years. But what makes me mad is having to put up with her, she's not even my daugher, she just happened to marry my son. Tomorrow is Vasily Ivanovich's birthday. My dear Vasya. Our friendship gets weaker with each passing day. It seems like we're no longer friends, just people who happen to know each other. We have less and less in common every day, and it's weakening the bonds of our mutual friendship. Most likely we will eventually go our separate ways especially when the time comes for me to leave the walls of the institute once and for all. For the time being I'm still part student, I don't attend classes, but I'm still on the rolls.

But that awful time will come when I will have to banish the institute from my mind once and for all.

So what? Not everyone can have a higher education. The way things have worked out in my life, I'm unable to continue my studies. After all it's not my fault that I was born into a particular family at a particular time. I'll just make my way through life some other way. So what if I wind up with just a high school education, just a general one without a a vocational skill, but it could have been worse. Especially in my situation. It doesn't at all mean that I've reconciled myself, that I accept what happened. I'll just take some time off, straighten out some things with my family and then I'll put up a fight. I'm not that old yet, though to look at me I could pass for half again as old as I am.

I've got some fight left in me. I'll go on the offensive, that's the only way, if I don't I'll be lost in the shuffle, they'll trample me underfoot, and rub me into the dirt.

Maybe I'll take a gamble and try my hand at literary work. Time will tell. Patience and hard work, keep your nose to the grindstone.

12/22/37. I never had insomnia before in my life, but now I have to note a strange phenomenon that has taken place in me. I haven't slept for three nights now. It's now 5 in the morning and it's the 23d, not the 22nd, but I wrote 22, it's still evening to me.

I decided to visit Vaska today, I have to note that ever since I dropped out, I enjoy each visit less and less. Today I felt downright awkward going to see him. He wasn't home, but I left him a present and a letter wishing him a happy 22-nd birthday. Just to let him know that I've not forgotten him and still respect him like before. 5 a.m. My eyes are so tired from reading, it's like they've been sprinkled with sand. If I went to bed now, I'd probably toss and turn a little and go to sleep. But I make a point of staying up. I have to go get in line at the information office by 5:30. Have they sent mama somewhere? With tomorrow being a day off they'll be accepting parcels I need to get some things together for her, at least some fresh linen and a piece of bread, I doubt they give them too much to eat, not to mention clothes. Who knows, maybe in 6 hours when the information window opens they'll give me some shocking news. She's dead, though most likely they'll say she's been exiled and tell me to wait for her to write. That'll be the end of the parcel and she'll go away hungry, exhausted, in dirty linen, and worrying sick that something's wrong with me, I had 2 whole weeks, why couldn't I manage to get a parcel to her. This whole thing weighs on my heart like a stone. I just wish it would come to some kind of conclusion, the sooner the better, living without knowing is worse than enduring any hardship I could imagine.

At first I dismissed it all with a wave of the hand and decided to let things go their natural course. I figured I was helpless to do anything. Now I'm thinking maybe I should fight back. To engage in an uneven battle, who knows what might happen, sometimes people win, even when they're the underdog.

The main thing is just to find out what's going on.

[...]

If it's just a matter of the passport, I just might be able to put up a fight. If there's something else involved there's probably no hope.

12/25/1937. A winter day in Moscow. My watch showed 5 a.m. when I went outside on 12/23. It's relatively quiet. A thin carpet of silvery snow covered the streets, the roofs, everywhere its gentle flakes fell. A light, ice-cold wind brought a flush to my cheeks. Everyone in Moscow is still in bed, there are no footprints in the carpet of snow. At the intersection, the policeman on duty paces back and forth with measured steps. His round Cossack hat and the overcoat of his green uniform are covered with a thin layer of snow. On the main street the hunched-over figures of an occasional passer-by show black in the distance. Now and then a truck or, more rarely, a car, roars past on the main Ring Road. By getting up so early I had hoped to be first in line at the information bureau, but it turned out that the line had started forming at midnight. I signed on eleventh. And it turned out that another line with another list had formed on the 24-th for people wanting to have a parcel given to someone. I signed on tenth. At 11 a.m. I learned at the information window that Yefrosiniya was here. My spirits improved a little and I went home thinking about tomorrow's parcel. I spent 40 rubles buying things, arranged and packed everything with loving care and by evening the parcel was ready. 5 a.m. on the 24th. The same morning landscape as on the 23d, but this time there were not just a couple dozen people in line but over 400. They were forbidden to gather at the exits. People with bundles and bags stuffed full of food stood out in front of the entrance of the large building in a line a half kilometer long. The broad stone staircase was scattered with people standing, sitting, and sprawling on the steps. Faces worn out from their sleepless night the rumble of voices. Every minute new people would come and sign onto the list.

The 461st, an old woman, says to the man who's taking down names, "Write it on my hand, sonny, I've got a bad memory, I forget everything." She licks her palm all over and holds out her hand. As he writes the number, the ink bleeds out and turns her palm blue.

I check to make sure the original list from yesterday is still valid and start to leave.

"Oh my lord, look at all these people." Someone was speaking Ukrainian. Hearing the familiar words I turned around. A short woman in a gray coat was standing next to me. Big round eyes sparkle and a peglike nose pokes out from under her big black scarf.

"What number are you?" I ask in Ukrainian, to initiate a conversation with someone from home.

"Three hundred thirty, I'm sure I won't...before they close...there's no point getting my hopes up."

"Who do you have in there?"

"My sister. She came to Moscow to look for her husband, he had joined the army somewhere near Moscow and she hadn't heard a word from him. But she didn't have a passport, no one out there in our village has a passport. So they arrested her here and she's been in there over a month now. Her husband came back from the army and she was gone. She has a 15 month-old baby at home and our mother is old. I can't find out a thing, not even where she is. I've been here a whole week now, living in my coat, just spending my nights at the train station, and during the day I go around trying to find where she is, everywhere I go they just throw me out, they don't even want to talk to me, and they don't understand me anyway. So I thought: maybe I'll get in this line for parcels."

I walked home, with an uneasy feeling lingering from the conversation.

I came back by 9, bringing a basket. People were crowded around the entrance waiting to turn over their parcels.

"Who's taking down names?" a well-dressed woman asks, trying to catch her breath after her brisk walk.

"I am. Your name?"

She gives it. "You're number 760." A shade of surprise and despair flashed across her flushed face.

People started to form a line according to their numbers on the list.

"First."

"Here I am." "Your name?" "Sivorukhin."

"Stand there."

"Second." "Here I am." "Your name?"

"Stand there," etc.

A long, winding line of miserable-looking human figures, hunched over from the cold. Some stand alone, silently thinking to themselves and judging from the expression on their faces their thoughts are not happy.

Others gather into small circles and listen to people tell their sorrows.

I went up to one of the groups. "I'm 32, my son is 9," began a young-looking woman. I looked at her and thought I wouldn't have given you a day over 22.

"It's not his fault he forgot the law allowing gynecologists to make house calls and continued his practice. When the other law came out banning abortions he stopped doing it, but it was a shame to throw away his instruments. And they were just lying there, not being used. Naturally they found them during the search, he hadn't tried to hide them. They took the instruments and my husband. They sealed the room, and threw me and my son out onto the street. It's a good thing my mother lives in Moscow, so we have a place to stay. But we don't have anything to wear, our things are in the room and so I'm going around in my summer coat and my son has none at all."

"Did you go see the prosecutor?"

"I've been everywhere. The investigator, two prosecutors, the police office, no one will even listen to me."

"The prosecutor just gave me a nasty grin, leered and said, 'Don't worry, you'll survive till the trial.'"

317

"And it's been going on for almost 3 months now."

"I already asked them to put me in prison with him," the prosecutor laughed and said,

"Some punishment that would be for your husband."

"I just wish they'd hurry up and have the trial. They'll convict him and send him away and I'll go with him."

She knows he's guilty I thought.

"What about the boy?"

"He'll stay with my mother, I can't help him anyway."

A special line formed right at the entrance for pregnant women and people with children. There were about 70 of them. The big huge bellies of the pregnant women. The babies squealed and the older ones whined. One woman came with two. A little baby and a boy of four.

The pregnant women and the ones with children get preferential treatment. In the morning they go first, then as they come through the day they are allowed in line after every fifth person.

10:00. It's about time for them to start. But alas! They're in no hurry. A reinforced police squad paces unhurriedly back and forth in front of the tightly closed door. 10:30. The people are restless, some start complaining. It's no use. 11:00. They let the pregnant women and the ones with children inside. At 11:30 they start accepting parcels. They don't have any reason to hurry. Their conscience is clean, and it's no concern to them that dozens won't get their parcel.

It wouldn't be quite fair to blame them and say that they're not meticulous enough. When the clock shows 4 in the afternoon they very meticulously stop accepting parcels. And no requests, pleas, or tears can get them to accept even one extra parcel after 4 o'clock.

A tall, thin woman with a hook nose, elongated like her whole face, came in the building carrying a baby bundled up in a warm blanket. I noticed her because I had seen her once before. The first time was on the 9th when I was waiting in line for information, and she had looked just the same then as she did now. An abrupt, resolute way of moving, sharp facial features, wide-open gray eyes. Energetic. A short, broad-collared jacket made of imported cloth reaching to her knees was wrapped tightly around her stately figure; its broad collar hung down to her waist. Tightly pressing the silent little creature to her breasts, she forced her way through the crowd to the window. The baby was that age that when they're hungry they wake up and give signs of life. She was holding a small parcel in her right hand. When she made it at last to the window, she was covered with sweat. She gave a name and, stretching out her long neck, she stared, unblinking, at the man as he checked the card file to see if there was someone there by that name.

"Yes, he's here, but we can't accept parcels, he's not allowed to get any."

"Why not?"

"We're not told why. But we can't accept any parcels."

"Just something little, just one little thing?"

"I told you we can't. Next."

"Just a couple of onions, there's scurvy out there…"

Big tears flowed down her emaciated face. The current of human bodies bore her away from the window. The next one in line got a receipt and filled out a card. The people standing near the window are absorbed in their own private concerns, for them the world outside does not exist. They stare straight ahead at the window. Racked with sobs, the unhappy woman slowly made her way toward the exit. In spite of her tears, her face expressed determination and something else besides, not quite hate, and not quite despair. It looked like she could have killed herself on the spot or indulged in some savage act of vengeance, right then and there.

Then it was my turn at the small square window.

An inexplicable terror came over me. My knees shook and buckled under me, my fingers trembled nervously. My heart raced, I could feel each beat distinctly, not only did I feel them, but with each heartbeat I heard a roaring in my ears, as though someone right next to me was pounding on a drum. I gave my mother's name and, holding my breath, I stared without blinking through the window at the fingers of the middle-aged female clerk as they shuffled through the card file. And the thought flashed through my mind:

"And what if there's nothing there?"

A half minute of silence seemed an eternity to me.

"She's not in my file," said the woman indifferently. My eyes wandered, my face contorted into a stupid smile, and noticing that she was looking over to one side, I saw that there was another woman there, older than the first.

"Podlubnaya? Let's see. No, I don't have her here either. We don't have anyone by that name."

"But they told me…"

"At the time they told you," interrupted the younger woman, "we had her, but now we don't. Next."

I don't know what my face looked like at that moment. Most likely I was a sight for sore eyes, all flustered and confused, for the older woman looked at me and said gently, "Don't worry, I'll write you a note for the orderly at the window across the room, he can tell you where she is." And she pressed a scrap of gray paper into my trembling hand.

At the "window across the room" I learned nothing; they couldn't find her. I just stood there in shock for ten minutes or so, then it was like I had awakened from a bad dream. I grabbed my bag, hung my head low and slowly headed for the door, followed by the sympathetic, fixed gaze of the other people in the room.

It was only after I got home that I fully realized the meaning of what had happened. A huge lump in my throat cut off my breath. I lost control of my muscles. My head felt so heavy, I could hardly lift it. Just thoughts, thoughts, a whirlwind of thoughts.

There she is without a kopeck, literally without a kopeck, I knew because earlier that evening I had gone through the pockets of the coat she put on later when they arrested her, looking for change, and I hadn't found any. The 20 rubles she had, she had left on the bookcase. She doesn't have enough money to buy a 3-kopeck envelope and write where she is and what she needs. In dirty linen. Not a single parcel in 2 weeks. Scurvy. Poor health. Where is she? In a women's prison? In the hospital? Is she dead?! Have they sent her away? The orderly hadn't been able to give a positive answer to a single question. It almost would have been easier to take if she had suddenly died a natural death at home. Well, she died, death came, her time came and she died. But as it is, imagine how painful it must be for her out there, wondering what's the matter with me? I never particularly liked spirit. But I went and bought myself a 1/2 liter and got drunk. Really and truly smashed. All by myself. Glass after glass, and without eating anything to speak of. It worked. I lay down on the sofa and fell fast asleep. I woke up 5 hours later and looked at the table, where I'd left the half-drunk bottle. It was gone. I looked around the room it wasn't on the window sill either. Or anywhere else. There was a half-eaten crust of white bread on the table. Someone had washed the floor.

I realized that Liza, who had promised yesterday to come and wash the floor, had come and found me sleeping. And guessed what was going on. She hid the dishes, washed the floor and left.

And it's a good thing she hid the dishes. I had started getting dangerous ideas again and in the state I was in I might have polished off the rest of the sleeping potion.

To take my mind off things, I went out to Vaska's, where I spent the rest of the day.

As before, I still can't get to sleep at night. Like right now, the clock says 3:30 at night, or more precisely morning, and I haven't even gotten undressed. I haven't bothered to, because I know I wouldn't get to sleep anyway. The silence of night, without all the traffic noise, is conducive to intellectual work, to reading and writing. More and more often I'm faced with the question of where to go from here. Where should I look for work. what kind of work. The army. What about the institute, my studies. What should I do with my life, what should I apply myself to. It's an extremely urgent question, and it's beyond my strength to answer it to myself, much less to others. I go out to take my place in the information line.

I come back from my walk. It turns out the line hasn't formed yet, there's no one there. Of course who could stand outside for any length of time anyway in this freezing cold weather. Just walking briskly there and back, my feet froze stiff. My knees are freezing cold, too. I don't have any long underwear, just boxer shorts, and the frost bites at my knees like a dog. By the way, I forgot to mention a very interesting letter I got from Lukian Khymyny. Nadya, Kostya's sister, graduated from technical school and has got herself an internship at a hospital in Khanzhenkovo, right where Lukian lives.

Yesterday I got a letter from him, saying that Nadya is terribly ill. Well, I thought it must be the flu, or angina, what's a person most likely to get sick with, anyway? The flu or angina, of course. But after beating around the bush, hoping to soften the blow, he writes she's got the same thing her mother had, and I know that her mother was mentally ill.

It's a shock, but at the same time if you think logically, it makes a lot of sense:

There's mental illness on her mother's side of the family. The old folks said that her mother's mother i.e. Nadya's grandmother was ill. Her daughter, Nadya's mother was also ill. And for a long time, too. It used to come and go; she would be over it, but then something would happen to upset her and she would get it again. Her husband tried to shelter her he never yelled at her, he tried not to overburden her with work, he didn't tell her about any of his money troubles. That worked. In 1918 it was hard to create a normal, calm living environment. And that year was fateful both for Nadya and for her mother. In 1918, when Nadya was born, the disturbing signs had quietly been making their appearance in her mother. She was already ill by the time Nadya was born. In 1919 her mother could no longer think rationally. They had to send her to Kiev for treatment. But what treatment could you expect in those years of war and destruction?

After six months they received notification that Praskovya Pc
had passed away. They only learned the details later. It turne‹
they had simply poisoned her, just like that, the doctors had cor
futile to go on with the treatment, and at the same time they sav
in even sending her home to her native village, and they thougl
even be more harmful to her. So Nadya lost her mother when sḫ
a year old, and a year and a half later her father died too, in tḫ
typhus epidemic. Her brothers took care of her and raised her. I
brother Styopa came back from the army. The beet harvest was
Autumn. Rain. He caught cold. The lung infection affected his
lost his mind and became violent. I remember that unforgettaḷ
spent in the hospital at his bedside. He was in a straitjacket witḷ
tied securely to his bed. Wide-open and incomprehending eɣ
there babbling and cursing, and intermittently making frenziec
to get up. Then his mind would clear temporarily, and he would
the people there and ask them to untie him and give him son
drink. But then he would start saying one thing then switch ove
thing else, he'd shout, sing, and struggle, trying to free himseḷ
straitjacket.

They sent him to Vinnitsa, the district center. He got over it
married. He has a son and he's never had another spell, either a
violent one.

That family is organically predisposed to mental illness, but ɛ
the women are more susceptible than the men. Can it be that at
age Nadya will suffer the fate of her mother? Her mother had a
someone to take care of her. Who will take care of you, you poɽ
you don't get over this and it turns out to be chronic?

Just her luck. She grew up in misery and poverty. She workec
managed to get through technical school, you'd think that
things could only work out for the better in her life. To apply ɣ
learned about theory in practice. Settle down into her work. Ma
man, start a family and just carry on with her life. But no, not yɽ
what you want, but what you get, it's outside your will.

No one can tell what the future holds in store. They say it's
that word, "Fate," but if someone asked me what it is, I'd proba
able to answer, just as I couldn't answer the question as to what
is. Maybe there's no such thing. What happens in life is dicta
conditions in your environment. "Being determines consciousṇ
sciousness is determined by being, I completely agree.

322

1/1/1938. Well, 1938 has begun. What awaits me this year? Can it be that fate will not smile on me? I don't regret the passing of 1937. Nothing good happened, but there were plenty of bad things. My life fell apart, before it could get itself into some kind of harmony. Before 1938 I had a future ahead of me — my studies at the institute. Now this one dream of mine too, this bright nugget on the black background of my life, is no more. I've been robbed of perhaps what is dearest to me of all the precious things I had. My beacon has been snuffed out, the beacon that showed me the way as I made my way along the path of my life, a difficult, winding road, burdened down with obstacles, but the bright spot of light from the beacon drew me toward it and showed me the goal to strive for. Now there's no goal in sight. To live without something to work toward is like an animal, what kind of life is that. There's nothing, there's no one to give me moral support. It's oh, so hard to maintain your human dignity. If I didn't have the desire to observe how people live and see what will happen next, it probably wouldn't be worth going on.

It's so disgusting. I've even got chills and shivers running up my spine. What should I do tomorrow and the days to come? Look for work?? To sell my labor for 200 rubles a month. Well, then what? Who needs my head, with all its general knowledge, but nothing specific? Who needs my hands without a useful skill? Sure! But I still need to go out and look for work. A lot depends on finding the right job. And I need to look for a good one.

1/7/1938. If the work you're doing brings you peace of mind, you forget all the bad things and all your urgent business. I'm still not sleeping at night, but every night I devour a whole volume of some book or other, mainly. Right now I'm reading Ukrainian literature. Also I've been thinking seriously about starting a translation project, translating some Ukrainian fiction into Russian. This brings me some peace of mind. And by the way I've done more than just think about it, I've actually started working on translating Ivan Franko's *Zakhar Berkut*.[6] It turned out to be a lot harder than I thought it would be. I got all caught up in it and forgot about my dearest friend — my diary.

On December 28 at the information office on Petrovka I learned that Mama is in Novinskaya Prison, and the same day I went to the prison office and verified that she really is there. On the 29th I turned in the parcel. They are extremely scrupulous, so scrupulous I even rather liked it. Not only do they take each thing out of the parcel and examine each individual part under the light, but they also probe it with their hands as though checking its quality. I included some linen and 100 rubles cash. It relieved the heavy burden on my soul. She'll still be hungry but it won't be so bad now.

I can't make myself go over to the institute, make a clean break of it and sort out what I'm going to do from now on. With things being like they are I haven't got practically any documents and so I can't find work, and I admit I haven't really tried to look. And boy do I need to get a job.

You could call today an eventful day.

Kostya told me about an interesting thing that happened to one of the engineers over at the Moscow Regional Executive Committee where he works, and I also had the pleasure of experiencing an interesting thing that happened to me even though I didn't even go outside all day long. An event within the four walls of my home, in my quiet home setting.

I've known Liza several years and I've also known Katya Khabalova for several years. Territorial proximity, the possibility of seeing her every day drew me closer to Liza though my feelings if they exist at all are the same for both of them. Occasionally Katya would call me and set up a so-called date. These innocent meetings meant practically nothing. We'd have a heart-to-heart talk. Mostly about our work. These conversations took place mostly when something bad had happened to me. She'd find out about it and would do the best she could, in her still childish way, to make me feel better. It was interesting to observe this 17–year old schoolgirl, who hadn't seen anything of life yet, trying to calm me down with a few simple words or give advice, though her advice always came out childish and naive. I never felt oppressed by her presence, I felt free to behave naturally without playing those games that you're always having to play continually with people, I felt as comfortable with her as I did by myself, and loved to observe her and listen to her childish, still undeveloped views of life.

We didn't see each other very often, but in spite of that she hasn't forgotten me over the last four years, I don't see her for a long time and suddenly there she is, we get together and talk. I wasn't especially interested in her, I made no demands, asked for no commitments, and anyway, what kind of promises and commitments can you expect from a 9-th grade schoolgirl?

Liza knew of our acquaintance she knew that we used to see each other now and then, and in fact I always told her afterwards.

She was jealous, on what grounds I don't know, I never promised her anything and never made any commitment to her, of course we were

close, but this is no grounds for getting jealous. She did seem less concerned about the other girls who used to visit me. That's probably
because she didn't know them, but she did know Katya. She figured she
couldn't make any concessions to her. Every time I saw Katya she would
always needle me about it gently, but deep down inside she took it a lot
more seriously.

It was right in character that when they arrested Mama and I was left by
myself she got bolder, and she was a lot more direct in her comments to
me, she even started a rumor that I was going to get married in the near
future, no doubt about it, and to her. She started coming to my room and
acting like she lived there. I didn't particularly like it, but it did make my
life easier, and I said nothing for the time being. But finally the stubborn
rumors about marriage, all the interrogations by people who knew about
our amicable relationship started really getting to me. It took a lot of
nerve, and it was all connected with my misfortune, it was their glee at
what I was going through that I couldn't stand. People can be so mean.
You'd think I could expect sympathy and advice from my dearest friends,
the people I shared my thoughts with and told absolutely everything, but
these people for their own selfish interests, because they could gain some
advantage from all this, these former friends are glad about my misfortune. They are glad and are trying to use it for their own vile interests. This
event has convinced me once again that you can never ever trust anyone,
no matter what. Your best friend, your good pal one day, one fine day
when he can use you for his own selfish interests or he doesn't need you
any more because he can't get anything useful out of you, someone like
that, a friend you trust completely and share your soul with, you turn your
soul inside out for him, a "friend" like that one fine day becomes your
enemy, and a dangerous one too because he knows all your sore spots, he
knows your secrets. No. Schopenhauer was right when he said "If I know
a secret, it is my prisoner, if I tell it to someone, I am its prisoner."

An incident with Nikolai Golankin convinced me of this once. This was
another case that again proves the truth of what Schopenhauer said.

Today Katya called, she'd found out about my predicament, and also
she had to return a book that she borrowed from me last summer. I
invited her to drop by. In a half-hour she was here and we had a nice conversation telling each other all the news that we had accumulated over the
last 3 months.

A couple of hours later Liza came over. She saw Katya sitting there and
left without saying a word. That was all right with me because it gave me

the chance to let her know that she hasn't taken me over completely yet and that I'm still free to have any other friends I want.

She showed up again 5 minutes later all upset and asked me if I would be free soon. I got up from my chair intending to invite her to come in from the hall and take a seat so we could the three of us have a nice innocent conversation. I was curious to see what the two of them who apparently hated each other equally, would do when they met face to face. What I wanted to do might seem cruel, but I really did want to see. Fortunately, or unfortunately, I don't know which, nothing came of it, for when I stood at the doorway and bowed to her, she slapped me in the face before I could invite her in. It was a real sharp slap, the kind that doesn't hurt physically but can really injure your pride if there is someone there watching. This is what hurt, I sensed it clearly, and now I understand the true meaning and emotional significance of a slap in the face. I was at a loss for a second, it happened so unexpectedly. It would take a lot to surprise me, but I couldn't have expected such a thing from someone so meek that my friends called her a "rabbit." And more instinctively than rationally I just said, in a surprisingly calm voice, "A...All right, that's fine," as though someone had suggested something to me and I was agreeing to do it a little later. Naturally, she was all upset, and in the same instant I steered her around toward the door and accompanied her out into the corridor, quietly, without any noise, as though she had gone out on her own will, and I closed and latched the door!

Katya heard something and understood that there was a conversation going on out there, and even thought that something had happened but it was all on the other side of the partition, and it only took a few seconds, and when I regained control of myself and walked back into the room, calmly crooning a tune so as not to betray my true state of mind she was sitting there as red as calico, looking curiously at me. On the outside I was calm though the red patch on my cheek where she had slapped me gave me away, but my artificial gaiety and my carefree manner threw her off the trail even if she guessed about the slap, my appearance told otherwise, except for the cheek. But she could have just thought I was blushing from what had happened.

When I walked out of the room with Katya, to see her off, I was a little concerned, what if she's out there on the street and starts up some hysterical scene, that wouldn't be too pleasant. Everything worked out all right. What surprises me is I recall the slap with pleasure. This is the first time in my life something like that has ever happened to me. I've never even observed anything like it, much less experienced it myself. My pleasure in

326

the recollection surprises me, and even now after what has happened, I've enjoyed going over it again in my mind. Most likely it's simply because I looked at it from her point of view, what a stupid thing it was to do.

And when I came back home a half-hour later, to my surprise, which still surprises me, and instinctively I try not to show it, there's Liza sitting on the couch. She'd just gone up and taken the key from its hiding place opened the room and made herself at home. Speaking calmly and authoritatively, I stated my desire to have nothing to do with her in the future. Reproaches, accusations. She heaps accusations on me and starts listing all the good things she's done for me.

"If that's the way it is," she announces, "I'm going to just keep all those things of yours you left at my apartment."

"That doesn't surprise me, that's about what I'd expect from you."

And I really had anticipated that, if anything happened between us she wouldn't return my things. By the way, about those things. They'd wound up in her apartment after Mama's arrest, I had given her my more valuable things for safekeeping in case they came back to do another search and decided to confiscate my property. And here you have the result. The people I trusted most of all turn out to be such scoundrels inside that after the first little quarrel they announce their intention to keep my things. She even put on my jacket once, this old canvas jacket that she wore over to my place intending to leave it here, she didn't want to leave it even after I reminded her. And on and on, threatening revenge. People can be so mean. Anyone one fine day can turn into a scoundrel. Even my most faithful friend this diary here, could betray me, all it has to do is fall into the hands of some official. And some bureaucratic soul will make the necessary conclusions and set the punishment. Bureaucratic souls can ruin a man for nothing or more humanely give him the chance to destroy himself. Today Kostya told me about one example.

Petr Semyonovich Melnikov, an electrical engineer gazed with a sad and perplexed look in his eyes at the 90 rubles salary he'd been paid for a half month's work. It hadn't quite dawned on him what had happened, but when he took another look at the bills clutched in his trembling fingers, he rushed back to the cashier's window.

"What's the meaning of this? Where's...There's been some kind of mistake."

"Don't worry, Petr Semyonovich, here's the register, take a look. Your salary is 450 rubles a month, right?" The cashier's yellowish, wrinkled face smirked as he spoke and he poked his hook nose, saddled by a pince-nez, back into the yellowish paper of the payroll list. "For this half of the month you're supposed to receive 225 rubles," the cashier continued without lifting his head speaking slowly and deliberately and with exaggerated courtesy, and he pointed the newly sharpened pencil which he held delicately with his slender fingers folded against his palm, at the first column of deductions.

"150 rubles has been paid out by court order to Citizen Drynkina." After these words the brown skin of his dirty bald spot twitched and he slowly raised his head to stare wide-eyed at Peter Semyonovich which made his eyebrows go way up and wrinkles appeared across his forehead. Then, as though he had gotten the answer to some private question of his own he looked down at the register again and pointed his pencil at another column of deductions.

"45 rubles for a loan" and he raised his head again, to make sure that he was listening, but indeed Peter Semyonovich had stopped listening he started walking briskly to the exit, mumbling, "So that's what it is…"

And there was a sort of frightened look on his face, his gray eyes wandered in their sockets. As he ran through the factory door into the shop, an icy wind calmed the confused rush of thoughts in his head. When he entered the shop he looked calm on the outside, only his eyes and his lowered brows betrayed his recent shock. Without stopping or looking at anyone he continued walking with quick unsteady steps toward his and the shop director's office, behind the thin plywood partition. He sank down on the broad chair straightening his collar and tie as though there wasn't enough air for him in this cramped little kennel. The shop director was out and left by himself he let his thoughts wander and they flowed out from within, onto his face. He sat there without moving a muscle for over an hour, pondering deeply. He recalled his 31 years of life. His memories of childhood were the brightest and most pleasant of all, not because his childhood had all the conditions necessary for a good life, no, after all, what good does life have to offer for a peasant lad, but even the smallest childish prank stays in the memory as something special and what a child might see as a misfortune, a grown-up recalls as something good. The death of his father and mother in the typhus epidemic. Life with his older brother, a joyless and difficult life. His work and his studies at the workers' school. His student years at the Energy Institute. It was only thanks to the motivation and the energy that gushed out of him like a spring that he managed to become an engineer.

Right up to his graduation from the institute he never once had to deal with love problems. He didn't know women, he avoided them. Finally he became an engineer, he had more free time, and he started seeing a woman who had latched on to him. What does that mean, he started seeing her? He went to the theater and the movies with her a few times, she started visiting him in his apartment which he shared with a friend. He never liked her, but there wasn't anything better in sight. He had very little money, just an old suit, and one thin overcoat to wear both summer and winter. She latched onto him, he paid some attention to her. Exactly 7 months after he met her she had a baby. Their relationship was over. Court, witnesses. It's the law, citizen Melnikov, the law. And the "judges" the court bureaucrats, intimidated, hypnotized by the big campaign about taking care of the children, they sentence him to pay 1/3 of his salary. Of course all the bureaucrat cares about is saving his own skin, it's better to overdo than not do enough. In this case, and in general with things being the way they are these days everyone just takes your word on something like this. Where, with whom, when some prostitute had a good time doesn't concern them, what's important to them is who she points the finger at and all she has to do is pick someone at random and say he's the "father" and the case is decided in her favor.

Appeals, petitions, nothing worked. They just docked his pay without asking him. Pay? Pay who?! Feed who?! What did he do to deserve this shame and disgrace?! The Party Committee. The secretary just gave a little smile and shrugged, spreading his palms out on both sides. He didn't say a word, but his mocking eyes spoke eloquently: I may be able to do some things, but on this one I'm helpless. It's the law. A court order. He looked calm when he came out into the shop where the workers were, even tried to make jokes, he'd come to some firm decision.

He paid off all his debts. He paid everyone he owed anything, to the last kopeck. There were 10 rubles left.

The night before his day off he didn't sleep. Thinking over his life. In the morning his bunkmate went out of town to see some friends. He wanted to go hunting. But his rifle was broken. Peter Semyonovich waited until his friend had gone. He took down the Berdan rifle and started to repair it. He unscrewed the different parts, and screwed them together again. Beads of sweat poured down his high forehead but he kept at his work. Finally at 3 in the afternoon he finished. He sat back to think everything over one more time. He laid out all his documents on the table, all the copies of his appeals. He looked through them, thought, and his hands dropped helplessly from the table.

"I'm not the only one, there are a lot of people just as bad off as me and you can't break down a stone wall by beating your head against it. No one can get any justice." And two huge tears dropped unintentionally onto the papers spread out on the table. His throat tightened and he couldn't breathe. Spite. He felt like crying, but he hadn't cried before now. What lies ahead?! Work?! For what? For who? And what chance was there of conducting a normal private life with such a disgrace hanging over his head. Who would believe me. Everyone will say that since the court decided that means you're guilty. It's the truth and his lips curled into a sneer. He attached the cartridge, loaded with coarse shot. What's been good about my life? Nothing. I lived hand-to-mouth, even starved, endured cold…Suffered…And what next? More of the same. No. Either live and enjoy life, or die. He cocked the gun.

Yes, yes. Let the damned law know, let the people who made such a stupid law, and made such a big deal about it, know that no matter what the issue, you have to be sensitive with a living human being. This will give the people concerned something to think about. But I die a completely honest man. He propped the barrel up against his chest, pointing at his heart, and pulled the trigger with his foot. Death came instantly.

1/11/1938. There's so much for us to bear and endure, both me and Mama. I was so shaken by today's news that I forgot all my elegant expressions. I can't think straight, only isolated words burst from my chest.

I got to see her today in "Moscow Prison No. 3," as they call it officially. Tears streamed down from her aged, wrinkled eyes, she had trouble getting the words out. "The NKVD troika[7] has sentenced me to eight years." How horrible, 8 years. It's so easy to pronounce, but so hard to live through. And for what?! The official category is "for concealing social origins," but how can you call it concealing when all the official powers knew about her social origin all the way back in 1934. And they say that there is justice in this world. There is no justice in the world anymore, justice died together with the good people, and the devil will leave in peace the scoundrels. The law. I'm not an anarchist by nature and I respect the law, but how can such injustice be done in the name of the law. They consider her a danger to society. You'd think they'd caught a bandit, but even bandits get lighter sentences than that. Well, so what, you can't break down a stone wall with just your head. Can this be the end of justice on earth. No there will be justice. Many people have perished in the name of justice, and as long as society exists, people will be struggling for justice. Justice will come. The truth will come.

NOTES

1 These jokes are in Ukrainian.

2 (Polish) sausage.

3 The first elections to the Supreme Soviet.

4 Nikolai Alekseevich Nekrasov, 1821–1878. Nineteenth-century populist writer. He is best known for his book *Who Can Be Happy and Free in Russia?* depicting the hardship of Russian peasantry.

5 Alla Ivanovna Vorontsova is talking.

6 Ivan Franko, 1856–1916. Classic of Ukrainian literature. Franko's novel *Zakhar Berkut* depicted the life of Transcarpathian Ukrainians of the thirteenth century.

7 A committee of three persons, organized in February 1930 to direct the operations of dekulakization on the district level; on each were the first secretary of the district Party committee, the president of the executive committee of the district Soviet, and the local official of the OGPU (the State Security). With time, these exceptional committees became institutionalized and were transformed into special courts without appeal. During the second half of the 1930s these troikas were renamed "special colleges" (*osoboe soveshchanie*) of the NKVD.

PORTRAIT OF LYUBOV SHAPORINA
SURROUNDED BY PROPS FROM HER PUPPET THEATER

LYUBOV VASILIEVNA
SHAPORINA

Lyubov Vasilievna Shaporina was fifty-eight years old in 1937, living in Leningrad. The time described (1935–39), is truly Shakespearian: it is "out of joint." In a poignant image, she sees herself inside a painting by Bryullov, Pompeii's Last Day.

Shaporina's diary is, above all, a chronicle of the times of terror, in the martyred city of Leningrad, which had been enduring a wave of arrests and mass deportations that began after Kirov's assassination in 1934. It is a diary of resistance, not in the political tradition (the city was the scene of one of the last public demonstrations of the opposition), but in the time-honored Russian intellectual and cultural tradition that has sustained throughout history a highly ambiguous relationship with the political power structure. Lyubov Shaporina was the founder of the Puppet Theater and the wife of the famous composer Yury Shaporin. Her world was deeply rooted in the prerevolutionary intelligentsia, those who returned from emigration and thrived in Soviet reality in spite of everything. Her pen describes how the celebrities succeed one another; we see them at the pinnacle of their glory, or fallen low.

In order to resist and survive, the diarist often abandons the present and retreats into reminiscences of her "tsarist" childhood or of the short period of emigration in France where Shaporina seems to have lived between 1925 and the early 1930s. Implicitly dedicated to Alyona, the little daughter who died in 1932, the diary is a requiem for the one who, to cite the diarist's own words, "chose for herself the better fate"—not to live the civil war of "1937," or the Great War, which Shaporina foresees with great lucidity at the time of the signing of the German-Soviet Non-Aggression Pact.

DIARY OF LYUBOV VASILIEVNA SHAPORINA
Notebook 1: March 1935–22 October 1937

March, 1935

They interrogated me for five-and-a-half hours, and M. Yudina,[1] who knew about it and who had been waiting for me to call, rushed out to Det-skoe, since she was sure that I had already been arrested and that she would have to bring me a parcel. On March 15 Vasya hurried to Moscow, wasted five days there and got nothing done, and then when he came back he started calling the NKVD agent in charge of the case. That same evening (March 22), he was summoned to Liteiny.[2] On March 16 Yu[ry] A[lekseevich] [Shaporin] telegraphed the NKVD—asking that the daughter of the Vladimirov family, which was being sent into exile, be exempted, that she was Vasya's common-law "wife." This was a lie, but it was the only way to save the girl. They called Vasya in to the NKVD and a dignified, high-ranking functionary started out by reproaching him: "You ought to be ashamed, Vas[ily] Yur[evich], you seem to want to wind up like Nikita Tolstoi.[3] You're compromising your fathers, this marriage is a fraud." Instead of standing up for himself, Vasya caved in immediately and agreed with him and promised to be a good boy from then on, thus compromising both his own statements and his father's request. They got him, so to speak, by bluffing. Then they started questioning him about my brothers. Which one of them had been a naval agent in Bulgaria? And the other one had been a volunteer, hadn't he?

Vasya concurred on that too—though neither Vasya nor Sasha had ever been agents for the Whites, and they had never fought the Reds.

Such an admission could have been dangerous, but fortunately the agents were perfectly aware of the truth.

With the NKVD you have to act as though you know what you're talking about, as though you were just passing the time of day, and most important, not let yourself be intimidated.

How was Vasya, at 19, supposed to know all that? How could he not be intimidated? I recall very vividly my conversations with the Chekists[4] in 1931. Just passing the time of day.

That you must not name names, though there are some you can—and those because you know perfectly well how close they are to the NKVD.

Though they are very well placed indeed in the world of the theater. Yes, sir!

334

In general the best thing is to look look dumb and completely self-confident.

People can't see beyond their own backyards.

Slaves, slaves in everything they do. Toadies to the very marrow of their bones—it's so painful. It never even occurs to them, the Takorins, that my grief over Alyona is alive, that she is gone—that I can't forget it. With them, if there ever was anything, it's all gone now. And as for acknowledging my grief, the thought never crossed their minds, not once. not even once.

4/21/35. Vasya is still not back. What is going on in their minds, in their hearts, it's a mystery to me.

Evgeniya Pavlovna told me that Starchakov[5] is outraged at Yu[ry] A[lekseevich Shaporin]'s behavior. Not only for what he did to me; it was simply inexcusable for him to come to Leningrad for practically 10 days and not stop in at Detskoe to see the Tolstois and Starchakovs, who were such good friends of his. And the plot he hatched up with Piotrovsky to redo the libretto in the Puppet Theater behind An. Nik's back. Is it really that awful to say something to someone's face? But no, they have to say nasty things behind their back. It's so deceitful.

When I was going through my papers I came across a draft of my letter in verse written 10/23/16! I had written it to Yury [Shaporin].

Talent and love are incompatible with each other. Ability to work and genius too.... It wasn't that stupid a thing to say, really.

And I'm horrified at how easy it was for Vasya to abandon his work at the first opportunity and rush off to amuse himself.

I ought to just leave well enough alone, to wash my hands of it once and for all.

When I think back over the way my life has been since 1918, I am amazed at myself: how I could have put up with Yury for so long, living under the same roof? And I feel such contempt for myself.

Today was Palm Sunday, the weather was wonderful. I went to the cemetery. Every time I go, I squint and think back on that road in St. Germain. Especially on a clear, sunny, spring day like this one. The Seine Valley. My dearest darling, my darling Alyonchik, what have you done to me! My God, it was so wonderful.

I'll never get over it, and none of it can ever be brought back. I only forget myself and my grief when I'm working with the marionettes, it's like a dream, and I'm transported into a fairy tale.

That's why I'm so eager to do a good job on this. I mustn't forget Alyona's wonderful way of putting it: "getting into a fog."

March, 1935.

The month of March, it was like some terrible, nightmarish avalanche
coming through, destroying families and homes in its path. It is all so
unreal: it came, and it's still here, right before your eyes, but you still can't
believe it. Lida Bryullova (Vladimirova) called on March 13, but I wasn't
home; I call them on the 14th, their apartment mate answers and says that
L. P. is out taking care of things, they're leaving on the 16th. Where? "To
Kazakhstan. All three of them." I went to their apartment at 3:00. The
room in shambles, just bare walls. We had been there a month ago for tea.
It had been so cozy.

Lyuba comes and goes, taking things away, packing. They are perfectly
calm, especially Lida and Natasha. Though they look awful, they're so thin
and pale. Natasha was doing some washing, singing happily as she
worked.

On March 12 they got an order to leave on the 15th, they barely managed
to wrangle themselves a one-day extension. They managed to sell the
piano and the wardrobe, and they farmed out various things to acquaintances. A ticket for Atbasar. Lida told about her last day at Theater of the
Young Spectator (TYuZ), where she had worked as a manager for twelve
years. They gave her an emotional sendoff, or rather, said their last
farewells. "TYuZ does a good job with funerals for its employees, whoever
they might be, from janitors to performers. They're very moving and sincere. And now I've had to live through my own funeral, only without the
singing."

Since there was a precedent with Nikita, Vasya proposed to Natasha,
and the poor girl agreed. She was so desperate to finish her studies, and
what is there for her to do in Atbasar!

The 14th: Vasya sat in their apartment in the shadow of a tall Gothic
chair, all miserable and barely holding back the tears; time was ticking
away, but he just couldn't bring himself to propose. I was in a ridiculous
position, since I had talked with Lida about it before he came. And they
had answered that this was the only way out. The night before, Mitya
Radlov, who was in love with Natasha, had also proposed marriage, but
she had refused, it was his love she was afraid of. It was time for us to go.
Finally we were left alone for a minute and I took advantage of the opportunity and told him to hurry up, and he went and found Natasha some-

where in the hallway and in five minutes everything was decided between them. At Nikita's advice he started calling the NKVD; they told him that they need confirmation from his father, when they get it they will let the girl stay. On 3/16 Yu[ry] A. [Shaporin] came and called the NKVD. He rushed to Moscow and botched the whole thing. Yury has been calling all week long, but they still haven't taken any action.

On the 15th Vasya left. He told me that he had walked the streets, crying. When he was at the train station sending his telegram there was a young man next to him writing a telegram and Vasya read over his shoulder; it said: "To Mr. Bubnov, a copy to Stalin, My father's being sent into exile. With only two months left before graduation, I beg you to allow...." Naive fool.

I went to see them every day, I was there on the 16th, too, just before their departure, I regret I couldn't see them off. We had the last rehearsal of the Chapygin play. I stayed there a long time, waiting for a telegram to come from Moscow and save them. There was absolutely nothing left in their room by that time, we were in Veronika's room. Dear Z. Ya. Matveeva brought them some felt boots. Right at that time the newspaper *Vechernaya Krasnaya Gazeta* (The Red Evening Gazette) carried an item entitled "Bird Day." "On this day all school children, Young Pioneers and Komsomol organizations will build starling houses and set them up in gardens and squares, so that when the birds come they will find shelter all ready and waiting for them!" Touching. Meanwhile tens of thousands of people of all ages, from newborn babies to old women in their eighties are being thrown out in the most literal sense of the word onto the street,[6] and their nests are destroyed. And here we get STARLING HOUSES.

On one of my visits to the NKVD, I was sitting there waiting my turn, and a lady came in carrying a girl about two years old. A lovely, little, blue-eyed girl, she was smiling, but two big teardrops glistened on her cheeks. She had asked for some guy, evidently her investigator. "I can't go tomorrow, I have absolutely no money, how can I take my little girl anywhere without any money?" "Sell your things." "I'm trying, but how can I sell anything in just three days, tied down like this?" He left, and she started kissing the little girl, putting all her love into those kisses, and saying the whole time, "Whose little eyes are these, Mama's, and whose little Tusya is this, you're Mama's too," and kissing her again, obviously drawing strength from her love. I couldn't bear watching her. The investigator led her off somewhere, and I don't know how it all ended. I sat in my investigator's office; an elderly lady was at the other table, all I could see was her cheeks and her glasses. "Citizen, hurry up and choose," said the investigator rudely. She answered irritably, "How can I choose, I don't know anyone anywhere." "Hurry up, citizen." "Well what about Vologda, can I go to Vologda?"

So this old woman goes to Vologda, and then what? Right there in front of me a woman threw herself at the investigator: "We have to leave tomorrow, but they won't let my husband out of prison, what am I supposed to do?"

They sent Tverskoy into exile, the man had worked in the theater since the beginning of 1914, and had been awarded a title of merit, but he had been an officer in the war against Germany, and rumor had it he had been an adjutant to Kerensky,[7] though I doubt it myself. He had worked in the Petrograd Department of Theater and Performance since the beginning of 1918. He had never been on the side of the Whites.

I went to say good-bye to him. His apartment was empty. Just a single chair standing in the middle of the room. "So, L[yubov] V[asilevna], another new stage in life. When you went abroad, I thought you wouldn't be back, now it's my turn. I wonder if I'll be coming back." He was going to Saratov, where he had been invited before. And now he was writing to his relatives. Now that his passport had been taken away, he couldn't work in the theater any more. The mathematician Prof. Kovantko, El. Serg. Kruglikova's nephew, is in the same predicament—he went to Tomsk, where he had been offered a position, but now he doesn't have a work permit. Starling houses, Bird Day.

I kept going to the NKVD, but without success. I arrived and the investigator started yelling, "What on earth can you be thinking, citizen, you think we have time to send telegrams to everyone?" And then he left.

The Vladimirovs' friend went to Moscow, she went to the milit. prosecutor's office and the telegram was sent.

4/28/35. Every spring I find myself thinking in verse. The poetry comes to me in response to some strange associations. I recall one time when I was in Nanteuil, Houdain I woke up saying these words to myself: "and they sway when they walk like a boat on the sea, feet churning the sand, camels passing by me." It was very early, about 5 in the morning, and percherons[8] were plodding past along the street under my window, slowly lifting and dropping their huge feet. It was the workers on their way out to the fields. The words had came to me in time with the sound of the horses' hooves. This morning I woke up repeating the words: "And life presses down on us like a straight road with no goal in sight, like a feast at a stranger's table."⁹ And I kept repeating those lines over and over as I woke up. Finally, when I was completely awake, I understood the meaning of the words; I recalled my sad life in its entirety, the sad days I am living through now.

5/12/35. I'm not afraid of death. What I dread is the thought that the things I cherish and hold dear will be of no use to anyone, that they will be discarded, burned, and given away to strangers.

I opened the trunk, I'm alone now in the apartment, and I've been going through Alyona's little dresses and socks. Each precious rag is a page in the diary chronicling the days of her short life. This white voile dress, with the little flower basket embroidered on the front, I made it out of my blouse in Nanteuil. M. Paul photographed her in it in Mme. Michel's garden. P. [illeg.] came, and we couldn't control our delight in her improved health; she looked so much better, she had grown so much, how pretty she was! Her little pink jacket, little Vasya's embroidered Romanian shirt.

One summer, maybe it was in 1932, we had dinner at the Tolstois', just the adults. We're out on the balcony, drinking tea. Suddenly Alyona appears with just a skirt on, and a blouse with a pink sash. I kissed her. "I got all dressed up," she says, "and here I am." My golden angel, the only light of my life. My God, why was my joy and happiness taken from me?

My little girl was so full of life, even right up to the last day of her illness. And that day, the anxiety and pain in her eyes during those last minutes of her life. No, I can't.

[…]

7/6/35. […] Life goes on, it tangles around you like a ball of yarn and you have no time to think or share in the grief of others, all you can do is try to ease your own private sorrows.

I organized that puppet theater for the third time. But it's so hard, and I don't know whether I will succeed in doing what I want to do. There's not much money and I have to do something popular to make a profit, so I have to put aside my Russian epic. The Russian epic is an export product. Oh, if only we understood, those of us whose job it is, that we need to work for export. I give practically no time to Vasya, he's started getting very hostile in his reactions to my comments. All I have to do is say something to him about his études and he loses his temper and starts yelling at me.

Today he started some still lifes—wildflowers on a background of blue and green. I didn't agree with his choice of color. He flew off the handle and started yelling, but he fixed the étude, and then later on he says, "Nevertheless, your presence and comments are very useful to me."

No matter what Vasya paints, his father praises everything—and the result is just trash.

I know how useful my suggestions are to him! Vasya is very talented, but he's still very inexperienced, though like Chupyatov he does have a high opinion of himself.

[...]

Yury corresponds with Vasya, but never once does he say to give his regards to me. I don't exist.

A touching telegram came (from Vasya's father) for his birthday on June 1, also one from his guests. It's so easy to simply brush aside all sorts of concerns about his health and development, his education, not to give a thought to anything beyond purely financial support, to correspond, send telegrams—and that's how it's been, since Vasya was 8 years old.

There's been a rift in the Tolstois' family happiness and I doubt any of them has any idea of how serious it is. It is so hard to take, I feel personally upset and hurt. I had gotten so used to see their family as an oasis amid the general sadness everywhere, that this rift has really depressed me. Here's what happened: a few days before Easter Nat[alia] Vas[ilevna][10] went to stay with her sister in Moscow. I thought there was something very strange about that and I mentioned it to the Starchakovs.

He didn't say anything to me, but later his wife admitted that N.V. had found some love letters and they'd gotten into an ugly fight.

Golovina told me that it's all Shatrova's fault. She'd been staying with them last summer, and right when Nat[alia] Vas[ilevna] was about to leave for the Caucasus, Ev. M. [Shatrova] sprained her foot (she probably faked it) and stayed behind and A[leksei Nikolaevich Tolstoi] didn't leave her side. Grandma had told me about it at the time. Nat[alia] Vas[ilevna] took it very hard. She came back from Moscow a month later terribly thin. Apparently a lot of tears had been shed. Though she looked cheerful enough. They're setting up an apartment in Leningrad for the children to use—she enrolled in the institute and will also work there. All this quarrelling has been an awful ordeal. I doubt Nat[alia] Vas[ilevna] has any idea of how sorry I am for her.

[...]

10/25/35. There's something wrong with my heart. It aches, I feel it all the time and it keeps me from working; there's a constant ringing in my left ear and I can't concentrate. Can it be that my time has come? Once someone told my fortune and said I'd die at 55. So it's time. I'm not sorry to leave this life, it's nothing but deception and lies anyway, and I'm not afraid of death. What hurts is to die unknown, without having completed any of the things I started. I failed to influence Yury [Shaporin], to get him to work, and I couldn't get Vasya on his feet either; I did nothing for myself and my work at the puppet theater is unfinished; I didn't achieve what I had planned.

And it hurts that everyone who loves me is far away, and the people here can't be bothered. Where's Sasha, what's the matter with him, my dear, beloved Sashok.

He's nowhere to be found, there's no getting to him.

But what really terrifies me is Vasya's future. He has no will at all, he's just like his father.

I'm afraid that Chupyatov's influence on him is getting more and more harmful.

They got him so thoroughly trained to conventionality in color that if you left him up to his own devices, in direct contact with nature, he wouldn't be able to make head or tail of it. He spent 2 months outside Luga and came back with 12 études, and none of them betray the slightest trace of nature. Nature was just an excuse to do the étude.

Everything was done in yellow—and that was in July and August, when there wasn't a single yellow leaf, everything was uninteresting and conventional to the utmost degree. Now he's taken up sketching. Yesterday he spent the day at home sketching, and by evening he had come up with a picture of a melon (from a drawing); that's called exploring form. I understand, but still, why destroy every unmediated perception, every direct, individual vision of nature? For Vasya, who is so susceptible, not to influence, exactly, it's more like hypnosis. It's terrible.

And I don't know what to do about it—there aren't any schools. He needs to le retremper au réalisme. But I can't talk with him, the jargon he uses with me is simply indescribable. That's what I get for all my concern, for all my grief.

And so you'll leave without having seen anything through to the end, without saying your farewells.

What an awful, degrading life.

11/8. Alyona and Vasya were raised the same way. Vasya saw more of my work life, but what a difference in their characters. Everything in Vasya is alien to me, incomprehensible, but I understood Alyona so well, everything in her was so dear to me, so close to my heart.

When Vasya is sick or hurt, when he cries, I feel disgusted and resentful.

The other day I felt ill, we called the doctor and I stayed at Kanonerskaya overnight—he got all worried: "That really upsets me. Don't you understand what an effect it will have on my state of mind if you keel over?"

Alyona had an insatiable thirst for knowledge. When she read *The Prince and the Pauper* she made me review the whole history of England and tell her about it; fortunately I chanced on Kipling's fascinating history of England. She never let her Petit Larousse" out of her sight. When she read something from Russian history, she always wanted to know the whole historical context.

Vasya doesn't want to know anything and he doesn't read at all. It's beyond my power to make him read. At 20 a man needs to be motivated from within. Yesterday Vasya showed me a sketch for a still life that he had started on his own. A mortar in the shape of an elephant with a green wine glass on a little table.

All the objects had been arranged in a fan shape (drawing). That's how Chupyatov draws, he claims that since the earth is round the axes of objects can't be parallel. That's just ridiculous, of course. On something with a total area of 50 centimeters! I tried to convince Vasya that if he wants to get anywhere in art, then now, while he's still studying, he needs to be governed strictly by what he sees in nature, in real life. I showed him a still life of his, a watercolor of the same objects that he had done in 1933, and it had been done with such loving care. I showed him drawings by Vrubel" and Van Gogh (his favorite artists)—how they turned to nature without becoming naturalists. The only true talent comes from presenting nature as perceived through your own brain and vision. But mannered and forced conventionality leads nowhere. Vasya lost his temper and yelled at me. But he discarded that drawing and started over. He needs me to be there. But alas, I can't give him that any more. Our material situation these days is such that we would not be able to live without my salary. Though prices have gone down a little, the cost of living is still quite high.

The Tolstoi household has collapsed like a house of cards. My God, how easily people destroy what is dearest to them, just for the sake of pure

physiology. Twenty years of life as Nat[alia] Vas[ilevna]'s soul mate, talented, grown children, a home, a whole way of life, everything down the
drain, gone to wrack and ruin, and for what? Love, passion? Nothing of
the sort. Is this genuine feeling? At 53, the old man felt a need for passion.
He told Starchakov: "I want to love, to love someone, anyone." He became
infatuated with Timoshka, Max Peshkov's[13] widow. She wouldn't yield.
Nat[alia] Vas[ilevna] found some verses A[leksei Nikolaevich] had written
to T[imoshka] and that's where the whole thing started. That's when she
went to Moscow, she went to see Timosha and offered A[leksei Nikolae-
vich] to her, saying that all she cared about was his happiness. Timosha
refused. Nat[alia] Vas[ilevna] decided to leave Detskoe, and that was where
she made her mistake. She said to me: "We'll have a wonderful apartment,
I will study, then I'll go to work [illeg.] I will think only of myself. Caring
for others is just a waste of energy. You have to be selfish. I'll get myself
some fine linen, the kind courtesans wear—I want to really dress in style,
I want to live only for myself."

That was the truth, but at the same time she still hoped that A[leksei]
N[ikolaevich Tolstoi] wouldn't be able to manage without her. She
installed Lyudmila Tarsheva in Detskoe and left. At the end of August
Lyudmila dropped by, she and I were always on very friendly terms, well
not friendly, but I was always well disposed to her. Her breakup with her
husband, the death of her stepson surrounded her with a kind of dramatic aura, she was in need, she worked, she was ill. I always felt somehow
sorry for her. And Nat[alia] Vas[ilevna] got along very well with her. Lyudmila told me about Nat[alia] Vas[ilevna]'s idea of hiring her to work as
A[leksei] N[ikolaevich Tolstoi]'s secretary and take her place as a hostess,
etc., and A[leksei] N[ikolaevich] also asked her to take over the household
accounts from the cook.

They offered her a salary of 300 rubles, plus room and board. L[yud-
mila] came to ask my advice on what to do. She was frightened by the Tolstois' casual, frivolous way of doing things. She needed to turn in her resignation at the library of the Writers' Union, where she worked.
[...]

Her leave from the Writers' Union ran out and they asked me about her,
to no avail. I knew nothing. Once Elena Iv. was giving Nat[alia] Vas[ilevna]
an English lesson, and A[leksei] N[ikolaevich] came and there was a terrible scene. Nikita was present at the time, and he tried to stop his mother.
Then Al[eksei] N[ikolaevich] left for Czechoslovakia, and weeping onto

Fadeev's[14] lapels he confessed his lover's ecstasy; he drank himself into a stupor and upon his return to Moscow he got a divorce and married Lyudmila. This is one time you can say "The tale is long in the telling, but short in the doing." Our new 53-year-old Ruslan found his Lyudmila.[15] I come back home from town one day, and Starchakov calls me: "Want to hear the latest news? Al[eksei] N[ikolaevich] is getting married, guess who's the lucky bride?" "Timosha?" "Worse, Lyudmila!" Yes, come on over, I'll tell you everything." N. V. had called him in and showed him a letter. But even before the letter Al[eksei] N[ikolaevich] had met with Nik[ita] Radlov[16] and asked him to tell Tusya that he'd gotten married and would soon be sending the divorce papers!

Starchakov was shocked: "Tell me, you know a thing or two about life, how can you explain such an act? What is the old man doing to me? I mean, I'm the one who brought him into the leadership, and in a day or two he would have been one of the main leaders, in Gorky's place, People's Commissars would be knocking on his door. They haven't been to see him yet, he'd invited Bubnov, but he didn't come. He would have come tomorrow. The patterns of life are very important. He had everything: a country house where everyone visited them, a full cup, a beautiful wife, a house fit for entertaining Wells or Bernard Shaw.

"These patterns must not be broken. Lev Nik[olaevich Tolstoi] fled Yasnaya Polyana in a quest for the truth.[17] Al[eksei] N[ikolaevich] hooks himself a floozy and heads off to Kislovodsk just like someone in a Leikin story.[18] It's one thing to fall head over heels for an Ulanova, and run away to Nice. Now there's a real statement! But Lyudmila, who's slept with Nikita and many others too, she gets a trip to Kislovodsk. Politically a bad move. People won't take kindly to it and he'll soon feel the effect.... Gorky won't be inviting him to bring Lyudmila over."

But evidently it's not turning out that way. We've been hearing rumors that he put on a huge banquet in Moscow in Lyudmila's honor. Masses of people. And Timosha responded with a banquet of her own. And that idiot Avgusta Peltenburg writes her husband that she's sincerely glad at Alyosha's[19] new happiness. Utterly without talent, but she's got this fantasy that Alyosha is going to make her a director.

[...]

11/21/35. I remember once I was in Saint Germain. Alyonushka was sitting on my lap. She put her arms around me, drew my head down to her shoulder and rocked me, singing, "Lullaby and good night, sleep, my beautiful baby." What happiness, my only happiness in life. My darling, beloved girl. I'm working for three, I'm busy all the time, I put on two shows in a single month. "Moidodyr"[20] and [what was written in the journal? – Ed.] *Literaturnoe obozrenie* (Literary Review) on the 17th, that took up all my attention and I didn't come home for three days on end. On the 18th I'm on the train, and there are two little girls in the car with me. They weren't like Alyona at all, but all my worries and preoccupations vanished in an instant, leaving only the raw, unrelenting pain.

Gross[21] has died. I feel so sorry for him. His life burned itself out so early, that repulsive old hag just walked all over him. In 1931–32 we were included in a writers' cooperative, and I used to run into him all loaded down with shopping bags, loaves of bread. It shocked me: "What are you doing V. N., dragging all those things around, it's bad for you." Each time he answered the same way, "Something came up, purely by chance, Palladochka couldn't do it today, the maid couldn't either...." and that "by chance" recurred every single day. Rolls, kerosene, potatoes, he used to drag it out to Detskoe all by himself.

Knowing he was ill, I went to see him on Easter, before the morning service. He was in bed. He wanted to quit his job and go on disability, since he wasn't up to the daily commute anymore. At home he could earn some money working on articles.

Pallada butted into our conversation: "but you do understand that we just can't live on 150 rubles." She made him keep on working right up until the pen fell from his hands.

[...]

12/17/35. [...] Alyona was a continual joy. Eyes flashing, hair flying every which way, all flushed with happiness. How could fate be so cruel, so unmerciful. And here I am alone, all alone, like a rowboat on the ocean. Alyonysh, why did you leave me. I just don't have the strength to bear it. Soon it will be three years already. Three years. And here I am alive. And my heart is empty and it hurts, it hurts so much.

[...]

Starchakov: Soviet literature should be left fallow and its writers should be destroyed like glanderous horses. Forbid them to write for at least 10 years.

Our literature is all overgrown with weeds, Lavrenyov,[22] Fedin[23] and others grazed their way through. The thistles grow taller than a man's head. Fallow.

Read Blok's[24] diaries and you'll see what an immature human being he was. He put on a demonic pose in public, but then he'd come home and write: I got some sausage for 10 k.

In the old days adults had a concept of honor, duty, responsibility. Now even Blok's generation has substituted conscience for honor, convenience for duty.

3/15/36. Yesterday Meyerhold gave a speech with the sensational title "Meyer[hold] against Meyerholdism."[25] The first part was an amendment to the *Pravda* articles. Quite a few brilliant passages. One statement that provoked thunderous applause was: "Soviet subject matter is often a smoke screen to conceal mediocrity." We need Soviet classics, as Com. Stalin said.

There was also laughter over the principle of the Pope's infallibility. Obviously people with shattered nerves have a need to believe in the infallibility of their Leader. People don't have the strength to figure things out for themselves. Their nerves were overstrained by the war, and it's nice to have someone giving you some thought, sinner that you are. And such a faith can allow no room for doubt.

They did their best to disgrace Shostakovich.[26] Yesterday was his rehabilitation. The famous "it's just chaos" has been replaced by "bold experimentation." There's a parallel with the agronomist Tsytsin, to whom Stalin said: "Be bolder in your experiments, we will support you."

A great master, Sh[ostakovich] — a thinker. Here are some of the things M. said that hit the mark:

"The path to simplicity is not an easy one. Each artist goes at his own pace — and they must not lose their own distinctive way of walking in the quest for simplicity.

"Experimentation should never be confused with pathology.

"What we need now must be discarded later.

"The angry, cruel headlines of the *Pravda* articles trumpet the high standards of the Party, standards for improving taste.

"All these articles attack critics who are still sitting out in the bushes, I don't know what they are doing in there....

"There cannot be a separation of form from content.

"The highest form of poetry is tragedy, if there were no suffering in life, there would only be such anguished longing that we all would go hang ourselves before our time.

"My path, realism, is anchored in the conventional theater. In the discussions of the theater, Okhlopkov[27] repented of his sins. He stripped naked, took a birch rod and flogged himself on the behind. Where can he go after that, how can he live the rest of his life?

"I may confess my errors, but I will never renounce my principles. And if something so unlikely were to take place, if I were to renounce the path I have set for myself, I would still have in my wallet the words of my teacher, the great master K. S. Stanislavsky:[28] 'Avant tout il faut faire de la musique.'"

[…]

9/16. A. O. Starchakov complained to me of old age. You ought to be ashamed, I tell him, just like Turgenev,[29] who starts in at the age of 30, complaining in all his letters about the frailties of old age. "Turgenev had a somewhat easier life than we do, whole bunches of his friends weren't being shot to death before his eyes," was his answer. "Or haven't you noticed?"

9/21. In Peterhof. It's so beautiful here. The palace looks even better without the fountains than with all those rushing streams of water pouring down everywhere. In fact it really is better. A fairy tale frozen in time, la belle au bois dormant [the sleeping beauty]. Here things don't seem to belong, it's a vision of the past, like the church in Kolomenskoe. And the sea! It may be just a puddle, but still it's the sea, and of course the spirit of Peter lives on in these parts. What will become of Vasya. Once in Sevastopol, long ago, Dasha Kv. himself read Yury's palm and said: "You have a lot of talent; it might develop, but then again it might not." It's the same with Vasya. I have the sense that you have to keep him reined in and ignore all his vipères et crapauds, as Alyona and I used to call his constant cursing and grumbling. When I came back from my trip, I found him completely satisfied with himself after failing his exams. He and Natasha will work together, have people over, etc. When I was gone they ordered a 250-ruble dinner to celebrate his failure, and invited Nikita and his wife, Ina and Natasha Kn. and her sister. They had a grand old time, went out in the middle of the night for a ride in Nikita's auto, and stayed up until 6 in the morning. I can just imagine how much fun it must have been, just them by themselves, with no grown-ups and with money to spend.

I set him to work painting: a large still life with a pumpkin and a black elephant. He did a beautiful job, the work of a mature artist, though I did have to constantly correct him and point out his errors. But what he had done for his exam was indescribable. Pathetic, utterly without redeeming value, you would never guess that it was Vasya's work. I don't get it. He was scared that he'd be accused of formalism. I asked Brodsky to look at his work. I helped him drag the canvases over there, and then I sat in Solovy-ovsky Square waiting for the verdict. Anyway, it scares me. What if I die? Who will give him direction, who will be willing to ignore his cursing and his complete indifference?

When will he get up and stand on his own two feet, morally and intel-lectually? He's even more of a dishrag than Yury [Shaporin]. Though Yury did have a certain amount of discipline from the his studies: the high school, university and conservatory.

9/28/36. New Peterhof. It's my last full day here and I'm so sorry to have to go; it's like jumping into cold water—all the worries and cares, all the rushing around after the peace and quiet here, the total solitude, the leisurely walks along the seashore. It reminds me of those long days I spent in Larino with Mama, the two of us alone together, the autumn days spent reading, drawing, going for walks, dreaming. Every day I go to the fountains very early in the morning. I'm the only one out there that early. La belle au bois dormant. The gold of the statues recalls their ancient models and in my mind I see the princess's servants; the cook snoring away, sprawled out like Bacchus in his rose-colored niche, next to him a young page kissing a Fräulein, a girl getting ready for a swim, I could even picture Perseus as a kitchen boy chopping up a chicken. The luxuriant, enchanting greenery of the trees completes the scenery.

A fountain splashes somewhere in the distance, the leaves rustle beneath my feet, the leaves pour down like golden rain.

It is so wonderful to dismiss all thoughts and ideas and give myself over to the intoxicating beauty around me. When I think back on my life, I real-ize it was only in nature that I found my few moments of true happiness. And it was nature that always healed my wounds. I will never forget Brit-tany—the ocean, the abandoned chapel, Kermanya[?]—the church where I would sit for days on end, sketching. The clock would chime out, you could hear sighs coming from inside the wall; the huge, rusty key belonged to me alone. Then Rome in 1912. The sky over the city, the forum, the villa Madame, Santa Maria-Dominica—the marvellous mosaic. I glanced out the window just now. The moon is out. It was on a night like this in early Sep-tember that Nadya Verkhovskaya and I rode over to our beloved Pogoreloe on horseback. In the moonlight the yellow leaves of the lime trees in the park looked like fine silk lace. The guard there tried to stop us, but then he realized that we were the young ladies from Larino. We were both 17, but I remember it as though it were yesterday. We started back; a thick white fog had risen above the Dnepr valley. We let the horses run; it seemed as though we were rushing along some fantastic white sea, with the moon shining somewhere, far away; Larino park appeared through the veil of fog like a dark island in the distance. We could barely see each other. Oh, it was so wonderful. [...] Nadya came to stay with us in the summers for several years in a row, when we were 15, 16, 17, 18 years old, until her marriage. We had no other friends, no suitors, and I have never experienced such a pure, sincere enjoyment of life with anyone as I did with her. And we were always talking philosophy. We had such a thirst for knowledge. Nadya spent hours reading the correspondence of Byron, she had already had mastered English by then. And how beautifully she played, Chopin, Mozart; how she sang. I heard Chopin's 7th Waltz played once this winter, and I nearly burst into tears. [illeg.] The way Nadya played it made an impression that will stay with me my whole life. There are people who are somehow passionate, full of life, people like Nadya, like Anna Mikh. Zherebtsova. And I feel a kind of gratitude to them in my heart. But such people are few and far between. One time Nadya and I stayed up all night philosophizing. Our favorite pastime was watching the sunrise. We climbed out the window, went up in the belfry, wandered around while Larino slept.

[...]

While I was here I read the much-praised memoirs of Custine.[30] What nonsense. A superficial, narcissistic Frenchman, not very intelligent, but pretending to be, spends a little too much time listening to the courtier Prince Kozlovsky's liberal platitudes and his pretentious abuse of his motherland, and he's off to the races, putting down everything he sees without the slightest knowledge or understanding. The sphinxes aren't real, they're just copies, and the statue of Peter is no good (he didn't know that it was done by Falconet), and Petersburg can go to hell, why was it ever founded anyway, and the birches are scrawny and weak, "Now just imagine some of our chestnut trees here," and the white nights[31] are unpleasant, and the political system just makes it all worse. If he doesn't even understand the role of Peter and Petersburg, what else can you expect from him? But he was praised to the skies here, seeing as how he tears down everything Russian, and whether any of it is justified or not, it doesn't matter, just so he can tear things down; the only thing he liked was Nicholas I.

The Bolsheviks will get even more credit for inculcating patriotism in the Russian people. It's about time. And so comes the end of my peaceful existence. I have to get down to work.

[...]

It's awful, no one is writing anything, people are just enjoying life. People used to write when they got old, they'd start preaching. Now preaching's out of fashion and writers are just enjoying themselves, that's all. Old man Shishkov sits out on his balcony with no shirt on, throwing together hackwork film scripts. Al[eksei] Nik[olaevich] has given up writing altogether—it's been over 2 years since the second part of his *Peter*[32] came out. It's wrong. Once you start preaching nonresistance and abstinence, it's time to serve us up a work of art.

Well what do you think, A. O. [Starchakov], I say, evidently your wish is coming true and Russian literature has gone fallow.

Al[eksei] Nik[olaevich] redid all his books for a children's publisher. They did it on board a ship, he, Lyudmila and the secretary, they hastily redid the engineer, Garin, with a secret agent knocking on the wall the whole time.

Will it be long now? He was under a tight deadline to deliver the manuscript to Moscow. Just imagine Lev Nikolaevich Tolstoi taking *War and Peace* and handing it to his wife: "All right, Sonya, cut it down for me."

[...]

1/30/37. Yesterday at the Belkins' Petrov-Vodkin[33] says to me in a whisper: "I made a point of not going to the meeting where we were supposed to come out in favor of a death sentence for the Trotskyites.[34] Well, late at night I get a phone call. 'Come on, K[uzma] S., make yourself heard.' 'All right,' I say, 'of course. What are people pushing for?' 'For sentencing them all, the whole government administration and the Party leadership too.'" I was getting my hair done yesterday at the hairdresser's. The radio started broadcasting Vyshinsky's speech for the prosecution. My Figaro spread his hands in the air, leaned over toward me and whispered, "I can't make any sense of it—the entire leadership!"

They used to teach them in the schools about a traitor named Sukhomlinov who lived during the reign of Nicholas II—they use him as an example to illustrate the breakdown of the monarchy. Now there are hundreds of Sukhomlinovs, beside whom he is a little boy, just a puppy.

Each People's Commissariat has in its leadership a traitor and a spy.

The press is in the hands of traitors and spies. They are all party members who have made it through all the purges. Ladybugs like Nasanin were sent into exile, people like Stolpakov were shot, murdered; meanwhile, for the last 15 years, there's been a continual process of decay, treachery and betrayal going on, and all of it in full sight of the Chekists. And what about the things that are not being said at the trial? Think how much more terrible they must be. And worst of all is the very openness of the defendants. Even Lafontaine's lambs tried to justify themselves before the wolf, but our wolves and foxes—people like Radek, Shestov, Zinoviev, old hands at this business—lay their heads down on the block like lambs, say "mea culpa" and tell everything; they might as well be at confession.

Feuchtwanger wondered why everyone is so forthcoming—how naive can you get! What's hypnosis for, anyway?[35]

Here I recall that scrap of paper that Logvinovich showed me in Vyazma in 1917. Everything in it was clear, the only thing I didn't understand was how they could socialize the land, divide it up, and then turn around and reestablish private property so to transfer it into new hands, Zionist ones this time. And suddenly it turns out that Mr. Trotsky already had everything figured out in advance, it was all ready to go, the machinery was already in place. Amazing! But as always with the Jews, it hadn't been planned carefully enough and was bound to fall through. They construct their grand schemes, but forget who's in charge. Mordechai had intended to slaughter all the Persians in three days, he sacrificed his niece in the attempt, but still nothing came of it in the end. And that's the way it always is. They took it into their heads to eat the Russians for dinner, figuring they're just pigs anyway. Just you wait, my dearies, the Russian people will show what it's made of yet. The Russian people, creators of such songs, such music. Where such phenomena as the Palekh[36] artists can exist.

[...]

8/27/37. I look at her in her coffin, I look and look and more and more clearly I see her alive, warm, my own dear Alyona. Of course she chose for herself the better fate. She did not have to experience grief, disillusionment, misfortune. She always felt my infinite love for her. I protected her from all distress, except for Vasya. And what would life have had to offer her? Tender, sensitive, how could she have survived? What was in store for her? My God, how I would like to believe in the immortality of the spirit, to believe that I will see her again, somewhere out there. Alyona was everything to me. What a terrible feeling — knowing that happiness is no longer possible for me. Ever. I can be content, can experience occasional pleasure, but I will never, never be completely happy. I keep getting the feeling that I'm inside the Bryullov painting: *Pompeii's Last Day*.[37] Columns falling all around me, one after the other, there's no end to them; women run past me, fleeing with terror in their eyes.

Utter exhaustion.

The puppet theater is my salvation.

And Palekh. How lucky I was to meet those people, to witness that way of life, magical and unreal, like something in a fairy tale. I want to go there again. To take another look at that art that simple peasants brought down to us through the ages. That's something that Alyona would have appreciated. She would have been 16 1/2 now, a real beauty. And I am so utterly, completely alone. Alone.

10/10/37. The nausea rises to my throat when I hear how calmly people can say it: He was shot, someone else was shot, shot, shot. The word is always in the air, it resonates through the air. People pronounce the words completely calmly, as though they were saying, "He went to the theater." I think that the real meaning of the word doesn't reach our consciousness — all we hear is the sound. We don't have a mental image of those people actually dying under the bullets.

You hear the names: Kadetsky, Vitelko, a singer who'd just recently performed in competition. Nat.[alia] Sats — the director of the Moscow Theater of the Young Spectator.[38] And many others.

What I just can't understand is the cruelty of exiling the wives of people who are arrested. A physicist is exiled to to Vladimir, to a concentration camp, and his wife, Marusya Shostakovich, to Alma-Ata. Malakhovsky hasn't been sent into exile yet. People tell rumors about him that are so horrible that you have to cover your ears — but his wife is in Alma-Ata already; from there they are sent out to the "regions," i.e., into the bare desert. Evgeniya Pavl[ovna]'s life is like that of a baby mouse with a cat sitting right above her, waiting for just the right moment to finish her off.

> There's intoxication in battle,
> In standing next to the abyss...
> Happy is he, who 'mid the fight
> Was able to find and know all this.[39]

I am one of those happy ones, but that state, the gloom of the abyss, is exhausting, terminally exhausting. Like walking through a cemetery pitted with freshly dug graves. Who will fall in next, will it be you? And it's already so commonplace, you're not even scared anymore.

The puppets are my refuge. A fairy tale. A living fairy tale.

God forgive the living and give rest to the dead.

10/22/37

On the morning of the 22nd I woke up at about three and couldn't get back asleep until after five. There were no trams, it was completely quiet outside, except for an occasional car passing by. Suddenly I heard a burst of gunfire. And then another, ten minutes later. The shooting continued in bursts every ten, fifteen or twenty minutes until just after five. Then the trams started running, the street resumed its usual morning noise.

I opened the window and listened, trying to figure out where the shots were coming from. What could it mean? These were not the usual noises from the factory.

It was definitely gunfire. But where? The Peter and Paul Fortress is nearby. That was the only place where they could be shooting. Were people being executed?

After all, between 3 to 5 in the morning it couldn't be a drill. Who were they shooting? And why?

This is what they call an election campaign.[40] And our consciousness is so deadened that sensations just slide across its hard, glossy surface, leaving no impression. To spend all night hearing living people, undoubtedly innocent people, being shot to death and not lose your mind. And afterwards, just to fall asleep, to go on sleeping as though nothing had happened. How terrible.

In Yaroslav Province, right where we used to live, everyone who had had anything to do with the church was arrested, all the priests, church elders, pastors, etc., etc. In Detskoe Irina came home from school and said, "They told us there are mass arrests going on right now. We need to rid ourselves of undesirable elements before the election!"

* * *

Notebook 2: 2 November 1937– 24 October 1939

11/2/37. How can you find the strength to live, if you let yourself think about what's going on all all around you? Pas de forces, as Lid. Iv. wrote about Vasya.

On the 20th I come back from work, and Natasha and Vasya open the

353

door and rush into my arms. Evgeniya Pavl[ovna] has been arrested, and Ira is here with us. Irina looks terrible. Her face is so swollen from tears that you can't even see her eyes, and there are big blue circles around them. She was at school, and they called her out of class. Ev[geniya] P[avlovna] only had time to say good-bye to her and tell her that she had been sentenced to 8 years of hard labor; the crime: being the wife of an enemy of the people (without a trial or investigation) – the investigation was done without her knowledge. Mara was sobbing uncontrollably. E[vgeniya] P[avlovna] had also told them: "Go to Lyub[ov] Vas[ilevna]." Irina rushed to the Lensovet,[ʰ] got a pass to see the prosecutor, Shpigel, burst into (her words) his office and told him everything: "How are we going to live without our mama?" Shpigel answered: "What about the Spanish children? How do they get by? The charge and the arrest are jus-tified, why don't you go to your grandmother's in Moscow, m/b your grandmother will take your sisters too; we'll wait five days, if you can't arrange things for them, we will come up with something."

But they came up with something immediately, without waiting, and at 6 p.m. some people from the NKVD came to Detskoe, picked up the little ones and took them to the NKVD children's placement center at 66 Kirov Street. When they told me that on the phone, I was just shocked. We had put on shows there before and the teachers had told us about the chil-dren. They are delinquents, neglected children. There are children with a long record of incarcerations. There are murderers in there. What could we do? Mara with her bad heart. The poor girls, what they've had to go through: in the morning their mother is taken away, and then they're picked up and taken to a place that is no better than prison.

Irina was shocked, though I tried to ressure her that it's not so bad in there.

I don't understand anything, it all seems like a dream to me. In the morning they were still a family, and now there's nothing, everything has shattered.

How can a girl bear all that – but Irina is no ordinary child. During those days she showed the strength of someone far beyond her years. That same evening N. K. Komarovskaya called me. She had been in Detskoe after the children were taken away, and it had made a terrible impression on her. It was as though someone had died in the apartment. She advised me to take all their little mementoes and hide them as soon as possible.

After three days of tireless efforts, Irina managed to get them to leave her all the rest of the property. Shpigel would not see her again, but sent her to an NKVD investigator. That investigator sent a different one out, he drove Ira out to Detskoe, unsealed the apartment and turned all the property over to her, to the utter amazement of the maids and all the neighbors. On the 2nd I went with her to 66 Kirov Street. The house manager was only too glad to turn the children over to me immediately. "How are you related to them?" he asked me. "I'm not, I'm just a neighbor." "But do the children know you, m/b they won't want to go live with you?"

The next day the children were settled in with me.

Starchakov was arrested in 1936, at the beginning of November. They kept changing their mind about parcels, first they allowed them, then they didn't. He and Evg[eniya] P[avlovna] had been having serious problems with their marriage.

I could never understand how such a brilliant, intelligent and clever man could be so crude, so nasty and coarse at home.

All it took was a few drinks and he'd lose all sense of propriety and go into a jealous rage. The jealousy was completely unfounded. Just before his arrest they had been at Popov's. Gavrila walked them home.[42] The moment they walked in, A. O. [Starchakov] grabbed a volume of Shakespeare and threw it as hard as he could at Evg[eniya] P[avlovna], hitting her in the face. The bruise covered half her face. And he didn't have to be drunk to behave that way. For the next five days or so he kept on beating her and yelling at her, using the foulest language. A month after his arrest, a new set of ordeals began for Evg[eniya] P[avlovna]; She started receiving official notifications, demands for payment of alimony from some old affair of his, for reimbursement of advances paid for work that wasn't finished, and they inventoried her property. All this just embittered her against him even more. Recently she said to me, "You know, sometimes I think how cruel I am for abandoning A. O. [Starchakov] to the mercy of fate. But I feel nothing for him but a terrible resentment."

On August 1 they made her sign a promise not to leave town and she was fired from her job. She found work, they had their own typewriter.

They arrested her and did a search, they turned up the children's letters, Mara's letters from the hospital.

Why do you keep all this junk, when they learned that she had an invalid child at home, they returned her passport. Evg[eniya] P[avlovna] wrote a letter to Stalin, to no avail. And on October 29 they took her and sent her into exile immediately.

In January Irina's grandmother received a letter from Evg[eniya] P[avlovna], who was in the Tomsk concentration camp—it was a cheerful letter, to the extent that was possible, and included a request for money and a parcel. I bought everything she asked for, got together some old things of mine, and sent 80 rubles in Mara's name (they're allowed 20 r. a month), and that's the last we've heard — no answer, not a word.

5/27/37. The children told me about it: When they took Mama away we cried and cried, then we went out for a walk. Suddenly Vasya runs up and says that some people have come for us, a man and a lady. I (Mara) would-n't go, I just refused. I cried and ran into the other room. But the lady kept trying to persuade me, she said that they have a really nice school, and the children are nice too. They took us in a van, they took Mama away in a van too, the same kind of black Maria[43] that they took Veta Isaevna Dolukhanova-Dmitrieva away in. There were a couple of very nice girls there, Iskra and Svetlana Ryazantseva. Their mama had been arrested too but they'd let her keep their little brother who was 6 months old with her. We slept together in the same bed and cried at night.

It was only today that I finally got up the nerve to ask them about their first days without their mother.

Most likely they themselves, at 7 1/2 and 9 1/2, are not fully aware of the shock that they endured during those days. And how many others are there like them.

[...]

11/20. Ira went to see the prosecutor, Shpigel, she'd gotten a pass the day before. Her whole throat was inflamed and she had a fever. Shpigel kicked her out. "What are you doing hanging around here for? You don't watch out, we'll sign you into the orphanage."

11/21. There was a concert at the Philharmonic, and the orchestra played Shostakovich's 5th Symphony. The whole audience leapt to their feet and erupted into wild applause — a demonstration of their outrage at all the hounding poor Mitya [Shostakovich] has been through.

Everyone kept saying the same thing: "That was his answer, and it was a good one." D. D. [Shostakovich] came out white as a sheet, biting his lips. I think he was close to tears. Shebalin,[44] Aleksandrov[45] and Gauk[46] came from Moscow, the only one missing was Shaporin. Can anyone be more disorganized than poor Shaporin. And Vasya, alas, is the same way. I ran into Popov: "You know, I've turned into a coward, I'm a coward, I'm afraid of everything, I even burned your letters." At the end of one of my letters, by the way, I wrote "Ev[genyia Pavlovna] is no longer in Detskoe, and Galya and Mara are staying with me!" It's absolutely terrifying! Natalya Vasilievna tells me: "Good for you, for taking the children. If it weren't for my apartment (she lives in a special apartment building for government officials) I would have taken one of them." With N. I. Komarovskaya, it's if it weren't for my heart, etc.

11/22/37. The joys of everyday life. I wake up in the morning and automatically think: thank God I wasn't arrested last night, they don't arrest people during the day, but what will happen tonight, no one knows. It's like Lafontaine's lamb—every single person has enough against him to justify arrest and exile to parts unknown. I'm lucky, I am completely calm; I simply don't care. But the majority of people are living in absolute terror.

12/12. Quelle blague! I went into the booth, where supposedly I was going to read the ballot and choose my candidate for the Supreme Soviet—"choose" means you have a choice. There was just one name, already marked. I burst out laughing uncontrollably, right there in the booth, just like a child. It took me a long time to compose myself. I leave the booth, and here comes Yury, stony-faced. I lifted my collar and ducked down into it so that only my eyes were visible; it was just hilarious.

Outside I ran into Petrov-Vodkin and Dmitriev. V. V. was going on and on about some irrelevant topic and laughing wildly. Shame on them for putting grown people in such a ridiculous, stupid position. Who do we think we're fooling? We were all in stitches. Those booths with their red calico fig leaves.

All the different offices and businesses conducted study meetings for the elections. Someone raised the question: Do you have the right, after getting your ballot, to go home and think over your choice? The answer: Of course you have the right to go home, sit down and spend a couple of hours discussing all the ramifications of the questions, and then afterwards you can come back and put your ballot in the box.

[…]

2/6/38. Yesterday morning they arrested Veta Dmitrieva.[47] They came at 7 in the morning, locked them in their room and conducted a search. They made a call to the NKVD: "Nothing here." Veta said goodbye to Tanechka (age 4), she said, "When I come back, you'll be all grown up."

My girls (Mara and Galya) were outside in the courtyard, they saw them putting Veta in the Black Maria. They came back in tears. Anisimova (the ballerina) has been arrested. I just feel sick—from the accumulated weight of all the crimes in our country.

They seize their victims and the victims disappear, a great many of them without leaving a trace. Starchakov, Milyaev, Zhenya's father, an old man of 77, Nechai-Tsarskoselsky, an old servant, a Pole without a single relative still living in Poland. Who needs all this?

Evg[eniya] Pavl[ovna] is in Tomsk. The Tomsk prison is a special camp. What threat could she pose to anyone, this unhappy woman who raised her children in such a way that they didn't utter a word of complaint when their father and mother were taken from them. They haven't gotten over their fear yet. Mara said once, while reading *Buratino,*[48] "How is it Papa Carlo doesn't know how to find the country where all the happy people live? I thought everyone knew it's the USSR!"

3/11/38. [...] The great, great Dostoevsky! We now see, not in a dream, but right before our eyes, that great herd of devils that entered into the swine, we see them as they have never been seen before in all human history.

All through history people have always struggled for power, have plotted revolutions.

Robespierre destroyed all the dissidents, but NEVER in the world have people and parties struggling among themselves worked to destroy their own homeland. Over the past twenty years all those members of our government have inflicted famine, pestilence, plague on their people, and sold the country off wholesale and retail.

And this whole Yagoda[49] inquisition. What we read in the papers is bad enough. But what about what they don't put in the papers. And what about that feeling I got, those premonitions I told Vasya? Now all he can do is shrug. Now Yezhov,[50] there's a smooth operator for you.

I hope that my other predictions will come true too and the emperor will be left standing there with no clothes on.

People in Moscow are in such a panic, it's made me sick, literally. As the old women say, it's gotten to my heart. Irina's aunt, a lawyer, said that every night two or three defense lawyers from her office are arrested. Morloki was arrested on December 21, and on January 15 Leva, our simple-minded theater fan and prop man, was exiled to Chita. At that rate they might as well arrest the table or sofa. Straight into exile without an investigation. When Lida came on February 1 with a parcel for him, she was told "Chita 15." And you won't find any articles now in the legal code that say what it is you have to avoid in our befouled fatherland. When you read about all those mysterious murders—Gorky, Max,[51] the dying Menzh[insky?],[52] etc.—you can't understand who needed the lives of all these people and what they needed them for. The only one they needed, the only really dangerous one was Stalin, plus Voroshilov,[53] Kaganovich[54].... They could have killed them a hundred times over, poisoned them, done anything they wanted to them, but no one has even made an attempt.

What can you make of all this? Where is the truth and where are the lies, and whose mill is all this water flowing into? I think Hitler's, m/b Chamberlain's, too, since England always has to tremper dans toutes les vilenies, whereever there's a profit to be made.

But it is unbearable to live in the middle of it all. It's like walking around a slaughterhouse, with the air saturated with the smell of blood and carrion.

What a splendid label for the country: indissoluble union.

And through it all, the eyes of the Mother of God look down on me from the beautiful mosaic in the St. Sophia cathedral in Kiev: I'd like to visit Kiev again in the spring. When you look at that beauty you forget the devils, if only for a minute.

3/21. I call and ask for for E. M. Tager,[55] and they tell me that she has a high fever, I knew she had angina. After a whole day of ordeals with the government theater administration and three trips to Smolny to see Gribkov, hungry and exhausted, I go up the stairs to Tager's apartment. Masha opens the door, and I go in; the door to E. M's room is open, which is unusual. "Isn't your Mama home?" "Where is she, in the hospital?" "No, Mama's not in the hospital, she was taken away by the NKVD." They came on 3/19 at 11 p.m. and stayed until 6 in the morning, searching the apartment; they went through everything. Her old aunt says: "I think they were looking for weapons, they checked all the coats the rack, all the dresses." They didn't find anything. They took E. M.'s letters to her father, written over 20 years ago. The letters are very interesting, she had wanted to write a novel, the story of a family. [In the margin: Zabolotsky has been arrested.][56]

They took the old bible, and when her aunt asked them to leave it, they answered, "What for? Religion is the opiate of the people."

So now there are just the three of them left: two ancient old ladies, her deaf mother, 73, and her aunt, age 77, and 13-year-old Masha. What will become of them? I dreamed up a scheme: to get permission from the repertoire committee to stage *Vaska* and get an advance for it from the accounting office. And it would go to her old aunt by proxy. But of course I failed. When I arrived at the repertoire committee, with an innocent look on my face, Pavlovskaya already knew everything. I'd gotten so used to the idea of staging *Vaska*, I'd gotten so immersed in Novgorod history and suddenly everything is off. I feel as though I've been knocked out of the saddle.

[...]

4/18. I went to the church at Znamenye (in Detskoe) twice — for the morning and the evening services. How I love that marvellous service: what wonderful words.

It used to be that no matter what a man became in life, he would always have with him these words he heard and learned in his childhood: Grant me to see my own sins and not oppress my brother, for blessed art thou for all eternity. If Vasya had learned the words of this prayer, had really let them sink in, would he be so malicious to everyone, would he be able to gloat so over other people's misfortunes! They've closed practically all the churches.

All that's left in Leningrad is the Greek Church, the Reformed Andreevsky Cathedral, the Nikolsky Cathedral and the church of Prince Vladimir. The majority of priests have been sent into exile. Obviously religion really scares them — or is it some kind of Masonic anti-Christian hatred? I want to order a bas relief of Alyona from Konovalova,[57] have it done on a white marble cross. I'll move Alyona and Mama to the Nikolskoye cemetery at the Alexander Nevsky monastery, where Grandpa is, I'll have a monument set up to Alyona and in my will I'll ask to be buried at Alyonushka's feet and to have engraved at the base of the cross the words "I see your magnificent mansion, O my Savior..."

What a fine prayer, a howl of the human spirit [...]

Konovalova told me, quoting F. G. Berenshtamm, that Koni's last words were a request to have a wooden cross placed over his grave. A few years ago F. G. commissioned Konovalova to carve that cross in the Russian style, the House of Scholars wanted to erect the cross on the anniversary of Koni's death. K. P. was unable to complete the work herself, since someone got scarlet fever in the apartment where she worked. It was completed by an old craftsman, a woodcarver.

But after all that they didn't put up the cross anyway.

It really bothers Vasya sometimes that I don't go out to the movies or the theater. Impressions just slide over them, the young people of today, without making any impact on their conscious mind. They've grown up in these terrible conditions: the words "arrested," "shot" don't make the slightest impression on them.

But what about us, who grew up among civilized human beings, not wild animals—but then why slander the poor animals.

Here's what I can't understand: Yagoda was shot, and he, and his action, and his stooges were disgraced. You'd think, if you reason it out, that all those absolutely innocent people, like the hundreds of thousands of members of the nobility who were exiled in 1935 for the death of Kirov (who was murdered by Yagoda) ought to have been allowed to return.

But what happens is the reverse: Now after they've served their five years or three years of time, they all are resentenced to new terms of the same length and sent even farther away. Does this make any sense?

5/1. They've started prepping us again for elections in the RSFSR. What is the point of using up such enormous amounts of money and paper—all the paper that we have in the country—for this? Who are we trying to fool?

The Party activist was telling us about the First of May, and I recalled a very funny story. I don't remember what year it was, we were living in Vilno and the Skosyrevs were planning a home theater production. M. Skosyreva, née countess Mavros, was countess Smionich in her first marriage. She was very ambitious and worked hard to advance her husband's career, and the show and the party were being put on for the governor, Von Val.

They performed *The Mouse—La Souris—*, I don't recall the author. As the youngest actress, I naturally played the older, virtuous Clotilda, my governess was played by Nata Kuzmina-Korvina. The performance took place at the beginning of May, but alas, Von Val didn't come, he had taken ill. It turned out, as gossip would have it, that on April 18 (which was May 1, new style), a lot of workers had been arrested for striking, they had all been locked up in the courtyard of the police headquarters. Val went over there and beat the workers "in the snout" with his own hands. The next day his whole face swelled up and looked terrible! No one could stand him and everyone gloated about it.

P.S. Lelya, who has an excellent memory, tells this story differently: on May 1 some workers tied a red flag to a goat's horns and had turned her loose down German Street. The police set up a sweep to catch her and also all the workers, who were then arrested, it was claimed, for political activities on the First of May. They were all driven into the courtyard of the district police office for a flogging; Mikhailov, a doctor, was summoned to examine the workers before the flogging and give his authorization. Val was present and supposedly participated. Afterwards Mikhailov himself was lured off somewhere and flogged.

I'm so frustrated with Vasya, and with Natasha too. That boy is so unbelievably callous. They live like rentiers, only working when they absolutely have to, they have no serious interests and make no effort to improve themselves. He'll never amount to anything, because he doesn't work at it. He used to listen to me before, he'd argue with me, but he'd follow my advice. Now all I have to do is say a word to him, and Natasha is up in arms, she sets him against me, and I have to listen to all kinds of incredible things from him, the kind of things that Alyona and I used to call des vipères et des crapauds.

My only comfort is the children, though they're not my own, they're so good, so affectionate and refined.

Vasya is no artist, he's been at it over four years now, and he still can't even do a quick sketch.

[...]

6/3/38. Among Alyona's papers there's a remarkable letter she wrote to herself on 9/12/29, she was 8 years old.

On the top: "Look for some money this morning. Alyona Sh." Then the letter: "I need 10 kopecks to buy a money box, that Mama has hidden in her secret drawer and also ask her to give me 5 or 10 kopecks to put in the money box. When I buy it, I'll ask Alyonushka for 4 kopecks for candy. Alyona!"

And on the day I die it will all be burned or thrown into the garbage. The photographs of Alyona, too, all those precious things, and her hair, that still has a smell of life to it, even now.

People used to keep things and pass them down from generation to generation, archives were preserved and history was created. Now the present day denies the day that has passed, yesterday's leaders are shot today, everything that remains from the day before is destroyed in the minds of the young.

Papa inculcated in me a deep respect for all these scraps of paper, these notes left from yesterday. He saved Nadya's photograph and a lock of her hair and kept them in his wallet his whole life through. Vasya's letters, too, and I still have them. If Vasya Yak. were here, but what is the younger Vasya to me? Alyona was the one I loved.

I got to thinking once, about why I hardly ever go out or have people over, why I live the way I do, as though I'm just riding a train somewhere.

And I suddenly realized, very clearly, that from the moment of Alyona's death I lost all my taste for life. I'm not living, I'm just filling up the days that remain to me. I've lost my interest in other people. Only when someone suffers some misfortune, then I feel the need to help, I feel closer to the person.

What was most important in my life left with Alyona. The joyful tie I had with life was severed forever. Maybe if Vasya were kind and tender, if I felt that he loved me, it would be different. But he's so cold.

Alyona, Alyona my darling, all my joy, light of my life.

And any, life everywhere, all around me, is nothing but misery too.

8/30/ 38. [...] All day today I've been thinking about what would seem to be a trivial speech I heard at our theater collective. The speaker was a local man, still young, blond with regular features — a high forehead and light-colored, steely gray eyes that sparkled with an inner light. The speech was part of the commemoration of the 20th anniversary of the Komsomol.

When he started his speech it became clear that he had absolutely no command of language. He spoke so badly and coarsely that the members of our collective started snickering, and it was only with the greatest difficulty that they held back their laughter. Phrases like: "a Congress of youthful youths, youthful youths the embittering struggle of youth against capitalism. The youth will present a gift for the 20th anniversary of its motherland to its mother. N. Ostrovsky conducted a civil war in his bed,"[58] and ainsi de suite. I was afraid there would be a scandalous scene, but he finished up quickly and said, "and now I'll tell about myself: in 1921, at the age of 17, I went as a volunteer to the Afghan border. The English were arming the bandits. I learned how to operate a Lewis machine-gun — the bandits were going around in bands of 1000, 2000 men."
[...]

1/24/[1939]. Yesterday I went to *Sleeping Beauty*, starring Ulanova. A charming fairy tale. Perrault and everything done in the style of the 17th century — marvellous music — it was all like a dream, a deep sleep that completely rested and relaxed my whole being. And you forget the whole all-Russian ugliness of life. And what is it leading to, this moment that we are living through? Why do we find ourselves so quickly returning to the years 20 and 21? Everything has disappeared, why? The city is freezing for lack of coal and firewood. Our theater is using the building of the Tram Workers' Park. You'd think that, even if they won't give you any books, you'd at least be able to get some coal. There's not any, not a speck, they don't even give it out through official channels, and there won't be any before summer. There's no firewood. No electrical supplies, no stockings, no cloth, no paper. If you want to buy some manufactured product you have to spend all day in line, and stay overnight too. The Vecherkovskys left Detskoe to get in a line. They went back to check in at 2 p.m., at 4, 6, and 12 midnight, and 6 a.m., after which they just stayed in line, and they came back ecstatic — they had gotten ten meters of sateen each!!

Salaries are being cut everywhere, from workers to writers and composers.

The factories are standing idle for lack of fuel. The newspapers are in ecstasy about our happy and prosperous life and the advances being made in worker discipline.

Was ist das? For shame. Improductivité. After all, we had all the necessary conditions for the experiment. And what came of it? Did the magic trick fail, or what? Or is it the reverse, maybe it was too much of a success. So far all the predictions have come true.

It's so sad. Vergogna [shame].

Koltsov[59] has been arrested. And he was praised to the skies. And what about must be going on in Al[eksei Nik[olaevich]'s mind? Lyudmila said that he had been very close to K[oltsov] recently.

When they visited us in November they liked the girls very much and L[yudmila] promised to send them 1000 rubles as a gift for the holidays. I have yet to see it. And you'd think he might recall all the favors A. O. [Starchakov] did for him, about those articles that St. wrote for him.

2/19/39. I went to Kuzma Sergeevich [Petrov-Vodkin]'s funeral. If he could have been present at his own funeral, sensitive and impressionable as he was, he would have been shocked. The funeral procession arrived at Volkovo at around 7 o'clock. It was dusk, and it got dark quickly, so it soon became impossible to see people's faces.

They set the coffin down by the grave and opened it. People were crowded around in the darkness on the low hills around the grave and on the exposed earth.

Complete silence, except for the grave diggers talking among themselves. They lit a lamp, mounted on a pole, and someone held it over the

364

grave. Its light slid across the face of Manitser, who was supporting Mariya Fyodorovna. She climbed up onto the pile of earth, leaned over the coffin and stroked K. S.'s forehead several times, tenderly and lovingly. I sensed that she was crying. Papusya is all alone now, all alone. She kissed him. Lenochka kissed him. The silence of the grave. And muffled sobs.

Again the grave diggers' voices, arguing about how to lower the coffin. The band struck up a funeral march. They grabbed the ropes, pulled the boards out from under the coffin and started to lower it, but suddenly it slipped and tumbled into the grave upright, and the lid flew open. My heart froze. I ducked behind the crowd and turned my back. I thought he was going to fall out of the coffin. Then the loud cursing of the grave diggers again, as the band launched into a spirited performance of the "Internationale." The sound of the clods of earth hitting against the coffin. The apologies and excuses of the drunken grave digger.

And that was all.

All of Kuzma's compositions were full of a striking harmony of lines, and the people in his pictures seem to be listening to some kind of inner resonance. He understood Europe and had a profound feeling for it, but the Russian icon painter in him overpowered the Western influences. His red horse[60] came not from Matisse, but from Palekh and beyond, from the 16-th century.

He was very intelligent, but with a certain unexpectedly rustic, lyrical twist. A peasant mysticism and belief in sorcery. He told me several times about a certain meeting of Valflo during the first years of the revolution. The main speech was about religion. There were Marxists, priests and rabbis present. Back then it was still possible to speak freely about such things. He gave a speech too, he was in top form and apparently spoke very passionately about faith. During the break he was surrounded by people and he felt the strength draining out of him, he turned and saw that there were rabbis all around him, touching his jacket. "I could actually feel the currents and fluids draining out of me." He was a believer in Cabala, in its existence. And at times it seemed to me that he might have been a Mason. He loved experiments. Once, one of the last times I visited them on Kirov street, we got to talking about religion. He reviled Christianity as a degenerative, antiartistic religion that had been set forth in the world by Jews, to destroy the world.

K. S. [Petrov-Vodkin] loved paradoxes. What we need now is a new religion, a religion that leads to God, but is strong and joyous, too.

He couldn't stand Jews, and he suspected everyone of Jewish origin, even Matveev.

I. I. Rybakov died — in prison. Mandelshtam died in exile.[61] People everywhere are ill or dying. I have the impression that the whole country is so completely exhausted that it can't fight off disease, it's a fatal condition. It's better to die than to live in continual terror, in abject poverty, starving. When I go out into the streets looking for something I need, all I can do is repeat the words over and over to myself: Je n'en peux plus. Lines, lines for everything. Their faces are blank, they go into the stores and come out with nothing, they fight with each other in the lines.
[...]

2/20/39. Hitler took Czechoslovakia, he sent an ultimatum to Romania, you get the impression that he's just cutting processed cheese, and no one says a word.

The only one who could have protested was Russia.

2/28/39. I dreamed of Alyona today: there's a phone call, I pick up the receiver and ask "Who's there?" A voice comes from far, far away: "It's me, Alyona." "Where are you, where are you calling from?" "From prison," comes her voice, it sounds so very weak, she's speaking in a bass voice, as she used to, for fun. Then a lot of questions of some kind, but I don't hear anything more. I go around to different prisons looking for her, I go into some building and ask a woman in a fur hat who's going in too, "Do you know whether there are any children in this prison?" She doesn't answer. I go down a marble staircase with a red carpet runner. A large room, all kinds of people and suddenly a bunch of children come in, girls, they're walking two-by-two and Alyonushka is with them. She's taller than the others, she's wearing something light-colored, I rush over to her and she gives a shy smile, without looking at me. I kiss her, kiss her hands, she's pale, there are dark rings around her eyes and they're sunk back in their sockets, but she's in good spirits. I ask the girls if Alyonushka is sad, how she's doing. The kids all say, interrupting each other, "No, it's fun here, Alyonushka isn't sad." I kiss her, again and again, and then everything disappears. Oh, Lord, that voice coming to me from such a distance, It's me, Alyona.

I'm all alone, so completely alone. To love someone as much as I loved Alyona, and then to lose her. You could smash your own skull, but here you are alive.

Alyonushka, my darling, help your poor Mama.

Such anguish, and it's everywhere, all around me.

3/20/39. I forgot to write in January about Vikt. Litvinov's return. It turns out he made it to Moscow safe and sound, took a walk around the city and then headed toward the main telegraph office to send a telegram to Novorossiisk, to the theater there. As he was crossing the street he stopped for a car that was passing by. Someone in the car saw him and he was arrested on the spot. It was a government car. They held him in prison in Moscow and Leningrad for 7 months.

He didn't do any work there, but did a lot of reading, he read Anna Karenina four times. He gained some weight and looks pretty good.

During that time the things that he had left at the Moscow Train Station were lost and he was informed that they had been sold, including his summer coat. His books were stolen from the dormitory, and some of them were burned. He was released with no restrictions, and they accepted him back in the conservatory, renewed his stipend and gave him a room in the dormitory again. Did they really need 7 months just to check him out? "Man," the word does not resound so clear and proud,[62] it's a quantité négligeable.

3/23. These days when I read the papers, filled with ecstatic cheers and hosannas for the XVIII Party Congress, I recall the song of the baby rabbits from *The Enchanted Colony* by German Matveev, which I put on last spring in the hand puppet theater. The rabbits sing:

Hip hip hooray, hip hip, hooray!
We have a burrow, a place to play.
What a lovely home, my gosh!
Long may it stand, our dear galosh!

Then the music changes to a melody taken from Lyadov's *Gray Wolf*.[63] The baby rabbits eat a piece of the galosh and decide that they are the strongest animals in the forest. These hurrahs sound ridiculous, especially now, with little Hitler striding across Europe like Gulliver over the Lilliputians.

And he doesn't even do battle, he just strides along, driven along by the sheer force of his iron will, before which everyone gives way. Like the waves of the Red Sea before Moses. What next? We also gave way. If you follow it to its logical conclusion, the moment of the most monstrous treachery in the world is at hand.

The stage is set.

And how terrible that it has befallen our poor generation to bear witness to it all. Helpless witness.

3/29. Hitler has taken (?) is taking (?) Danzig. They used to say "Great is the

God of the Russian land." But first of all, we are not the Russian land, we are the anonymous Union of SSR, and secondly why should God save us? How easily people betray their faith, how easily they forget all their moral principles. Informing has become the key to everything. Informing has destroyed the countryside. [...] I always feel this burning shame for Russia, and it hurts. The frogs who chose themselves a king.

I foresee the suffering of people like Vasya L. and the others, who feel the pain of a love for their country that was too strong.

But maybe our great God will take pity on us for the sake of those righteous martyrs, for the sake of those millions who are in captivity.

What insane, desperate cowardice not to speak a word of truth at that congress. How much more convincing it would have been just to come out and say: yes, comrades, the whole country is naked, there are no manufactured goods, there's not enough coal, there's not enough food — and then explain why it is so.

But a deliberate lie doesn't fool anyone.

Le mensonge ne peut pas durer. [The lie cannot last].

4/9/39. Easter Sunday!

I think this is the first time in my life I haven't gone to the morning service. There's nowhere to go. There are just 3 churches left in the city, all are completely packed, there's no Easter procession, and you won't even hear the words "Christ is risen" spoken on the streets. And I'm simply exhausted. For two-and-a-half months now I've been without a maid, and I have to fix breakfast and lunch for the children, keep the stove going, bring kerosene, be at the theater by 11 and work at home on the staging. I took the children in the heat of the moment and I don't regret it for a minute, but I didn't reckon on the limits of my own strength or my means. And there's not enough of either.

I did go to church the other day — it is so good to get away from all the cares and demands of everyday life. I cried bitterly and felt the tears washing away the troubles and cares that had built up over my soul like a thick crust, cleansing me. I thought about poor Evgeniya Pavlovna and all those hundreds of thousands of mothers sent into exile, who know nothing about the fates of their own children. Can you imagine a more barbaric torture? [...]

I saw Khodasevich at the premiere of "The Snow Queen." She had been at Al[eksei] N[ikolaevich] Tolstoi]'s house for dinner with Koltsov, a Spanish general and his wife and some other Spaniards. A few days afterwards Koltsov was arrested. They claimed to have discovered that he had been one of the most important international spies for a great many years.

Tolstoi was utterly shocked—they had become very close friends. When they visited us in November, Lyudmila said, "We've been trying to avoid any contact with high-ranking officials. Either they turn out to be saboteurs, or they are just not interesting." They were like a man sitting behind the wheel of a car going full speed, 500 kilometers an hour, he hangs onto the wheel with both hands, shaking, he doesn't even look to the sides anymore, all he can think about is how to keep himself alive. "We had been very close to Mikh[ail] Efimovich [Koltsov]—You never know what's going to happen next."

[...]

4/28/39. I picture the body of Russia covered with purulent abscesses— everywhere confusion, negligence, sabotage, squabbling, denunciations. Everyone is busy doing all those ugly deeds, major and minor, that you have to do to your neighbors; with all this firewood and kindling, you can't see the woods, you can't see anything bright and holy, you can't see Russia itself.

I look at the faces of people standing in lines a verst long, dull-faced, embittered, haggard, not a single thought on their minds.

They, these people, can stand in line for hours, days, all day and through the night, there's no limit to their patience. It's not patience, but stupidity and the maniacal thought: they're giving out herring. Is your herring really so important to you that you can't live without it?

No, it's autosuggestion, and it kills off everything else. To inform, commit a vile act, to destroy your neighbor, to curry favor—this too is a maniacal thought. Yesterday I went to see *Don Juan*, what music, what a finale. A rest from all your cares. And how distant and small do they seem, all those pathetic people from the State Theater Administration who are trying to do me harm. It's like looking down at the earth from the Eiffel Tower. Sviridov was just here, he played his music for Ruslan. We got to talking. He's a fine and talented young man, and unlike all the others, he doesn't speak in hackneyed formulas.

He told about stopping in a church yesterday, he hadn't been for five years and his visit left him with a feeling of joy, though he's not a religious man. The candles, the smell of incense, the faces of the icons, the silence, the recollections of childhood. He's very talented, though he's still under the strong influence of Shostakovich.

4/29. I'm walking down Furshtadskaya Street and Liteiny Boulevard and I run into a woman carrying a basin full of sauerkraut. I run over to her, as everyone does these days: "Excuse me citizen, where did you get the sauerkraut?" This winter there's no sauerkraut anywhere, at the market it costs 7 r. a kilo (pineapple is 20 r. a kilo) and there are huge lines for it.

"Where I got it, they won't give it to you," came the proud reply. I laughed. It's all clear. Right down the street is the special food distribution center of the NKVD. Our masters are a streptococcal infection eating away at the organism of the country. They can even pick up a serving of sauerkraut for their services.

7/8. Moscow. A. Ya. Brunshtein, whom I visited yesterday, said something really remarkable—in reference to A. Tolstoi—"it's important to know what serves as the meridian of a man's life. You can live at the Paris meridian, the Greenwich meridian, or you can draw your meridian from your own, beloved center of gravity, your navel. All he ever talked about was himself about his plays, about how they're being suppressed, etc."

Clever and perhaps true.

She talked about the ordeals she'd been going through as a writer. They made a film based on her story "Pink and Blue." 4 days were left in the shooting, it had already cost 1 mln. 200 thous. Everyone said it was wonderful, then a new director, Dupletsky, is appointed, and he just throws away everything, without even looking at it. That's all the past, what we need is contemporary material. Writing something about school life, they latch onto the Spanish war, then some disaster takes place in Spain, and that's the last you hear about any film scripts.

I asked her for a contemporary Soviet play. She doesn't even want to hear about it. She'll write up something out of Hoffman for Obraztsov and me. Take it or leave it. I want, she says, to rest and heal my wounds. Only death will heal mine. Vasya. With all his ability, not a single step forward, he won't work and he's completely under Natasha's thumb: "boy-husband, servant-husband, one of his wife's pages." Worse, just a kitchen boy.

[...]

It's better not to even talk about your own wounds, that just makes them hurt worse. I hear rumors that Meyerhold was arrested on June 20, there were vague accusations of espionage.[64] Can it really be, that with a man so important, a man who is so well known throughout the world, there's no other way of taking action than to arrest him? For shame. Then again, shame is not smoke, it won't burn your eyes out.

Just before his arrest there had been a conference of directors in Moscow. Meyerhold was greeted with ovations, he was a resounding success, but there was nothing about it in the newspapers. And M[eyerhold] had gotten terribly drunk at a reception in the Kremlin and said loudly to Yury Al. [Shaporin?], "They won't let me go to Leningrad, either Molotov is too fond of me, or it's too close to Butyrki Prison."
[...]

8/24/39. [...] The nonaggression pact with Hitler, with Germany.[65] What nonaggression? What, are the Germans afraid we're going to attack them? Last fall V. S. told me with tears in her eyes something she'd heard from the editor of a military journal: The German newspapers are writing that Russia doesn't have an army any more, that they have to hurry up and carry out their mission.

Why should they hurry? The Russian people are lying flat on their backs, "with a heavy stone on top of them, lest they should try to rise from their coffin." There they lie, some drunk, some sober, but all of them so worn out from suffering that they've lost all semblance of a human countenance.

A nonaggression pact—at what a price!

"To save the revolution" Lenin paid indemnities, it's easy to give away other people's property, he gave away whole seas, what can we give away this time? Ribbentrop wouldn't go for any old trifle. [...] Most likely all our raw materials, oil, coal, etc. will go to Germany. We are the manure that fertilized the noble soil of Germany. Hitler's hands are untied. Poland will come next after Czechoslovakia. The threat to France—to France, our second Motherland. After the Brest Treaty,[66] I was riding the tram somewhere, I saw the Summer Garden flash by the windows, it etched itself onto my memory. There's a young French woman of about 35 sitting next to me, all in black, and she says: "c'est lâche, c'est lâche, que va devenir la France," and the tears just pour down my face, I know, that nous sommes des lâches, look where Lenin's betrayal has led us.

Seventeen million exiled, how many shot, a starving, enslaved peasantry, and now a second Moscow-Brest Treaty with Germany. And how many have emigrated? *Pravda*'s lead article about the signing of the treaty ends with the words: "From this day on the friendship between the peoples of the USSR and Germany, which had been stifled by the efforts of the enemies of Germany and the USSR, shall have the conditions necessary to develop and flourish." What? What is this? Who are these enemies? What about the still-warm corpses of the people murdered in Spain and Czechoslovakia? — The bastards. I just can't.... I am overcome with such unbelievable spite, hatred, scorn — but what can I do? They're all gone now, all the journalists who had a voice and a head on their shoulders. Radek, Bukharin, Starchakov. A. O. [Starchakov] was such an intelligent man, is he still alive? He was charged with an attempt on Voroshilov's life (and he confessed).

We know that people under Yezhov, and not only under Yezhov either, confessed to crimes that had never taken place.

Shchedrin[67] couldn't have dreamed up anything like this. I can just imagine Ribbentrop's scorn as he sits on the train, looking through the window, into the window of the car, the russische Schweine-Schurken, who betrayed their country, who ALLOWED SEVENTEEN MILLION PEOPLE TO BE IMPRISONED IN THE CAMPS. AND HE'S ABSOLUTELY RIGHT.

I saw the floor of the room where he [Starchakov] was interrogated; it was all covered with blood. They beat him on the cheeks. A[nna] Akhmatova told me that her son had said that there were such brutal beatings last June, in '38, that people's ribs and collarbones were broken. Starchakov was so proud and intelligent — what must he have had to endure, to admit to such a crime! It's frightening to imagine. Was he shot, or is he still alive?

Akhmatova's son[68] is accused of a plot to assassinate Zhdanov.

Poor Boris Stolpakov was shot back in '34 for the "attempt" on Kirov's life, when Yagoda plotted Kirov's murder and set a false trail to mislead the public about it. Bobrishchev-Pushkin, Zinoviev (or was it Zakhariev, I don't remember) and two other young men from the old nobility were shot along with Stolpakov.

It's very clear now why they had to get rid of Kirov, who was an honorable and forthright man. The German Gestapo needed only pawns. That photograph in *Pravda* tells it all: on the right the stupid, bloated snouts of Stalin and Molotov, and on the left von Ribbentrop standing like Napoleon with his arms folded across his chest and a smug grin on his face. Yes, we've lived to see the day. The triumph of communism! A lesson for all times and all peoples — this is where a government of "workers and peasants" will lead you!

I believe that the only honorable course of action for any true communist and revolutionary would be to send a bullet through his brain.

And what about you, INTELLIGENTSIA?

Gavrila Popov told Vasya: well, thank God, at least there won't be any war for five years, I can write my opera. [...]

His *Spain* was removed from production several days before Rib[ben-trop]'s arrival.

Yesterday Konovalova was at Gorin-Goryainov's, he got a lot for a dacha. He's happy that there won't be any war and he "has to hurry up and get started on the construction." Maybe they'll bring back private property. Our paradoxical Aunt Lelya was onto something when she said, referring to the destruction of peasant farms and gardens, "It's all being done for Adolf." Also, "We are beating out game for the fascists."

What should we be doing? The only thing I know for sure is that in the theater we ought to be concentrating only on things Russian. Russian history, the Russian epic, song. To teach it in the schools. To familiarize children with this, the only wealth that is left to them.

But where are the authors? Where is poor El[ena] Mikh[ailovna] Tager, who understood that so well, and who loved it so? What a cruel joke of nature, that she and I, pureblooded Russian members of the intelligentsia, had such an agonizing love for that priceless Russian treasure. E. Danko — her father a peasant, her mother a noblewoman — she despises the Russian epic, in her opinion the bogatyrs[69] were negative types who supported the feudal system! How ridiculous! She raves about Hoffman. Baryshnikova, our best puppeteer, is the daughter of a very wealthy merchant, most likely a former peasant; she despises everything Russian, and there are so many others like them. Slavery, the German yoke, wouldn't it be better if it were just out in the open? Let there be a German Schutzmann standing on every street corner lashing out right and left with a rubber truncheon at Russian louts, drunkards and toadies. Maybe then they'll understand where the crabs spend the winter [understand a thing or two].

But only "maybe." We are all in the paradoxical "phase" — as Pavlov put it.[70] There's more to come!

And meanwhile there's no sugar, out in the country there's no butter either, no boots, no manufactured goods, no transportation.

[...]

9/5. Ev. Yak. Danko was here with Yanson. E. Ya. spent her summer vacation in the House of the Arts in Detskoe, the former house of Tolstoi. G. A. Lavrenyov was staying there too. When they heard the rumors about the murder of Raikh,[71] Lavrenyov went to the military prosecutor's office and came back with this version: Z. N. [Raikh] got a phone call summoning her to Moscow, supposedly to get some news about Vs[evolod] Em[ilievich] Meyerhold]. She arrived late. The murderers followed her. She was found with her eyes gouged out, apparently the murderers believed the old superstition that the last thing a dying man sees is imprinted on his eyes.

Ev. Yak. said that Lavrenyov is a terrible man, apparently only too well aware of what goes on in the NKVD. The news about Starchakov is sad: he was shot as an enemy of the people. I don't want to believe it, Lavrenyov couldn't stand him, I recall him telling me he was a troublemaker, a man with an unsavory character. They worked together at one time, somewhere in Central Asia, and evidently that's where their mutual antipathy originated. A. O.[Starchakov] called Lavr[enyov] a ravenous shark. [...]

10/24/39. [...] I came back from vacation on the 6th. Beginning 7/29 I stayed at N. V's place on Seliger Lake, I went to Palekh, and came home from there. On the 29th I took a small boat to the steamship dock at [illeg.]. The ship was late, and I waited for it in a decrepit old bathhouse by the lake there, for some two-and-a-half hours. The lake reflected the pink sunset, stars appeared in the sky and twilight set in. It was quite cold. The ship, an overnight stay in the House of the Peasant. A whole day at the Ostashkov train station. Some three hours in Bologoye, until 2 a.m. Shuya, overnight at the janitor's. An evening ride on horseback to Palekh. Sunset. A marvellous moonlit evening — the smell of autumn in the woods, the earth, the faded leaves. Golden, luminous birch copses. I breathed in deeply, savoring that aroma and the recollections of Larino, our horseback rides in the autumn woods, that it brought me.

A day in Palekh. A snowstorm blew in overnight, and by morning there were snowdrifts half an arshin [fourteen inches] deep. I put on felt boots, a huge sheepskin coat with a big collar, and a woolen scarf on my head and went by carriage to Shuya — a five-hour trip. The wheels clogged up with snow. Zorka could barely walk. Both of the artel's cars had been appropriated for military use. That is, one of them was, the other had had its tires removed. You can see how ready for war we are. Though from what you hear and read in the papers we've been preparing for a good 20 years now.

Another whole day in Shuya, I spent the night in the room of that same janitor, Chebynina, after a verst-long hike along the railroad, trudging through the deep snow that covered the ties. Finally, the sleeping car, the 28–hour trip home, and, finally, my warm bed, a chance to sleep off my vacation.

And the whole trip has left me with the feeling I've been on the road to calvary.

The people groan, and the monotonous sound spreads over the surface of our beggared life and fills the air, covering the whole country.

[...]

I was sitting in the train station at Shuya; it was evening. A group of workers with knapsacks on their backs stood in the middle of the waiting room, smoking. You're not allowed to smoke in the station. A policeman went up to them and said something to them, then he snatched a cigarette out of the mouth of one of the workers and threw it on the floor. There was an uproar. They surrounded him — "You say he's got no right? Go ahead and talk all you want, but keep your hands to yourself."

It looked as though they would come to blows any minute. The policeman just barely got away. A young man in a tattered quilted jacket and denim trousers was lying on a bench. He pulled himself up and sat there hunched over with his head hanging down, making a low, moaning noise. Maybe he was singing, I don't know.

The policeman showed up again and started trying to get him to leave; you're not allowed to spend the night in the station. He wouldn't go. The station manager himself came out. At this point the man jumped up and started cursing both of them out. He gave them a piece of his mind. "You just keep it up, and we'll put you in the slammer." "Go right ahead, you so-and-so's, arrest me, at least in prison they give you bread." I must have heard these words dozens of times. An old woman in a black shawl sitting next to me. She piped up, "They're not afraid of anything; you can tell they're workers, and obviously from the city; out in the countryside, where I come from, no one would have said a word. Oh, it's not easy on the Collective Farm, you get nothing for your work, there's nothing to wear, nothing to eat, everyone is just crushed." The old woman comes from the other side of Nizhny, and she's just repeating the same old song that I've been hearing my whole trip.

I'm on my way to Palekh; it's evening. There's not a single dog in the villages. I recall last time — dogs would rush out of each hut barking their heads off at people as they passed. I mention it to one of my drivers, (an old stableman from Palekh), "Yes, you see, there's nothing for them to eat, and plus they've got nothing to guard either, they can't steal the skin off your back."

Palekh is in decline. In 1938 they arrested Al. Iv. Zubkov, the organizer and chairman of the artel. The reins of management were taken up by Bakanov, a young Party member, who had fought for this with all his might and most likely was responsible for Zubkov's arrest. With Zubkov's arrest, the NKVD started meddling in the business of the artel. They removed from the library all the materials that our brilliant Chekists thought were "religious" — antique illustrated Bibles and pictures of cardboard that were even older — copies of Novgorod frescos, ancient icons and copies. All this (according to I. I. Vasilevsky) was burned. All these priceless things had served artists as models for their works, as their ancestors had used seventeenth-century bibles. Under Zubkov the artel had its own representative in Moscow, Vasilevsky, who had gotten them commissions from all over the country. He was removed under the pretext that he was the son of a priest — and that having an agent was just an unnecessary waste of the artel's money. Vas. had earned a 700-r. salary. Now the artel sits idle for lack of commissions and Bakanov has reoriented it toward mass consumption, something that Zubkov fought against tooth and nail.

I was staying at Bazhenov's, but towards evening I went to Nik. M. Parilov's, who had done *Saltan* for us.[72] Parilov is a peasant by origin, and Bazhenov is a member of the intelligentsia, though he's half-literate; they represent completely different aspects of Palekh. Bazhenov is more talented, but Parilov is more original and his "style" comes straight from icons, which he had to paint himself. Bazhenov learned the style through study, he was an eleven-year-old boy when the revolution came. Parilov is a face-painter — i.e. his specialty was painting the faces on the icons; even in his sketches, the faces were done remarkably well, painted in the traditional way, over white foundation paint. Bazhenov's sketches for the puppets were not that interesting or original. They served me tea with sugar and candy, i.e. with the sort of thing that only good hostesses have on hand. His wife complained about the hardships of running a family farm: "We don't even know whether we'll be able to keep our cow; since we are private individuals farming on our own, they didn't give us any meadowland. And you can't buy hay anywhere." As for Nik. Mikh., he complained about the lack of opportunity for artistic work. There aren't any commissions from theaters, or for illustrations, the price rates for lacquer work have been reduced, and the older skilled craftsmen have stopped painting boxes — the young ones copy postcards and cheap prints. Par[ilov] took me around to the studios. It was already quite dark, and there was no one there; he took me around the rooms, opening boxes and drying ovens, showing me both the boxes and the originals that they were copied from. A postcard photograph of a tiger; the box has a tiger too, slightly stylized and shown next to a palm tree. Another one is even worse, without any stylization whatsoever. In the morning Markichev showed me all kinds of boxes — each one cruder than the next—one in particular made an impression on me: Gorky and a group of children, just their heads, with an oblong-shaped bouquet of utterly tastelessly done flowers underneath them. One box, painted by the old master Speransky, was an exception: a large (about 40 cm.) picture of King Lear. On top you see the king with his retinue and his daughters, and each of the 4 sides has a different scene. The storm, with the clouds painted in gold against a black background, and the golden rain, was just stunning. What use has a peasant from Vladimir for Shakespeare and what use has Shakespeare for him? In the same place Markychev showed me a small, oval miniature box made by Bakurov, illustrating devils. Golden snow with a black troika on a dark blue background. Just marvellous work, if I had had a hundred rubles to spare, I would have bought it for sure. Parilov showed me his painting *The Kolkhoz Hippodrome*, it's 1 ½ meters long. Palekh horses harnessed to sulkies run across the foreground. The crowd is shown in the center of the background and around the edges. If this painting were exhibited in Paris at the gallery of some marchand de tableaux, it would be a colossal success. Du Douanier Henri Rousseau with his incredible naiveté. All the faces were painted in detail, just like those on icons, there was no overall composition, the people were just standing in a row, all the women's skirts painted alike, with the inevitable single fold down the middle. Parilov is stifled as an artist, and undoubtedly he's not the only one. A snowstorm blew in overnight, and by morning the snow had accumulated to almost half an arshin! We barely made it to Shuya—the snow clogged the wheels. They gave me some felt boots and an enormous sheepskin coat to wear.

All along the road, as we passed through villages, and in Shuya itself too, I admired the carving around the windows and attics, and along the roof edges. I brought home a ceramic flask, or rather, a vase, from Palekh that Iv. Markichev gave me. Silvery flowers against a black backgound. What extraordinary, perfect taste these people have.

All this ought to be recorded on film, it's the art of the past, and who in the Collective Farm would think of decorating his home? I asked A. V. Kotukhin, an excellent old craftsman, how they found the time to carve window casings. His answer was: "You come home from the studio (he had been an icon painter) all tired out, and to amuse yourself, for the good of your soul, you pick up a board and carve whatever comes into your head." That's why there's so much variety in their work.

One more day in Shuya.

The last time I went out to a restaurant in the morning to have breakfast, I observed how people were nourishing themselves. At 11 in the

morning: 2 glasses of vodka, 2 bottles of beer—which people drink
salt—and a bowl of cabbage soup. During the time I ate my l
another group of 3 downed 1 ½ liters of vodka, countless bottles of
and one serving each of soup or a main dish. These were evidently
nomic planners," some sort of "bosses." Tall boots and short ja
trimmed with lambskin. Their ugly faces gradually became flushed
were having some kind of conversation about business. People lik
have their own special jargon.

Everyone drinks, there are drunks everywhere. They lie aroun
pigs. My trip left an absolutely awful, even excruciating impression
everyone in Palekh has been depressed since A. I. Zubkov's arrest. It
ribly hard to build, but oh, so easy to destroy.

NOTES

[1] Maria Venyaminovna Yudina, well-known pianist, or Maria Petrovna, an actress. It could not be established whom Shaporina had in mind here.

[2] The Liteiny Boulevard in Leningrad where the central administration of the NKVD was situated.

[3] Aleksei Tolstoi's son.

[4] General name for "employees of the State security." See "Chronicle of th Year 1937," note 65.

[5] Aleksandr Osipovich Starchakov, journalist writing, among others, for *Izvestiya*.

[6] After Kirov's assassination, thousands of Leningrad inhabitants were expelled from the city and deported.

[7] Aleksandr Fyodorovich Kerensky, 1881–1970, head of the Russian provisional government from July to October 1917.

[8] Big French draft horses.

[9] A slightly modified quote from the poem "Meditation" (1938), by Mikhail Lermontov.

[10] Aleksei Tolstoi's spouse.

[11] French dictionary.

[12] Mikhail Vrubel, painter, 1856–1910, one of the most original and tragic fig ures of Russian art history. Died in a madhouse. Vrubel was one of the m protagonists of the symbolist movement in Russian art.

[13] Gorky's son.

[14] See "Chronicle of the Year 1937," note 11.

[15] Ironic reference to Pushkin's tale in verse "Ruslan and Lyudmila" (1820).

[16] Nikita E. Radlov, Soviet engraver and caricaturist.

[17] Lev Tolstoi left his family and died in November 1910 in the stationmaste

house in Astapovo.

[18] Nikolai Aleksandrovich Leikin, 1841–1906, journalist and writer. Shaporina refers here to Leikin's stories about the merchant class.

[19] Diminutive for Aleksei [Tolstoi].

[20] A tale in verse for children, by Kornei Chukovsky.

[21] This name could not be identified.

[22] Boris Lavrenyov, 1891–1959, one of the "fellow travellers" of the Soviet 1920s. His civil war novel *The Forty-first* inaugurated the scheme of the "two camps," where love unites — and eventually destroys — lovers belonging to two opposite camps.

[23] Konstantin Aleksandrovich Fedin, 1892–1977, author, among other works, of *Cities and Years*, one of the first major novels of Soviet literature.

[24] Aleksandr Blok, 1880–1921, major symbolist poet.

[25] See "Chronicle of the Year 1937," note 63.

[26] Dmitry Dmitrievich Shostakovich, 1906–1975, renowned Russian composer. Shaporina refers to the devastating campaign of criticism of which Shostakovich was the object after the performance of his second opera, *Lady Macbeth of the Mtsensk District*, in 1936. On 27 January 1936 a lead article appeared in *Pravda*, entitled "Chaos instead of Music: On the Opera *Lady Macbeth of the Mtsensk District*," accusing the composer of "Meyerholdism," leftist chaos, naturalism, pleasing the foreign bourgeois public. At the source of the campaign was Stalin himself, who had been irritated by the performance.

[27] Nikolai Pavlovich Okhlopkov, 1900–1967, well-known Soviet theater director, producer, and actor. He directed the Moscow Realist Theater between 1930 and 1936 and played in films such as *Lenin in October* and *Lenin in 1918*.

[28] Konstantin Sergeevich Stanislavsky, 1863–1938, founder with Nemirovich-Danchenko of the Moscow Art Theater, theoretician of "psychological realism" in theater.

[29] Ivan Sergeevich Turgenev, 1818–1883, one of the greatest nineteenth-century Russian authors.

[30] Reference to the marquis de Custine, author of *Lettres de Russie: La Russie en 1839*. His work was published for the first time in 1843, after a two-month visit to Russia. It was rediscovered in the USSR during the Cold War, but in underground publication. Custine's writing has been compared to Tocqueville's *Democracy in America*.

[31] On summer nights it does not get dark in the northern latitudes where Leningrad is located.

[32] Aleksei Tolstoi's *Peter the First*, a historical novel, which earned the author tremendous fame.

[33] Kuzma Sergeevich Petrov-Vodkin, 1878–1939, famous painter, master emeritus of the arts of the RSFSR.

[34] Reference to the Second Moscow Trial ("Trial of the Seventeen") of 23–30 January 1937.

[35] See "Chronicle of the Year 1937," entry of *Izvestiya* of 30 January 1937, and note 15.

[36] Palekh is the location where traditional Russian lacquer boxes were crafted. For recent analysis of this "tradition," see Svetlana Boym, *Common Places: Mythologies of Everyday Life in Russia* (Cambridge, Mass.: Harvard University Press, 1994), 106–109.

[37] Karl Bruyllov, 1799–1852, who enjoyed immense popularity during the first half of the nineteenth century. He was acclaimed during his lifetime as the great master of Russian painting, precisely for *Pompeii's Last Day*.

[38] See Shtange's diary, note 3.

[39] Verses from Alexander Pushkin's drama *A Feast During the Plague* (1830).

[40] The first elections to the Supreme Soviet after the adoption of the new Stalin Constitution.

[41] Soviet of the city of Leningrad.

[42] Gavrila Nikolaevich Popov, 1904–1972, Soviet composer, author of the *Music of the First October Years* and the *Third Symphony: the Heroic*.

[43] Black vans of the NKVD, which served to transport arrested people.

[44] Vissarion Yakovlevich Shebalin, 1902–1963, Soviet composer. Author of the symphonic poem *Lenin* (1931).

[45] Aleksandr Vasilevich Aleksandrov, 1883–1946, Soviet composer, who wrote the Soviet national anthem and organized in 1928 the Ensemble of Songs and Dances of the Soviet Army. Shaporina could have in mind two other Soviet composers: Boris Aleksandrovich Aleksandrov, 1905–? the son of Aleksandr Vasilevich, director since 1946 of the same Ensemble of Songs and Dances of the Soviet Army, or Anatoly Nikolaevich Aleksandrov, 1888–? author of romances, sonatas, symphonies, and music for theater and film.

[46] Aleksandr Vasilevich Gauk, 1893–1963, Soviet composer. From 1936 to 1941 Gauk was the principal director of the State Symphony Orchestra of the USSR.

[47] Veta Isaevna Dolukhanova-Dmitrieva.

[48] Pinocchio.

[49] See "Chronicle of the Year 1937," note 30.

[50] See "Chronicle of the Year 1937," note 47.

[51] Peshkov, Gorky's son.

[52] Vyacheslav Rudolfovich Menzhinsky, 1874–1934. Of Polish origin, member of the Russian Social-Democratic Workers' Party since 1902, Menzhinsky was one of Dzerzhinsky's first assistants at the Cheka. From July 1926 to May 1934, he was the president of the OGPU (State Security). He was also a member of the Central Committee of the Communist Party since 1927.

[53] See Shtange's diary, note 5.

[54] See "Chronicle of the Year 1937," note 51.

[55] Elena Mikhailovna Tager, 1895–1964, poet and prose writer. Expelled from Leningrad by the Cheka in 1920, she could return to the city in 1927. In

1939, she was arrested and accused of working for the "Fascist Intelligence Service." She spent ten years in the Kolyma camps and six further years in exile. She returned to Moscow in 1954 and was rehabilitated in 1956.

[56] Nikolai Alekseevich Zabolotsky, 1903–1958. Major Russian poet, arrested on March 19, 1938. After a fabricated trial for "anti-Soviet propaganda," Zabolotsky remained in labor camps until 1945 and was allowed to return to Moscow in 1946.

[57] Klavdia Pavlovna Konovalova, 1893–1942, sculptor and puppet maker. She graduated from the School of the Society for the Encouragement of the Arts in 1917, and from Vkhutemas in 1927, and taught at the Theater Institute in Leningrad. (Information from Charlotte Douglas, New York University.)

[58] See "Chronicle of the Year 1937," note 2.

[59] Mikhail Efimovich Koltsov, 1898–1942? writer and journalist, author of the *Spanish Diaries* (1938) relating the civil war in Spain. He was arrested shortly after the publication of this work, like many other participants in the Spanish war.

[60] Reference to Petrov-Vodkin's painting *The Bath of the Red Horse* (1912).

[61] Mandelshtam died in a Far-East labor camp on 27 December 1938.

[62] Reference to Satin's famous line in Maxim Gorky's play *The Lower Depths* (1902), "Man -- this sounds proud."

[63] Anatoly Konstantinovich Lyadov, 1855–1914, Russian composer and director, professor at the St. Petersburg Conservatory of Music. Lyadov was the author of symphonic pictures on Russian folkloric themes and arrangements of Russian popular songs.

[64] See "Chronicle of the Year 1937," note 63.

[65] The German-Soviet Nonagression Pact was signed in Moscow on 23–24 August 1939.

[66] Reference to the Treaty of Brest-Litovsk, signed between Germany and the Soviet government in 1918, by which Russia lost the Ukraine, its Polish and Baltic territories, and Finland.

[67] Mikhail Evgrafovich Saltykov-Shchedrin, 1826–1889, major Russian nineteenth-century satirist.

[68] Lev Gumilyov, born in 1912, son of Anna Akhmatova and the poet Lev Gumilyov, historian and orientalist. Arrested a first time in 1935, he was liberated and arrested again in 1938. While in exile in 1944, he volunteered for the front. He defended his doctoral dissertation in 1948 and was arrested again in 1949. He was liberated and rehabilitated only in 1956 and started to publish his scholarly work after 1961.

[69] Valiant knights in the Russian epic tradition.

[70] Ivan Petrovich Pavlov, the famous physiologist.

[71] Zinaida Raikh, actor, and Meyerhold's wife.

[72] Shaporina refers to a Palekh lacquer box, containing a motif from Alexander Pushkin's "The Tale of Tsar Saltan" (1831).

COVER OF FRELIKH'S DIARY, WITH PORTRAIT OF PUSHKIN

OLEG NIKOLAEVICH FRELIKH

In 1937 Oleg Nikolaevich Frelikh was fifty years old, living in Moscow and working as an actor in the theater.

"Two men live in myself and each reacts in his own way to the surrounding world," wrote Oleg Frelikh in the last pages of his diary. The (unconscious?) Faustian paraphrase did not apply only to the man himself, whose daily life consisted in being "another," an actor in the Kamerny *theater and the* Komsomol *theater. Oleg Frelikh, recording in two small notebooks, with the same even writing, his diurnal and nocturnal existences, was keeping two parallel diaries.*

This duplicity, which Pascal saw as inherent in mankind as a whole, is even truer for our diarist, who, it seems, is a being with many secrets. First of all, there are the apparent secrets, like his ellipses that make visible what is unspoken but essential—or is it self-censorship, a gap of memory, the powerlessness of the diurnal logic to relate the "fantasy" of the dreams?

Then there is the secret buried in Oleg Frelikh's conscience, which, via his unconscious, suddenly rises to the surface under his pen: the trial for murder experienced by the dreamer refers to an actual episode, though in real life the author escaped responsibility. Declared incompetent for trial, by reason of insanity, Oleg Frelikh underwent psychiatric internment for several months for the murder of his lover, committed in the fall of 1917.

However, the true secret of Frelikh's duplicity lies, we think, elsewhere: in the irremediable nostalgia of the "patient," beyond any politics or ideology, as a letter addressed to his wife in 1929 seems to indicate. The letter insists on his pro-Soviet commitments, even quoting "evidence": as member of the Committee for Socialist Emulation in the domain of theater production, he expressed his readiness to print out business cards testifying to this activity.[1] Frelikh was of noble descent and had been rubbing shoulders with the artistic and intellectual "all Moscow" of the prerevolutionary era. But his nostalgia is, above all, sensual: not only the clicking of hooves on the asphalt has disappeared from the city, but also the "fragrance of the past." "Gone, the scent of fir that filled all Moscow at Christmas time. Forgotten, the perfume of incense, the sour odor emanating from the cabmen's coats, the mushroom market, with its smell of wet earth."[2] Out of touch with modernity rather than with the regime, the renowned actor is also an internal émigré who questions himself: "Does this mean that something is wrong with me? Or was I simply not born at the right time? Or rather: I don't like being on the side of the victors? Yes, the latter is the correct explanation."³

We have decided to publish Frelikh's second — nocturnal — diary, that is, to choose the reality of dreams over the "real" reality because of the harmony that is offered here between the content (the dreams) and the form (the diary). They draw on the same set of rules: the blurring of perspective, the disappearance or reversal of logic and common sense. In this context the question whether the diarist "tells the truth" becomes incongruous. At the same time, history pervades the dreams of Oleg Frelikh: his "Speculations on Rembrandt" coincide with a large Rembrandt exhibition held at that time in Moscow; he dreams of Bukharin at the very moment when the latter comes up before the courts. The fading away of Bukharin's face depicted by Frelikh shows us that sometimes the dream tells the truth while reality lies.

We learn from Frelikh that resistance to terror can be deeper than a retreat into contemplation of a beautiful landscape or reading a classic work of literature; it takes its place in the unconscious as well. And what of the little dream of immortality experienced by our last diarist, which meets the desire-epigraph of the first one, Fyodor Shirnov — "May this here thing live on forever" — completing the circle of our diaries?

DIARY OF OLEG NIKOLAEVICH FRELIKH

White Guard

Early dusk. A low hill. Some people, I don't know who they are, but they're not strangers either. A man wearing an officer's cap comes out on top of the hill from behind, walks halfway around, then starts down. I chase after him and grab him from behind, but without turning around he reaches back with one hand, seizes me, and carries me down the hill on his back. We're in a small, low-ceilinged room (a mud-walled hut or grotto). There's a large pane of glass, like a shop-window, and behind it I see a group of people. A schoolgirl, an elderly lady with an air of prerevolutionary Russia about her, a group of men in bowlers and officers' caps. There's something unreal and mannequinlike about all the people in the window. Their eyes stare straight ahead, utterly lifeless, and they look like they're made of mica. "They're on our side," the man in the officer's cap tells me. "On our side...." I repeat mechanically. "You can shake their hands...here's one," continues the man in the officer's cap. I see a hand lying on the sofa behind me. I can't tell whose body it belongs to and I don't turn to look. I take the hand and recoil in disgust: it's worse than dead—all soft, as though it were stuffed with sawdust, and the skin feels like a glove. It's such a disgusting sensation that I try to force myself awake. I awaken for a second, but the dream takes over again and I'm standing on the edge of an abyss, and the familiar head of the man in the officer's cap rises out of it. I hit it as hard as I can with a hammer, it disappears and rises again. I hit it again, and again I try to wake up.

Again I awaken, but again not completely. From above me, an armchair in a white slipcover comes whistling through the air and falls, gripping with all four feet onto the floor in front of my bed. It's so terrifying that I make a desparate third attempt to wake up and this time I succeed.

(December 1934)

Retribution

Years ago I murdered my lover. I got away with it, the crime was not discovered. The only way anyone would find out about it was from a particular clue that I myself didn't know. I have a German-style helmet that I keep around. Somehow I attracted the attention of a policeman and was arrested; they took my helmet and cut into the lining and found something there that they used to establish beyond a doubt my complicity in Vizarova's murder, committed many years ago.

And now I'm on trial. It's taking place outdoors, in a large clearing, and a huge throng of people has gathered to watch. The malicious, gloating voyeurism of the people, their desire to catch the murderers, to get all the details, to make them confess. "Murderers" because I didn't act alone, but in collusion with my other lover, an insignificant, deceitful woman, who had the same face and figure as Vizarova. I know that the newspapers are all reporting: "Murder on such-and-such a date, such-and-such a year...." I'm tied to a chair. Both of us struggle to escape. I'm tormented by the thought: how did they find out about me? Why was the policeman so interested in the helmet? And when he looked behind the lining, what did he find there that gave me away? How will my accomplice bear up under questioning? Will she break down? And Mama's in Moscow.... It will be so easy for them to catch her: they'll just come to her apartment and inform her that they've solved the case, everything has been brought to light, and all she has to do is tell what she knows. Mama wrote me a letter: "I've tried to get help from (a certain important person who takes lessons from her), but they told me there that though they'd like to help me, nothing can be done here. The only thing you can do is to appeal afterwards for a reduced sentence. They say that your case is being viewed differently in Kiev, and that a lot of people there are on your side."

I sit here all depressed at the thought that I have something weighing heavily on my soul again, and I realize that crime in this day and age is inevitably followed by retribution. The retribution dogs your heels for years, but, sooner or later it catches up to you. And it is forever.

(January 24–25 1935, twenty years later)

An Empty Soul

I've got money, a whole lot of cash. And life whirls around, everything is topsy-turvy, you can't stop it or set it right. I'm on a binge, throwing money away right and left. I buy my lover a big, beautiful fringed shawl made of white silk. I take her my present. She is standing there completely naked, all pink, and she smiles as I wrap the shawl around her. Then I take a big antique pistol and shoot her three times. The pink living body becomes a corpse right there in my arms and assumes the repulsive materiality of death. And this materiality destroys my soul. My soul is empty. I'm going to shoot myself now. Not from grief or desperation – these are for living men – but from emptiness. And I'm not at all afraid to cross over into death, even right this minute. I don't know how to handle a pistol, I fumble with it and load it with three bullets (they feel like beans to the touch) – and I shoot. No fear, no curiosity about death, no will to die. Nothing at all.

(14 April 1935)

Monster Cat

Twilight, but the lights haven't been turned on yet. Someone says that he saw our orange cat in the garden, the one that was lost. They go out there to look and come back with him in a basket. I peer under the lid and recoil in horror and disgust. Sure enough, the orange cat is in there, he's alive, but at the same time there's nothing "human" in him. He's ten times smaller than a normal cat, he has a blank look in his eyes, and there's dried blood encrusted on his lips. What happened? Someone explains: evidently he took a fall and ruptured something. After that he stopped growing and started to shrink, shrivel up and lose his vigor and his mind, and all this time he's been wandering around in the garden, unable to

386

find his way out. It was terrible—though the monster was so much like the cat we'd lost, in fact he had nothing in common with him. All his former intelligence and vibrant charm was gone.

(no date)

Israel

On the table in front of me is a small box, about fourteen inches square. It has a large round glass window that allows you to see what's inside. A man is sitting in a low armchair. He's dressed all in black. Huge black eyes stare out of his gaunt, suffering face, his black hair falls down over his forehead. His brow is furrowed with the excruciating strain of his thought. The man sits with his bare feet stretched out in front of him, each one soaking in a glass basin full of warm water. The atmosphere in the box that imprisons the man is like that of a greenhouse, otherwise he would not survive. His feet are pitted with open sores, in places the flesh has come off and the bones are exposed. The man's thoughts are tormenting him, his mouth twitches. With difficulty he stands up, takes a step, raises his head to the sky and, pausing after each word, as though sending up a challenge, intones, "Was willt du, Izrael?" [What do you want, Israel?] There is no answer.

(26 April 1935)

Lares and Penates

A room, rather large, crammed full of boxes and trunks. But this disorder does not arouse a feeling of desolation or unease. Quite the opposite, everything feels solid and permanent, it's comfortable and homey here. You don't even mind the cobwebs and the dust, it reminds you of your childhood here. Mama, Grandpa, and Grandma do not appear in the dream. Nothing at all happens in the dream, there's just the scene and a calm, unhurried voice explaining the objects: "These are lares and penates.... All of us have them in our lives, they give us that warm feeling of belonging that makes life worth living. But they leave the room, they leave life (they die?), taking that warmth away with them, and man is left alone in his spacious, bleak, unheated room.... He can shout and cry out then, but no one will hear him anymore...."

(24 October 1935)

In The Year 1789

I am Louis XVI. My wife, Marie Antoinette, is asking me to let her go out for a drive on the streets of Paris. I know how dangerous it is, but how can I turn this woman down? She has a kind of extraordinary fragile charm. It's as though she's not alive, but made of fine, delicately painted porcelain. And there's an air of cold, absolute perfection about her. I give my permission. She leaves. I'm left alone by the large, quiet window, but I know beyond the shadow of a doubt that this silence is deceptive and that in a few hours Paris will explode in revolution.

(no date)

Freedom

I've committed some kind of crime for which I could be severely punished under the law. I am fully aware of the consequences. So I flee. At first the feeling of the chase is exhilarating, I'm getting away with it. Then, no longer conscious of any immediate danger, I run through green valleys, across the slopes of low hills covered with soft grass, under the spreading cupolas of lime trees. The lighting is soft, muted and joyful. I have reached a place where there is no authority, and various groups of people have come together and are living out the short time they have, knowing that soon power will come and put an end to anarchy. I know this too, but it doesn't keep me from luxuriating in the feeling of limitless, unobscured freedom. It is only in sleep that I have fully savoured this "feeling of freedom." In my waking hours I could never imagine all the sweetness of this ideal anarchy. I vaguely recalled that back there in the world I had fled, I had left my loved ones, responsibilities, the need to explain something to someone.... Then I forgot everything and now here I am, a man without memories, surrounded by strangers to whom he is not bound in any way, from whom he expects nothing, and freedom fills the sky above us. And the air is so pure!!

One of my most unusual and enchanting dreams.

(no date)

A Terrifying Woman

Night. The city. Lights.

I'm outside, opening a letter addressed to me. It's from a woman named Strelova. She accuses me of negligence in connection with some business affair with her and her partners. The letter starts out with accusations and sarcasm, but by the end they've turned into irate, hysterical curses. Hatred writhes in every line. Holding the letter, I go into my room. The room is high-ceilinged and spacious. A curtain across the middle divides it into two halves. It's dark, but a light shines from the other side of the curtain. And I see the silhouette of a female figure standing there motionless and

tense. Then I hear a rustle. I ask, "Who's there?" The rustling stops immediately. I get scared and, sensing something evil, I repeat: "Who's there?" I
draw back the curtain and see the woman is standing there looking at me
with a kind of diabolical glee. I understand that it's she, and she's here for
revenge. I scream in terror, and she screams at the same time and rushes
toward me. Lurching backwards, I let the curtain fall, and hear the sounds
of a scuffle. I realize that the maid is in the room and is restraining her. I
groan out loud and Olga wakes me up.

A terrible dream. It gave me a real sense of the human defenselessness
against dark, evil forces. I was all alone in the dream, no one needed me.

(no date)

Evening Has Come...

I look at myself in the mirror. The face I see is not mine, but I like it, and I
know that it's mine. A thin, nervous face, deeply lined. Dark brows. Large,
dark, sparkling eyes. And hair that has gone completely gray. This surprises
me. I think, how did that happen? Where did the time go? And as though in
answer to my unvoiced question, I hear a gentle voice coming out of the
darkness of the twilight, saying, "Evening has come...." And I understand
immediately — it's my evening that has come...I comprehend the concept
of time: a human life fits within the span of a single day: it was morning, the
sun shone, children played, the day passed, and evening came. How simple
it is! My whole life, all of it is just a single day, and I must reconcile myself
with the fact that it is over now and evening has come.

(December 1936)

Speculations On Rembrandt

A large house, a lot of rooms, all [illeg.]. An unwelcoming, grayish-
bronze light (as in the novel *Nana*). I have two rooms at my disposal, but
they're not adjacent. As I look them over, I get the feeling that I'm not
alone in there. Finally, reaching under the sofa, I feel someone there, he's
curled up into a tight ball. I sense the disgusting physical presence of an
unfamiliar and hostile creature. "Just look at that!" I say in disgust to
someone there, who is supposed to clear him away.

Meanwhile there's a stir of excitement in the other rooms: some
smooth operator had acquired for practically nothing a Rembrandt that
had been lying around somewhere, he had arranged an exhibit of the
painting and made thirty thousand pure profit

(11 June 1937)

Fokin Alley

Some rich old woman, waiting petulantly for her lover. Her body is young and white, with a very ample bosom and a disgusting, aged face. Someone's pushing me toward her, but with a proud, easy feeling of freedom from all material temptations (the old woman's money) I shout, "I spit on your money! I don't need it!" And I spit.

Then I'm out in the gloomy, gray, completely uninhabited city with its tall buildings and narrow streets, I'm looking for something (an apartment?) In a dark alley someone tells me that it's here, in Fokin Alley. Well, all right. But there's something else I need to find too, and now I'm at a cemetery. The sky is lead-colored, too, as it is in the city, and the cemetery itself looks like a city: there are no trees at all, just a dense crowd of high stone tombstones and crypts, all huddled up against each other. I open one door, a second, a third....

(17 June 1937)

Fortune-Telling

Konstantinov arrives. It turns out that Belevtseva is his wife. She has also come and has stopped somewhere nearby. I go outside and see her coming toward me. We greet each other, and I jokingly invite her to come and walk with me under the window, so that Konstantinov will see us together. Then we sit down on a bench and she insists on telling my fortune. She takes my hand and examines my palm, and a dark shadow comes over her face, then she takes my other hand and looks at it.

"Well?"

"Misfortune. Nothing but misfortune in your life, though there's a small glimmer of hope in the other hand."

"You mean I'm in for bad luck?"

"Misfortune, misfortune."

(July 1937)

Lies

I'm in a large, dimly lit hall. A dark painting is hanging on the wall, the work of some Old Master. Suddenly, through the gloomy colors of the picture, I distinctly see the face of Bukharin. I shout, "Hey, look, look there!" People I hadn't noticed before turn around, but the features fade away just as quickly as they had appeared, and it's just an ordinary painting again. But I saw it! I know it's not that simple! I feel the lies that permeate everything around me, and an awareness of the dreadful injustice of life weighs heavily on my soul.

(7 March 1938)[1]

The Church

A huge pile of laundry. People are turning it over to a coarse-looking man, who says, "Why give it to me? I'm just a no-good bum." But it's clear that he is a good worker and can get away with talking that way because he's fully aware of his own worth.

Walking back across a large field covered with snow. Night. A small low-roofed wooden church is visible on the horizon. The sky over my head is dark blue and sparkling all over with little golden bees who disappear, then appear again. It's the Milky Way. It's enchanting, very beautiful.

(December 1938)

Flight

My uncle and I, who are from the wealthy Moscow bourgeoisie, decide to flee from the revolution. This uncle, a small, dark and energetic man, is unlike any of my real uncles. We make our escape during some show in a Moscow theater (that isn't like any of the theaters I know in Moscow).

. . . .

. . . .

It's a moonlit night, and we're walking along some low mountains. Below us is a river, and we can just make out some people swimming in it. Who are they? Friends or foes? My uncle pretends to be a guard from the local area, and speaking deliberately simply, he yells down to the people swimming. One of them yells something back, and judging by his robust, confident tone of voice, we realize that there was a battle here recently, that the Reds won and now they're taking a swim to refresh themselves. We turn hastily onto the high road, which has tall trees growing alongside it, and head off in the opposite direction, trying to restrain our steps and walk as quietly as possible. The road goes along the foot of a mountain that blocks the moonight and it's completely dark here. But the need to get out of danger as quickly as possible makes us terribly nervous, we can't restrain ourselves and take off running. Immediately we hear the sound of hoofbeats, they're coming after us! Closer and closer. We run through the darkness, they're gaining on us and to throw them off, we swerve off to the right, up under the mountain

. . . .

Morning is breaking when we enter the city. It's some kind of international city: there are both Reds and Whites here. They're close on our trail, so we hurry to take cover in the first building we see. It's the Chinese Consulate. "May we see the consul?" "Yes, they're both receiving, both the consul and the deputy." We go into a room, and see two Chinese women there. The older one is the consul, the younger is the deputy. I start speaking loudly and excitedly, but the older woman signals me with her eyes, and says pointedly, "Don't say any more than you have to." I realize that her deputy is not to be trusted, and immediately lowering my voice, I mumble something completely incomprehensible. Our enemies are searching for us, we see them passing by outside the windows, but we feel completely safe, and with a kind of willful bravado we carry on a light-hearted, superficial conversation with the Chinese women....

. . . .

My uncle and I have made ourselves at home here; I'm leafing through a very elegantly produced journal that contains some pseudo-scholarly research on Chinese antiquities, written by [illeg.]. It's amazing. I know that [illeg.] knows absolutely nothing about the subject and I am struck by his casual, clever charlatanism. One of the Chinese women gave me a finely crafted ring with a portrait of her on it, to remember her by

. . . .

We continue onward. Now we are in a ship's cabin that's being cleaned by a maid, a very attractive girl. She is explaining something, and as she talks she rustles her flimsy apron, which has large crimson roses embroidered on it. Her movements excite me and I go up to her and take her by the shoulders. But she immediately breaks away angrily and moves away from me with a hostile expression on her face. I'm hurt; I tell my uncle, "You see, uncle, I'm over the hill, women aren't attracted to me anymore."
  (January 25, 1939)

Grandpa
  Grandpa stands there and asks petulantly, "Well, did they?"
  Some woman who's related to me (though I don't know who she is) tries to calm him down, she says they've already called.
  "Who did they call?"
  "Your sisters."
  It turns out that Grandpa has three sisters? That's strange! I never knew that.

"I thought you had just one sister, Grandpa, Aunt Sasha, and one brother, Uncle Dorya?"

"Aunt Sasha is no sister of mine."

"Well, that's right, you have different mothers.... But what about Uncle Dorya?"

Grandpa's eyes turn dry and hostile. "He's no brother of mine."

I'm shocked. But I hear a phrase, it sounds like something out of a book—"The explanation is right here."

And there's a large, high-quality book in front of me. Excellent paper, illustrations.

A picture of a large room with a vaulted ceiling, globes, stars, gloomy arches. The light falls on the face of a romantic-looking, long-haired youth on bended knee. It's Uncle Dorya. "But of course—he was an astronomer!" I recall.

It's an exhibition hall for statues of great astronomers.

The caption explains: "The last statue is a man who seemed brilliant on the outside, but who was a nobody. It was easy for his country, with its observatories in Baku and in Penza, and in many other cities too, it was easy for such a country to insist on having a statue of him included."

So that's it! So I ought to understand that he renounced his relationship with Uncle Dorya out of shame for his brother. But no, that's not it: Uncle Dorya himself was always cold and miserly with his brother, that explains what my grandfather said. And I say to someone,

"His daughter, Aunt Anya, was a miser too. Once Mama was in a pinch and asked her for a fifty ruble loan, and she answered that she didn't have any money available at the moment, though she was a millionaire. I was seventeen or so at the time...."

"You were twenty," someone corrects me, and I'm surprised that the time can be pinned down like that.

(9 February 1939)

The World of the Soul

I'm dead. Like a sigh of relief: "At last I've finally died!" A feeling of incredulity: so life does go on after all?...And such a feeling of liberation! Such freedom!

My soul looks down from somewhere above at the body it has left behind. This man (the body) does not look like me at all.... My soul is overjoyed: "That's not me." (My soul's joy is understandable: the moment

393

it left its body, the body stopped looking like the man who had worn it. That means that the face had been the gift of his soul).

And a new feeling awakens in me, a feeling I never experienced before, complex, powerful, intense and creative. As though the newly freed soul spread out its huge, powerful wings. A new world opened up before me. A powerful, joyful, triumphant, boisterous world, waving its wings, and it is the only real world. It's like a revelation. The world of the spirit, hidden from human eyes, but incommensurable with our world in its meaning, its joy, its free ideas, its inexhaustible creativity, I understand that such a world cannot be anything but immortal.

I begin to understand everything, but it's such a fresh and irrepressible flow of discovery. It burst out at me from this world, so forcefully that I'm frightened. I cannot bear this, it's beyond my strength to take in so much all at once. It's as though I'm closing a curtain that had opened wide before my eyes. I think that such a dream couldn't just be the mere product of my psyche, the human soul does not have the capacity to project ideas of that magnitude, even in sleep. That means that the dream comes from a world outside of me, a world that is unquestionably immortal.

(17 June 1939)

NOTES

[1] This information is drawn from Oleg Frelikh's biography by Rachit Yangirov "Zhizn vslukh i pro sebia" (To Live Aloud and for Oneself), published in the journal *Moskovsky nablyudatel* 10 (1992): 52–63.

[2] Ibid., 55.

[3] Ibid., 61.

[4] 7 March 1938 was the sixth day of Bukharin's trial.

CPSIA information can be obtained
at www.ICGtesting.com
Printed in the USA
FSHW010508210819
61243FS